DATE DUE

DEC 6 8 1999

The Troubled Birth of Russian Democracy

Photo: Meeting in Moscow on March 10, 1991.
Manezh Square in the capital became the arena of
demonstrators' passions. Called together by the
Democratic Russia Movement, tens of thousands of
Muscovites came there to express their feelings toward the
Union referendum and the coming rise in prices and to
support once again the position of the chairman of the
Russian Federation of the Supreme Soviet, B. N. Yeltsin.
(Photo credit: D. Sokolov, TASS)

The Troubled Birth of Russian Democracy

Parties, Personalities, and Programs

Michael McFaul
Sergei Markov

Hoover Institution Press

Stanford University
Stanford, California

Hoover Institution Press Publication No. 415

Copyright © 1993 by the Board of Trustees of the
Leland Stanford Junior University

First printing, 1993
99 98 97 96 95 94 93   9 8 7 6 5 4 3 2 1
Simultaneous first paperback printing, 1993
99 98 97 96 95 94 93   9 8 7 6 5 4 3 2 1

Manufactured in the United States of America

The paper used in this publication meets the minimum requirements of
American National Standard for Information Sciences—Permanence of
Paper for Printed Library Materials, ANSI Z39.48–1984. ∞

Library of Congress Cataloging-in-Publication Data

McFaul, Michael, 1963–
    The troubled birth of Russian democracy : parties, personalities,
and programs / Michael McFaul, Sergei Markov.
          p.   cm. — (Hoover Institution Press publication ; 415)
    Consists chiefly of interviews with various Russian personalities.
    Includes index.
    ISBN 0-8179-9231-6 (alk. paper). —
    ISBN 0-8179-9232-4 (pbk. : alk. paper)
    1. Political parties—Soviet Union.   2. Soviet Union—Politics and
government—1985–1991.   3. Political parties—Russia (Federation)
4. Russia (Federation)—Politics and government.   5. Politicians—
Soviet Union—Interviews.   6. Politicians—Russia (Federation)—
Interviews.   I. Markov, Sergei, 1958–   .   II. Title.
III. Series.
JN6598.A1M35   1993
324.247'009'048—dc20   93-393
                                                        CIP

Contents

Preface

In 1988, when the Democratic Union was founded, the monopoly of the Communist Party of the Soviet Union (CPSU) over organized political activity had begun to erode. In August 1991 it collapsed. What kaleidoscope of parties, movements, and forces will fill the political vacuum created by the CPSU implosion is still uncertain. Several political parties and movements with distinct ideological platforms and tactics, however, had already begun to emerge before the CPSU's collapse. This book is a snapshot of the spectrum of political forces, movements, and parties that existed in Russia in 1991.[1] Compiled here are interviews, documents, and analyses that provide an introduction to those political forces, ranging from the radical Democratic Russia Movement to the neocommunist United Workers' Front.

This book is not a survey of all political parties, movements, or clubs in Russia.[2] Rather, we have selected a small group of parties and movements that were the most prominent in Russian politics in 1991.[3] As the situation in Russia changes, the people and parties discussed in this book may fade from importance, while other new faces and forces will emerge. In organizing this book, however, we have tried to select those people and parties that played historic roles during the dramatic years leading up to the August coup in 1991.

The rapid pace of change in Russia has frustrated our ability to record, study, and understand the history and development of Russia's democratic (and antidemocratic) movements, arguably one of the most important events of the twentieth century. Although most events discussed in this book occurred during 1989–

1991, they already seem like ancient history. Moreover, many of those events and the personalities who participated in them are still unknown to many in the West, for most previous scholarship on Soviet politics focused on the inner workings of the CPSU Politburo, not the development of informal political activity outside official structures.[4] The demand on scholars and politicians (both in the West and Russia) to understand the present and future situation in Russia has left little time to retrace and explain the origins of this second Russian revolution.

As such, this book aims to add to the data base about this important period in Russian history. Unless recorded beforehand, political history is always told from the perspective of the winners. Even in the interviews in this book, completed during the spring and fall of 1991, the nuances and perspectives on the historical development of the political parties and movements had already been influenced by Boris Yeltsin's increasing success. Follow-up interviews after the coup demonstrate how a single, contemporary event can radically reshape the way in which we understand the past. Although this book makes no claim to correct for this inevitable recasting of history, we do hope that these interviews and documents from a particular, defined moment in time will help historians and political scientists understand the context and flavor of these revolutionary times on the eve and in the wake of the August 1991 putsch.

With few exceptions, both authors participated in the interviews, all of which were conducted in Russian. Before beginning each interview, we explained that the text would be published in a volume of interviews of political leaders. From each organization, we interviewed the most active and/or prominent political figure, which was not always the official chairman or president of the organization. Given space limitations, all interviews had to be abridged. Michael McFaul translated and edited these interviews; he also wrote chapter 1 and is solely responsible for any errors or omissions in these sections.

In calling this book *The Troubled Birth of Russian Democracy*, we do not assume that Russia's transition to democracy will succeed. As discussed in detail in the following chapters, major obstacles now impede democracy's development, and antidemocratic forces threaten the Russian democratic project altogether. If a democratic system does not take hold in Russia, the historical period discussed in this book—a period in which democratic structures and institutions were emerging—may help illuminate the reasons why.

Acknowledgments

The information for this book was compiled under extremely difficult circumstances. Russia was in the midst of one of its most volatile historical moments, as we were pestering some of the main actors in this drama to sit down with us and recollect where they have come from and where they are going. In addition to those people whose interviews appear in this book, we would like to thank the following people who granted us interviews during an extremely hectic time: Andrei Antonov, Mikhail Astafiev, Vladimir Boxer, Igor Chubais, Maksim Dianov, Vladimir Filin, Telman Gdlyan, Kirill Ignatiev, Boris Kagarlitsky, Valerii Khomyakov, Igor Korovikov, Vera Kriger, Pavel Kudiukin, Vladimir Lunin, Vyacheslav Lyzlov, Anatoly Medvedev, Alexander Obolensky, Alexander Ogorodnikov, Lev Ponomarev, Galina Rakitskaya, Ilya Roitman, Ilya Shablinsky, Lev Shemaev, Vyacheslav Shostakovsky, Alexander Shubin, Dmitrii Shusharin, Yurii Skubko, Mikhail Sobol, Sergei Stupar', Alexander Sungurov, Alexander Terekhov, Anatoly Zheludkov, and Victor Zolotarev. If this book could have been a thousand pages long, all these interviews would have been included.

Many people provided invaluable information, contacts, translation assistance, and logistic support in Moscow. In particular, we would like to thank Iva Chernobrova, Elizabeth Cousens, Vyacheslav Igrunov, Yana Ilina, Tatyana Krasnopevtseva, Alexander Kuznetsov, Vladimir Kuznetsov, Alexander Lebedinsky, Julia Lugovaya, Lina Markova, Kelly Smith, Irene Stevenson, Alexander Suetnov, and Niiole Tochitskaya.

Also, we would like to thank Steven Fish, Andrei Shutov, and Nikolai Zlobin, our colleagues in a weekly seminar at Moscow State University, for their constant intellectual stimulation regarding the historical events that we all lived through and analyzed together.

Third, we would like to thank John Raisian, director of the Hoover Institution, and Charles Palm, deputy director, for sponsoring this project, and Joseph Dwyer, deputy curator for Russian and East European Studies at the Hoover Institution, for facilitating the production of this project. We applaud John Raisian, Charles Palm, Joseph Dwyer, and the Hoover Institution in general for their commitment to documenting this important period in Russian history. We also want to thank Patricia Baker and the entire editorial staff at the Hoover Institution Press for their patience and support in completing this project. We also would like to thank George Breslauer for reading and commenting on the entire manuscript.

Final production of this book took place when we had assumed other responsibilities and affiliations. For indirectly supporting this project, and being patient with both Sergei and me as we ducked away to finish editing this book when we should have been doing other things, we would like to thank the International Research and Exchanges Board, the Center for International Security and Arms Control, the National Democratic Institute for International Affairs, the University of Wisconsin at Madison, and the "MacNeil/Lehrer NewsHour" team in Moscow.

We wish to thank especially Lina Markova and Donna Norton
for allowing this book to happen.
In preparing this book, we were away from our respective homes
in Dubna/Moscow and San Francisco for more time than we should have been.
For understanding the importance of historical moments, even when they
interfere with the more important parts of life such as family and friends,
we dedicate this book to them.

chapter one

The Origins of Party Formation in Revolutionary Russia 1985–1992[1]

Self-organized political associations, be they political parties, civic groups, trade unions, or parliamentary factions, constitute a central component of a democratic system.[2] For most of the Soviet Union's seventy-year history, self-organized political association was either suppressed, co-opted, or impeded. As the "leading and guiding force of Soviet society, the nucleus of its political system," the Communist Party of the Soviet Union ordered and controlled almost all political activity in the state and society.[3] Organized forms of dissent in the Soviet Union[4] have a long history, however, ranging from overt antigovernment actions such as the demonstration on Red Square in 1968 protesting the Soviet invasion of Czechoslovakia to more subtle forms of informal organization such as football fan clubs or Russian cultural associations.[5] But whenever dissent groups attempted to organize overt, independent political associations, they were quickly stopped by the Soviet regime. Within the Party-state apparatus, some Western observers who identified political interest groups, lobbies, and factions concluded that the Soviet system was becoming more pluralistic.[6] Yet characterizing splits within the Politburo or interministerial battles as indicators of Soviet democracy only rationalized repression and obfuscated oppression in a regime that actively quashed independent association and, more generally, civil society.

Gorbachev's Reforms from above
Ignite Sparks from Below

On becoming general secretary of the Communist Party of the Soviet Union in 1985, Mikhail Gorbachev began to temper the Party-state monopoly on the Soviet polity and economy. After twenty years of *zastoi* (stagnation) under Leonid Brezhnev, revitalizing the system required radical action, not minor adjustments.[7] After a year of tinkering with the old tactics of *uskorenie* (acceleration) and discipline, Gorbachev began to respond innovatively to the Soviet crisis with policies like *glasnost'*, *perestroika*, and *demokratizatsiya*. Gorbachev's agenda, however, aspired to create neither a democratic political system nor a capitalist economy. Gorbachev's liberalization of political processes aimed to stimulate a restructuring of the Soviet socialist system.[8] Glasnost' and democratization were means for stimulating perestroika, not ends in themselves.[9] In prompting grass roots political activity with these liberalizing policies, Gorbachev hoped to create an alliance for change between reformers at the top of the Party and "the people" from below against the entrenched Party bureaucrats who opposed reform.[10]

By reforming the ancien régime, however, Gorbachev unleashed revolutionary forces ultimately bent on destroying the old order.[11] After decades of repression, independent political associations flourished in the late 1980s, first as clubs, then as fronts and movements, and ultimately as independent political parties.[12] Initially these groups in Russia were devoid of any obvious political content, focusing instead on cultural renewal, urban remodeling, environmental issues, or scientific questions.[13] Gradually, however, politicized committees or factions crystallized within these apolitical organizations.[14] When politicized members from these informal social groups began to interact with one another, overt political associations coalesced.

Properestroika Clubs

Informal[15] political associations first formed in the spring of 1987, after the plenary session of the Communist Party of the Soviet Union amended Articles 70 and 190 of the criminal code dealing with anti-Soviet agitation and propaganda. Taking their cue from Gorbachev's call for a more open political dialogue, young leaders of the intelligentsia—academicians from institutes, journalists, and low-ranking communist functionaries—convened political discussion groups, including, most notably, the Club of Social Initiative (KSI), Club Perestroika (in Moscow and Leningrad), Democratic Perestroika, Perestroika 88, Obshchina (Commune), Grazhdanskoe Dostoinstvo (Civic Dignity), and the All-Union Socio-Political Club.[16] Many of these groups later joined in a loose coalition called the Federation of Socialist Social Clubs (FSOK), founded in the spring of 1988. Agenda items of these discussion groups included the relationship between the plan and the market, the role of the church in a socialist society, and Soviet relations with the West. In the early years of organization, these properestroika groups rarely challenged basic concepts such as socialism or the one-party state. The program of the Federation of the Socialist Social Clubs, for instance, stated that "restructuring is the beginning of the revolutionary process, the essence of which is the establishment of the original democratic principles of socialism."[17] For these groups, the problem was not socialism; at issue was the poor practice of socialism by conservative apparatchiks within the CPSU. To correct this situation, the Communist Party had to be reformed, cleansed, and redirected but not destroyed.

The Democratic Union

During the era of properestroika clubs, a second, more radical, political current coalesced around dissidents returning from exile in 1987 and 1988. Initially, these kinds of groups returned to traditional dissident themes such as human rights and morality.[18] Like their contemporaries at the state-run think tanks, the political activity began with weekly discussion groups, the most important being the "Democracy and Humanism Seminar" organized by Valeriya Novodvorskaya, Igor Tsarkov, and Yurii Samodurov. But unlike Democratic Perestroika or KSI, these informal associations quickly moved beyond improving socialism as their mandate and discussion as their method.

The Democratic Union, an outgrowth of the "Democracy and Humanism Seminar," even declared itself to be a political party in May 1988, the first opposition party to the CPSU in seventy years (see chapter 2). A coalition of liberals, social democrats, anarchists, and even Communists, the Democratic Union was, however, unified behind two outrageously radical concepts for the Soviet Union in 1988: dismantling the cult of Leninism and creating a multiparty democracy. The Democratic Union did not seek to help Gorbachev reforms succeed but rather advocated the overthrow of the entire Soviet system.

To introduce these concepts into Russia's political discourse, the Democratic Union (DU) took to the streets without parade permits from the local communist authorities. Its first major demonstration—at Pushkin Square on August 21, 1988, marking the twentieth anniversary of the Soviet invasion of Czechoslovakia— was immediately dispersed by hundreds of Komitet Gosudarstvenoi Bezopasnosti (KGB) agents. More than a hundred DU leaders and sympathizers were violently arrested and detained. Undeterred, the DU also organized unauthorized demonstrations in September 1988 to commemorate the beginning of the Red Terror (on

September 5, 1918), in December 1988 to celebrate the international day on human rights, and in April 1989 to protest the T'blisi massacre.

Stepping beyond the bounds of perestroika both ideologically and tactically, the Democratic Union was shunned by Russia's liberal intelligentsia still hoping for reform from above.[19] But the shock value of the DU's open defiance of the Soviet regime reverberated throughout the other informal discussion groups. Eventually the mainstream would follow in the DU's wake.[20]

Russian Nationalism

Resurgent Russian nationalism constituted the third political current to emerge in these early years of glasnost'. Most notably, Pamyat', a reactionary national patriotic group headed by Dmitrii Vasiliev, organized one of the first noncommunist demonstrations in May 1987, a full year before the left took to the streets[21] (see chapter 3). Pamyat's message was blunt and frightening: Russia must rid itself of ethnic impurities, most notably Jews, and foreign ideas such as communism and capitalism in order to return to its nineteenth-century greatness. The appeal was both anticommunist and antidemocratic.

Neocommunism

A fourth force, communism, appeared somewhat later than these other trends within the burgeoning Soviet civil society. Allegedly, this political force also emerged from below, beginning with the letter "I Cannot Give up My Principles," published by Nina Andreeva in March 1988 in *Sovetskaya Rossiya*.[22] This letter, which represented the ideological treatise for those conservative Communists upset with the direction of Gorbachev's reforms, led to the creation of the neo-Stalinist group Edinstvo. The following year, the conservative communist organization the United Workers' Front (see chapter 10) held its founding congress in Leningrad, thereby establishing, at least theoretically, a communist social movement not controlled by the state or the Party.[23]

Most believed, however, that Nina Andreeva's letter was supported (if not written) by senior conservative figures in the Politburo of the CPSU.[24] Likewise, the United Workers' Front was created not by workers but by CPSU functionaries with the implicit sanction of leading conservatives such as Yegor Ligachev.

The Nineteenth Party Conference and the Creation of Popular Fronts

The publication of Nina Andreeva's letter, coming only a few months before the opening of the Nineteenth Party Conference in June 1988, served to catalyze an alliance between Gorbachev and the Politburo reformers from above and reform-oriented informal associations from below. Encouraged by Gorbachev and even logistically supported by liberal Komsomol and Communist Party district branches, informal associations organized weekly meetings to discuss the proposed theses to the upcoming conference. Most significantly, FSOK convened a conference of several informal organizations that produced a document called "Public Mandate for the Nineteenth Party Conference."[25] To ensure that Gorbachev's reform package would win approval at the Party conference, informal organizations began conducting campaigns to promote liberal delegates such as Yurii Afanasiev and Gavriil Popov.[26] Finally, as a means to influence the course of events at the conference, the informals convened public demonstrations, including most notably the weekly meetings organized by Obshchina (Commune) and Grazhdan-skoe Dostoinstvo (Civil Dignity) on Pushkin Square during May and June 1988.[27]

Despite the hype, the conference was a major disappointment for activists in the informal movement.[28] The most important event at the conference may have been a sharp exchange between Boris Yeltsin and Yegor Ligachev that served to heighten Yeltsin's popularity.[29] Outside the conference hall, however, public monitoring of the event further politicized Soviet society. As Boris Kagarlitsky, one of founders of the Federation of Socialist Social Clubs, reflected,

> The conference's massive significance lay in the fact that the public gained an immediate opportunity to observe the clash of various political views and was able to understand the differences between one political leader and another. In short, the Party conference raised the masses' level of political competence.[30]

An important, unintended consequence of the political activity surrounding the Nineteenth Party Conference was the formation of popular fronts in major cities throughout Russia. Modeled after the Estonian Popular Front, these fronts represented a major step toward consolidating new political forces outside the state and the Party. In Moscow, the idea of a Moscow Popular Front arose in June 1988 and was formalized during conferences of informal groups and associations, including the Federation of Socialist Social Clubs and the All-Union Socio-Political Club (VSPK) on August 21, 1988. In the fall, the Moscow Popular Front elected a Coordinating Committee, which then organized a founding congress on March 2, 1989.[31] Powerful fronts had also been organized in Leningrad, Yaroslav, Stavropol, and Khabarovsk.[32] Inspired by grass roots activity in other cities, which at this stage often exceeded the work of informals in the capital, front organizers in Moscow and Leningrad even began to plan and organize an All-Russian Popular Front.[33]

At this stage, popular fronts in Moscow and elsewhere still lacked the ideology to oppose the basic principles of Gorbachev's perestroika. Although highly contested, the Moscow Popular Front passed a resolution at its first organizational meeting espousing democratic socialism.[34] Old revolutionary slogans such as All Power to the Soviets and Land for the Peasants were resurrected as an obvious affront to the CPSU-state bureaucracy, but the 1989 Moscow Popular Front charter still listed "respect for ideals, peace, free democracy and socialism" as its principal concerns.[35] The Moscow Popular Front did take some positions regarding specific policies, such as support for the development of cooperatives and "democratization of the state and social life."[36] But the front never directly challenged the course of perestroika. Rather, the focus of activity was still support for reform, however vaguely defined, as carried out by the system in place.

In addition to the popular fronts, other nonrevolutionary, reform-oriented organizations formed in the summer and fall of 1988. In 1987, a handful of young activists from several informal associations founded the Memorial society, an organization dedicated to commemorating Stalin's victims.[37] In 1988, prominent figures such as Yurii Afanasiev and Andrei Sakharov became active in (and eventually took over) the organization. Soon thereafter, Memorial branches sprouted in every major Russian city and several major cities in other republics.[38] Also in the fall of 1988, the Moscow Tribune, a group of prominent individuals from Moscow's liberal establishment, held its founding congress.[39] Like the Moscow Popular Front, this organization sought to assist in the development of Gorbachev's reforms.

Elections 1989

Elections for the Congress of People's Deputies of the USSR provided the next major catalyst for populist politics in the Soviet Union. As they had during the Nineteenth Party Conference, Gorbachev and his reform faction within the CPSU leadership encouraged informal political activity as a means to help elect reform-minded deputies, that is, *communist* reform-minded deputies, to the People's Congress. Having decided that beheading the CPSU apparatus was too dangerous, Gorbachev sought to resurrect Soviet governmental structures as a counterweight to the entrenched Party labyrinth. As Anatoly Sobchak, one of the democratically oriented deputies elected to the first Congress of People's Deputies, explained,

Only much later did I realize why Gorbachev manufactured such a complex and utterly undemocratic but ingenious electoral system. The apparat, firmly and reliably entrenched after generations of Party selection, wouldn't allow democrats a single chance to win direct and justly weighted elections carried out by secret ballot. A well-oiled system of bureaucratic procrastination, mutual back scratching, controlled media, money from Party and state budgets, the power to pluck from regular jobs just about anyone needed for the campaign, paid support groups— these guaranteed success. But Gorbachev and his brain trust tossed the apparat into alien conditions where the Soviet tradition didn't work. Elections within public organizations and the USSR Academy of Sciences and the division of the country into territorial and national-territorial electoral wards opened up many new possibilities.[40]

In seeking to empower new state institutions such as the Congress of People's Deputies, Gorbachev also tried to create a new power base for himself by becoming president of the USSR. The Soviet leader believed that Gorbachev the president could become as powerful as and more legitimate than Gorbachev the general secretary.

Most informal organizations (with the exception of the Democratic Union) viewed these elections as an opportunity to promote reform from within the system. Cumbersome registration procedures filtered out almost all noncommunist candidates well before the vote.[41] Moreover, elections were held not only on a popular level but also within organizations, professional associations, and workplaces, guaranteeing hundreds of seats to communist organizations (the CPSU and the Komsomol, for instance, each received one hundred slots) and impeding "independents" from making candidate lists.[42] Consequently, few candidates from noncommunist political organizations managed to get on the ballot.[43] Of those who did, Sergei Stankevich, a leader of the Moscow Popular Front, was the only informal movement candidate to be elected to the new legislative body.[44] Organized support for other progressive candidates, however, proved critical to the electoral successes of Yurii Afanasiev, Ilya Zaslavsky, Andrei Sakharov, and Boris Yeltsin. Informal organizations also launched negative campaigns against conservative CPSU members. As a result, several prominent CPSU leaders were *not* elected into the Congress of People's Deputies, including, most notably, senior figures from Leningrad and Kiev.[45]

Surprisingly, informal political activity did not end after the 1989 elections, as popular fronts throughout Russia continued to hold rallies in an attempt to influence the agenda of the congress, scheduled to open in May. In Moscow, the parade grounds next to the Luzhniki sports stadium served as a regular meeting place between newly elected deputies and the mobilized electorate, beginning with a massive precongress meeting on May 21, 1989.[46] The Moscow Popular

Front and Memorial alternated as hosts to these daily demonstrations of more than 100,000 people at which deputies would report on the activities in the congress at the day's end. Although difficult to measure, the Luzhniki meetings appeared to influence congress proceedings.[47] In particular, the failure to elect Yeltsin to the Supreme Soviet was met with outrage at Luzhniki, where a resolution was passed threatening a massive strike if Yeltsin were not elected.[48] The curious compromise by which People's Deputy Kazannik stood down from his election to the Supreme Soviet so his slot could be given to Yeltsin resulted in large part from organized popular support for Yeltsin at Luzhniki and elsewhere in Russia.

Within the congress, the most progressive deputies organized themselves into a bloc called the Interregional Group of People's Deputies, which included such prominent figures as Yurii Afanasiev, Gavriil Popov, Telman Gdlyan, Arkadii Murashev, Andrei Sakharov, Anatoly Sobchak, Sergei Stankevich, Boris Yeltsin, and Ilya Zaslavsky. Despite this array of leaders, however, the group constituted only a small minority within the Congress of People's Deputies and therefore had little influence on the congress's proceedings.[49] Yet the group did formally unite famous liberals in a legally recognized opposition movement. Noncommunist political organizations were becoming less informal and more legitimate.

Elections 1990

In a pattern similar to the activity around the Nineteenth Party Conference and elections to the People's Congress of the USSR, the election process for deputies to the Russian Congress of People's Deputies as well as local and district soviets reinvigorated grass roots political activity. In these elections, held in March 1990, hundreds of thousands of candidates ran for tens of thousands of seats. Although restrictive nominating procedures still impeded free and fair elections, the "democrats" now knew better how to manipulate the system.[50] Through the election process to the USSR People's Congress, groups like the Moscow Popular Front and its successor, the Moscow Association of Voters (MOI), became professional campaign organizations. Although still denied access to newspapers, radio, or television, these groups grew adept at organizing mass demonstrations, disseminating leaflets, and mobilizing support networks for progressive candidates. Their task was made easy by a public eager to participate.

Initially, hundreds of voters' clubs organized around individual candidates. As the nominations process required a meeting of more than five hundred people to gather and then endorse a candidate, these local support groups were essential to getting on the ballot. Enthusiastic public participation, however, produced as many as a dozen candidates for one position in a city soviet, making distinctions between progressives and conservatives difficult. Besides a few Democratic Union candidates (the party as a whole boycotted the elections), the Communist Party was the only overtly partisan affiliation in the election besides "non-Communist." Even this divide—Communist versus non-Communist—did little to differentiate candidates, for some of the most radical candidates (Yeltsin, Popov, Stankevich) were still Communist Party members, while many conservatives ran as non-Communists.[51]

The task of distinguishing good from bad, or democrats from Communists, was eventually assumed by a coalition of candidates and activists called the Democratic Russia bloc (see chapter 8). Meeting in January 1990, leading figures of the opposition agreed to coordinate their activities within this republicwide movement. After establishing a campaign headquarters run by the former core organizers of the Moscow Popular Front and the Moscow Association of Voters, Democratic Russia, or DemRossiya, called on candidates to submit their credentials for review. If approved by a review committee at the campaign headquarters, DemRossiya would include the names of unknown candidates on posters and leaflets with more familiar figures like Yeltsin, Popov, and Gdlyan.[52]

This effective strategy established a near majority of DemRossiya deputies in the Russian parliament and pluralities in the Leningrad City Soviet, the Moscow City Soviet, and a handful of other city councils.[53] Radical organizations on the left (Democratic Union) and right (Pamyat') that did not join the DemRossiya coalition fared miserably at the ballot box. For the first time in seventy years, Soviet legislative structures were composed of people from different political associations.

Party Proliferation

At roughly the same time that DemRossiya coalesced in preparation for the elections, other, more tightly defined political organizations began to form new political parties as alternatives to the CPSU monolith. Although the Democratic Union had played such a role for two years, the DU program was too radical for professional politicians, and DU tactics had failed to mobilize popular participation. To focus people on political programs rather than rally chants, and to take politics off the streets and into the parliaments, leaders from some of the first discussion clubs now worked to create Western-style parties.

The first impetus for a massive opposition party came from within the CPSU, when the liberal wing of the Party formed the Democratic Platform (Dem-Platforma) (see chapter 6). Originally a club of young communist intellectuals led by Vladimir Lysenko and Igor Chubais, the notion of a liberal platform *within* the Party soon attracted such prominent figures as Yeltsin, Nikolai Travkin, Vyacheslav Shostakovsky, Yurii Afanasiev, and Gavriil Popov. Because affiliation with the Democratic Platform provided a forum for liberals within the Party yet did not jeopardize Party membership, the organization had garnered more than a million supporters within the CPSU only two months after its inaugural congress in January 1990.

The Democratic Platform's original mandate was to prepare and then present an alternative Party program to the CPSU Twenty-eighth Congress, held in June 1990.[54] Sensing that the silent majority among the rank and file of the CPSU supported reform, Democratic Platform leaders initially believed it a mistake to abandon the Party and alienate these potential supporters. By March, however, it became clear that Gorbachev would not allow any alternative program to be presented at the June congress. Instead of offering a new direction for the Party, most of Democratic Platform's leadership used the congress to stage their resignations.

Only thousands, not millions, followed them. The silent majority within the Party stayed silent, unwilling to risk their careers and Party perks. The Democratic Platform continued to exist outside the Party, but newly elected officials such as Yeltsin (now chairman of the Russian Supreme Soviet), Popov (chairman of the Moscow City Soviet), and Anatoly Sobchak (Leningrad's chairman) soon became too subsumed in governing to engage in Party politics. As Yeltsin argued in refusing to join any party, forty years of CPSU politics was enough for one lifetime.[55] Shostakovsky and Lysenko eventually reconstituted the organization as the Republican Party of Russia in November 1990, but only a fraction of original Democratic Platform supporters joined.

Nikolai Travkin, a gruff, no-nonsense proponent of radical reform, preempted the DemPlatforma exodus from the Communist Party by several months to form his own Democratic Party of Russia in the spring of 1990 (see chapter 4). A former construction boss, Travkin emphasized organization as the key to mobilizing a mass party to rival the Communist Party.[56] By the fall of 1990, Travkin's party claimed to have more than fifty thousand members, with branches in all major Russian cities. Travkin was big on organization, mobilization, and party cards but short on ideas beyond anticommunism. Moreover, in a society where social groups and classes were poorly defined and rapidly changing, Travkin's party lacked a cohesive social base on which to build. The party's greatest strength—its charismatic leader—was also its greatest curse. Although Travkin's abrupt oratories had genuine populist appeal, his centralized party structure and disciplinary leadership style alienated many of the party's key figures, including Gennadii Burbulis (Yeltsin's future first deputy prime minister), Lev Ponomarev and Arkadii Murashev (both DemRossiya cochairmen), and Garry Kasparov.[57]

The repeal, in February 1990, of Article Six of the Soviet constitution, which guaranteed the Communist Party's "leading" role in Soviet society, prompted Russia's Social-Democratic Association (the successor organization to Democratic Perestroika) to form the Social-Democratic Party of Russia (SDPR) in May 1990 (see chapter 5). Unlike Travkin's party, this group of young intellectuals devoted enormous energy to producing a one-hundred-page party program. Russian social democracy added many caveats to West European social-democratic orthodoxies. Although sympathetic to the ultimate ends of European social democracy, the Social-Democratic Party of Russia realized that Russia must undergo a radical transformation to capitalism before notions about social welfare could be entertained. As SDPR cochairman Oleg Rumyantsev explained, "Social democrats in the West are concerned with 'socializing' capitalism; we, on the other hand, are trying to 'capitalize' socialism."[58]

However intellectually stimulating, these abstract theories did not resonate beyond the urban intelligentsia. Although the Social-Democratic Party had found a clearly defined social base in the liberal, urban intelligentsia, it was a small one. Throughout 1991, the SDPR continued to function as a prototype of a Western political party, working especially effectively in the Russian parliament.[59] But that party and the dozens of other political parties that formed during 1990 never mushroomed into mass, republicwide parties.

The Russian Christian-Democratic Movement combined high-profile personalities (Father Gleb Yakunin and Victor Aksiuchits) with Russian Orthodox ideas to found a party with a specific orientation and social base, but competing Christian-democratic organizations slowed membership drives (see chapter 7). The two constitutional democratic parties (the Cadets) suffered a similar fate, relegating them to intellectual discussion groups. The Party of Free Labor, a political club for Russia's new entrepreneurs, commanded real economic resources; the Russian People's Party, led by Telman Gdlyan, united several populist leaders; and the Peasant Party, led by Yurii Chernichenko, is oriented toward a large social group, giving all these parties a potential future. None, however, has managed to attract more than a few thousand followers.

Several historical legacies, structural impediments, and tactical blunders have stalled party development in Russia. First, their timing was poor: Parties flourish during elections; all of Russia's new political parties were formed *after* the March 1990 elections.[60] As a result, the vast majority of people's deputies elected as "democrats" had no institutional affiliation beyond the soviet.[61] Several parties managed to form factions within soviets, but these party affiliations proved to be weak and fluid. Because deputies neither owed their seats to party associations nor were connected to any party obligations outside the soviet, the noncommunist parties have played only a small role in setting the agenda of these legislative bodies.

Second, for obvious historical reasons, Russians distrust and disdain the concept of "party." After seventy years under the tyranny of Party cards, Party membership, and anti-Party crimes, few have been eager to join another party, communist or otherwise. Moreover, because Yeltsin remained independent, others followed his example, believing that a democratic government could function without parties. This neutrality by some of Russia's most well known figures

(Yeltsin, Popov, Stankevich, Sobchak) seriously retarded the development of party affiliation.[62]

Third, the structure of Soviet society has impeded party building. In a society where miners demand markets and private property, owners of the means of production cling to arcane state planning principles. Thus parties have had difficulty defining individual agendas that appeal to specific social groups or classes because a propertied bourgeoisie is only just emerging. The program of the Social-Democratic Party of Russia, for instance, states that the party shall be based on the "new middle class."[63] But this middle class does not yet exist in Russia.[64] Parties, of course, can be oriented toward other kinds of social bases besides class. That most of Russia's new political parties are focused on discovering their class base, however, suggests that the legacy of seventy years of Marxism may be difficult to forget.[65]

Fourth, as in many other nascent democracies, there were simply too many parties,[66] as throughout 1990 major parties were formed monthly. When splits within these new parties occurred, the opposing factions simply created new splinter parties. Russian democracy has been stalled by too much democracy.

Finally, parties need elections to focus mobilization and present political platforms. Because most parties were formed after the March 1990 elections, they have not yet had the opportunity to compete. In June 1991, when elections were held for the posts of Russian president and mayor in Moscow and Leningrad (now Saint Petersburg), some democratically oriented parties considered running candidates.[67] Realizing their own weaknesses and the dangers of splitting the "democratic" vote, however, most opted to support Yeltsin. Since then, all elections have been postponed.[68] When coupled with the lack of significant representation in the soviets, Russia's new parties have had few practical functions as of 1992.

Democratic Growing Pains

The slow organization of Russia's new parties jeopardized the democratic victories of the March 1990 elections. In the Russian Supreme Soviet the lack of party discipline within the DemRossiya coalition allowed the more cohesive Communist Party bloc to stall reformist legislation. As esteemed economist Nikolai Petrakov observed in November 1990,

> As far as democracy is concerned the period of nonattachment to any party is over. I think it's high time for democratic leaders within power structures to join hands with democratic organizations. Let's face it, the fact that Yeltsin is not allied with any party does not help reach agreement within the Russian parliament.[69]

In Leningrad, a bitter fallout between City Council Chairman Anatoly Sobchak and the noncommunist majority in the council had virtually stalled the government by the summer of 1990.[70] Moscow's City Council reached a similar impasse in the spring of 1991.[71] By quarreling more among themselves than with the Communists, democrats were allowing their governments to crumble and their reputations to corrode.

Division among the democrats, however, was only part of the problem. After several months of participation in soviets at all levels, the democrats began to realize that the government structures they now occupied were inefficient, powerless, and situated in a political and economic context still dominated by the Party-state apparatus. The greatest impediment to effective, democratic government, then, was the very structure of the Soviet system. As Gavriil Popov concluded after six months as chairman of the Moscow City Council, "It would be an utter delusion to think that a complete rebuilding of the USSR can be done without changing today's Soviet system, whose basic features were formed in 1917. Our political system is as outdated as our command economy."[72]

First, with almost thirty thousand soviets in the country and roughly twelve hundred municipal soviets, there were simply too many legislatures and legislators to legislate effectively.[73] The Los Angeles City Council has fifteen members; the Moscow City Council has five hundred deputies. Such numbers made decisions impossible, prompting several prominent city and district soviet leaders to call for smaller numbers of deputies in each soviet.[74] Second, the vague division between legislative and executive power also blocked effective government, prompting the creation of a Russian presidency at the republic level and mayors in Moscow and Leningrad.

Yet even if the institutions of government could be revised, they still remained powerless when compared with the Party-state labyrinth. No matter how good the legislation, the Soviet ancien régime could still block its execution.[75] Many within the democratic camp who had decided to assume governmental positions in city and district soviets began to question the effectiveness of their strategy.[76]

Right-Wing Resurgence

At the same time that the democratic forces were experiencing a paralysis, the right was regrouping. Conservatives discontented with Gorbachev's leadership of the CPSU began to form their own organizations. The organizers of the United Workers' Front conspired with conservative CPSU apparatchiks to form the Russian Communist Party (see chapter 10). Although still affiliated with the all–Soviet Union Party (the CPSU), these Communists collected their own dues, printed their own party cards, and wrote their own platform. Reviving nineteenth-century schisms between Western liberalism and Slavic nationalism, the Russian

Communist Party attempted to forge a coalition between national patriotic groups like Pamyat', Otechestvo, and the Russian Writer's Union and neocommunist organizations like Edinstvo, the United Workers' Front, and Communist Initiative.[77] As Alexander Prokhanov, one of the coalition leaders, proclaimed, "The Communist Party of Russia and the national patriotic movement need each other."[78]

At the Union level, conservatives also were regaining ground. Within the USSR Supreme Soviet, Colonel Victor Alksnis and Yurii Blokhin formed Soyuz, an alliance dedicated to preserving the Soviet Union at all costs (see chapter 11). Soyuz vehemently attacked Gorbachev for losing Eastern Europe and allowing the disintegration of the Soviet Union. Support for Soyuz in the USSR Supreme Soviet forced Eduard Shevardnadze's resignation in December 1990 and put Gorbachev under severe attack. According to outspoken Soyuz leader Colonel Victor Alksnis, both Gorbachev and Yeltsin had to step aside if the Soviet Union were to avoid civil war:

> Today [February 1991] I'm contemplating the creation of a truly public salvation committee, one not designed to save socialism, like the Russian Communist Party's top man Ivan Polozkov wants. The committee I'm thinking of should save the union as a state. If we don't stop the perilous degradation we'll be plunged into civil war. A nationwide salvation committee is the way to do it. . . . But neither Gorbachev nor Yeltsin should be members.[79]

Within the highest echelons of the CPSU, Gorbachev's clashes with Yeltsin in the fall of 1990 fueled sharp criticisms of the general secretary's leadership. To allay these fears, Gorbachev appointed hard-liners Victor Pugo (as minister of internal affairs) and Boris Gromov (as Pugo's deputy) to his cabinet in December 1990 and shortly thereafter named Gennadi Yanayev as his vice-president and Valentin Pavlov as his prime minister. Suddenly, Gorbachev the centrist had surrounded himself with a very conservative government.

Outside the Soviet parliament and the CPSU Politburo, a third conservative force, the Centrist Bloc, came together in June 1990. Headed by Vladimir Voronin, the leader of the A.D. Sakharov Union of Democratic Forces, and Vladimir Zhirinovsky, chairman of the Liberal Democratic Party of the USSR (see chapter 12), this coalition of two dozen organizations claimed to be the compromise alternative to the conservatives in the government and the radicals in the democratic movement.[80] In reality, however, the Centrist Bloc enjoyed close ties with the leaders of the conservative faction in the CPSU, prompting speculation that the Centrist Bloc was in fact a creation of the KGB designed to discredit other democratic parties and coalitions.[81] The appearance of this group, however, coupled with conservative resurgence in both the Soviet government and the Supreme Soviet, gave the appearance that democracy and the democrats were in retreat.

The Consolidation of Democratic Forces

Right-wing resurgence eventually stimulated consolidation among Russia's democratic forces. Most important, the Democratic Russia bloc regrouped in October 1990 to form the Democratic Russia Movement—a united democratic front consisting of DemRossiya parliamentary factions, new political parties, civic organizations, and individuals (see chapter 7). The movement's six cochairs combined leaders from the Interregional Group of the USSR Supreme Soviet (Popov, Afanasiev, and Murashev) with noncommunist people's deputies from the newly elected Russian parliament (Victor Dmitriev, Lev Ponomarev, Father Gleb Yakunin). Although most major democratically oriented political parties joined the coalition, the core of DemRossiya activists came from the nonpartisan Moscow Association of Voters.[82] Famous orators stirred the crowds at demonstrations, while behind the scenes grass roots organizers captained the unwieldy front. The ideological spectrum within the movement ranged from Green Party revolutionaries to neoconservatives, but DemRossiya remained united behind one objective: the destruction of the communist dictatorship. Unlike the positions adopted by past popular coalitions, Democratic Russia openly opposed the government in power. Polarization between right-wing Communists and radical democrats was crystallizing.

Bickering between Russia's new democrats stalled early DemRossiya activities and quickly discredited the coalition. Only after the invasion of Lithuania in January 1991 did DemRossiya solidify into an effective opposition capable of mobilizing an already politicized population. The numbers attending DemRossiya functions grew from tens of thousands at the demonstration to protest the Baltic massacres in January to hundreds of thousands at rallies to demand Russian glasnost', support the striking miners, and resist the union referendum in February and March.[83] Finally, and most dramatically, hundreds of thousands took to the streets on March 28, 1991, to support Yeltsin in the face of his impeachment as chairman of the Russian Supreme Soviet.[84] This rally, declared illegal by Gorbachev, precipitated a major standoff between Red Army soldiers and Russian democrats in a dress rehearsal for August's resistance.

Although Democratic Russia made huge progress in early 1991 in constructing a united democratic front in major cities throughout the Russian Federation, coal miners in the Kuzbass, Donbass, and Vorkuta again demonstrated the power of organized labor when they went out on strike for the second time in two years in March 1991 (see chapter 9). Claiming that the government had reneged on obligations negotiated during the last strike in 1989, the miners' demands this time around were more political, including the resignation of the Soviet government and Gorbachev.[85]

The crescendo of popular demonstrations organized by Democratic Russia, culminating in the March 28 showdown in combination with the crippling miners' strike, dramatically altered the balance of forces between the center (the Soviet government) and Russia (Yeltsin and Democratic Russia).[86] Reflecting on this period of history, Yeltsin recalled that "the consolidation of democratic forces began at that time, and by April they managed to set up serious barriers to those favoring totalitarian methods."[87] Having turned to the right in December to appease the right, Gorbachev now turned back to the left to seek Yeltsin's assistance in ending the coal miners' strike and negotiating a new union treaty. The result was the "9 + 1 Accord," an agreement between Gorbachev and the leaders of nine republics to begin new negotiations on a Union treaty.[88]

After the March showdown, the 9 + 1 Accord, and Yeltsin's landslide election victory as the first president of Russia in June, many in Moscow believed that street rallies *against* communism had to give way to legislative proposals *for* democracy and economic reform. To deal with the new situation, people and parties started realigning according to ideological orientation. The Social Democrats and Republicans, which had attempted to merge for several months, now formed a single party organization with a left-of-center orientation in more than a dozen Russian cities. The Democratic Party of Russia (Travkin) united with the Russian Christian-Democratic Movement (Victor Aksiuchits), the Constitutional Democratic Party–Party of People's Freedom (Mikhail Astafiev)[89] to form the bloc Narodnoe Soglasie (Popular Accord)—a coalition that advocated radical economic reform and, at the same time, the preservation of the strong Union state. As in earlier postelection lulls, Democratic Russia once again showed signs of collapsing. Neither ideologically engaging in debates about capitalism or social democracy nor aspiring for elected office, the logistic technocrats within Democratic Russia believed that the front should disintegrate just as Solidarity had in Poland once a multiparty democracy had been established.[90] In contrast, leaders like Yurii Afanasiev, who had profited politically from DemRossiya's success, advocated its transformation into a mass opposition party with a radical reform agenda.[91]

During this period of reshuffling, a handful of prominent CPSU liberals led by Shevardnadze and Alexander Yakovlev joined with Moscow and Leningrad city bosses Gavriil Popov and Anatoly Sobchak to form the Movement for Democratic Reform (see chapter 13). These senior government officials hoped to unite reformers in the CPSU with the major democratic parties and movements challenging the CPSU from without. As a cofounder of both DemRossiya and the new movement, Popov was considered the linchpin in forging this coalition.

During the summer, Alexander Rutskoi, the new Russian vice-president, also took preliminary steps to form the Democratic Party of Communists of Russia on the basis of his Communists for Democracy faction in the CPSU. Although intent on creating its own party, Rutskoi's political organization actively supported the formation of the Movement for Democratic Reform coalition as a more moderate alternative to Democratic Russia.[92] At the other end of the spectrum, Colonel Victor Alksnis hinted that Soyuz would also form its own party. Although still fluid and underdeveloped, the basic components of a multiparty democracy—protoparties of all major ideological orientations—were taking shape.[93]

The August Putsch

The greatest obstacle, of course, was the centralized CPSU-state bureaucracy, which still controlled or at least obstructed Russian political and economic life. The Communist Party of the Soviet Union had never been a true political party, and few believed that it would or could make the transition into one. Rather, the struggle between those defending position and privilege within the ancien régime (albeit hidden behind new language and names) and those seeking to dismantle the communist system would be a long and arduous process. Momentum was clearly on the side of the opposition forces, but battling with the old system was still a trench affair, full of half victories, minor setbacks, and compromise. As Sergei Stankevich cautioned, "Democratic forces in the Soviet Union must steel themselves for a long period of uneasy transition. During this period we will have no choice but to accept the coexistence of hardly compatible persons, ideas, and institutions."[94]

During three days in August (19–21), one pole of this bipolar political balance suddenly collapsed. Instead of quietly condoning huge reallocations of financial resources from CPSU treasuries to private banks run by former Komsomol apparatchiks, Russia's democrats were now sealing Central Committee offices and confiscating Communist Party dachas. The trench warfare predicted by Stankevich had given way to blitzkrieg.

Destruction of the old order resulted from a combination of unwillingness to continue to rule from above and willingness to organize and overthrow the ancien régime from below. After only two days of the putsch, indecision among the leaders of the old order was apparent. Their tactical blunders and logistic errors demonstrated that they were never certain of their ability to rule. Equally important to their failure, however, was how detached these Party lords had become from Russia's new political scene. Polarization had permeated not only the Russian parliament and the Moscow City Council but the military, the KGB, and society as a whole. When an organized opposition, not the complacent and terrorized Russia of the Brezhnev era, responded to the coup attempt, this condition of dual sovereignty gave Russians, and especially Russians in uniform, a choice as to whom to support.[95]

A political movement experienced in mass mobilization proved essential to the resistance.[96] DemRossiya quickly used its phone networks to assemble hundreds of activists at the White House (the Russian parliament building) only a few hours after news of the coup had been received. By the following day, DemRossiya had organized two massive demonstrations, one at the White House and the other at the Moscow City Council, in which tens of thousands of Muscovites defied Red Army regiments to defend their democratically elected leaders and institutions.[97] Around the White House, Yeltsin loyalists from within the military organized a Russian national guard. Inside the White House and at the Moscow City Council, democrats of all parties and organizations manned phone lines and fax machines to propagate Yeltsin's decrees throughout Russia and the world. The Russian Supreme Soviet even convened an emergency session to approve Yeltsin's decrees. This legal alternative to the coup leaders' decrees gave military commanders the excuse not to fulfill orders.[98] Although Yeltsin personally led the resistance to the coup, he would not have succeeded without an experienced opposition movement, a democratic parliament, and a newly politicized people supporting him.

Russian Political Parties after the Coup

After several months of hesitation, Boris Yeltsin moved to fill the power vacuum created by the August coup by consolidating executive power in the office of the Russian presidency. On receiving permission from the Russian parliament to rule by decree, Yeltsin reconstructed an executive authority that has tried to assume responsibility for virtually all aspects of government.[99] Especially after the Soviet Union was dissolved in December 1991, the president's office has become the only true political power in Russia.

This situation has presented dilemmas for Russia's young democratic political parties and opportunities for Russia's neocommunist and neofascist political organizations, which have proliferated since the banning of the Communist Party in Russia after the August coup.[100] Within the democratic movement, the Democratic Russia coalition began to collapse after the fall of communism. Ideological and tactical cleavages, which had earlier been suppressed in the name of unity, crystallized after the disappearance of a common enemy, resulting in the splintering of the democratic front into several parties and blocs.

First, and most fundamentally, parties and movements have split over the issue of preserving the Soviet Union and the Russian Federation. Within Democratic Russia, Yurii Afanasiev has articulated one extreme by calling for self-determination for all those nations seeking independence both within the Union and within the federation.[101] At the other extreme, Nikolai Travkin's bloc, Narodnoe Soglasie, stated that independence of autonomous regions from the Russian Federation is nonnegotiable, whereas preserving the Soviet Union should be pursued by any means necessary. Blaming DemRossiya's radicals for promoting the collapse of the Soviet Union and the dissolution of the Russian Federation, Travkin's bloc finally quit the Democratic Russia coalition in November 1991.[102] Outside Democratic Russia, Zhirinovsky's Liberal-Democratic Party, Soyuz, and the emerging neocommunist organizations have all, to varying degrees, advocated restoring the Soviet Union and preserving the Russian Federation.[103] The confluence of interests between the Narodnoe Soglasie bloc and these organizations has created a new, albeit strained, alliance between former foes. In response to the creation of the Commonwealth of Independent States, these various political forces combined in a prounion demonstration on Manezh Square in Moscow in December 1991. Subsequently, Mikhail Astafiev and Victor Aksiuchits—two of the three party leaders of the Narodnoe Soglasie bloc—joined with several other nationalist groups to convene the Congress of Patriotic Forces on February 8, 1992.[104] Since then, these former members of Democratic Russia have worked closely with nationalist and neocommunist organizations to forge a new front dedicated to preserving the Russian Federation and ultimately reviving the Soviet Union.

Nikolai Travkin, after a brief flirtation, decided not to follow his partners from Narodnoe Soglasie in forming an alliance with nationalist and neocommunist groups. Instead, Travkin sought more moderate allies outside Democratic Russia, which, nonetheless, championed the idea of strong state. In March 1992, the Democratic Party of Russia signed a cooperation agreement with the newly formed People's Party for a Free Russia headed by Alexander Rutskoi.[105] This party, founded on the second day of the coup, united former Democratic Platform members who had refused to quit the Communist Party and were now without a party.[106] In May, the Russian Union of Industrialists of Entrepreneurs formed a political party, the All-Russian Union Obnovlenie (Renewal), cochaired by Arkadii Volsky and Alexander Vladislavlev. These three parties then joined with the parliamentary faction Smena and several other independent political leaders to found Grazhdanskii Soyuz (Civic Union) in June 1992.[107] Although not supporting the re-creation of the Soviet Union, this coalition of *gosudarstvenniki* (statists) has advocated the preservation of a strong Russian state.

A second major divisive issue among the new political parties and movements relates to the method and pace of constructing a capitalist economy. Although divided internally,[108] Democratic Russia as a whole has assumed the most radical position on economic reform, arguing that only immediate price reform and rapid privatization will succeed in destroying the Soviet command economy. To this end, Democratic Russia formed the Social Committees for Russian Reform in December 1991 that were tasked with promoting the economic reform package of Prime Minister Yegor Gaidar.[109]

Not surprisingly, the new neocommunist organizations that have emerged out of the banned CPSU have denounced Yeltsin's economic reforms, privatization in particular. Some former Communists have joined with the Socialist Party and the Federation of Moscow Trade Unions to form the Party of Labor.[110] Like the coalition formed to preserve the Russian Federation, this new alliance includes activists from the democratic movement as well as functionaries from the old communist regime.

The Grazhdanskii Soyuz coalition has assumed a position somewhere between these two extremes. Coalition members support privatization and the market generally but disagree with the method of reform advocated by Gaidar's government. Most important, Grazhdanskii Soyuz advocates a method of reform that will not destroy Russia's industrial base. Regarding privatization, they argue that directors and managers should become the new owners of their respective enterprises rather than outside (and especially foreign) buyers. Regarding price reform, Grazhdanskii Soyuz has supported free prices but not on all goods, particularly not on energy. Finally, this coalition has promoted continued subsidies to major Russian enterprises, arguing that their bankruptcy will cause massive social unrest and the collapse of Russia's industrial base.

A third issue dividing old allies and creating new coalitions involves the level of support that should be rendered to Yeltsin's government. The coalition opposing Yeltsin's government is made up of those who advocate the Soviet Union's preservation and oppose market reforms. Extremists on both sides of these issues—neonationalists who advocate preserving the Union and neocommunists who oppose market reforms—have formed several new political movements and parties united solely behind their disdain for Yeltsin.[111] These organizations have joined forces to organize biweekly demonstrations in Moscow and elsewhere to protest Yeltsin's economic reforms and the dissolution of the Soviet Union.

Democratic Russia continues to support Yeltsin and his government but at the cost of fomenting another major split within the movement. Given the depth of the economic crisis and the threat of new fascist movements, the pragmatic bloc within Democratic Russia, in conjunction with the Republican Party and the Social-Democratic Party, has argued that all democratic forces must continue to be supporters, albeit critical ones, of the new Russian government.[112] The radical wing of Democratic Russia, including most notably Yurii Afanasiev, Leonid Batkin, and Marina Salye, has moved into formal opposition to the government, claiming that blanket support for Yeltsin will nurture an authoritarian regime.[113] Grazhdanskii Soyuz, although less didactic than the Afanasiev group, has also warned Yeltsin that he cannot rely on its support without major changes in his economic reform strategy.

Party quandaries over whether to support or oppose the new regime are exacerbated by both the lack of party representation in the Russian parliament, the Yeltsin government, and the local soviets and the decreasing power of the legislative branches of government. Because elections to the Russian Supreme Soviet and all other soviets took place before most political parties had organized, they are not constituted along party lines. Party factions subsequently formed in these legislative bodies *after* their election, but faction members do not owe their parliamentary mandate to their respective parties. In this situation, parties and movements that seek to oppose an executive decision have little recourse within parliament or other government institutions. They still must resort to the politics of opposition practiced earlier against the communist regime: demonstrations, strikes, and demands for the government's resignation. Moreover, though some parties claimed to have influenced the composition of Yeltsin's new government, no senior figure has an official party affiliation.[114] Consequently, parties and movements are expected to pledge their support to Yeltsin without tangible political paybacks. Finally, as executives gain power both nationally and locally, they rely less on support from either the soviets or the population, the two arenas in which political parties and movements have influence. The combination of these factors has severely limited the role of new political parties in the postcommunist Russian polity.

Conclusion

Whether this diminished role of political parties and associations is temporary or permanent remains uncertain. The emergence of a multiparty political system was only beginning to take root before the August coup. Thereafter, the magnitude of the economic crisis confronting the current Russian regime, coupled with the other impediments to party formation already discussed, may postpone further articulation of parties and instead concentrate political power in the executive branch of the new Russian government.[115] Most new party leaders realize that Russia's democratic government will acquire legitimacy only if the new regime can deliver on popular demands for economic improvement.[116] If the economic reform fails, so too will Russia's experiment with democracy.

Democracies, however, cannot survive over the long run without organized competition between political parties. As the following chapters demonstrate, prototypes of Western-style political parties as well as trade unions and social movements already have histories and agendas. If Russia continues to aspire to creating some form of democracy, political parties will play an ever-increasing role in the construction of this new political system.

chapter two

The Democratic Union

The Democratic Union (DU) was the first noncommunist political party to form in the Soviet Union since 1917. Of all the political movements and parties that emerged in the late 1980s, the Democratic Union had the closest ties to dissident movements and individuals from the previous era. The idea for the creation of the Democratic Union grew out of a series of Democracy and Humanism seminars that were organized in the summer of 1987 by dissidents recently released from prison. Valeriya Novodvorskaya, the chairperson of the seminar and a political dissident who had spent ten years in and out of psychiatric wards, was one of the principal initiators of the new party. Unlike other political discussion groups at the time, the Democracy and Humanism seminars united older dissidents who had dared to take moral stands against the Soviet regime with a younger generation of radical activists who sought to pursue concrete political objectives.[1] This coalition united to form the Democratic Union.

The organizational committee of the Democratic Union, which convened toward the end of 1987, included Novodvorskaya, Yurii Samodurov, and Igor Tsarkov from the older generation of dissidents as well as younger activists such as Yurii Skubko and Victor Kuzin.[2] As described in detail in the following interview with Victor Kuzin, the Democratic Union then held its inaugural congress May 7–9, 1988, in Moscow and Kratovo, a small town outside Moscow where Sergei Grigoryants, the editor of *Glasnost'*, had a dacha. Although the police and the KGB harassed the delegates, dispersed their meetings, and arrested many of the participants, the congress managed to discuss and approve a political platform. Most important, the platform called for the creation of a multiparty political system and an economic system based on multiple forms of ownership. At the time, these demands were extremely radical, representing a direct challenge to the CPSU monopoly on political and economic power. Most observers, whether in Moscow, Paris, or Washington, believed that the Democratic Union would not last long.[3] Speaking at the Nineteenth Party Conference in the summer of 1988, Mikhail Gorbachev categorically ruled out the possibility of a multiparty system.

Members of the Democratic Union, however, refused to be intimidated. The radical tactics of the organization were commensurate with the kind of revolutionary change the group promoted. Most dramatically, the Democratic Union began to stage illegal demonstrations on Pushkin Square in Moscow, including a massive rally organized on August 21, 1988, the twentieth anniversary of the Soviet invasion of Czechoslovakia. At this meeting, several Democratic Union leaders, including Victor Kuzin, were arrested. For the next two years, the Democratic Union pushed the limits of Gorbachev's glasnost', publishing its own newspaper, *Svobodnoe Slovo* (Free Word), disseminating anticommunist platforms, and organizing antigovernment rallies. Although supported by only a small minority, DU radical stances and tactics made it easier for more moderate groups, movements, and parties to enter into opposition democratic politics later.

The Democratic Union, although resolutely committed to radical tactics as a means of fighting the communist system, lacked a common ideological platform. Calling itself a political party in opposition to the Communist Party of the Soviet Union, the Democratic Union actually resembled a united front of several ideological orientations, including a "liberal" platform, a social democratic platform, and even a communist faction.[4]

After enjoying two years in the political vanguard of the Russian (and Union) democratic movement, the Democratic Union began to splinter in 1990, with many of the DU's original ultrademocratic principles undermining the organization's cohesiveness. First, Democratic Union activists from republics other than Russia drifted away from the organization as national fronts and republic-based parties formed. Second, branches within the Russian Federation began to claim their autonomy and independence from the Moscow-based leadership. For instance, after holding the founding congress of the northwest division of the Democratic Union in Leningrad June 18–19, 1990, Ekaterina Podoltseva and Valeriya Terekhova led a motion to suspend the transfer to Moscow of any funds raised locally through membership fees.[5] Third, the further articulation of ideological platforms provoked increased conflict between factions. As more associations and parties emerged, factions within the Democratic Union joined their ideological counterparts in those organizations.[6]

In addition to these divisions, the Democratic Union's viability as a cohesive and influential organization was constrained by two decisions, one organizational and one tactical. Organizationally, the same ultrademocratic policies that fostered regionalization also hindered decision-making procedures within the group. At the Second Democratic Union Congress, held January 27–29, 1989, the DU Central Committee was abolished and replaced by the more democratic Party Council after numerous members complained that the party was too centralized. Moreover, the party has never had a chairperson or cochairs. These decentralized structures made decisive and unified action for the Democratic Union increasingly difficult as the issues faced by the movement became more complex. By 1991, DU meetings resembled anarchic debating matches at which few concrete decisions were ever taken.

Tactically, the DU's most controversial position centered around whether to participate in governmental and institutional structures created and maintained by the communist system. At the second congress, the majority of delegates spoke out against DU participation in elections, supporting instead creating alternative government structures. Again, in Chelyabinsk during October 7–8, 1989, the first council of the Democratic Union recommended that the party boycott the 1990 elections, arguing that participation only legitimated communist rule. The party eventually split into two factions—the radicals and the realists—over this issue. Led by Novodvorskaya, the radicals advocated increasingly confrontational tactics, while the realists recommended that party members take an active role in the parliamentary processes at all levels of government.[7] A handful of the realist faction, including Victor Kuzin, were elected to city and district soviets.

The division between radicals and realists became crippling after the "Letter of Twelve" scandal. Before the opening of the Fifth Democratic Union Congress in Moscow, January 18–20, 1991, a group of twelve Democratic Union activists, including Novodvorskaya, signed a letter that advocated the overthrow of the Soviet government by any means necessary, including armed struggle.[8] The letter became the central issue of the congress. Most of the leadership denounced the letter, but fifty-six DU members, including twenty delegates at the congress, supported it.[9] Ultimately, the divisions between those for and against the Letter of Twelve precipitated the dissolution of the Democratic Union as a political party. A moderate faction split from the party and joined Democratic Russia.[10] Individuals have continued to participate in various political forums, and several local DU branches still convene. The Democratic Union, however, carries out few functions as a unified party. Almost everyone in Russia's democratic movement recognizes the Democratic Union's vital role in defying the communist regime, introducing radical ideas into the Russian political discourse, and, thereby, changing the terms of the debate about reform and revolution.[11] But the party proved incapable of adapting to the new political situations that developed in 1990 and 1991.

Victor Kuzin

Victor Kuzin was one of the original founders of the Democratic Union and, as he explains in the interview, a young, active participant in the Democracy and Humanism seminars as well as the political group Club Perestroika. Later, with his friend Yurii Skubko, Kuzin formed Perestroika-88, a more radical version of Club Perestroika. In 1987, Kuzin was also one of the founders of Memorial.

Trained as a lawyer, Kuzin emerged as one of the Democratic Union's most articulate and outspoken leaders. He frequently spoke at Democratic Union demonstrations and was arrested several times in 1988 and 1989. Although vehemently anticommunist, Kuzin organized the social democratic faction within the Democratic Union, believing that the state and society had to play a role in caring for the poor.[12] Tactically, Kuzin has consistently represented the pragmatic position within the Democratic Union, supporting peaceful change rather than violent revolution. Kuzin supported the notion of a dual front against communism both within and without government structures. For this reason, he ran and was elected as a people's deputy to the Moscow City Council, the only Democratic Union member in the city's government.[13]

As a people's deputy, Kuzin has continued to be an outspoken critic of both the Communists and the new ruling democrats. His most controversial campaign in the city government concerned the appointment of General Komissarov as Moscow's chief of police. In November 1990, Kuzin's Commission on Justice, Human Rights, and Law and Order nominated Komissarov to replace General Bogdanov, the communist-appointed chief of police in Moscow who had actively repressed anticommunist demonstrations and political activities in the city.[14] In January 1991, however, Gorbachev's new minister of the interior, Boris Pugo, claimed jurisdiction over Moscow's police force and blocked Komissarov from entering the headquarters of the City Administration of Internal Affairs with police officers from the Union Ministry of Internal Affairs (the MVD).[15] To protest Pugo's action, Kuzin and several other people's deputies conducted a hunger strike in the spring, which succeeded in convincing the Russian government to try to assume jurisdiction. After the putsch, however, Popov appointed his own candidate, Arkady Murashev, to the post, claiming that Komissarov was not qualified for the post in the new postcoup situation.[16] In response, Kuzin's entourage staged another hunger strike.

The Komissarov affair and other similar occurrences catalyzed major opposition to Popov's government within the Moscow City Council.[17] As demonstrated in the following interview, Victor Kuzin has been one of the main critics of the Moscow government.

Interview with
Victor Kuzin (May 1991)

· ·

When did you first decide to become politically active?
We thought about politics a long time before we acted. We always perceived the vital necessity of genuine action against totalitarianism, but having been suppressed by this totalitarian monolith since birth dampened my enthusiasm. Young people with beliefs like mine did not dare do anything under the conditions of that [Brezhnev's] time.

But there comes a time when a person grows up and becomes mature. For us, this change was not merely a fad but an internal necessity. We were all thoroughly absorbed with the struggle against totalitarianism. In 1979, we created a theoretical circle, but it was soon discovered by the KGB. Although the founding of the theoretical circle was an insignificant event for our country, it was very significant for us personally, for it meant that we had finally dared to do something. However, we all suffered as a result of these actions. The KGB began to follow us everywhere. They threatened us, tried to co-opt us, and even tried to recruit me as their informant. Of course, I rejected their offers. At the time, I was in my third year at the university, and I was very surprised that there were no repercussions for refusing these KGB offers.

I graduated from Moscow State University with an honors diploma and entered the Institute of State and Law of the Academy of Sciences as a postgraduate student. I hoped to remain at the African Institute, where I had been a technical assistant. I planned to study the political ideology of Africa and had even written my thesis on this subject. The authorities at this institute, however, made it clear that I would not be able to work there.

I then found a job at a law office. However, I felt uncomfortable with the job because in such offices one must become an adviser on how best to violate the law rather than how to comply with it. I felt morally compromised and soon quit. Then I worked at the Central Economical Scientific Research Institute under the State Planning Committee of Russia until I was dismissed in 1988 because of my political activity.

We had reinitiated our political activity in the spring of 1987 with the publication of the independent, unlicensed magazine *Point of View*, which I published jointly with Yurii Skubko and one of my friends. The main contribution of this publication was its criticism of the Soviet system and of Gorbachev himself. At that time, people were optimistic and largely supported Gorbachev's policies.

However, we were very critical of Gorbachev's reforms. We stressed that only the facade of renovation was taking place and that the system itself was close to its death. The authorities were attempting only to save the system, not to achieve true democratic reform.

Now we must suffer the consequences of these policies. The real value of Gorbachev's *perestroika* was revealed by the bloodshed that has plagued Azerbaijan, Karabakh, and Lithuania. Now even those who supported Gorbachev, our famous "men of perestroika," have realized the folly of these policies. However, the price of this realization has been extremely high.

In those early years, who else was active?

Practically all dissidents, such as Lev Timofeev and Sergei Grigoryants, were active. These human rights activists were incorruptible and continuously opposed the system. But before the creation of the Democratic Union, there were already several organizations made up not only of dissidents but also of new people. [At the time] the most radical groups were Memorial and Perestroika-88. Soon thereafter, many nationalist organizations in Moldavia and Ukraine adopted the ideology of the Democratic Union, and, in the early stages, some of them joined us—for example, Leonid Dobrov in Moldavia, Anatoly Dotcenko, who is an influential representative of Rukh [the Ukrainian nationalist movement], and many other Ukrainian nationalists. They eventually left the Democratic Union, not for any political reasons but on the pretext that the Democratic Union was an imperialist [i.e., all–Soviet Union] party.[18] They left our ranks for fear they would be reproached by their nationalist countrymen because everything that originates from the center is met with suspicion in the republics. Because the role of the Democratic Union was to launch the process, we did not object to their exit.

When was Memorial created?

The first initiative was made on November, 14, 1987. In the summer [of 1987] the meeting "Public Initiatives for Perestroika" had taken place. It was organized by the procommunist youth who allegedly were close to Yeltsin. Most important, this meeting also drew together dissidents and was not simply a Komsomol gathering. People from the seminar Democracy and Humanism, from which the organizational committee of the Democratic Union emerged, were also there. Club Perestroika, Rumyantsev, and others who later composed the moderate wing of the democratic movement also participated. This group never went outside the limits of the law. They haggled for concessions with district Communist Party committees. We worked differently. We rejected all their [Communist Party] restrictions because if one just dances to the tune of the existing order, then it makes no sense to organize.

When you say *we*, to whom are you referring?

We were the radicals who had participated in the meetings mentioned above. At that time, none of us were members of only one organization. We also actively participated in the work of a discussion club called Club Perestroika. When questions about our principles arose, such communist-inspired leaders as Rum-yantsev, Mikusev, Yankov, and Danilov were reluctant to take more radical stances. They preferred to stay within the limits allowed by the Communists. Some communist-inspired leaders thought that democratization needed to be initiated by the Communist Party. We partly accepted this approach; however, we also used all other means available to achieve our ends.

Thus, two factions existed. The radical faction always wanted to attract the dissidents into Club Perestroika, and the representatives of the moderate faction were very opposed to these overtures. Eventually, a split took place. Our radical wing won the support of most of the rank-and-file members of the discussion club. During one of the sessions in November or December of 1987, our radical resolutions were approved by the majority. At this point, the moderates became frightened and left the session, hoping to break it up. We regarded their withdrawal as inappropriate and continued the session and elected several dissidents onto the coordinating council of the club. This act finally exhausted the patience of these moderates, and they began to act autonomously and secretly. They then formed a new organization called Democratic Perestroika. We responded by forming our own group called Perestroika-88. At this point, Sergei Grigoryants joined us.

This was a time when the radical elements of many democratic organizations were coming together. Yurii Mitiunov, who became the first correspondent for "Radio Liberty," Yurii Skubko, Misha Kovalenko, who later formed the radical faction within Memorial in November 1987, and I began to collaborate. The initiative to form Memorial was first announced at a meeting called "Public Initiatives in Perestroika." It was Yurii Samodurov who had the idea of preserving the memory of the victims of repression. We decided this was necessary to expose the repressive essence of the regime, to begin to document the crimes of the regime, to give practical assistance to the victims of repression, and to agree on a strategy for legally rehabilitating those who were not yet rehabilitated. We united in support of this agenda.

However, by the end of 1987 or early 1988, the differences between the moderate and radical wings of Memorial had emerged. The moderate wing was led by Yurii Samodurov and Lev Ponomarev, who had been in Memorial from the very beginning. [Victor Kuzin led the radical wing.] The radical wing made it clear that all political repressions from 1917 until 1988 should be investigated. Our opponents wanted to confine investigations only to Stalin's repressions.

These debates sharpened only at the latest stage. In the beginning we could not fully disclose our positions, especially while meeting with the public, because we would have shocked many people. We, therefore, only talked about the political prisoners.

On November 14, 1987, we formed a picket on the Staraya Arbat. We immediately were removed by the Fifth Department of the KGB. We were held for four hours, fined fifty rubles, and information about our actions was passed on to our workplaces. Of the ten of us at the demonstration, four carried placards and made up the picket itself, while the others were in the crowd to look for KGB agents, observe what happened to the picket line, and quickly report the outcome to the Western mass media because our Soviet mass media would not help us in any manner at that time.

At this point, the authorities were faced with a dilemma. On the one hand, Gorbachev himself was criticizing the regime. Thus, in one sense, our initiative was a development of Gorbachev's own policies. On the other hand, Gorbachev himself ordered the police to arrest us.

We attempted to educate the public so that ordinary people could understand the contradictions of this policy. Every week, we held small demonstrations in the center of Moscow so that people could observe our arrests. We also invited correspondents to the demonstrations to ensure that everything was filmed. Our demonstrations won the support of many people.

Among the events having a decisive impact on the development of the democratic movement of Moscow, one should mention the meeting for the de-Stalinization of society held on March, 6, 1988, at Oktyabrskaya [October] Square. There, for the first time, the fusion of the old dissidents and the new democratic groups occurred. At the meeting, we carried such slogans as Liberty to the Political Prisoners! Down with Political Repressions! Down with Privileges, and Down with the KGB. At that time, these were very radical slogans. Misha Kovalenko and myself distributed leaflets all around Moscow with the hope that people would at least come and watch. As Gorbachev allegedly also opposed the privileges of the nomenklatura, repressions, Stalinist crimes, we argued that people should be able to carry signs condemning these evils.

On the day of the meeting, the police had cordoned off the square and closed local stops on mass transit. We [Kuzin, L. Kovalenko, and Skubko] met elsewhere and then took a cab to the square. We jumped out of the car with our placards turned upside down and proceeded to the center of Oktyabrskaya Square, which was filled with KGB officers and police but no public crowd. Interestingly, there were many men in uniform but no one below the rank of lieutenant colonel. The square itself was blockaded with approximately forty cars and trucks. Just as we arrived, people from the Democracy and Humanism seminars emerged from the metro but were immediately arrested. We were also arrested, even though we had not yet shown our placards.

Along the perimeter line [formed by the police], a huge crowd stood and observed our arrests. News of this event spread throughout the city. After this meeting, many dissidents and democrats realized that perestroika was a fraud and that Gorbachev and his team were merely pursuing their own aims.

When did Yurii Afanasiev, Andrei Sakharov, and other such well-known people join Memorial?

This problem is connected with the existence of two poles within Memorial. After we attempted to picket in 1987 and were dispersed, some members of our group became very pessimistic. To galvanize the movement, two strategies were proposed. The first proposed that our public demonstrations should continue, regardless of the arrests and repressions, so that our efforts would continue to be covered by the media. We hoped that people would begin to think, "What strange things happen in this country! Gorbachev has proclaimed de-Stalinization, but the people who want to focus public attention on the victims of repressions are arrested!"

I agreed with Skubko and Kovalenko that we should continue such acts of defiance. If we acted amid the people, they would see how the government responded to us and would sympathize with us. This public support would then influence the state structures. It would be a long process, but it was a strong stance.

Our disagreement with the other position [in Memorial] centered around the issue of whether to perpetuate the memory of the victims of repression of only Communists or whether to include non-Communists and the enemies of Communists as well. We [the radical position] treated 1917 as the Bolshevik coup d'état directed against the people and the state. But Communists in Memorial had a different view, some because of their spiritual beliefs in communism and others because of their Party instructions to lead and direct the [Memorial] initiative. Among the latter was Vladimir Lysenko, who is now a people's deputy of Russia, and Lev Ponomarev, who is frankly speaking a non-Communist who became a Russian people's deputy as a close friend of Sakharov's. However, after he was elected as a deputy, he quickly became close to Lukyanov.

These people took a different approach to our tactics. This group—Lysenko, Ponomarev, Sheboldaev, and Samodurov—decided go out and recruit famous people. So Ponomarev, a doctor of physical and mathematical sciences and a close friend of Sakharov's, along with Samodurov began to visit famous people like Afanasiev, Popov, the actor Ulyanov, the publicist Karyakin, and others who then signed a letter in support of the Memorial initiative. In principle, this was not a bad thing, but we stood for different methods and found ourselves in the minority. All the people they approached were Communists. Thus, they were not sympathetic to our idea that we should preserve the memory of political repressions of the White Guard, of those who lost their lives in the Kronstadt uprising, of those who protested at the Putilovsky factory, of those who died in the famine, of the deportation of whole nations, and so on. Finally they agreed to sign our declaration, but they demanded major amendments to make the document less extreme. Moreover, we affirmed that the initiative should be concerned not only with the past but should also be directed at the present to defend people from political repressions and to help those political prisoners still in jail today.

It was around these issues that a real struggle took place at the founding congress of Memorial, which was held in January 1989. By this time, the

Democratic Union already existed and had been suppressed on the basis of the seventieth article of the penal code. Afanasiev did not want to discuss these issues at the founding congress. There were declarations submitted that demanded the liberation of political prisoners, but he removed them. More concretely, there was a resolution calling for the abolition of all the penal codes being used against Democratic Union members. He did not want to discuss this issue at all. There were also several resolutions expressing support for Armenia, but he used all means possible to remove them from the agenda.

This conference was saved by the Memorial delegation from Leningrad. This group, hardly known in Moscow, began fighting for the adoption of these resolutions and thus saved the cause. As a result we adopted an extremely radical version [of several resolutions] that I think made the Central Committee men tremble.

Thereafter, however, people like myself lost interest in the Memorial initiative. We had lost our influence there to strangers who began to take the organization in a different direction. However, the Democratic Union introduced into Memorial the necessary political vocabulary to describe our political reality, overcoming the so-called Orwell syndrome in which everything is labeled with opposite names and people's lives are conditioned by illusory concepts in an illusory world. In our documents, we had defined our state system as totalitarian, which at that time was an unthinkable thing to say. But not everyone agreed with us.

Let's return to the origins of the Democratic Union. How did the idea of a political party arise?

Soon after the creation of Memorial, the idea of uniting, forming some kind of nucleus, and then creating a party emerged. We created an organizational committee [for the party] in late March or early April. Its permanent members were Valeriya Novodvorskaya, Igor Tsarkov, Eduard Molchanov, Andrei Gryaznov, Alexander Eliovich, Evgenaya Debrianskaya, Yurii Skubko, and myself. In May 1988, we held the first congress of the Democratic Union.

We prepared the documents for the congress openly and without hindrance by the authorities. We also published the date, agenda, and draft program of the congress. The program turned out to be very promising, though it had been written in a hurry by many different people. It was more radical than the program of the People's Labor Union [NTS]. Regarding political matters, we called for the liquidation of the CPSU monopoly, the creation of a multiparty system, a parliamentary system, an independent court, freedom of the press, liquidation of the KGB, and complete repudiation of the criminal Leninist ideology. We declared that Leninism is the ideological foundation of totalitarianism. At that time, these statements were considered acts of sedition.

Among those at your first congress, did you have socialists and liberals present, or just one ideological orientation?

Socialists participated because we are a union. We believe that all conventional ideological groups should be represented if they concur with certain principles of civilized politics. These principles at a minimum include an independent court, a parliamentary regime, a multiparty system, a free press, and independent trade unions.

At the first congress, we had many liberal democrats. However, people came from different organizations as well, including supporters of Eurocommunism such as Eliovich and Gryaznov. We had very different views, but the model of "party-building" permitted us to unite people with different ideologies. Because there was a very small number of radical people from which to draw, it was important to unite these various political ideologies. It was especially important because if liberal democratic views were dominant, then the social democrats and Eurocommunists would not join us.

How did you know who to invite to the inaugural Democratic Union congress from other cities?

The Democratic Union did not emerge from a void. Its birth was preceded by a period of formation of different groups and initiatives. These groups developed their independent activities and formulated their own position with respect to the system. Some adjusted to the system, some criticized it, and some decisively fought against it. The latter group were the people who united to work for the Democratic Union. Only a few dared to take this step. This fact explains why the original Democratic Union was composed of many decisive but adventurous people, rather than people disposed to do the real party work. We even had several people with criminal records.

With this collection of people, we began to work. The congress was planned for May 7–9 to coincide with the May ninth holiday period.[19] Of course, from the very beginning, the members of the organizational committee were under continuous surveillance by the KGB. The congress was held in the flat of Bogachov into which 160 people managed to squeeze. Outside the flat stood many police and KGB.

Alexander Lukashov began our meeting by reading our political report. He was later killed. Valeriya Novodvorskaya then made her opening speech, and many people supported her initiatives. Vladimir Zhirinovsky also showed up at the congress and made a most unintelligible speech, after which we realized that his mission was to create obstacles to the formation of our party. Retrospectively, it's interesting to connect these actions [of Zhirinovsky's] with his present bid to become president of Russia. Only thirty minutes into the meeting, the police knocked on the door and demanded to be let in. We refused to open it even for Sergei Grigoryants, who came late. We feared that if we opened the door to let Grigoryants in, the police would invade. That first day ended very late. We closed by distributing drafts of documents, statutory principles, and our first program with the aim of discussing them the next day at the various flats around Moscow.

Then, on the third day, May 9, we planned to meet again as a whole at the editorial office of *Glasnost'*, which at that time was located at Grigoryants's dacha. On the seventh, we had left our session under KGB escort. As we filed out of the apartment, KGB agents followed each one of us ten meters behind. They did not detain us physically, but the psychological pressure was enormous. On the next day, we assembled at various flats according to the committee. We had sections on politics, the economy, ideology, constitutional questions, and culture. On this day, the police began to deter us with a series of obstacles. For instance, when I was at the meeting on political issues, the police stormed our apartment after only one hour of work, asking for identity cards. Remarkably, all of our people who were visiting Moscow for the congress had their identity cards in order. Formally, however, they had the right to delay all the residents who did not reside in Moscow.[20] As a lawyer, I tried to defend our guests by arguing that you cannot enter a man's home without his permission and demanded that they leave. They eventually agreed to leave the flat but waited for us on the street. When we left that evening, a huge crowd of policemen were waiting at the exit, demanding to see our passports. They let all the Muscovites go but held all out-of-town residents.

Alexander Chatov and I spent that night at the police station to watch what was being done to those arrested. We demanded to know the legal basis of the detention. They showed us a very old instruction from the Internal Ministry, which called for "the deportation of prostitutes from Moscow." This made us furious.

Having argued with the police throughout the night, I then went directly to Grigoryants's dacha at about six in the morning. The congress was scheduled to continue there at twelve that day. I arrived at the dacha and fell asleep only to be awakened early that morning by Yurii Petrovsky [one of the *Glasnost'* editors], who informed me that the police had arrived to arrest us. I went downstairs and saw that the house had been surrounded by police. They claimed that Grigoryants illegally occupied the dacha and therefore had to leave immediately.

Inside, we decided to take some preventive measures such as barricading the doors and windows and closing the useless extra shutters. Outside, they constantly demanded to be let in, but we refused, saying, "No, you cannot, this home does not belong to you." Grigoryants, who had been going inside and out, was suddenly seized, thrown into a car, and taken away. We then understood that they planned to storm the house. Suddenly, Bill Keller from the *New York Times* rang. I told him what was happening, that Grigoryants had just been taken and the assault was about to begin. Immediately thereafter, our telephone line was cut. They forced their way in, breaking windows and doors, perhaps expecting us to resist. They arrested us and took us to the Ramensky Department of the Internal Ministry. Naturally, they plundered the editorial office, taking several computers, type-writers, archive materials, and the dacha, for which he had paid a fantastic sum. We were tried for disobedience. The trial was held very quickly with only one judge. No fines were given, only detentions. We were given five days, Grigoryants seven. To protest our arrest, we all went on a hunger strike. It was my first five-day hunger strike.[21] When the main contingent of the delegates arrived at the congress, the house was surrounded by police. One old man then proposed that the congress convene on the premises of a rural soviet [council]. This, apparently, was another scheme of the regime because the hall closed on the delegation exactly one hour after they had arrived. They managed to finish the congress outside [near a railway station] with a tight circle of KGB officers surrounding them. Again, at this session, Zhirinovsky began to pretend to be a member of the coordinating council, but no one trusted him, and he was eventually asked to leave. After this episode, he began to criticize us severely.

What were your tactics after the congress?

At this first stage we had one task: to enlighten people about basic democratic values. Again, you must remember that for that time, these were very seditious ideas. Even criticism of the leading role of the CPSU was radical, while to stand for a multiparty system, private ownership, an independent and uncensored press, or the liquidation of the KGB was unthinkable. All the people who are now united in Democratic Russia regarded us as provocateurs and extremists; they fiercely criticized us with words in the same way that the Communists did with batons. Objectively, they worked for the same cause.

What were your relations with the Moscow People's Front, which emerged shortly after the Democratic Union?

The People's Front emerged in the summer [of 1988], but people who joined both the Democratic Union and the People's Front came from other earlier organizations such as Perestroika-88, Democratic Perestroika, Memorial, and Club of the Social Initiatives.

What was the general attitude of the people in the Moscow People's Front to the Democratic Union then?

Generally, their attitude toward the Democratic Union was skeptical and even hostile. These people, the honest people among them, understood that we set forth needed slogans and demands. On the other hand, they did not have enough spiritual will or firmness to stand along with us. Many people sympathized with us internally, but organizationally their reaction was critical, skeptical, and hostile. At several of their meetings, they described us as provocateurs, but for the most part, these speeches fell upon deaf ears.

The Moscow People's Front and other groups like it engaged in political activity within the framework permitted by the laws of the totalitarian state and the totalitarian constitution. If they were told no, they did not do it.

How did you organize your meetings?

[Unlike the Moscow People's Front] all our meetings were forbidden. We did not solicit permission for holding meetings because we considered the political system to be internally hostile to us and totally illegal. In our program documents, we declared that we shall adhere to guidelines [on congregation] set forth in human rights declarations and international agreements. We respected acts and legislation of the Soviet Union only so far as they did not contradict these agreements. We, however, did observe all the rest, including the constitution. We thus declared a nonviolent war on the regime.

Needless to say, the authorities did not like this. This explains why they vigorously repressed us for the whole period of our development. First, in the autumn of 1988, there was an attempt to bring an action against the members of the Leningrad organization. The same kinds of actions are resuming against us now.[22]

As for our activities, we gave weekly talks to which all were invited. Most people would not commit [to the party] because no one knew how Gorbachev's perestroika would end. As a result, we attracted people not of intellectual force but of firmness in their position. This characteristic persists among our members today. We have considerably more "fighters" than people capable of normal analysis of the situation and tactical flexibility. We suffer from this.

Formally, the aims of the Democratic Union seemed to have been achieved. We declared ourselves to be a party for the transitional period from totalitarianism to democracy. The external signs of parliamentary democracy—the parliament, the multiparty system, the independent press, the formally independent court— are all apparently available. In fact, all this is nothing more than an attempt to create the external facade of a formal democracy, but in fact there is no democracy. All this is but a screen behind which the former master and lord stands.

So we agitated and not only in Moscow but also in other cities. We tried to make people understand that this regime has not changed but is based on the former principles. This was not evident because perestroika was developing progressively. However, the attitude of the regime toward the Democratic Union exposed the essential nature of the regime. Those groups that carried out their activities with permission from the district communist committees and consulted with the authorities showed the good side of the authoritarian regime. But those such as the Democratic Union, who acted within the framework of the rules, showed the negative side. From the beginning, we rejected violence. We rejected the imposition of an idea [communism]. And for this, we were beaten.

This was our main task. We had to convince people of their right to choose their methods of opposition to the regime. These methods do not suppose any allegiance to Gorbachev or Yeltsin. Rather, these methods must be based on the certainty of popular initiative that can call into question the acts and words of the authorities. Democracy is strong not because a crowd adores a leader but because each individual has his own point of view.

How did you publicize your activities? How did you communicate to people, for instance, that you were holding a demonstration on Pushkin Square?

We had no support from the press at all. The mass media regularly berated us.

We found support mainly in the Western mass media. The first Soviet publication that wrote about us in a more or less neutral manner was *Ogonyok*, but this article was written much later. We eventually began our own newspaper, but that also took some time. Initially, we distributed leaflets.

If we planned a demonstration, we always informed the Western mass media and they willingly attended our meetings. This was our only defense because the authorities were afraid of any public scandal that would compromise Gorbachev's line. This is why the retaliations against us were moderate and measured.

How did new members find you?

Strangely enough, the Communists helped us. The first publication about our constituent congress was very critical. The author stated that we had a fascist faction in the Democratic Union. Deliberately, they published the telephone number of the flat where the constituent congress was held.[23] Supporters called us!

We also communicated with representatives of other democratic organizations who knew us well. They gave out our addresses to those interested in knowing more about the Democratic Union.

Why did the Democratic Union never become a mass organization?

We never intended to become a mass organization. Our organization offered no material advantage for becoming a member. On the contrary, membership led to repressions, unemployment, and other harassment. Other organizations enjoy a certain level of tolerance, and their members are elected as candidates and deputies for the government bodies. But we believed that membership in an organization should not be united by external rewards but by the internal conviction of the truth of its cause and a readiness to struggle for these ideals. These are virtues lost in our society. The Bolsheviks virtually killed these impulses among our people a long time ago. In our society, people's actions are guided by fear or by temptation.

Our society and state are fraught with moral and spiritual degradation. Those who had ideals were considered abnormal until very recently. Perhaps this situation is not unique to our society. But it explains our small membership.

The growth of our organization was also restrained by the great demands of membership. We wanted people who were committed. We would not want our people, finding themselves in jail, to betray their colleagues and reject their ideals. We placed our ideals above all else. Because the bearers of such virtues are a small group, our organization is small.

Our members are not angels, however. We have had many problems. We have had to part with many people for various different reasons. Some attempted to grow rich at the expense of the party. This is very normal, but it hurts the organization. Now we are suffering great difficulties because of our tactical inflexibility. As a result, we are losing our clout in political life. I do not mean the value of our ideas. On the contrary, their value now is generally accepted by most within the democratic movement.

This acceptance has occurred not because these ideas are ours but because we borrowed them from the experience of the Western democracies, where they have proved effective for decades. We wrote in our first program that we do not consider ourselves pioneers. We use only what has already worked. Our main contribution was to launch the mechanism of democracy, that is, to make this democratic movement itself a somewhat autonomous force.

By the way, Gavriil Popov [the mayor of Moscow] is a leader of this post-Bolshevik type because he believes the people should support him regardless of whether or not they understand what he intends to do. Such populism is a continuation of bolshevism, though from the opposite wing. This is a very regrettable trend. Again, there is no complete freedom of information, and, even more, I am becoming increasingly convinced that one should not trust anyone who came from the communist system, including Popov. It's absurd to endow them with absolute power.

The Mossoviet [Moscow City Council] is not against the mayor, it is against a mayor with unlimited powers. Popov wants to deprive the Mossoviet of its powers and become totally independent of the deputies and the electorate. He can be criticized, but he would be indifferent to criticism because there will not be any real threat that he will be removed from power. Popov also carried out a policy aimed at splitting the deputys' body itself. He frustrates any attempt at collaboration and blocks any decision that does not agree with his views. He is a very authoritarian person.

Postcoup Reflections (October 1991)

How has the political situation in Russia changed since the coup attempt in August?
However strange it may seem, the postputsch situation has changed our situation very little. The political process has changed in outward appearance, but its essence has remained the same. We used to say that a certain part of the CPSU nomenklatura remained in political power, slightly changing the content of their activities but still maintaining a monopoly on the political process. But now they are trying to seize key positions in the future market economy. It means that they will be leaders. But it also means that they can nominate candidates and provide victory to their protégés at elections. In our country the power of money is monstrous, and the power of rich people is tremendous.

But this may be not the most depressing and disappointing phenomenon in our postputsch situation. More important, you must understand what a certain group of our democrats are doing. Even before the putsch, we had no illusions about their commitment to democratic ideals or the pursuit of a policy to establish a legal regime that would make real the bourgeois idea of equal opportunities.

But we expected that they at least would be able to fulfill the task of establishing a parliamentary democracy that would allow energetic, enterprising people to start a business or sell their labor. But we see nothing of the kind.

We are convinced that these so-called democrats belong to another nomenklatura that I have always called the "nomenklatura democrats." We know that these people were narrow-minded. We know that people like Sobchak and Popov are Communists, though lately they had no Party membership cards. They are Communists not because of their sympathy to this ideology but because they had been involved in the nomenklatura cover-ups. It means that there are compromising facts that can be used to blackmail these people. For that reason they will support the interests of these circles whether they want to or not.

This tendency revealed itself in the Moscow City Council headed by Popov immediately after the elections. We saw that the system of power in Moscow, which was controlled by the democratic Moscow City Soviet to some extent, began to be destroyed. De facto, it has been destroyed, though it is the only legal power in Moscow. We have the city soviet de facto, which looks like a democratic body, but it is democratic in name only. If we examine the city council's policy and the staff of the leaders, we will discover that they are either Communists or people connected with Communists. They are not only Communists but also belong to the nomenklatura.

Who is among them? Take, for instance, Bryachikhin—the former first secretary of the Sevastopolsky CPSU District Committee. Or [Boris] Nikolsky—the second secretary of the Georgian Communist Party Central Committee, who was certainly involved in some way with the Tbilisi events.[24] Another one is [Nikolai] Karnaukhov. Most of the other staff people, with several exceptions, came to the Moscow City Soviet during the times of [Victor] Grishin, the notorious CPSU Central Committee Politburo member, and Saikin, his protégé. It is necessary to change these old people, for they can not work in a new way.

Under the old regime, when the likes of [Vladimir] Kryuchkov and [Boris] Pugo were in power, it was difficult to replace these people. Popov did not attempt to neutralize them and confer their powers and functions to democrats. Even after the putsch, when Popov even had the power to occupy the building on the Old Square [Staraya Ploshchad] that had belonged to the CPSU Central Committee, he did not replace these people. Naturally then, he faces a certain opposition within the city soviet, where our work is most active. Look at the way the city hall works; they keep everything top secret. We learn about certain decisions taken by the [executive branch of the] city council weeks or months later. We have learned that state flats in state-owned buildings have begun to be distributed among the nomenklatura. Popov or [Yurii] Luzhkov [the vice-mayor] are doing it. This process is taking place despite the critical situation in our city housing. The government's attempts at improving the food supply in the city also have been pitiful.[25] We realize that Moscow is not a separate state and that it is impossible to change everything for the better until change takes place in the rest of Russia. However, some measures can be taken. The city council could receive a tremendous profit by leasing buildings and/or privatizing properties. But the city government uses the buildings it confiscated [after the coup] in the wrong way. For instance, the new mayor's office is located in the old CMEA [Council for Mutual Economic Assistance] building.[26] It is a very comfortable building designed to accommodate international representatives. Why was this building not leased to foreign firms? If it had been leased for hard currency, the profit would have amounted to one-third of the city budget in rubles. We might have been able to give assistance to those people living below the poverty line. But Popov says that they are loafers who do not want to work and that only those who cannot work should be assisted. In fact, he does not support them either.

Popov also talks about the necessity of a decisive transition to the market, but he does not carry out this transition. Much time has passed already, but he has yet to take some measures to privatize shops. He asserts that the decisions of the Moscow City Soviet are inhibiting him and that there are enemies of democracy in this body. Popov capitalized on the democratic Moscow City Soviet as a politician, but now he aims to bury the Moscow City Soviet because we criticize him.

How did he seize power? He snatched up the Moscow KGB and then appointed his assistant, Evgenii Sevostyanov, to be the new head of this organization. Then he illegally took control of the militia, violating the constitution and laws of Russia. He says that he is a democrat and therefore invents various pretexts to justify his usurpation of power.

It is clear that he is simply concentrating power in his hands when he says that he needs [Arkady] Murashev, a civilian, as chief of the Moscow militia.[27] Popov claims that generals [professional police officers] cannot stay there because they showed themselves at a disadvantage during the putsch. In fact, this is typical demagogy because in reality different generals took different actions. On the one hand there were those who backed the putschists, and on the other hand there were those who backed [Marshal] Shaposhnikov, [General] Kobets.[28]

By the way, the manner in which Moscow's government acted during the putsch was extremely vague. It is not clear, for instance, why Luzhkov did not give the order to build up concrete defenses around the White House.[29] It was in his power. There are a number of concrete structures and parts production plants subordinate to the Moscow government.

For some strange reason, Luzhkov issued an order to deliver tremendous quantities of foodstuffs into shops on the day of the putsch. Much is vague here. Luzhkov's first statement on the coup was not distributed immediately; nobody knew about it. And what is the most interesting is that the committee formed to investigate anticonstitutional activities during the coup examined the actions of Mirikov, the chief of the Moscow militia. The committee established that, during

August 19–20, Mirikov followed Luzhkov's orders. At the same time the committee established that during those days, Mirikov did not take a single step to counteract the putschists. Thus, a lot of questions arise.

We would have had many more facts on this matter if the Moscow militia had been headed by a law-abiding person who would have sought to maintain law and order in Moscow. But it was not done. The fact that Komissarov is a person devoted to democratic values, though he is a general of the militia, was not doubted. He is a highly qualified professional who has a complete conception of how to improve the functioning of our police. When few civilians dared to criticize the CPSU, he made a statement that it was a criminal organization during testimony before our committee last November.[30] We knew very well that, during the 1980s, Komissarov, who was the minister of internal affairs of Osetia, Georgia, proved himself to be inclined to using noncoercive measures to settle conflicts. We knew that he was given orders to resort to coercive measures against mass disturbances, but he refused and preferred other ways of settlement. The total sum of this person's traits of character makes him extremely valuable and fit for the post of the Moscow police chief. Popov, however, did not want an honest, independent professional in this position because he was afraid that such a police chief would reveal facts compromising himself and Luzhkov.

Popov is unscrupulous. What is going to happen when he concentrates all power in his hands (now that the KGB and the Moscow police are subordinate to him), while he is attempting to gain control of the office of the public prosecutor? We are going to struggle against him. We have tried to explain to Yeltsin the situation, and he has realized there is a problem.

Popov and Luzhkov, the so-called Moscow government group, are merely Mafia. Popov has not bought all of us because we are so many, but he has managed to buy a great many deputies. He keeps saying that the Moscow City Soviet has been wasting money, that deputies' salaries are very big, but the average salary of a city hall worker is 2.5 times higher than that of a deputy.

Popov's people have prevented the five hundred Moscow City Soviet deputies from working effectively. They have disorganized our work deliberately in order to get rid of the Moscow City Soviet altogether. Before, Communists used to interfere with our work in the same way. But after August 19, the Communists have disappeared so we do not feel any opposition on their part. Popov's team is the only disorganizing force left. While Popov does not seek to revive communism, his actions can give rise to confrontation with the masses, which can lead to establishment of a terrorist regime. These people are moving to capitalism, but how?

At present, Popov, Sobchak, Shevardnadze, and Yakovlev are trying to resurrect the nomenklatura system that has been defeated.[31] I can not explain present events otherwise.

Document

. . . .

The following document is the political program adopted by the Democratic Union at its founding congress in May 1988. At the time, it was the most radical anticommunist program and the first to advocate the creation of a multiparty democracy.

Declaration of the Democratic Union Party

Man is born free, and there is no ideology and no social idea that could compensate him for the loss of this freedom. Man's inalienable right is the right to doubt, to quest, to disagree with the majority, to dream, and to uphold his own beliefs. In effect, freedom is the right to oppose. Since October 1917, we gradually have been denied this freedom until we were deprived of it altogether. This denial has determined the entire course of history of this country.

The Communist Party's monopoly on truth, on political power, and on society's economic and intellectual life has led what once was a rich country to the brink of bankruptcy, its people to material misery, and one of the world's greatest cultures into spiritual decay and mediocrity.

The October coup of 1917 was made possible by the underdevelopment of a democratic culture and civil awareness of broad popular masses, inherited from the period of Russian absolutism. The monopoly on power, which has destroyed individual sovereignty as well as civil society and which is the foundation of the totalitarian system, must be overcome. Otherwise, the country will undergo social upheaval as a result of ecological catastrophe, ideological and moral breakdown, and political disarray. The millions of victims sacrificed to totalitarianism and the tragic experience of many nations have demonstrated that there is no alternative to a democratic society. Totalitarianism is the principal cause of the most severe crisis that has hit our society and become especially aggravated during the 1980s. Not only individual criminals or groups of criminals, but the entire system of partocracy [sic], is the primary source of popular misfortunes.

The Communist Party, which has exercised undivided rule in the country and which has declared its ideology to be the only key to absolute truth and "heaven on earth," led the people down the path of tragic mistakes and crimes. A permanent hell was established in the name of achieving this "heaven on earth." The more the regime killed, tortured, and persecuted people for their convictions, the more it lied about the imminent creation of a society in which there would be neither violence nor murder. But the road of lies and crimes does not lead to such a society.

No one has the right to decide for the people which path society should take. Only the people themselves can choose this path through agreement and the free expression of their will. But lest the principle of power by the people and for the people be an ideological illusion, a minority disagreeing with a decision by the majority must have a legal opportunity to campaign extensively for a different social system. Democracy differs from bankrupt democratic centralism because of precisely this—the absence of a system to suppress a minority.

We no longer want to live by the dogmas of "great ideas" for the happy future of unknown successors. We want a worthy life for ourselves and our fellow citizens today and declare a decisive break from the totalitarian past. Setting ourselves the goal of achieving a democratic society, we form a political party called the Democratic Union, which unites people of different political convictions—from democratically minded Communists and Social Democrats to Liberal and Christian Democrats. Despite all our ideological differences, we believe in the unconditional value of individual freedom and are committed to the principle of pluralism once formulated by Voltaire: "I find your opinion thoroughly alien, but I am prepared to sacrifice my life for your right to express it."

Democracy for us is not a slogan or an empty call but the form and essence of a social system based on political, economic, and spiritual pluralism, a multiparty system with a free press and independent labor unions. We are committed to the idea of the state being above all parties and to the principle of primacy of personal rights over the interests of the state.

Our social, moral, and political position is based on the renunciation of violence as a method of political action, no matter what wonderful and humane goals may be cited to justify it. This is why we denounce not only Stalin's wholesale terror but also the red Bolshevik terror that was unleashed in 1918, as well as genocide against the peasantry during collectivization. We consider the harassment of dissidents, which has continued to this day, to be criminal.

The path to democracy lies through the deideologization of the state and equal rights for both the currently dominant ideology of the Communist Party and all other ideologies and views.

Advocating a radical democratic transformation of society, we define the substance of our activities as political opposition to the totalitarian state system in the USSR. We do not seek confrontation for the sake of confrontation and do not repudiate sensible cooperation with the state, while not agreeing to ideological and moral compromises. We consider it our direct duty to wage a decisive ideological and moral struggle against forces within the ruling party that seek to block the way to pluralism and humanity. But at the same time, we declare our support for those members of the Communist Party who seek to take advantage of their position in the ruling party to effect democratic reforms in fact rather than in words.

Even the insignificant changes for the better that have been brought about currently by the national leadership are no guarantee against a relapse into Stalin's or Brezhnev's times. The main guarantee—the realization by the people of their rights and their readiness to uphold these rights—is even far from being realized. The existence of a democratic opposition is an essential condition of the nation's revival. We oppose physical and moral violence on the part of repressive agencies serving the ruling nomenklatura with the full power of moral and ideological resistance and confidence in the righteousness of our cause. We are prepared to cooperate with other forces sharing democratic ideals and convictions.

We believe that the state should not prevent religion from constituting a moral guide for the people.

We want our country to assume a worthy place among other powers—not through the force of arms but as a result of the greatness of its spirit. This was a dream nurtured by its great humanists and enlighteners—Gertzen, Tolstoy, and Dostoevsky. But for this dream to come true, we need to relinquish voluntarily imperial ambitions and gains. A people who oppresses other peoples cannot be free. Therefore, we strongly condemn the USSR's policy of expansionism.

After having existed for seventy years as a totalitarian state, all of us have to repent, sincerely and openly, for the evil that has been done. This will not humiliate us but will cleanse us. We believe in the unsquandered energies of our people and their capacity for rebirth.

Adopted by the First Democratic Union Congress
on May 9, 1988

chapter three

Pamyat'

Although patriotic clubs had existed well before 1985, national patriotic sentiments were some of the first political ideas to surface publicly under *glasnost'*. As early as 1987, "patriots" began holding public demonstrations and propagating their materials at Pushkin Square in Moscow and the Rumyantsev Garden in Leningrad, well before the "democrats" appeared on the streets.

Pamyat' (the Russian word for memory), however, is not a single organization but a number of national patriotic clubs and organizations that have periodically united and divided.[1] The common principles that unite these organizations have been (1) a desire to awake a national revival of the Russian nation and (2) a belief that a Zionist-Masonic conspiracy is destroying Russia's greatness.[2]

Although dozens of factions and clubs exist throughout the Russian Federation and among Russian ethnic groups living in other former Soviet republics, two of the most famous include Otechestvo, based in Saint Petersburg and Moscow, and the national patriotic front Pamyat', headed by Dmitrii Vasiliev in Moscow. Compared with other patriotic groups, Otechestvo is a moderate organization focused principally on preserving Russian traditions and cultures. The national patriotic front Pamyat', in contrast, resembles a paramilitary organization, complete with military training and secret membership. The group claims to have branches in more than thirty Russian cities.

Despite their high profile, patriotic organizations fared miserably in the 1989 and 1990 elections. Those who did win elections—most notably Alexander Rutskoi, the former Moscow deputy chairman of Otechestvo and now the Russian vice-president—quickly distanced themselves from the radical elements of Pamyat' organizations.[3]

Beginning in 1990, some patriotic organizations began seeking alliances with neocommunist groups. Although starting from very different premises, these two groups share a hatred for the West and a desire to preserve Russia's imperial greatness. After the Communist Party was banned in August 1991 and the USSR was dissolved in December 1991, their cooperative activities greatly expanded, and the visibility of nationalist and patriotic organizations has increased commensurately. Beginning in January 1992, Pamyat' organizations have participated with neocommunist groups in public demonstrations against the Yeltsin government. On February 8, 1992, several Pamyat' groups participated in the Congress of Patriotic Forces, which brought together nationalist Communists (i.e., the parliamentary faction Rossiya), nationalist democrats (i.e., the Christian-Democratic Movement of Russia), and Alexander Rutskoi, the Russian vice-president, who many hoped would be the leader of the nationalist communist coalition.[4] The following day, the two groups—nicknamed the "red-and-browns"—joined forces to stage an anti-Yeltsin demonstration in Moscow.[5] Whether this marriage of neo-Communists and neonationalists can continue to function, however, is uncertain. The historical lack of unity within the nationalist patriotic camp suggests that holding together a united front with neo-Communists will be difficult.

Dmitrii Vasiliev

Dmitrii Vasiliev, the leader of the national patriotic front Pamyat', is the most charismatic and well-known figure in all the nationalist and patriotic organizations. Before entering politics, Vasiliev was an actor and photographer. When addressing audiences he frequently dresses in traditional Russian clothing. His followers wear black uniforms.

The interview took place at the semisecret headquarters of the most prominent Pamyat' organization in Moscow. As we entered the offices, two bare-chested men covered with tattoos escorted us to the vestibule to Vasiliev's office. In the vestibule hung the Pamyat' flag, red canvas with black lettering. The word *Pamyat'* was spelled out with Old Church Slavonic letters, making the middle letter, *m*, look like a swastika.

We have purposely limited our editing of the following text so as to preserve the manner and "logic" of Mr. Vasiliev's words. We have not included any documents or political programs as Vasiliev's organization is against programs, ideologies, and platforms. The group even refuses to call itself a political organization.[6]

Interview with
Dmitrii Vasiliev (*June 1991*)

. . . .

How did you decide to get into politics?
There are two ways of getting involved in politics—out of desire and out of
necessity. I am an actor and a stage director by nature. I also write, though it is
for others to decide whether my writing is good or bad. Anyway, I have an urge
to do it. I am also a photographer, and, as a hobby, I like to farm. Surprisingly
even to myself, however, I have gone into politics, something for which I did not
even prepare myself, as I never thought that I would have to be concerned with
rescuing my country, my fatherland. I had to do it, though, because they [the
Communists] drove the people into a billiard pocket. The way Russian people
live is not even slavery, since the slave owner at least feeds the slaves. The
Communists have victimized the nation by failing to provide adequate food,
ruling by ruthless tyranny and violence, while accusing the previous system—
monarchy—of all these sins.

However, the monarchy, in contrast, ensured a natural, vibrant, beautiful,
and healthy life, generating immense spiritual and moral development. The
Communists, having arrogated the right to condemn and demolish everything not
created by them, have become so brazen that one can no longer tolerate their
political boorishness in any form. Naturally, therefore, one must protest. There
are two alternatives: be a communist slave, a victim of the Communist Party
midwife that has invented Marx, Lenin, and the entire gang of criminals who
have drowned their own people in blood, or fight them.

But as soon as I rose to fight, I naturally had to study the mechanism of the
disease; I had to investigate the germ that started it all. I began studying the
sources of communist ideas that have begun to conquer the world. Quite involuntarily, I traced them to Zionism. They are inseparable: Zionism-Judaism and
communism. One stems from the other and vice versa. All the postulates are the
same: Zionists have hegemonic claims on the world and their theory of racial
superiority just as the Communists do. The Communists summon the devil, Satan,
to help. This makes them the diabolical scum attempting to set us at odds with
God because our state is atheistic according to communist ideology. All this
enables me to conclude that their power is from Satan. They are forcing their
system of government on us to spread their rule over one-sixth of the globe.
These are hegemonic aspirations. This is also expansionism—efforts to foist their
world outlook on the great many people inhabiting this country.

Naturally enough, this made me think about what was happening, and I asked myself how come that such an anomaly as the communist doctrine has been able to triumph in the world and, in particular, in Russia. This naturally led me to an analysis of the Paris Commune. It turned out that those were all Masonic deeds, purely Masonic—all those Marats and Robespierres. That, too, was a secret political concept not of the majority but of a minority reduced to a party striving to achieve world domination. As I studied Masonry, I became ever more convinced that Masonry is the bridge from the Zionist idea of global domination to the expansionism of communist ideology under communist slogans, all those idiotic slogans invented by that bearded idiot Marx and no-less bearded Lenin. They staged a bloody orgy in the world. When I began to think about it all and when I spoke about Zionism and Judaism, I was not referring to all Jewish people in general. I spoke about individuals, I spoke about specific people. There are more riffraff among the Russians who have betrayed their nation, betrayed their people and still betray them, serving the Communists, licking their asses, and lacking the courage to mutiny. All nations have mutinied, while the Russians are still sitting idle and sleeping. I realize that there is little you can do against genocide, but today even children are dying from malnutrition. So, why are you sleeping? Why are you sitting? How much longer can we tolerate all this mess? One has to be an animal, not a human being, to be able to put up with all this.

This kind of patience [in the Russian people] also helped my awakening, pushed me to act. I am a Russian, I respect members of any ethnic group, but I do not like scoundrels of any ethnic backgrounds. Scoundrels are an international notion, they are the underworld of ethnic contacts. Why should I respect them?

I was immediately branded an anti-Semite. This was just because I dared to denounce Zionism. However, Zionism is not at all some characteristic of the Jewish people because Jews themselves are the victims of Zionists, and, incidentally, Jews suffer more from Zionists than from anything else. This is because ordinary Jewish people are a bargaining chip in their game. Take, for instance, Eichmann of the Third Reich. He was a Jew by nationality, but he exterminated Jews in concentration camps. It prompted me to take a look at national socialism and examine what it was. I began to think, "Can a theory of racial superiority and impious concepts appear in a Christian nation?" No! I began to explore [Christian] religions and I found nothing like it there. But Judaism has it! All this, correspondingly, comes from Zionism, that is, the political fiber of the nation and people, the upper crust, as Marx would say, of the Jewish bourgeois oligarchy. It was Jews themselves, however, that suffered. Jews were killed through the fault of Jewish leaders, while the blame was shifted entirely on the Germans. They say that the Germans are to blame. Yes, they are. But why don't people admit that the ideologue of that extermination was a Jew? Today, they [the Zionists] speak about communist expansionism, but the movement's ideologue was Marx, a Jew. They fail to mention that he was a Jew.

This is a taboo [to mention such things]. Jews have done it all, invented it all, covered themselves with blood, but we are supposed to keep quiet. My attitude toward Marx the Jew, Lenin the Jew, Trotsky the Jew, and the like is just the same as my attitude toward the Russian villains that served them loyally and did it all for them. They are equally guilty. None of them is more guilty or less guilty. People betraying their history and traditions are just as guilty.

As soon as I started to say that I am a Russian, they began branding me a Fascist. However, this is a compliment for me because Fascist means a bundle, a bunch, unity, and there is nothing terrible about this word. It only sounds bad for illiterate idiots, just as the notion of anti-Semitism does. I can easily prove that I am not an anti-Semite because I love Arabs, and the Arabs are the main Semite group. So, how can I be accused of anti-Semitism? How can I be accused of Judophobia [sic]? Can anyone charge that I have ever made a programmatic speech against the Jewish people anywhere? If you can prove it, then call me any name you wish. I am prepared to answer back. But you can't prove it because it never happened. I am a reasonable person, and I understand everything. Even if I were a crafty politician, I would have never done it. I would have acted by totally different methods. Do I look like an idiot to do something as silly as this, especially as I have studied the experience, say, of the Roman Empire, Hellenic civilization, Byzantine, and the Third Reich? The charges are groundless. This is again a deliberate campaign by a press afraid of the ethnic self-awareness reawakening throughout the world, which is the foundation of strength and prosperity of any state and calm and stability in the world. When a nation is strong in spirit, respects its national history, and is educated enough to understand the fundamentals of its culture, it naturally projects this love and respect to any other nation because its cultural level is so high. Amid barbarians, no civilized state can survive because it will be swamped and eaten.

Advocating these views, I have been called so many names, but this did not stop me and, on the contrary, only convinced me that my position is right. And I began to wage an active struggle because I am aware that in the struggle between evil and good, where the battlefield is the human heart, as Dostoevsky said, the world is on the brink of death, and evil is increasingly plunging the world into aggression, which first develops at individual-to-individual level and then escalates into interethnic and continental conflicts. This must not be allowed. This is why we began our work.

When did Pamyat' begin its work?
In the 1970s. At the time, there were also cosmopolitan dissidents, but they didn't care for our ideas. They still fought the communist dictatorship in their own way; it can't be said that they didn't do anything. Nevertheless, they stood on cosmopolitan positions, while we took purely national positions in our struggle.

The whole situation [in the country] has forced me into politics. Strange as it may seem, I am a man that is kind by nature, and I simply don't want to be involved in all this. I want to work on land, I want to see kind faces, admire nature, and do whatever I like. But I cannot do this today because God has entrusted this responsibility in us. Having said *a*, I must now go down to the end of the alphabet. Otherwise I would be a coward. In short, things should be brought to their logical conclusion. What happens next is hard to say.

I have explained our predicament even to Zionists who have visited from Israel. I always tell them, "Drop your idiotic idea of conquering the world! Can't you see that nothing comes out of it, nothing but evil and hatred toward you, ever since the Crucifixion of Christ? You will only exacerbate the situation and make people start beating you in all nations at the same time. So far, you only have been beaten locally, but you are now bringing the world to a frenzy. This is true even in countries that seem to have been very loyal to you and treated you normally, countries where there has never been a Jewish question. Even these nations are increasingly on edge because they are realizing that there is a hegemonic effort to subdue the national interests of every state." I tell them, "Imagine the entire world rising up in arms against you and charging at you. Imagine what will be the outcome. You, as a people, will cease to exist. Do you want this? Is it your secret goal? Maybe you are masochists prepared for self-destruction. But I tell you that this is your problem. We have different problems." I am a Russian, I am more interested in the Russian issue, more interested in the Russian history and culture.

What are your political activities? How do you struggle against Zionism and the Masonic movement in Russia?

You see, it is easier with Zionism. It has an ethnic idea and for this reason, it is possible to find one's bearings. It is much more difficult with Masonry because Masonry involves traitors of the [Russian] nation. A Mason can sit alongside you, look exactly like you, and nonetheless be up to treachery. This makes it much more difficult. As a matter of fact, the entire communist model of the state is patterned on the Masonic lodge. Reports by informants go from the bottom to the top, and orders come from top to bottom. The entire communist doctrine and communist administration in this country is modeled on this Masonic pyramid. Everything is done secretly, and the Communists leave no loose ends. If you write a letter to the Communist Party, no one will reply to you because they say, "This is not the custom here." Why? They held power illegally for seventy-three years in this country. But who perpetrated all this for seventy-three years? Against whom can a lawsuit be filed now? Was it a legally unaccountable organization? Why did you then assume the right to destroy, knife, strangle, and shoot people and do all this in secret? The rank-and-file Communists are uninitiated ignoramuses. They were mere executioners. Those initiated into the Masons are up top, sitting tight, and watching from above. Policies now change this way and now that way—for no apparent reason. You don't know what to think. First, one guy with bushy brows sits here, teaching us, day and night, how we should love communism and socialism, but then a metamorphosis occurs, perestroika is announced, only to be followed by catastroika [*sic*] and then revolution. And it happens this way all the time. This means that there is some planned nature in all this and that the masses do not know by which methods, at what rate, or by which conditions our society develops when everything depends on the winks of top leaders. Since there are no visible causes to explain changes in this or that structure, this means that they are hidden in the corridors of power. One can only judge what is happening in the country by what they are scheming. It is a different matter, however, when it comes to proving that someone is a Mason. This is difficult. Only a fellow member of the Masonic lodge can do this.

But what are your methods of struggle?

Their own, Masonic tactics, only with our own substance.

That is, force?

Absolutely. You see, I have realized one thing, namely, that all these liberal notions about the world are sheer rubbish. For instance, the child in your family becomes too naughty. You let him get away with it once, twice, and thrice. But he keeps fooling about and pours boiling water on your head. That's it. You are scalded, and skin peels off your face. This won't happen if you punish him as soon as he starts mischief. It's another matter as to which method of punishment to use—persuasion, a belt, or something else. But there still has to be a measure of punishment to stop improper actions.

Are you implying, then, that the people are like children?

Of course! The people are children and the country is the mother. The people are the children, and the head of state is the father of the nation, who should raise them. Everything turns on him—how educated he is, how competent, cultured, honest, and decent he is. This is the principle underlying monarchy, which is why our state under monarchy grew ever stronger while love flourished in the nation. Now, love has been replaced by hatred because it is the political ambitions and egocentrism of political leaders that are flourishing, while the people are only fed promises in order to win them over to various political platforms. The promises are later forgotten, and only political ambitions remain, which turn very fast either into a dictatorship or some other absolute. All this results in a political leader leading the country ultimately either into a dead end or bloodshed. In contrast, a monarch is first of all a Christian, a believer serving godly interests, writing not human-drafted laws but Christian postulates. This has a wholesome effect on the nation if the sovereign is noble. This is not the case now. Basic thousand-year-old morals and ethics connected with Christianity are absent, replaced by a mean and damned communist morality. There can be no communist morality, as morality is one and the same everywhere. And there can be no Soviet spirituality or Western spirituality. There is only one spirituality, one that emanates from the Holy Spirit, which consists in observing Christian values and the postulates of the Christian cause. I dream of opening my eyes one day and seeing

Russia, as in the past, as a land of geniuses. Today it is the most infamous, police-run, communist regime, hunting talents by means of the KGB and Interior Ministry, killing, knifing, strangling, and shooting its own people.

How did the national patriotic front come to exist?

Spontaneously. It is even hard to explain it because, at first, it had the nature of charity functions, enlightenment seminars, and the like in the 1970s. It was only gradually, after we studied documents shedding light on the country's tragedy, that our political awareness crystallized. By 1985, we had probably achieved political and civic maturity. On October 4, 1985, we held the first political event on the subject titled Oh, Moscow, How Much Does Your Name Hold for the Russian Ear! We read "Protocols of Zion Sages" there, hitting Zionism and [Victor] Grishin hard and setting the general tone of our movement.[7] On May 6, 1987, Saint George's Day, we held the first demonstration on Manezh Square, the first large unauthorized demonstration during the seventy years of the Soviet regime.[8] The column of demonstrators included some six hundred people. But how many were on the sidelines, I could not guess. I was concerned about the people watching, as we were aware that the demonstration could be greeted with fire, all the more so as the demonstration was being held on Manezh Square under the Kremlin walls.[9] To safeguard against a government crackdown, I concentrated some ten thousand people along the periphery of the square. They were invisible demonstrators. I instructed them that if any action was taken against the central group of activists, they should stream onto the square from all sides, surround the demonstrators, and leave by alleys, still encircling the demonstrators so that nobody could be arrested. But everything worked out fine. Yeltsin even received us. He was not that impressive. Judging by what he said and how he spoke, I perceived him as a devout and impassioned Communist. This is why I cannot understand the current infatuation with Yeltsin. I generally do not distinguish between the Communists; they are all spiders in a jar. They are all like this, only one has already thrown his Party membership card out of the jar, while another still keeps his under his armpit. It is only the forms that are changing, while the substance remains the same.

We need to change our ideology in the country and dismantle the one-party system. We need to have an assembly of the land. All social groups should be represented there as they were in the assembly of the land in the past. It is still too early to speak of monarchy because society is not yet ripe. But in order to move toward it, social classes or estates must be created anew, determined by birth or occupation, not economic position, in order to bring these estates up to higher cultural levels like it was in the past. The peasants' estate, the workers' estate, the nobility estate, and the middle-class estate should all be elevated to a corresponding level, and their best should represent them in the assembly of the land. These representatives should not be appointed by anyone but suggested by the people themselves. It is not party interests that should be defended in the assembly of the land because a party is the same as ideology. We have a million democratic parties today, but they are all still permeated with communist doctrines. They cannot imagine any other path of development other than the one they have known for the past seventy years. This is true of even the monarchist parties. Incidentally, there can be no monarchist parties by definition. They are all Communists by their convictions, all of them. They speak about monarchy, but they do not even understand what it is. This represents the horrible tragedy of the political movement in this country because it is assuming a surrogate nature. Whereas previously communism was very much manifest, it is now taking cover in some democratic organizations, and this is what makes it frightening. This all happened before—on the eve of the February revolution and the October coup. The same old scheme is now being repeated. Of course, the man in the street is impressed, but he does not remember anything and has never known anything after all the brainwashing in school. Now he just turns on another brainwasher—the television—and does nothing else.

What can you expect from such a society? Which political games do you intend to play with it? You should not play games with our society right now because it is very dangerous. The democrats have stirred up the crowd, but they do not understand what will be the final outcome. The mob itself will crush them and swallow them. Why? Because the Communists are holding the democrats by the throat. They do not leave them any chance to move because all the store shelves are completely barren. Why should the people need any sausage-and-vodka philosophy if there is no sausage and vodka in the store? Tomorrow, the democrats will all be gulped down. Why? Because they are absolutely immature politically. They all declare inviable principles and make unmanageable promises. They dangle out lots of promises but this is ridiculous. In such a country as this, one can promise nothing to anyone. The tsar was wise: he just floated a draft law as a trial balloon to reach the lowest levels, and as it went the full way from top to bottom and from bottom to top, it gained weight and substance. Now, we have a political cacophony.

Meanwhile, the West goes crazy, subsidizing everything without even realizing whom it subsidizes. It is the West who let the communist hydra grow after the Paris Commune. The West is a traitor; America and the West have betrayed Russia. They do not even understand the kind of games they are playing by supporting Communists. This spells tragedy for America: either a red flag or a flag of another state will be hoisted there very soon as America will be bought up, lock, stock, and barrel. America has a catastrophic balance-of-payments deficit and disastrous liabilities. They are bluffing prosperity because they no longer pay any attention to anything but making a faster buck and enlisting foreign investments while the people may starve to death. Why? Because the powers that be there realize what America really is, and they inflate the image of the American establishment, which is nothing but camouflage. How do they do it? By means of Hussein's treachery, for example, through provocation. For America, this is not a war, it is a carte blanche won by America today. Hussein's act of betrayal was a deliberate move to somehow reinvigorate the situation in America, on the one hand, and bolster Israeli presence and Israeli influence in the region. These are all nothing but games. Hussein is just a traitor, an agent provocateur. He is either a fool, a madman, or a political adventurist. What did he do to the Intifada that had by that time united the entire Arab world? It choked up entirely and instantaneously. This also enabled Israel to enhance its influence in the region. In addition, he depressed the Arab world and exacerbated the Arab crisis. What is the positive function of this procommunist Hussein? The war was a downright provocation—a collusion to help Bush, which had our consent. We were not involved, but we helped maintain the situation.

Are there any affirmative political forces in the United States?

I believe that the situation in the United States is fairly complex. My impression from meetings with Americans is that there are good forces there, although, alas, the show is controlled by the Zionists there, and they prevent ethnic forces from gathering momentum. Just like the Soviet Union, America is a caldron of very many ethnic groups. So they [the Zionists] are preventing ethnic development. Incidentally, how can America, which established its domination and influence just three hundred years ago, be cited as an example for us to follow? We have been around for thousands of years. I find it ridiculous to look at America as an experience for us to draw on. Secondly, we increased our strength without destroying our native populations, while America practically destroyed the Indians, driving them onto reservations. Should we borrow this bloody experience? I believe that America is an extremely unfortunate example, all the more so as it helps the Communists today so actively. Bush is a very dubious figure for me.

Do you have contacts in the West?

This is a kind of question which is put to us by the KGB and the Interior Ministry. I prefer not to answer it, just as I prefer not to discuss the question of our membership.[10] When people ask me, "How large is your organization?" I always reply, "Large." Likewise, when asked about our structure, I always answer, "We exist and, at the same time, we don't. That's all." In this way I have preempted all your questions. This is all I can say on this score.

Returning to political tactics, does the national patriotic front aim, first and foremost, to bring pressure to bear on the authorities, while remaining in opposition to them, or do you hope to come to power?

No. We are not struggling to seize power. Rather, we are struggling to change the system of power. Today, in this country today, we do not have "power." We have a form of government. Power is bestowed by God. In an atheistic state, there can be no power. It can only have a form of government. And because its power does not come from God, I have the full moral right, as a Christian, to press for changing this form of government. This is what we are doing.

Which organizations do you view as your rivals?

There are many such organizations, but they are almost worthless. You see, the number of all these parties and associations is so great because three people have gathered and decided to make a revolution, and so they go out on the streets and hurl bombs, and that's it, that is their entire party. Or they collect one million signatures, which does not mean anything.

What are your relations with monarchists?

I believe that Pamyat' members are the only monarchists in the Soviet Union. Pamyat' declared that we should return to a monarchy before these other organizations existed. Moreover, a monarchy cannot be based on parties. It's just another piece of nonsense, designed to discredit the very essence of monarchy.

What are your relations with other patriotic organizations?

They have not joined Pamyat' because they are afraid of being slandered. I do not recognize such patriots. We have been through the baptism of fire, worked out our political orientations, and gained political experience. All too often, these other organizations are just high school boys. They come to us and say, "We are a monarchist party."

I tell them, "My dear, first, get rid of this kind of terminology and say that you are not a monarchist party, but monarchists." Then I ask, "What kind of monarchists are you?"

They immediately reply, "Constitutional monarchists."

I tell them, "There is no such thing as a constitutional monarchy. It's just another piece of trash. A constitution and a monarchy are mutually exclusive. A constitutional monarchy is something invented to enslave the people to an even greater extent."

They then respond, "Then we are for an absolute monarchy." I retort, "Friends, there is no such notion either. An absolute monarchy is a dictatorship, the power of one person."

"What kind of monarchy is there then?"

"Ah, darlings, you ought to have started with this before calling yourselves monarchists."

This is how monarchist parties are born here. I am for an autocratic monarchy as the only right form of government, whereby legislative, judicial, and executive power is concentrated in the sovereign's hands, who then relies on the social institutions of the state to carry out his decisions. This is the meaning of autocracy.

You stated earlier, however, that the national patriotic front's primary goal is to reinstate an assembly of the land. What methods do you plan to use to achieve these goals? Do you recognize the methods of revolution?

Not at all. Political revolutions are nonsense, an alien strategy. They do not produce any result except for a very transient effect, only to be followed by a rude awakening and increased hatred toward the lightning changes. We favor a slow-but-sure approach, which means that we should first develop knowledge.

How can we talk of increasing popular self-awareness if knowledge is lacking? For what is self-awareness? It is greater knowledge. How can we increase self-awareness if we do not know our history, our traditions, our roots? We need to upgrade our awareness to be able to understand internal ethnic problems. How can one speak of changing the political system today if we have all this ignorance, primitive thinking, and low educational standards in our universities?

Luckily, I avoided our higher education system. But I study twenty-four hours a day—from people, from life, from books. They give me so many ideas and knowledge that if you are able to fit it all in your head, you don't need any university. Universities are needed to keep young people busy and detract them from practical work on the land. They study, then look for a job, then find a job and do not do anything on this job, while nonetheless being paid. They are all concentrated in cities, manageable and dependent. The powers that be find it more advantageous if people stay here and do some slipshod work, but be dependent on them, than gain complete independence working on the land. Because those working on the land grow produce, market it for money or payment in kind, and are thus independent. They have their own cellars crammed with food; they know that they can feed themselves, so they do not give a damn for others. If an energy crisis hits, they will burn candles and keep a furnace going. There is no hopeless situation for them. With horses, they need no tractors. They are independent. This is why the private property—land—is denied to people here. They now advocate privatization and tell people to go ahead and build their homes. But they do not give land to the people. Land, however, is given neither by a party nor by a state. It is given by God! It is our habitat. Throw a fish out of an aquarium and it will die. How can land be separated from man? This is why humanity decays in the cities, getting infected with diseases, killing itself, corrupting its conscience, failing to see the world in its harmony—simple sunrises and sunsets and birds singing. Everything in cities is artificial. They [the government] drive living nature into cages and behind store windows. They even sell us nature, conditioning us mentally to be completely dependent on them. Pamyat' is against this kind of life. We favor an organic human life directly from the earth, as the primary factor of living. Urban living is total nonsense.

Do you plan a gradual resettlement of people from the town to the country?

I want to tell you that the concentration of the human potential in cities is extremely dangerous for any state from a strategic point of view. The primary force, the main wealth, of any state is its people. But their concentration in cities makes a state strategically vulnerable. Just imagine if missiles are fired on Moscow? Hit all capitals and half the people on earth will be dead. This is why distributing your population evenly across your territory is wise for any state.

Living as we are, we burrow deep into the ground and destroy immense natural riches, destabilizing the situation on earth only to service cities and industry that are needed by no one. We are killing our own planet, we are killing ourselves. Why do it? The city does not give us anything, it only numbs our conscience. Moreover, a person needs contact with the heavens. In receiving a spirit descended from heaven, we form some invisible contact with outer space. The city cuts off this bond. Our entire life-style is changed with all this television and radio. It should be this way: as the sun sets, we go to bed, too, only to get up with the first rays of the sun in the morning. As nature reawakens, so do we, living in tune with nature, producing something until nature goes to sleep, and then we go to sleep as well. Everything went this way, the natural way, in the past. Now, everything has been turned upside down. Magnetism has increased, the effects of ionospheres and negative charges have increased. All this is affecting our awareness.

Take the homes we live in—concrete dwellings. Put a radio on the windowsill, and it will work better. But take it inside the room, and it will receive no program. The same is true with the head. If you sleep in a concrete house, you receive nothing and you give nothing. This is why you come out in the morning like a devil and can think of nothing but whom to bite. A wooden house and continuous contact with nature and with land are all we need. This is why we have had so many writers and poets born on the land and why authors flee cities to write their best works in the country, in contact with nature. This is because the word is part of nature. When we came to the city, we cut off our conscience and cut off the word.

This is why a land distribution program will make people more harmonious, pure, independent, strong, and rich. They will then not obey the state. And when they unite, there is no stopping them! In contrast, when they are all here [in the cities], with all the police in the cities, anybody can be apprehended, anybody can be hauled in on some pretext.

In this connection, what kind of economic reform does Pamyat' support?

Such a question is typical from a Soviet man! We all live under some programs! Are we cyborgs? People cannot live by programs. There must be no programs! They are all rubbish. The most humane program is the absence of any programs. This is because everything laid down in Christianity has already been formulated, and you are given the chance to learn everything else through your own experience. Learn, take advantage of your experience, and everything will be fine. But when you are handed down a program, you again act like a slave under it. What makes Pamyat' so effective is that we work without any program. We never know what we shall do next. We are drinking tea, and it suddenly occurs to us what we ought to do tomorrow. So we do it. And we succeed. Before they manage to prepare for it or prevent it, it's all over. The train has already left. We do not fit into a program. This is very important.

There can be no economic program as well. There is the natural course of commercial and economic relations, the natural course of farm produce and manufactured goods. This involves the town-country relationship, where everything is so natural that nothing has to be planned. It only needs that you do your job competently and produce quality products. Commodity-money-commodity, that's the whole cycle.

We favor the rejection of the communist program, with its collective farms and state farms, and advocate the free use of land. This is no program. This is a vital need. Get a plot of land, use it, grow produce.

To begin this rebirth, which writers and poets do you believe should be read?

As for historians, we should forget Solovev and Klyuchevsky. They should be known, but they present a very subjective view of history, very Masoniclike, very socialistlike, and I would even say communistlike, by the ideas and notions they profess. Alexander Nechevolodov adeptly blended historical documents, authentic testimonies by witnesses, and his own poetic enthusiasm with history. Or take Ivan Zabelin, a brilliant historian, Ilovaisky, a leading monarchist historian, or Kostomarov, who had his revolutionary vacillations and deviations but still retained an impartial and objective style of writing. Or take such an exceptional author as Zagoskin. His work is an amazing embodiment of historical and documentary material in poetry. Undoubtedly, Derzhavin is simply an amazing historian. We know him as a public figure, politician, poet, and so on, but he was also an extraordinary historian and a remarkable thinker. I should also mention Zhukovsky, who was a little misguided by Masonry but still was a sincere person, and Professor Platonov, a major expert on the troubled times. These are the principal authors who can give us a clearer picture of history. As far as objective descriptions of the lives and activities of our sovereigns are concerned, I would recommend Olderborg. Among the generators of ideas, I should certainly mention Dostoyevsky, who was able to combine the grief of national decay with the nation's spiritual strength along with fallacious revolutionary ideas and views— a wonderful phenomenon merging everything in himself, a person perfectly realizing the hopeless nature of historical shifts in this country and foreseeing the future but still remaining a committed optimist. Read *The Devils*. It is a picture of today. Of course, you should read Nikolai Gogol, the shining peak from the standpoint of both literature's artistic merits and civic activism. Nobody has since been able to conquer these heights. Finally, banal as it may sound, one must include Pushkin, but he is more a lyricist than a citizen.

What about modern writers?

You see, a terrible metamorphosis has taken place in the country of Soviets—in the world as a whole, too, but here especially—apparently because this is the focus of all the world's madness, and the Slavs' special mission is to demonstrate to all those living on earth the tragedy taking place here and thus show the world how it shouldn't live. Here, for instance, they divide artists into painters, graphic artists, sculptors, designers, applied artists, and so on and so forth. The implication is that there are no artists, no maestros, only dabblers divided into categories depending on their specialization. This leaves no art, just hackwork.

Nonetheless, if I am to mention noteworthy writers—not geniuses but talented writers prevented by the Soviet system from developing their genius—these are Belov, Astafiev, Rasputin, Abramov, and Rubtsov. They are a reflection of the times and, perhaps, if they had lived in prerevolutionary Russia, they might have become geniuses.

What about Solzhenitsyn? What is your attitude toward him?

Solzhenitsyn for me is simply a journalist. He is a real journalist who knows his ropes but nothing more than a journalist. He can skillfully use his information. If you could receive documents from the archives, you could write better books because your perception will be fresher and keener. And you won't be so monotonous. Imagery is what makes great literature; Solzhenitsyn does not have this quality.

As far as his program for reorganizing Russia is concerned, I simply do not support it because it is at odds with many of our traditions. As he sees it, we can do without monarchy, or take his indifferent attitude to Orthodoxy [the Russian Orthodox church]. Similarly, his idea that our state must be dismembered in order to be united is also misguided. In America they have a document, PL-86-90, which says that Russia must be dismembered. It is Brzezinski, if I remember it correctly, who disclosed it to the press, and it became clear to everyone what they wanted to do with Russia—dividing it into geopolitical districts rather than ethnic territories.

Do you advocate Russia's separation from the Central Asian republics or do you favor preserving the Soviet Union?

No separation by any manner or means! Unfortunately, our disgusting propaganda does not allow alternative views to be expressed. I keep in touch with nationalist organizations in practically all other republics, and nowhere do they want to separate from Russia, nowhere. Among ethnically conscious people, serious and educated people, no one wants to secede, neither in Armenia nor in Georgia. All this is being done by politicians to the detriment of their our people. It is like what happened with Armenia before the revolution when Lenin gave Turkey half of Armenia to please Britain. It was his payment to them for their having given him money for the revolution. The same is true of the western part of the Ukraine, the Baltics, and so on.

Are you satisfied with the results of your work?

I am satisfied with how our work is going, but I am not satisfied with the final results. So far, everything is too flimsy.

What kind of difficulties do you experience?

Wholesale treachery. This is frightening. The country has produced a huge number of ordinary turncoats, blatant national traitors. The cowardice of your associates is the greatest difficulty. In addition, the secret services have infiltrated our ranks. So I have to act also as security chief and do constant analysis. As soon as a new contingent joins in, I look at them very carefully, analyzing their old links and identifying the logical signs of the presence of agents inside our movement. And then I either remove them or follow their actions very closely. The third difficulty is the terribly low educational standards in the country from top to bottom. Russia has not known such intellectual drabness for a thousand years. Having graduated from a parish school in a village, a peasant used to know a thousand times more than our people know now. Now they say that our people then were illiterate. Rubbish! A lie! Pyotr Stolypin carried out an education reform whereby several hundred schools opened in the countryside during his reign. He brought culture and knowledge to the people, realizing that it was impossible to save the nation without it.

This decline can be seen even in parliament—the so-called cream of society. Just listen to the way they talk—totally illiterate. These are deformities of the language and culture, but a deformed language means, first of all, a lack of inner culture. Why the lack of inner culture? Because a person lacks knowledge. A clever politician will never put a new word into circulation without first analyzing it from all sides. Take, for instance, pluralism. On the one hand, it means diversity, and, on the other, in medical terminology, it is a gang rape watched by another gang. So, try to understand where we belong—to the rapists or to the raped. It seems to me that we are the raped. It can't go much further. If the national leadership demonstrates such low political standards and shows only political cunning, this country will never achieve political success.

As for ideological difficulties, I should also mention communist expansionism, which continues to grow, paralyzing the human conscience, psychology, and mind. Only now it has been transformed into a democratic shape.

Would you argue, then, that organizations like Democratic Russia are communist?

As I see it, it [Democratic Russia] is just a well-camouflaged outgrowth of one force inside one party. America has two parties—the Republicans and the Democrats. Eight years ago a poll was taken on differences between them. A girl in her fifth year at school answered that there was no difference. She was right; they all are subsidized by the same force. Since the American model of production is now being imposed here, we too are introducing a two-party system. There will be the Communists and the anti-Communists, only the anti-Communists will be communist-minded. After all the crimes they have committed here, one is naturally apt to ask, "How can you stay in power?" They are puppets, kept to cover up vested interests. This means that there is a system that subsidizes all this.

How is the communist nature of Democratic Russia manifested?

In the methods and pattern of their work and actions. For instance, I am told that the presidential form of government will change our life and we shall be better off. How come? Will one word, *president*, change everything? So, let's not elect anybody.[11] After all, an election costs 150 million rubles. I am told that everything will change when Yeltsin becomes president. Why isn't he doing anything today? Everyone around is down and out, and they claim that his election will change everything! It is important to them to change the sociopolitical structure and introduce a purely American model. Enormous funds are spent on it—200 million rubles to change a word [from *chairman* to *president*]—while 100 million people live below the poverty line. Every session of the Congress of People's Deputies costs 20 million rubles! Do you understand the absurdity of the system in this country? All is done in order to obtain credits from idiots in the West.

But they [in the West] are no fools! They do everything lest they have communism: "May Russia carry this yoke itself until everyone there dies! We don't want any bit of it, so [instead] take everything you want!" The West will make investments here. But we shall not answer for the Communists' debts. We shall send them to Swiss banks; let them withdraw money from accounts there. And they will ruin Switzerland because Switzerland hinges on the money from countries ruled by communist regimes. It is Switzerland that regulates the dollar exchange rate. The exaggerated rate of the dollar and the devalued ruble are a result of our capital being stored in Swiss banks. We are not idiots; we understand this. The exploitation of such a vast country and the siphoning off of its natural resources and funds bring astronomic billions in profits to Europe and the entire banking system of the world. If we evaluate all our property, capital, and basic assets that we have today, the value will be six to seven times higher than the present value of the ruble. But the press does not report this. This is because they get their money from the same bag, be it *Pravda* in Moscow or the *New York Times* in New York. It is the same worldwide syndicate of slander and public deception in the interest of capitalism.

If people begin to love me for opening their eyes to these activities, they [the capitalists and Communists?] will reckon with me. I will have to be destroyed. If I am physically destroyed, I will be a martyr. To avoid this, they will try to destroy me morally, by slinging mud, sowing slander, and practicing treachery in order to crush me. But I cannot be crushed! I am born for victory, and God is with me! He is the highest judge for me.

chapter four

The Democratic Party of Russia

As discussed in detail in chapter 1, the idea of creating a massive opposition party to the CPSU began to percolate among many liberal reformers within the CPSU at the end of 1989. At that time, the Democratic Platform was taking shape within the CPSU while activists from the popular fronts in Moscow, Leningrad, and elsewhere were also discussing the proposition.

The Democratic Party of Russia was the first attempt to create a political party of liberal reformers from the CPSU and moderate activists from outside the Party. The initial impetus for the Democratic Party came from the Leningrad Popular Front, headed by Marina Salye and Ilya Konstantinov, at the end of 1989. After the March elections, activists from the Moscow Association of Voters, including Vera Kriger and Lev Ponomarev, also supported the idea. Finally, in March 1990, when it became clear that the CPSU would not accept the Democratic Platform's alternative program, prominent leaders of this reform movement, including Nikolai Travkin, Gennadii Burbulis, and Arkadii Murashev, quit the Communist Party and advocated the creation of an alternative party. In April 1990, Nikolai Travkin formed an organizational committee for the Democratic Party of Russia.

During May 27–28, 1990, the first organizational conference of the Democratic Party of Russia convened. Lofty aspirations of creating a single, massive political party, however, were shattered on the second day of the congress when serious disagreements emerged among the party's leading figures. The major division erupted over the issue of leadership. Nikolai Travkin proposed that the party have only one chairman, as was the tradition with other West European political parties. Marina Salye, Vera Kriger, and Lev Ponomarev argued that the party should have three cochairmen to avoid the centralization of power. Travkin's faction won the debate, but the majority of the Leningrad delegates, along with Vera Kriger and Lev Ponomarev, quit the party over this issue.[1]

Despite this shaky start, the Democratic Party began setting up regional branches throughout Russia. With the exception of the Democratic Union, no other political organization had attempted to establish cells or local representatives, so the campaign initially had tremendous success. By the end of the year, the Democratic Party was unequivocally the largest noncommunist political party in Russia.

At the founding congress of the party, December 1–2, 1990, in Moscow, Nikolai Travkin was elected party chairman and the party's first draft program was approved.[2] The party's platform was vague and short, focusing more on "anticommunism" than on concrete proposals for changing the Soviet system. The congress also abolished ethnic factions within the party, stating that such divisions threatened to divide Russia and the Soviet Union.

The party suffered further splits at its second congress at the end of April 1991.[3] Although also motivated by personal clashes, publicly this split centered around substantive policy issues.[4] Dissatisfied with the draft program submitted for ratification at the congress, the "liberal" faction of the party, led by Arkadii Murashev and Garry Kasparov, submitted an alternative program.[5] Although nuances and emphases varied, the fundamental divide between the two documents concerned whether to support the preservation of the Soviet Union and the Russian Federation. Kasparov and Murashev supported the preservation of both but stated that republics (and autonomous regions) had the right to leave.[6] Travkin argued that the Soviet Union must be preserved at all costs. The congress sided with Travkin, with which Kasparov, Murashev, and several dozen other delegates quit the party.[7]

Travkin, increasingly convinced that the Union must be preserved, would not even entertain questions about independence for autonomous regions within the Russian Federation. During the summer of 1991, Travkin traveled to several other republics in his bid to form an all-Union democratic party, focusing particular attention on the rights of minorities—Russian minorities. Ideologically, the party moved further to the right (according to the Western political spectrum), becoming champions of private property and unregulated entrepreneurship. Several leading Russian businessmen, including Svyatoslav Fodorov, the world-renowned eye surgeon, began to support the party, as did conservative parties in Western Europe.[8] At the same time, Travkin remained committed to preserving a strong state, arguing that only a strong and unified state could protect private property rights and the human rights of minorities.

Travkin's resolute stance regarding the Union and the Russian Federation fueled tensions between Democratic Russia (DemRossiya) and the Democratic Party of Russia. Travkin had always disliked the idea of a coalition because the Democratic Party had been founded before DemRossiya. Instead, he urged others to join *his* party in a united front against the Communist Party.[9] Moreover, when local DemRossiya chapters began to form after its founding congress in October 1990, they relied almost exclusively on preexisting Democratic Party structures and individuals in several major cities. Travkin considered this coattailing dangerous to his party's development.

Soviet military actions in Lithuania and Latvia in January 1991 catalyzed democratic cooperation on all levels and helped to improve relations between Democratic Russia and the Democratic Party. Travkin and Valerii Kkomyakov, the head of the Democratic Party's Executive Committee, became members of the Coordinating Council of Democratic Russia at that time, while the party as a whole formally joined the DemRossiya coalition. In recognition of their special size and importance, the Democratic Party along with the Republican Party and the Social-Democratic Party were allocated more seats in the DemRossiya Council of Representatives than were other organizations.

The Democratic Party, however, was never an active partner in Democratic Russia, for there was tension between parties in the coalition and nonparty activists. Party leaders considered their parties to be the backbone of the coalition, whereas nonparty leaders considered the parties to be only a small fraction of DemRossiya's active members. These strains escalated after the coup attempt in August 1991 when the necessity of maintaining an anticommunist coalition withered. Once again, the most controversial issue revolved around attitudes toward the preservation of the Union and the Russian Federation. In the spring of 1991, Travkin joined forces with Victor Aksiuchits of the Russian Christian-Democratic Movement and Mikhail Astafiev of the Constitutional Democratic Party—the Party of People's Freedom—to form Narodnoe Soglasie, or Popular Accord, a bloc of parties united first and foremost by their shared attitudes regarding the necessity of preserving a strong Russian and, if possible, Soviet state.[10] In November 1991, this bloc of parties formally left the Democratic Russia movement, claiming that the radicals who controlled the coalition were responsible for the collapse of the Soviet Union and were now fostering the dissolution of the Russian Federation. According to Travkin, "The Democratic Party of Russia is stronger than the rest of the (Democratic Russia) movement" and therefore did not need the coalition affiliation.[11]

In December 1991, the Democratic Party held its third congress in Moscow with great pomp and circumstance. More than seven hundred delegates attended as well as observer delegations from Europe and Asia. During the congress, Stanislav Shatalin, an author of the five-hundred-day plan, was elected chairman of the Political Council of the party. Travkin lauded Shatalin's new role as well as the new membership of several other prominent Russian intellectuals and politicians as the beginning of a new era in the history of the party. At that time, given that the Communist Party had been banned, the Democratic Party was the largest political party in Russia.

Scandal, however, again crippled the party after the third congress. On receiving information about the Minsk meeting among the presidents from Russia, Ukraine, and Belarus that established the Commonwealth of Independent States, the Democratic Party hastily organized a demonstration denouncing the agreement.[12] In opposing the dissolution of the Soviet Union, however, the Democratic Party suddenly shared the political positions of people such as Vladimir Zhirinovsky and Victor Alksnis. When the Democratic Party held its meeting on Manezh Square, both Zhirinovsky and Alksnis attended, adding credence to the rumors about cooperation between Russian nationalists and the Democratic Party. Immediately thereafter, Shatalin, as well as one of the party's deputy cochairmen, Alexander Terekhov, quit the party to protest Travkin's dangerous relations with nationalists and Fascists.[13] Since the creation of the Commonwealth of Independent States, Travkin has advocated redrawing Russia's borders to reflect its precommunist territory.

Despite a brief flirtation in December, Travkin did not follow his Narodnoe Soglasie partners into the new nationalist coalitions. Victor Aksiuchits and Mikhail Astafiev were two main organizers of the Congress of Civil and Patriotic Forces in February 1992, but Travkin and his Democratic Party refused to attend, thereby dissolving the Narodnoe Soglasie bloc.[14] Instead, Travkin sought new allies, first with the People's Party for Free Russia (Rutskoi's party) and later with Obnovlenie (Renewal), the political arm of the Union of Industrialists and Entrepreneurs, cochaired by Arkadii Volsky and Alexander Vladislavlev.[15] On June 21, 1992, these three organizations joined forces with the parliamentary faction Smena, the chairman of the Moscow City Council, Sergei Gonchar', and Deputy Prime Minister Vladimir Shumeiko to found a new coalition called Grazhdanksii Soyuz (Civil Union).[16] This coalition consists of two large parties (the Democratic Party and the People's Free Party of Russia), a parliamentary faction (Smena), a powerful and organized union of industrialists (Obnovlenie), prominent people in Yeltsin's government (the vice-president and three deputy prime ministers), and charismatic and popular leaders (Rutskoi and Travkin).

At its founding, this powerful coalition united behind two main concerns: strengthening the Russian state and protecting Russia's industrial base.[17] As one of the first *gosudarstvenniki* (statists), Travkin and the Democratic Party fully supported the coalition's position on the Russian state. The coalition's endorsement of protecting Russian state enterprises and criticism of Yegor Gaidar's economic policy, however, again prompted splits within the Democratic Party. In particular, Alexander Sungurov, the chairman of the Democratic Party in Saint Petersburg, formed a "liberal" faction within the party to resist Travkin's courtship of Obnovlenie's "conservative" industrial directors,[18] which eventually left the Democratic Party of Russia altogether.

Despite these splits, the Democratic Party of Russia remains the largest political party in Russia, claiming more than fifty thousand members in 549 cities.[19] The party is represented at all levels of government and plays an active role in the parliamentary process. Since its inception, the Democratic Party has focused on preparations for the next elections.[20] Nikolai Travkin's name is often mentioned as a possible successor to Yeltsin, depending on which way the political pendulum swings during 1993–1996.

Nikolai Travkin

As noted above, Nikolai Travkin is chairman and founder of the Russian Democratic Party, and to many in Russia, the Democratic Party of Russia is synonymous with his name. Born in 1946 and educated at a teacher's institute in Moscow, Travkin worked for many years as a construction foreman, for which he received the Hero of Socialist Labor award. Because of his leadership qualities, Travkin was invited to attend the Moscow Higher Party School to receive training as a Communist Party functionary.

During perestroika, Travkin became an outspoken liberal within the CPSU. In 1989, he was elected to the Supreme Soviet of the USSR, where he helped to found the Interregional Group of People's Deputies along with other prominent reformers such as Yurii Afanasiev, Gennadii Burbulis, Telman Gdlyan, Arkadii Murashev, Gavriil Popov, Andrei Sakharov, Anatoly Sobchak, Boris Yeltsin, and Ilya Zaslavsky. In January 1990, Travkin was also one of the prominent figures who joined the Democratic Platform. In March 1990, Travkin won a seat in the RSFSR parliament as well. For the following two years, he devoted most of his energies into building up the Democratic Party. In January 1992, however, Travkin was named head administrator of the Shakhovskoi region of the Moscow oblast.[21] In accepting this position, Travkin hopes to establish a record of executive successes before the next elections.

Interview with
Nikolai Travkin (June 1991)

. . . .

When and why did you decide to go into politics?

It is connected with this expanded economic experiment. My first experience dates back to 1978, when my construction gang used some principles of the free economy. Our wages were not fixed nor were the salaries of administrative workers or engineers. We took on a construction project with a certain estimate, which we had no right to exceed, but it was the construction crew's decision as to how to split the estimate. We eventually expanded this experimental method of building. At first we had a crew of fifty people, then a small organization of two hundred people, then a construction trust of twenty-two-hundred people, and at the last stage a large-scale organization working in the Moscow region with sixteen thousand people. At this stage, we did not use any of our previous experiences from communism. In addition to the right to decide how to split the estimate, the collective was self-governing. We did not have to be governed by some general regulations as to how many workers to employ or what kind of holiday they should have. This was called an economic council. Later, when our experience spread throughout the country to other branches of industry, it was called the Council of Workers' Collectives (CWCs). The Council of Workers' Collectives, once a progressive organization, has evolved into a conservative one today.

The final stage of this project was in 1987–1988. Everything happened very fast because the crew itself had been developing these methods from 1978 to 1984. In 1984, the crew was transformed into other units, and its leader became the chief of a unit of two hundred people. In only two years, this unit became an amalgamation that belonged to the Chief Administrative Board enjoying the rights of a Republican Ministry, i.e., it was at a rather high level. But whereas at the previous stages political limitations at the city or district level did not really interfere with our work, at the Republican level a conflict between economic development and rigid Party and political structures pushed me into politics. It was very unpleasant. In 1988 I had to leave the construction business and spend a year in the Higher Party School. The following year, 1989, we had elections of the USSR people's deputies. I have been engaged in politics ever since.

How did you get elected as a USSR people's deputy?

In the first place I was quite well known as a reformer in the building industry. In 1986, I was awarded the title of a Hero of Socialist Labor. I attended two Party congresses and the Nineteenth Party Conference, at which my name became known. So, during the elections, I was nominated in many parts of the Moscow region.

You were one of the leaders of the Democratic Platform. Why did you leave this organization?
The Democratic Platform is a fragment of the whole chain which brought into being many different parties. The first link in this chain was the Interregional Group of People's Deputies. It functioned only at the congress of the USSR Parliament, but its political actions were of considerable importance for the entire country. Public opinion even came to identify the Interregional Group of People's Deputies with a certain structure. There were questions at the meetings: "Why don't you set up grass roots cells to give you organized support?"

This is why the second stage of the search for some common political force was the creation of the movement Democratic Russia. The idea for Democratic Russia preceded the Democratic Platform. It was clear to the organizers of Democratic Russia that having like-minded people in the parliament alone was not enough for doing the job because all other links, all soviets, all power structures, remained beyond the influence of the democrats. The Democratic Russia movement had a common program and expected candidates running for election both at the grass roots level for city and district soviets and at the highest level, the Russian parliament, to subscribe to it. The idea was to form a single structure of like-minded deputies who were supposed to pursue a common policy throughout the entire hierarchy of the organs of power. Then it would be possible to change something by legislative means. They [the Democratic Russia sup-porters] also were supposed to lobby to influence the executive bodies.

The idea was good, but it failed because everything rested on the movement and meetings. There was no permanent organizational work done. Eastern Europe's experience was misleading, too. People asked, "Why should we create structures and institutions if Eastern Europe succeeded in defeating communism through powerful democratic movements—the Round Table or Solidarity?[22] If they succeeded, we should do the same."

The weak points of the movement [Democratic Russia] already have become apparent. For instance, among the deputies at the Russian parliament who were members of Democratic Russia, people had very different views with only one thing in common—anticommunism. But how were we to carry out further trans-formations? Some people were in favor of private property, others were against. Some said that land could be sold, others that it could not be sold. Some were in favor of carrying out privatization in the normal way to ensure the best economic effect, while others said that privatization should not ignore social justice. In other words, there were all sorts of views on every issue.

This situation lead to the third step—the formation of parties. At first, the idea was to create a kind of a party within the existing structures of the CPSU that would be constituted of people who disagreed with the CPSU ideology yet remained within the Party structure. This was the Democratic Platform.

So from the very beginning of the creation of the Democratic Platform, you had the idea of creating a new party?

Yes, this was the case from the very start when the Democratic Platform was being created. The maximum plan was to create a party on the basis of the Democratic Platform in the following way: We would come to the Twenty-eighth Party Congress using the canvassing for candidates to get as many deputies' mandates as possible for people who supported us at the twenty-eighth congress. If we had more than 50 percent support at the congress, the deputies would give up the communist ideology of the Party and a newly oriented party would be founded based on the majority of the delegates at the congress. That was the maximum plan.

The minimum plan was the following: We would come to the congress and make an impression on a number of delegates. We would not be able to reform the Party or change its program or ideology, but we hoped that many would leave the Party accompanied by the division of Party property. The Party would be split into two parts. We made no secret of it.

However, once the election for deputies to the congress began, it showed that we could not expect either outcome, be it reforming or splitting the Party. Only several dozen of our delegates were elected. Before the plenum preceding the congress, we had approached Gorbachev with the idea that he should hear the opposite positions expressed by the Democratic Platform. He refused, however, to invite me to attend the plenum. [Vasilii] Shakhnovsky and [Vladimir] Lysenko attended, but they were not allowed to speak. Gorbachev and [Alexander] Yakovlev, in fact, had agreed to let me attend, but other Politburo members said no. So why should I remain in the Party if they would not even listen?

Following this episode, I left the Party. As the congress approached it became clear that nothing could be done from within the CPSU. We were just wasting time. I argued that we had no time to waste and instead should create another party. We decided that some people should leave the Party right away and begin to organize a new party, while others would leave the CPSU after the congress as a method for encouraging even more people to leave. But there was a gentlemen's agreement between all within the whole Democratic Platform that everyone would agree to join together after the congress.

Why did this plan fail?

When Yeltsin left the CPSU [during the congress] he refused to join any other party, claiming that he had made a pledge to remain nonpartisan during his election campaign for the chairman of the Russian Supreme Soviet.[23] Other major personalities such as Popov, Sobchak, and Stankevich decided to remain outside of parties because they were too occupied with government offices at lower levels.[24] Still others who left the CPSU at that time, figures such as Vyacheslav

Shostakovsky and Vladimir Lysenko, said that could not join "Travkin's party." This was how the Democratic Party had been labeled. It was all prompted by heightened self-esteem. So they started to form their own party, which later became the Republican Party.

Do you think that other attempts at splitting the Party from within might succeed? For instance, is this what Yeltsin had in mind when he chose Alexander Rutskoi as his vice-president?

I do not think so. The choice of Rutskoi had little to do with his membership in the CPSU or the Russian Communist Party because normal Communists understand that neither Yeltsin nor Travkin has any intention to begin persecutions against Communists. The choice of Rutskoi as his vice-president was connected with the main opponent in the presidential run—Nikolai Ryzhkov.[25] Who did Ryzhkov have as his running mate? He had Boris Gromov as his vice-president.[26] What kind of people gave support to Gromov? They were the military, Afghan veterans, people in uniform, and the disabled. It was necessary to neutralize him.

How does the Democratic Party of Russia differ from other parties?

The main difference is that nearly all parties have proclaimed the primacy of common human values. But when it comes to the key issues, such as the state system or the market, this primacy for others recedes into the background. With us this primacy permeates all of the party's ideological program. We affirm that an individual's interests are higher than the state's. Why do we start to develop the economy? Why do we build the state? To meet more fully the demands of the individual.

This conflict between the individual and the state is most apparent regarding military issues. How are we supposed to deal with military doctrine? The peculiarity of our economy is that 50 percent of it is devoted to military purposes. The individual gains nothing from this, so there must be a drastic cut there. Why can't we make this drastic cut? Because we have this doctrine of sufficient defense capability, that is, we must maintain military parity all the time. Well, if the individual suffers from this notion, it means that the doctrine is wrong. We can cut military expenditures if no one is threatening us. So maybe we could develop a different military doctrine: civilized countries do not threaten each other. There may arise a threat, like the one in Iraq, for instance. Then, the Soviet Union must take the initiative of creating united armed forces under the auspices of the United Nations to prevent such local conflicts. But the starting point of these kinds of decisions must be the primacy of the individual, that is, the primacy of the individual over society. There cannot be social interests that run against an individual's interests.

Let us consider the state system. Should Russia remain a single whole or should we adhere to the slogan To Each Nation Self-Determination Even If It Means Secession? What is the benefit of division [of the Russian state] for the individual? None. If Russia is split up into separate states, the burden of taxes for each person increases. The maintenance of Tatarstan's president is more expensive than that of the chairman of the Russian Supreme Soviet.[27] These splits run against the interests of the individual, so they should not be done. This is the most important issue.

[Another distinguishing feature of our party] relates to a sore point which we have been debating for over a year now—the Union. The question is whether or not we should have a Union at all. Most of the democratically oriented parties say, "No, the Union has no right to exist because it will lead to the revival of totalitarianism." We, however, argue that not only can the Union be—it must be. There are things which are cheaper to do together, and this is advantageous for each individual. But the Union must be a voluntary one. The center of gravity of power should be moved to the republics. The degree of republican sovereignty should be enhanced, but there still should be a Union, a federation.

With regard to Russia, others have posed the question, "Can Russia be divided or not?" If democracy is conceived of abstractly and not in relation to concrete conditions, then it [the division of Russia] sounds democratic, as each nation has a right to self-determination. But in reality this will lead to an endless chain of divisions and bloodshed.

More generally, these issues highlight a most serious difference of opinion among our democrats regarding the way of development we choose. We have two options. Eastern Europe has shown us one—the Velvet Revolution or varieties on the Velvet Revolution: when the old power does not flee, when they have meetings for three days, or when fighting breaks out as in the Romanian version. In all cases, the process was very fast. Everything looks ever so attractive—just a few days and all's done; you have democracy with democrats in power. The second path is a civilized one that the rest of the world follows: You have elections, and then one political power replaces another. Democratic countries vary from country to country, but the strategic development of society does not change and there are no sharp fluctuations.

We, however, make changes of 180 degrees. It is not just a change of one party's policy for another's, but it is a change of an entire social and political system. In any case, these kinds of changes should be achieved in the usual civilized way. Theoretically, if we won elections to all soviets in Russia, like-minded people would come together to write normal laws and form their executive power. Can we do this without war? Yes, we can. So if this is possible theoretically, why can't it be done in real life. What are we lacking? We are lacking an organization that permeates all levels of power within which there would be no contradictions. With the help of such a movement, we can win elections again, like we did in the Moscow City Council last spring. But, as the politics of the Moscow City Council clearly demonstrates, we then defeat ourselves by arguing all year long as to whether shops should be privatized or not. It is the democrats who argue between themselves; they are in the majority.

This experience demonstrates the weak points of elections based on a movement instead of a multiparty system. Generally speaking, we should have taken into account Eastern Europe's experience in a different manner. In Eastern Europe, the transitions have not been smooth either. [Vaclav] Havel is an idol, yet suddenly he is encountering opposition. In Poland [Lech] Wałesa wins the election, but then Solidarity breaks up into several parties and contradiction begins there as well. If a society's starting point is totalitarianism and its finish is civil democratic society, then along the way between these two points we must go through a stage of dismantling the totalitarian system. A movement is very effective in destroying the totalitarian system as it can unite everyone into a broad front on the basis of anticommunism. This is what happened in Eastern Europe. In our own society, people have united under one slogan—Anticommunism. But after the victory over communism people ask, "What shall we do next?" Some say that land should be dealt with in one way, others say it should be dealt with in another way. What comes first, social justice or effectiveness of the economy? So what seems to be a united movement breaks up into independent political parties of different orientations. These parties begin to argue, while the state and economy begin to deteriorate as totalitarianism is dismantled. This produces growing uncertainty in society, and enthusiasm is immediately followed by another disappointment. This is what is happening in Eastern Europe. We are following a similar path.

But for us, this path will not be bloodless. It will not even be like the one in Romania, let alone the one in Czechoslovakia. We have quite different institutions of oppression. Power here will not flee voluntarily like it did in those countries. Here it is sure to resort to tanks. So the peaceful, nonviolent form of transition is impossible here. Besides, even if it were possible, we should learn from the East European experience that you cannot disappoint society a second time. At the very outset, we must come to an agreement about our aims, about what we are going to create, about this intermediate stage. If we state clearly our objectives beforehand, we can go through this intermediate stage together with the movement and without making any stops until we reach our final goals. But when we reach this stage, we then must have narrower associations than the movement, that is, besides anticommunism, people must agree about what positive things they will do. This is why parties have emerged.

It is in this period of differentiation that the Democratic Party of Russia emerged with our main slogan of nonviolence. We are against the use of violence as a method of development. Other parties do not reject violence entirely. They say, "Yes, we are certainly against bloodshed and civil war, but let's stage a general political strike." But a general political strike in Russia is necessarily the first step toward a civil war. You cannot carry out a strike here easily and not because the authorities will use weapons against the strikers but because the strikers themselves will turn their peaceful political strike into a riot. There is already a shortage of everything in this country. A couple of work stoppages are enough for people to start looting shops.

How do you assess the activities of Democratic Russia?

Democratic Russia should be viewed on two levels. The first is Democratic Russia's administrative organs here in Moscow and its top leadershio—[Yurii] Afanasiev, [Arkadii] Murashev, [Lev] Ponomarev, [Vera] Kriger, [Vladimir] Boxer, [Mikhail] Schneider, and others. The second level is Democratic Russia organizations at the regional, city, or district level throughout Russia. In cities and rural areas outside of Moscow, there are no contradictions between our party and Democratic Russia because local party branches and the Democratic Russia movement are made up of the same people But in Moscow, we have all kinds of conflicts. Why? Because there no parties behind all these people in the Dem-Rossiya apparat. They are on their own. This top leadership of Democratic Russia is a destabilizing element in politics not only for society at large but for democracy. Moreover, if these people do not continue to promote passionate, confrontational politics, they will be quickly forgotten because they have no permanent, supporting structures. So instead, they always want to call meetings and coin slogans to excite people all the time.

Recently you created a coalition of parties called Narodnoe Soglasie (Popular Accord). Will this coalition serve as an alternative to Democratic Russia?

The Christian Democrats and Constitutional Democrats joined us in forming Popular Accord because we have no disagreements on the issues of the Union or Russia or violence and nonviolence. Right now, it would be wrong to quit Democratic Russia. Efforts must be made to pull this movement away from permanent meetings and channel it toward a truly democratic movement. In order to do this, it is necessary to make changes in the leadership of Democratic Russia. This effort is being made. We must seriously reconsider the role of the entire democratic movement. Yesterday the democratic movement was attacking. Now Yeltsin has won, Popov has won in Moscow. What is the point of calling meetings now? Now that democrats have assumed power, they also must assume the responsibility for initiating further transformations. Yeltsin has to take unpopular measures in Russia; there is no other way out. Unpopular measures will be accepted and bring results only if the government has got enough credit of confidence from the very start (and Yeltsin has it) and if this government is supported by some political force that can ideologically persuade people to endure the temporary deterioration of life. It is like having a tooth pulled out; it is very painful but one feels better afterward. Only democrats can be this ideological and political force. The CPSU and Russian Communist Party are going into opposition. They will criticize every step of the reform. Democrats, however, have not realized that they are beginning to operate on a different basis now. We must give support, not criticize. Democrats must become a basis of the public accord. Yesterday the democrats instigated passions, but today they must calm passions down. This is a very serious reappraisal. If democrats can make this transition, they will succeed. If not, they will fail. If Yeltsin loses the support of the democratic forces, he will resort to methods of command in the economy—including repressive actions.

What is a mechanism of ideological and political support for Yeltsin's reforms? It is a party with a disciplined structure. Of course, we must be aware of the specific features of our situation. We still have the functioning CPSU that is found in every workshop and on every farm. We must neutralize the activities of the CPSU in every workshop, on every farm. The Democratic Party's structure is determined today in many respects by the fact of the existence of the CPSU. We have structured our party in a very organized fashion. The situation makes us act so.

Why have such prominent figures as Lev Ponomarev, Vera Kriger, Marina Salye, Arkadii Murashev, and Garry Kasparov left the Democratic Party? Was it because of ideological differences or for personal reasons?

Salye, Kriger, and Ponomarev left for the simplest reason; it was over the question of whether to have one chairman or several cochairs.[28] Why did this question of cochairs arise at all? It was nonsense, as a matter of fact. A party is an organization, a business, in which there must be undivided authority. This undivided authority, however, must be established on a democratic basis. This notion of cochairs has emerged simply because there is little room on Olympus and a great many people who want to occupy a place there. The number of cochairmen usually relates to the number of leaders or stars. In the Interregional Group [of People's Deputies], we had five stars; hence, we had five cochairmen. In other parties, the ratio is three to three. This was the case here, too. These people believed that cochairs were necessary. They all came from popular fronts and voters' clubs. Their product was only meetings and demonstrations. They believed that the party would be just like that, only the meetings would be better organized. After an exchange of minispeeches, it became clear that we had very different ideas for our party. Since May of last year [1990], we had grown cool toward meetings.

Secondly, we stated categorically that the notion of cochairs would not be accepted as a matter of principle. Only one chairman was needed, no matter who. It had to be a person who would assume the responsibility and shame for failure.

Murashev and Kasparov left the party much later and for different reasons. Both Kasparov and Murashev are ardent advocates of [Vladimir] Bukovsky's ideology in this country.[29] They say that a transformation in a democratic manner is impossible here. Since the democratic way is impossible, then what is the other way? Why are they so convinced? Do they want a civil war in this country? No, they just do not consider the situation here carefully. When one travels abroad and just drops in here on occasion, then it seems that everything will be over in-between two trips to Italy and France. "They will make a revolution here and I

[Bukovsky] shall come back as a leader." As such, we have different attitudes. But [the departure of Murashev and Kasparov from the Democratic Party] is not a split within the party. Just two people have left, that's all.

Leaders of all other parties concede that the Democratic Party of Russia has more local organizations than any other. How have you managed to have more party branches than the others?

We have more branches because we have concentrated all our efforts on organization. At our [founding] conference in May 1990, we set the task for ourselves that we would not stage any actions or participate in any roundtables until some structures were formed. Everything else is just profuse political talk. We democrats are not a force yet, but we already shout, "Gorbachev, sit down with us at a table!" But who is there to sit with? I also ask, "Why should I sit down at a table with you, [Yurii] Afanasiev? Are there some political parties behind you?" He says, "Yes, all of Russia's democrats are behind me." [I reply], "Well, if it's all of Russia's democrats, then you better figure out who is who because I, like Gorbachev, think that all of Russia's democrats are behind me."

There is no organization, so no roundtable can take place until people [who would participate in the roundtable] represent concrete forces. We have been busy with the formation of these structures now for a year.

Does your party have a specific social base?

In this country now, no party rests on just one social basis. It's impossible. Everything is only black or white [communist or anticommunist]. What do social bases have to do with it? One part of society says everything must be left black, while the other one says everything must be changed to white. Workers, peasants, intellectuals all take different sides.

In our party, we have a wide representation of all social strata. For instance, within our party, 18 percent are workers, more than any other party. This is a small percentage, but they are professional workers, not lumpens [sic]. We also have many intellectuals—scientific, technological, and cultural workers—and many people with higher education.

What are the party's principal problems?

The main problem is its professionalization [sic]. We cannot remain amateurs any longer. We need professionals and functionaries. People must be trained. The most important professionalization follows from parliamentarianism [sic], from the parliamentary character of the party. We will be able to act only through legally elected organs of power and only to the extent that we receive mandates. If we have got ten mandates, then the degree of our influence is 10 percent. If we have 60 percent, then we will have decisive influence. To gain these mandates, we must learn to be more proficient by the next elections. We must learn to produce preelection platforms not only for the whole of Russia but for every city. For this we need training centers everywhere. We must concentrate sufficient intellectual potential to prepare our people in places like Tambov or the Tambov region. People who can solve a problem theoretically cannot always solve real problems in practice. So, we must prepare a team. Everything is being done for the first time. This country has no experience. This is why [Stanislav] Shatalin's membership in our party was a sort of a turning point.[30] This is a very serious step. This is the first time that a prominent, recognized intellectual has made a definite political choice. Following his membership, I made a trip to Siberia to visit academic towns everywhere. Immediately a qualitatively new wave of people came to our party. Soon afterward intellectual centers began to spring up. With Shatalin's coming to us, things have become much better.

What kind of relations do you have with Yeltsin and Gorbachev?

They are normal relations. I have no close contacts with Gorbachev; there have been just a few meetings. Even today, I still like this man. It is wrong to say, "Down with Gorbachev!" Gorbachev has done his job; he has done his part of the job. He has done all that he could do within the framework of socialism. Gorbachev led us for two or three years on this evolutionary development, but further on there must be a market economy and a multiparty system. We should thank him and do the rest ourselves. While Gorbachev is still in power, we must become a force; we must create structures and a powerful party to pick up power at this fence we have come to. Unfortunately, democrats have done nothing of the kind.

Gorbachev has come to the fence [i.e., to the end of his abilities], and we are shouting, "Go ahead, lead us on!"

He answers, "I have not promised to lead you farther! My potential is up to this point."

Yet, we yell back, "No, we want you to do the rest for us!"

This is wrong. It should be acknowledged that he has both done his job and exhausted his potential as a reformer.

As for Yeltsin, the political machine and opposition have changed him a good deal. However, a man's handwriting does not change. Suppose I have developed a handwriting, and then I had to write with my left hand for a while, as in opposition. Yeltsin came into the opposition from the power structures; he got his right arm broken. But when he was brought into power again, he got his plaster cast removed. He will retain his old handwriting, but something inside him has changed. So a lot will depend on the democrats, on whether they will watch his handwriting closely and make him feel that he cannot return to the old times. Or democrats today can try to appease him and very soon everything will go back to the old ways from which we were trying to flee. To my mind, Yeltsin had not five paths to choose but just two—either we go toward the civilized world or we return to the old times under the likes of Makashov or Ryzhkov or Zhirinovsky.[31] Yeltsin has chosen to enter the door into the civilized world. This is a necessary condition to become a civilized country, but it is not enough. Whether we will get there or not depends on all of us, not on Yeltsin alone. The Democratic Party cannot merely watch Yeltsin act. If we do so, we take tremendous risks because we too nominated him and have ensured his election to the best of our abilities. We will be held responsible if he fails. If Yeltsin makes zigzags we will respond to them with full awareness of our responsibility.

Postcoup Reflections (October 1991)

How has the situation in your party changed after the putsch?
First of all, our central objective changed drastically. The wall that we had been struggling to break down crashed dramatically. Second, certain forces that claim monopoly power and [advocate] a one-party system have appeared immediately. The leftist, radical Communists in the person of the Movement for Democratic Reform (DDR) already have begun playing the leading roles formerly occupied by the Communist Party. They are trying to subordinate all democratic forces and parties. If before the putsch one could only benefit from fighting against the one-party communist system, now opposition to the seemingly democratic monopoly becomes unpopular. We are accused of being splittists. It has become more difficult to explain that the multiparty system remains the most important objective.

Another problem is that we have to be in opposition to the democratically elected president and government bodies because a whole set of actions they have taken are bringing them back to the administrative commanding course that used to exist. Opposing Popov's or Yeltsin's decisions also does not add to our popularity. But I am sure that in future it will be clear who is right. Our stand remains the same; let us speak the truth and people will understand everything themselves.

The third point is the following: Before the putsch we could build up our party structures slowly. Now everything regarding organization of the party has become an urgent task to be solved immediately. That is why problems of the organization's technical equipment, telephones, fax communication have become urgent. The putsch showed us how important it is to be able to communicate instantly, to exchange information with the branches so that they know what is going on in Russia. We cannot afford to be taken by surprise again.

Elections are coming. They are going to be the first large-scale elections in the whole territory. Our party will be able to test its strength but not if we do not have a full understanding of the situation in the entire country. We realize that if we nominate the wrong people in some places, it will be a very harmful loss. The party branch in the region will lose as well as the whole party. We have to choose candidates more strictly. We have started their training. We will support only professionally qualified nominees so that if they win, they will be able to change the situation for the better. After the putsch, we have begun to work on a professional basis. During these two months, we have completed the party apparatus and the newspaper editorial staff. Our financial situation also has changed.

The hard days during the putsch affected businessmen here in Russia. Since then, we have managed to arrive at an understanding with them. If we used to have stable financial resources, now they are better than ever. It is clear that the party will be backed by professionals and businessmen. They regard us as their political ally.

Document

. . . .

The following statement founded the coalition Narodnoe Soglasie between the Democratic Party of Russia, the Russian Christian-Democratic Movement, and the Constitutional Democracy Party–People's Freedom Party on April 19, 1991. In November 1991, the bloc withdrew from Democratic Russia.

Declaration of Narodnoe Soglasie (Popular Accord)

The catastrophic deterioration of the situation in the country is due, on the one hand, to the monopoly of the Soviet Communist Party, which preserves the totalitarian system and, on the other, to leftist-radical inspired chaos. The intoxication with utopian goals pushes the rival forces toward mutual destruction, which is fraught with tragic consequences for the entire society. In these conditions, we should formulate a "third path"—the path of national accord, real emancipation, and creation.

We, representatives of democratic parties and political organizations, adhering to right-of-center (constructive democracy) orientations, put forward the following principles that can, in our view, bring constructive democratic forces together and pull the country out of general crisis:

- The priority of individual rights and freedoms over any others, in particular ethnic and corporate. Our duty is to protect individual rights and freedoms in every case, regardless of the reason given for their violations—federal, republican, or other interests.

- Constitutional guarantees for individual rights and freedoms, full responsibility of the state for maintaining law and order.

- Renunciation of left-wing and right-wing radicalism and all forms of political extremism: overthrows, upheavals, or other violence. Wholesome changes are only possible on the path of peaceful and speedy evolutionary reform.

- Deideologization of the state system and renunciation of communist ideology as a destructive utopia. But the struggle with the communist regime ravaging our fatherland should not lead to a struggle with statehood as such, for only a strong democratic state is the guarantor of human rights and liberties. We want a replacement of the political regime but not the destruction of statehood, as both right-wingers and leftists will die under its rubble.

• Desire for the Russian Federation's unity and territorial integrity, transformation of the USSR into a new federal state on territories that favor the preservation of state unity and on the basis of their voluntary signature of a federal treaty hammered out by them.

• Struggle not for sham sovereignty but for the decisive democratic transformation of the real center of power: federal structures. Our immediate political demand is new elections for a new state! A general democratic presidential election in a new federal state without delay!

• Economic freedoms—the foundation of individual civil and political freedoms. A market economy, sweeping privatization, free enterprise and private ownership, primarily land ownership, antimonopoly legislation, a taxation system stimulating production, state and public funds for the social protection of those in low-income brackets and the non-able-bodied, and coherent environmental legislation.

The goals behind the bloc's formation include

• Preparations for the next elections to take part in the race as a single political force with common candidates
• Joint political actions
• Coordination of the party's parliamentary activities
• Propaganda for the bloc's political platform
• Coordination of activities in the Democratic Russia movement
• Realization of the principles of free speech and freedom of the press

There are two political currents in the nation's democratic movement: the leftist-radical one, the actions of which lead to the destruction of the federal state and the partitioning of the Russian Federation, and the constructive-democracy one, which seeks to preserve the unity of the Russian Federation and create a new federal state. Both currents should have an equal right to self-expression within the framework of the Democratic Russia movement.

Signed:

For the Russian Democratic Party—
N. I. Travkin, chairman of the Russian Democratic Party and a people's deputy of the USSR and of the Russian Federation

For the Russian Christian-Democratic Movement—
V. V. Aksiuchits, chairman of the Russian Christian-Democratic Movement's
political council and a people's deputy of the Russian Federation

For the Constitutional Democracy Party–Party of People's Freedom—
M.G. Astafiev, chairman of the Central Committee of the Constitutional
Democracy Party (People's Freedom Party) and a people's deputy of the
Russian Federation

A congress of the Russian Democratic Party ratified the text of the declaration
with the exception of the first and final paragraphs. The two other parties ratified
the declaration in full.

April 19, 1991, Moscow

chapter five

The Social-Democratic Party of Russia (SDPR)

Although the Social Democrats did not officially form their party until May 1990, the cohesive core of this organization has been together since 1987. Many SDPR leaders began their political careers in the discussion group Club Perestroika, which formed in February 1987.[1] At this early stage, Club Perestroika served as a forum of ideas for reformers both within and outside the CPSU. The club had no political program and did not believe in confrontational tactics. But the biweekly meetings attracted activists from many different social groups, serving as a clearinghouse for future political movements. In addition to Club Perestroika, future Social Democrats played active roles in the All-Union Socio-Political Club and the Public Initiative in Perestroika conference held in August 1987.

By the end of 1987, different ideological tendencies within Club Perestroika began to crystallize. First, factions within the club formed around opposing attitudes toward socialism. The radical wing favored complete rejection, while the more moderate faction supported traditional social-democratic ideas. Second, tension within the club arose over tactics and the method of debate. The radical wing advocated open opposition to the Soviet regime, while the moderates aimed to reform the Communist Party and the Soviet state. The two factions finally split when the moderate wing of the club refused to allow the radicals to participate in Club Perestroika discussions.[2] The moderate faction later renamed the group Democratic Perestroika, while the radicals split to form Perestroika 88.[3]

In May 1989, leaders of Democratic Perestroika convened an intercity meeting to prepare for the founding of the Social-Democratic Association (SDA).

After struggling with the more radical Democratic Union Party, moderates such as Oleg Rumyantsev and Leonid Volkov seized the initiative and convened the constituent congress of the SDA in Tallin, January 13–14, 1990.[4] The SDA aimed to unite Social Democrats from all republics, but the hidden agenda at the Tallin conference was to form the organizational committee for the Social-Democratic Party of Russia. After the repeal of Article Six of the Soviet constitution, which guaranteed the leading role of the Communist Party in Soviet state and society, the Social-Democratic Party of Russia held its founding congress on May 4, 1990, in Moscow.

More than two hundred delegates representing ninety-four Russian cities attended this founding congress at which RSFSR people's deputy Oleg Rumyantsev, USSR people's deputy Alexander Obolensky, and people's deputy of the local soviet Pavel Kudiukin were elected to the presidium of the new party.[5]

At the Second SDPR Congress, held in Sverdlovsk, October 25–28, 1990, the party adopted a sixty-eight-page program called "The Path to Progress and Social Democracy," allegedly the first comprehensive party program written by any noncommunist organization in Russia.[6] As outlined in this document, the SDPR's constitution is based on three principles, "freedom, equality, and solidarity."[7] Freedom relates to the rights of the individual to control her own destiny, defend his individual liberties such as the right to speak, publish, and associate, and realize her full potential. These ideas resonate with many liberal party principles in the West. However, Solidarity refers to the obligation of Social Democrats to "understand their class interests" and then work toward achieving them by "helping each other."[8] "Consensus," not "struggle," is recommended as the best means to address conflicting interests. "Equality," as explained in the SDPR manifesto, also refers to traditional social-democratic values.

Regarding economic policy, the program outlines two paths to the market: the "democratic, civilized" form and the "predatory, Mafia-controlled" type. To avoid the latter, the SDPR supports private enterprise and a free and honest market but also advocates market regulation that serves the needs of society as a whole.[9] According to the program, civilized privatization requires that the state actively assist in the creation of a "new middle class" as opposed to the now-emerging "nomenclature bourgeoisie."[10] To avoid what it calls "nomenklatura capitalism," whereby the old captains of Soviet industry unilaterally privatize their companies and become the new chief executive officers, the SDPR has supported other forms of privatization such as auctions, workers' collectives, and employee ownership schemes.

Given Russia's unique political and economic situation, however, Russian social democracy has had to diverge from West European social-democratic orthodoxies.[11] According to Oleg Rumyantsev, "Our place in this spectrum [of Russia's political forces] is a bit left of center, that is, the 'social-democrat' [social liberal] niche."[12] This ambiguous characterization captures the dilemmas of social democracy in postcommunist Russia. Although sympathetic to the ultimate ends of West European social democracy, the Social-Democratic Party of Russia also has realized that Russia must undergo a radical transformation to capitalism before notions about social welfare can be entertained. As Oleg Rumyantsev explained at a press conference after the Sverdlovsk congress, "Social Democrats in the West are concerned with 'socializing' capitalism; we, on the other hand, are trying to 'capitalize' socialism."[13] Accordingly, the SDPR has supported radical economic reform thus far during the transition to the market. Once a functioning market economy is established in Russia, however, the SDPR program states that the party will then assume traditional social-democratic causes, such as defending workers' interests, developing a social welfare system, and promoting state regulation of the market.[14]

To realize this agenda, the SDPR program encourages active participation in elections, roundtables, and the parliamentary process, while chastising strikes, demonstrations, and "populist" actions.[15] In abiding by a moderate and legalistic strategy for reform, SDPR members have played active roles in drafting the new Russian constitution.[16] Although only four SDPR members are people's deputies in the Russian parliament, they have concentrated their energies in the Constitutional Commission; the secretary of the commission (Yeltsin is the chairman) is Oleg Rumyantsev, three other SDPR members serve on the commission, and many of the legal experts working on the commission's staff are SDPR sympathizers. As the draft constitution contains many social-democratic principles without once mentioning the words *socialism* or *communism*, conservative opponents of the SDPR have accused Rumyantsev of leading a legal coup d'état from within.[17] In addition to the Constitutional Commission, Social Democrats joined people's deputies from the Republican Party to form a sixty-member faction in the Russian parliament.[18]

SDPR leaders hope to extend their party's influence by playing an increasingly active role in government structures. As Oleg Rumyantsev exclaimed, "Two days ago [we were] dissidents, yesterday—informals, today—people's deputies, tomorrow—partners in a coalition government."[19] Since suggesting the idea at the massive demonstration on February 25, 1990, Rumyantsev has been one of the leading advocates of a Polish-style roundtable as a means of transferring power from the Communists to the democrats.

After the 1991 August putsch, the SDPR claimed to have played an active role in the formation of Yeltsin's new government. Allegedly, Yeltsin authorized the SDPR to nominate his new minister of labor, Alexander Shokhin, who subsequently became deputy prime minister for social issues.[20] Shokhin appointed former SDPR cochairman Pavel Kudiukin as his deputy minister of labor.

Outside government structures, the SDPR has supported cooperation between other democratic parties, including close coordination among the three leading parties, the SDPR, the Democratic Party of Russia, and the Republican Party of

Russia.[21] In the fall of 1991, the SDPR and the Republican Party initiated a plan to unite their parties, resulting in unified party branches in several cities (but not Moscow).[22] Leadership clashes, particularly between Oleg Rumyantsev and Vyacheslav Shostakovsky, prevented the two parties from completing the merger. The SDPR was also one of the founding organizations of Democratic Russia. Personality clashes, however, between the leaders of the Social-Democratic Party of Russia and Democratic Russia, and fears that Democratic Russia overshadows the SDPR, have frequently strained relations.

After the coup, relations worsened. Responding to rumors that Democratic Russia planned to become a political party, Rumyantsev as well as other party leaders viciously criticized the hegemonic aspirations of DemRossiya activists. The SDPR is even more critical of the Movement for Democratic Reform, asserting that the bloc of former CPSU dignitaries will only impede democratic reform and "democratic privatization." Still upholding the necessity of consolidating democratic forces, however, the SDPR joined forces with a faction of the Republican Party called the Social-Liberal Union (headed by Vladimir Filin), the Russian People's Party (headed by Telman Gdlyan), and the Peasant Party of Russia (headed by Yurii Chernichenko) to form the political bloc Novaya Rossiya (New Russia) in January 1992.[23] This new political coalition aspires to become a unified party that will occupy the left-of-center position in Russia's newly emerging political spectrum.

Despite the parliamentary work of its leadership and its active role in democratic coalitions and movements, the SDPR has had difficulty extending its message beyond the urban intelligentsia. The SDPR's detailed political program has appealed to a well-defined social base—the urban intelligentsia—but this base is small and relatively powerless.[24] SDPR activists have worked closely with workers' movements and independent trade unions, but sustainable ties have yet to form.[25] As for the middle class, the social group to which the SDPR party program is aimed, it is only just emerging. As such, the SDPR has yet to expand into a massive political party.

Unlike other new parties, however, the SDPR has avoided major splits within its ranks. In January 1991, Vyacheslav Lyzlov, cochairman of the SDPR branch in Moscow, formed a liberal faction within the party that later joined the Democratic Party of Russia, but only a handful of SDPR members followed him.[26] Personality conflicts between Rumyantsev and Obolensky also have precipitated tense plenums and congresses, but neither leader has quit the party. At the SDPR Third Congress in Saint Petersburg, May 1–4, 1991, Obolensky and Kudiukin were replaced by RSFSR people's deputy Leonid Volkov and Professor Boris Orlov as presidium members, signaling that the party had the ability to change leadership and not collapse.

The Social-Democratic Party has not grown into a mass electoral party nor has it withered away. Under difficult conditions, the party has managed to carve out a special position in Russia's new political spectrum. Once greater social articulation and economic differentiation occur under the market economy, the Social-Democratic Party has the possibility of finding a social base of support for its political platform.

Oleg Rumyantsev

Born in 1961 and elected to the Russian parliament when he was only twenty-nine, Oleg Rumyantsev is often referred to as the wunderkind of Russia's democratic movement. Rumyantsev was educated at Moscow State University and the Institute of the Economy of the World Socialist System, run by Oleg Bogomolov. Trained as a Hungarian specialist, Rumyantsev remained at the institute as a researcher until entering politics full-time. As mentioned above, Rumyantsev became active in the discussion clubs Club Perestroika and later Democratic Perestroika. In 1990, he was one of the primary forces behind the creation of the Social-Democratic Association and the Social-Democratic Party of Russia. Despite his age, he is the party's most famous and visible member.

Elected as an RSFSR people's deputy in March 1990, Rumyantsev has headed the Constitutional Commission since its creation.[27] The commission has produced a working draft of a new Russian constitution that has yet to be ratified.

Interview with
Oleg Rumyantsev (June 1991)

. . . .

How and why did you enter politics?

At the university I strongly disliked all the Komsomol activities. During my first year, I nominally participated in them. By my second year, I had already begun to conflict with the Komsomol authorities and purposely ignored the meetings.

This was during the late 1970s and early 1980s. It also must be said that I was a great lover of music, of John Lennon, and the ideas of pacifism. This music was also one of the factors which brought me to politics. In particular, on December 21, 1980, I took part in a ceremony in memory of John Lennon on the Moscow State University parade grounds. I remember well how this peaceful student gathering was broken up by a huge crowd of KGB officers.

Later, in the early 1980s, I went and studied in Hungary. This was the last factor that led to my involvement in politics, as I saw how there was more freedom in that country and more love of freedom. I listened to lectures and read books published there. Through these experiences, I began to understand many things. And though they then had Kadar's "goulash" socialism, the atmosphere there was strikingly free as compared with here.

After returning to my institute in Moscow and writing memoranda from the institute to directive organs, I understood that nothing could be gained by memoranda. I also understood that perestroika was nothing but the renovation of the existing regime. Then, in 1986, my friends from Hungary, the reformers from the Central Committee of the HSWP [Hungarian Socialist Workers' Party] invited me as an expert to their country as by then I was a political scientist studying not only Hungary but our own situation. They asked me to write a paper analyzing the concept of perestroika. Perestroika became public in January and June 1987, but I had received the request to write this paper before then.[28] I began to write this paper not by compiling materials but by constructing my own theory. I was trying to understand how a revolution from above could be carried out. The essay was published in Hungary but not in the Soviet Union. Later in 1987, when perestroika was introduced by Gorbachev as an official policy, I saw that there were many parallel ideas to my own.

Then I came to the conclusion that nothing can be gained by simply writing concepts and stating ideas. So in January 1987, after the Central Committee [of the CPSU] plenum on glasnost', I went to a Club Perestroika meeting. At this meeting I met some wonderful people, including Vladimir Kardailsky, Victor

Kuzin, a Moscow City Council deputy, Andrei Fadin, and Pavel Kudiukin. Thereafter, I became very active in politics, participating in the organization of discussions. Later, I organized a seminar called Models of Socialism, which served as a sort of intellectual club.

What was the initial objective of these activities?

The idea was this: it seems that glasnost' was proclaimed by the Party, but one still had to talk about everything in a whisper. The slogans of the period were Socialism with a Human Face, the Administrative-Command System, the Cleansing of Socialism, etc. The media was flooded with sycophantic articles from the "superintendents of perestroika" who all were beside themselves with the feeling of how progressive they were. In reality it was a laughingstock; it was the same bootlicking, only now they kowtowed to the new course. We wanted independent opinions, views, and discussions on bureaucracy, land reform, the national problem in Russia, and the church.

Our club was attended by dissidents like [Father Gleb] Yakunin, [Victor] Aksiuchits, and (Father Alexander) Men. Our speakers included [Nikolai] Petrakov, [Nikolai] Shmelev, [Evgenii] Ambartsumov, [Boris] Orlov, and [Leonid] Volkov. After a while, we realized that we not only had to gather and talk, but we also had to do something, that is, prepare some kind of programs. I had the idea of bringing together intellectuals from around the country to prepare a substantive political program to submit to the Nineteenth Party Conference [of the Communist Party]. I came up with this idea because something similar had been done in Hungary earlier. The Hungarian alternative program had attracted many people. Among its authors was a friend of mine, a Hungarian political scientist, Mihaly Bihari.

My idea was realized during a seminar series on models of socialism. We ran the seminar with much difficulty as it was very hard to attract political scientists to our discussions. They regarded us as a boys' club. Even at our liberal Bogomolov's institute, I had difficulty in attracting participants. [Alexander] Tsipko could not be persuaded to come, but Ambartsumov and [Igor] Klyamkin showed interest. Moreover, our meetings were sometimes attended by unkempt and unwashed people, not only intellectuals. They were not numerous, but they were there. We met in the Party committee room; the air was heavy there, but the ideas soared. People like [Lev] Sigal and [Andrei] Fadin, the future staff members of the excellent newspaper *Kommersant'*, Pavel Kudiukin, now a leading expert in the Supreme Soviet [RSFSR], Leonid Volkov and myself, future cochairmen of the Social-Democratic Party, and other founders of the Social-Democratic Party including Sergei Magaril, Oleg Obolin, Galina Rakitskaya, Sergei Markov, and Kirill Yankov.

So it was in the clubs, Club Perestroika and Democratic Perestroika, that the nucleus of the SDPR was formed?

Yes, but not only the Social-Democratic Party of Russia. More generally, I believe that these clubs were a serious intellectual center for the new democratic ideas. In addition to the SDPR, a part of the Democratic Union—Victor Kuzin and Yurii Skubko—emerged from these organizations.

How and why did the split between the future leaders of the Social-Democratic Party and the future leaders of the Democratic Union emerge?

It was in the air from the very beginning. In the fall of 1987, I left Moscow for a couple of months and went to Hungary. Upon returning, I noticed that new people with different orientations, objectives, and values had joined our club. It was not a question of personality; it was simply that I realized that there were different approaches, some more radical and some more moderate.

In October 1987, there was a big commotion at one of our meetings. Instead of discussing a serious political problem, or adopting some decision or resolution, we began having petty quarrels. We within the club did not understand what was happening; our ability to discuss issues evaded us and instead we began playing power games regarding who should lead, how to lead, and so on. Factions within the club began to coalesce. Retrospectively, these experiences served as a sort of university for politics, as we were all newcomers to real politics. In a way, our discussion club acted as a sort of parliament, preparing some of us for real parliamentary work later on.

Finally, however, I said that we had to put a stop to this bickering. I actually acted consciously to initiate one of the schisms as I wanted to end all quarrels. At one of our meetings, we decided that the nucleus [of Club Perestroika] should be called the Democratic Perestroika bloc, and from that time on, we took the initiative in our hands. At a meeting soon after the creation of this nucleus, we declared a moratorium on all discussions for a couple of months. We then began having seminars at our institute, resulting in two different series of meetings, major and minor meetings. At the larger meetings, resolutions were discussed, while at the seminars we discussed documents on "models of socialism." In many ways, our work in the smaller seminars was similar to the function of parliamentary committees, while the meetings of the Democratic Perestroika club resembled sessions of the Supreme Soviet.

This training was very important for us. It was our political school. We also began publishing the *Open Zone* magazine. Our own political and social journalists were developing, many of whom now work with other periodicals.

It then became evident that we were not simply a discussion club but a new phenomenon in the political structure. I wrote a book on the role of self-motivated movements and initiatives during perestroika. In this manuscript, I asserted that these newly formed social movements constituted a critical element in the formation of a civil society. These informal movements would then grow to play a role in higher politics. That much was clear even then. We were not an analogue to the Green movement or the 1968 revolution in the West, that is, we were not an alternative choice. Rather, we were an embryo of a new layer of larger politics.

Consequently, this was the reason why radicals, extremists, and provocateurs were repudiated from the movement, while a stratum of people like Yankov, Kudiukin, Markov, and Volkov, people who had the ability to participate in major politics, remained.

Therefore it was not coincidental that our club played a significant role not only in preparing for elections [in 1989] but in elaborating the problems, decisions, and documents for the future Interregional Group [of People's Deputies] in the USSR Congress of People's Deputies.[29] Gradually and painlessly we were pulled into major politics, first through our work with the Interregional Group, then through our success at electing some of our members to the Russian parliament, and lately through our work on the Russian constitution.

By its character and approach, our work on the constitution did not differ much from the preparation of the "Democratic Mandate," a document put forward by Democratic Perestroika [for the Nineteenth Party Conference]. It was the same model, differing only a little in composition. I can be absolutely sure of this as I have organized both of them myself. Availability of a computer did much to facilitate my task [of preparing the constitution], but the working principles were the same in both cases. Actually the process of shifting gradually from informal structures into larger political institutions turned out to be very natural for our party. The leaders of the Moscow Popular Front, the Moscow Association of Voters, and Democratic Russia have had and will continue to have a much more difficult time in making the transition as they are more prone to mass actions— rallies, demonstrations, protest marches—than parliamentary politics.

This split [between people prone to moderate parliamentary politics and people prone to radical, mass-based politics] has had and continues to have a harmful effect. We decided clearly from the start that we are not outcasts but are rather part of a civil society. This civil society should be structured using parties as a means to form and express the political will of the society. Because of this orientation, we believed that our informal movements and associations should aspire eventually to form real political parties. On the other hand, the Moscow Popular Front and its successor, Democratic Russia, chanted slogans such as Down with Parties! Only a General Movement, Mass Action, and so on. Actually all these slogans were a cover for the aspirations of a very narrow circle of persons who wanted to dominate the entire movement. Such was the situation in the Moscow Popular Front and now in Democratic Russia.

There was a third position, the position of the anarchists and the Boris Kagarlitsky group. I cannot find proper words for this tendency other than to say that they were very self-absorbed.

And the fourth position is that of the Democratic Union, which could be described as a kind of radical uncertainty. Even today, the Democratic Union expresses no interest in normal politics. When asked about the idea of participating in a roundtable with Gorbachev and democratic leaders such as Rumyantsev, the

Democratic Union's leader, Valeriya Novodvorskaya, says that she would like to turn this table upside down and spill jam over all those present at the table. For five years now, we have heard this brand of politics. Now is the time for more constructive approaches, such as that offered by our "Democratic Mandate." In offering an alternative program to the Nineteenth Party Conference, we were proposing a reformist approach. It was not a radical approach, but it was a half step forward instead of thirty three steps backward.

How and when did you decide that it was necessary to form a political party? And why did you decide to form a *social-democratic* party?

I think it was possibly in 1988, as the ideas I started to draw from when working on the "Democratic Mandate" were taken from Social Democrats, especially the East European ones such as Mihaly Bihari and Zoltan Kiracs from Hungary. Later, we drew from the documents of the West European social-democratic movement. By studying our counterparts in Europe, we developed a concept of democratic socialism. Despite his claims, Gorbachev was not adhering to this idea, so we elaborated the concept. At the time, it sounded like an alternative program that could move society forward, a half step forward. Eventually, Gorbachev took this half step and adopted the concept of democratic socialism. But then, we abandoned it and adopted the concept of social democracy. This was a little different in wording and essence, with the aim of pushing society forward toward a multiparty state.

In 1988, a network of Perestroika clubs began taking shape. An information system also was being developed. I had a computer at home that Volodya Kardailsky used. He would bring his children with him. My place turned into a headquarters for this information network. It soon became clear that we needed to form some kind of association, and thus the idea of the Social-Democratic Association [SDA] arose.

Preparations for the association proceeded for a whole year. We created four working groups that met four times a year. We were preparing ourselves in earnest for the formation of a real party.

In January 1990, we founded the SDA. In May 1990, we founded the Social-Democratic Party of Russia [SDPR]. We wanted to create socially active politics but did not want to cede this to the degenerating CPSU. Rather, we wanted to establish a modern social-democratic party that would develop the idea of social democracy in line with our present conditions.

How does your conception of social democracy differ from other social-democratic ideas? How is Russian social democracy unique?

We have a unique historical and psychological situation. At one time, the Bolsheviks were united with the Social Democrats. Herein lies the tragedy. But the Mensheviks were also Marxists. The whole complexity of the situation is related to this point: how can one build a social-democratic party in a country where the totalitarian regime stems from those very Social Democrats or at least from those whom we usually call Social Democrats? It is very difficult. But at the same time we realize that without a foundation, without a party of the new middle class, we will not move forward because the Party includes the lumpen but does not involve the middle class.

But to clarify matters, is it not true that West European Social Democrats do not consider your organization to be a social-democratic party? Are there difficulties in your relations with Western Social Democrats owing to this historic process? Many, in fact, have claimed that Rumyantsev is a liberal, not a Social Democrat. What is your attitude toward this?

[Italian prime minister] Craxi also calls himself socialist, though I think he is not. The heart of the problem is that the West does not understand what is happening in Russia and therefore applies Western standards to a non-Western situation. They are not able to understand how we can create social democracy here, on one hand, while at the same time express a completely negative attitude toward bolshevism and offer our own alternative policies to the CPSU. I recommend that you consider the latest results of polls of our delegates at the Third SDPR Congress. These polls revealed that the leftist radicals had quit the party; right-wing liberals had also left, leaving the party with a reformist orientation. And we are establishing our reformist approach both in policy and method. When West European Social Democrats criticize us for being liberals, they are simply wrong. Our attitude toward privatization and questions of property is very different from that of liberals. Just listen to Arkadii Murashev.[30] He espouses a purely liberal position that places *freedom* above all else. We, on the other hand, promote a triad of values that we consider interdependent: freedom, justice, and solidarity. From this triad, there arises a certain role for redistribution and a role for the state in the economy, which liberals would not support.

What is your current attitude toward Democratic Russia?

Of those delegates polled at our third [SDPR] congress, the index of support for SDPR was +92, for Democratic Russia +73, for the Republican Party +55, for Travkin's Democratic Party of Russia +21, and for the Socialist Party −22, worse than the Democratic Union. The CPSU came in the last place. This means that the Social-Democratic Party of Russia still feels itself to be a part of Democratic Russia. But we do not wish to be a toy in the hands of the MPF-MOI [Moscow Popular Front–Moscow Association of Voters] Coordinating Council of the Democratic Russia group, all people attempting to monopolize the democratic movement.[31] This tendency can be traced from 1988; you could write a special book about it. Their militant, antiparty spirit is expressed in the following manner: "We are the Coordinating Council of Democratic Russia; there are millions of people behind us. Parties are just a hindrance to us; Travkin, Rumyantsev, and Lysenko are just hindering our work." That is how some of the DemRossiya Coordinating Council members express themselves. We, through our parties and our image, gain prestige for the [Democratic Russia] movement, and then a bunch of apparatchiks in this movement start to say that we are a nuisance. This process is typical of other large-scale social organizations in which the apparat later subjugates the interests of the participants in the movement to the interests of the bureaucracy.

What is the attitude of the SDPR to the current policy of the Russian government?

Our party, and I in particular, took part in the development of a concept of how to proceed from the idea of state sovereignty to the declaration of state sovereignty. By the way, many of our people took part in the wording of the declaration on sovereignty—[Kirill] Yankov, [Yurii] Khavkin, [Pavel] Kudiukin, [Andrei] Bystritsky, [Leonid] Volkov. We devised a clear-cut concept, which was then accepted by Yeltsin, and now continues to be developed.

We realize that we have not yet attained the level of political culture in which relations between the leader, the voice of the government, and the supporting political forces are not shaped according to the principle "I like you" or "my assistant has a dislike for you" but according to the principle of real coalitions. That is, if we have been developing a concept together, if we elaborate anything together, we then go further together.

Regrettably, right now, the situation in our White House and around Yeltsin all too often resembles a monarch's court: what will be said at court? what will such-and-such lady-in-waiting say? or what will the court barber say? This is very unfortunate because it has introduced subjectivism into the decision-making process. Consequently, one cannot understand how decisions are being made and implemented.

However, we still manage to take part in some decisions. When I meet Yeltsin, I offer him advice. But these meetings do not happen frequently, and one has to surmount considerable obstacles to meet with the Russian president. It turns out that every decision is now taken at the level of Yeltsin and Burbulis. This is a far too undemocratic process. For that reason, the Social-Democratic Party gave support to Yeltsin during his election [for president] conditional on our participation in the formation of the new government. Yeltsin promised me that we will participate in the formation of the new government. However, when I mention this to Burbulis, he retorts, "Oleg, you are thinking too much in terms of categories of a civilized politics." I reply, "Well, let's make our politics civilized!" Why should we begin to play these little apparat games, informing against each other in a clandestine manner until society begins to complain? Rather, Yeltsin should define a new spirit from the very beginning. Unfortunately, the situation has not evolved in this way so far.

After Boris Yeltsin's election as president, politics in Russia entered a new era. What will be the principal tasks of the SDPR during this new political stage?

Our main task is to organize a roundtable.[32] Seventy-nine percent of the population favors this idea wholeheartedly, while another 14 percent supports a roundtable conditionally. The Coordinating Council of Democratic Russia, however, voted against the roundtable idea, arguing that it is impossible to have talks with Communists. These figures represent a major difference between our party today and Democratic Russia. Another example is our party's attitude toward calls for the immediate resignations of Gorbachev and the Union Cabinet of Ministers. Only 40 percent [of our members] supports this idea, whereas 100 percent of Democratic Russia activists favors their resignations. These figures underscore the moderate character of our movement.

We have entered a new stage of politics in which issues now will be decided in parliamentary, governmental, and municipal forums, without any more rallies or strikes. We Social Democrats are prepared for this as we were never advocates of political rallies. As for the future of our party, it is difficult to say. But we are not going to cease the activities. We shall continue gradually to become a party sharing power in the government.

Postcoup Reflections (October 1991)

What did the putsch mean for your party and what are the perspectives of the SDPR after the putsch?
I think that the main political consequence of the putsch for our party is that it has enabled us to clear the niche of the left center. The leftist communist ideology and demagogy are gone. On the other hand, anticommunism abruptly gained momentum, and, as a result, so-called democratic groups and parties have moved to the right. A bloc of civilized right-wing organizations of conservative forces has begun to take shape. For example, Travkin's party has left its position in the left center, which in fact belongs to us, and has moved into the conservative bloc. The putsch gave us an opportunity to become a consolidating force of the left of center.

On the other hand, the putsch has made it clear that people like [Alexander] Yakovlev, [Eduard] Shevardnadze, and others—who are as responsible for the disorganization, chaos, and disintegration in our country and who are accustomed to playing the role of democracy's defenders—also have disqualified themselves as a possible party of the left center or social-democratic type because they were a party of power. It is party of power according to its style and methods of work and psychology. It means that the putsch helped us to determine our social niche, cleared it for us, and let us see who would be our possible allies.

Second, the putsch showed us that we need an abrupt change in our party structure model, from a principally nonmass electoral type to a party of activists who can be elected by broad masses of population, especially, the middle class. The putsch has helped people to stop distrusting parties and politics. It also helped to convince a significant number of former CPSU members to take part in the work of new political structures. Thus, our party now has the opportunity to become a mass party.

chapter six

The Republican Party of Russia

The history of the Republican Party begins with the creation of the Democratic Platform, as almost all the Republican Party activists and leaders began their political activity in the Democratic Platform.

The idea for the creation of a liberal faction *within* the Communist Party percolated up from of activities of various Party clubs. Party discussion clubs, organized with Gorbachev's sanction to help resuscitate the CPSU, began to proliferate at the local district and city level throughout Russia beginning in January 1989. Soon thereafter, some of the most active members of these Party clubs formed an interclub Party organization with the aim of coordinating actions and sharing information. Among the founders of this coordinating group were Igor Chubais from Perestroika 88, Mikhail Maliutin from Socialist Initiative, Vladimir Lysenko from Memorial and Obrita, Georgii Gusev from Narodnoe Deistvie (Popular Action), and Sergei Stankevich from the Moscow Popular Front.[1] The coalition fell apart, however, in May 1989. The more radical faction followed Lysenko and Chubais to form Communists for Perestroika, while the more moderate wing maintained the inter-Party club. Factions within Communists for Perestroika also developed: Chubais established a social-democratic faction, and Alexei Prigarin founded a communist group.

As similar Party club activity expanded in other cities, activists organized a intercity club meeting in November 1989. At this meeting, the organizers decided to convene the All-Union Confederation of Party clubs and Party organizations January 20–21, 1990, with the goal of establishing a Democratic Platform within the CPSU.[2] Representatives from 102 cities and thirteen republics attended this conference, including such prominent figures as Yurii Afanasiev, Boris Yeltsin, Nikolai Travkin, Vyacheslav Shostakovsky, Gavriil Popov, and Arkadii Murashev.

Few ideological disagreements emerged at this founding congress, as the congress almost unanimously approved resolutions calling for the repeal of Article Six of the Soviet constitution, the creation of a multiparty system, the formation of liberal and conservative factions within the CPSU, and the admission of guilt from the CPSU leadership about totalitarian crimes of its past.[3]

Questions, however, did arise over tactics. One faction believed that the Democratic Platform had to work for greater democratization within the Communist Party.[4] Others, led by Arkadii Murashev and Nikolai Travkin, advocated the formation of alternative party structures to the CPSU immediately.[5] A third group advocated a two-front strategy both in and outside the CPSU.[6] As a compromise, the Democratic Platform created a commission to draft liberal, alternative documents for the upcoming Twenty-eighth CPSU Congress in July 1991, agreeing to postpone the question of leaving the CPSU until after this important meeting.[7]

Initially, the CPSU leadership indicated a willingness to consider the Democratic Platform's recommendations.[8] Commensurately, supporters of the Democratic Platform flocked to join the new organization. By March, Democratic Platform organizers claimed to have more than a million members.[9] However, the selection process for delegates to the congress, the expulsion of Igor Chubais (one of the founders of the Democratic Platform) from the CPSU, and the harsh criticisms of the Democratic Platform from official communist publications beginning in April 1990 demonstrated that the CPSU leadership had no serious intention of allowing an alternative program to be presented at the July congress.[10] Democratic Platform representatives were allowed to attend the March CPSU plenum, but they were not invited to speak or participate in deliberations.[11] At the congress itself, only a handful of Democratic Platform members, including Vyacheslav Shostakovsky and Boris Yeltsin, were allowed to speak. Most of the Democratic Platform's leadership, therefore, used the congress to stage their resignations.

At the second all-Union conference of the Democratic Platform, held in Moscow June 16–17, 1990, a resolution was passed calling for the creation of a new political party. At the meeting of Democratic Platform's Coordinating Council July 14–15, 1991, an organizational committee for the new party was established. During November 17–18, 1990, the founding congress of the Democratic Platform Party, renamed the Republican Party of Russia (RPR) at the meeting, was held in Moscow.

Thousands, not millions, joined the new party. The silent majority in the Party who had supported the Democratic Platform stayed silent, unwilling to risk their careers and Party perks. Moreover, newly elected officials such as Boris

Yeltsin (chairman of the Russian Supreme Soviet), Gavriil Popov (chairman of the Moscow City Soviet), and Anatoly Sobchak (Leningrad's chairman) soon became too subsumed in governing to engage in party politics. As Yeltsin argued in refusing to join any party, forty years of CPSU politics was enough for one lifetime. Finally, by November 1990, the Democratic Party of Russia, the Social-Democratic Party of Russia, and the Democratic Russia movement were already active, attracting away many of the Democratic Platform's early supporters.

Consequently, at the inaugural congress, the Republican Party had difficulty in defining its political niche. Even the name of the party resulted from its late entry into Russia's new party politics, as the two most popular names among the delegates—the Democratic Party or the Social-Democratic Party—were already claimed.[12] The name bears no relationship to the party's attitude toward a united federation of republics, nor does the party necessarily share the political platform of Republican parties in Western Europe or the United States.[13]

As a further obstacle to defining a party identity, the party's political orientation initially varied little from the social-democratic program.[14] Regarding economic policy, the Republican platform affirmed the necessity of creating a market economy. Noting that seventy years of Communist Party domination of the economy had caused all other social groups to "become completely estranged from property," it is now "a most important task to involve all main social groups in relations of ownership. This will provide the basis for bringing about greater democracy in society and create guarantees for the social security of citizens."[15] Noting that the Republican Party was oriented toward "the middle sections of the population—the skilled part of workers and peasants, intellectuals, and civilized entrepreneurs and cooperators"—the party nonetheless affirmed that "the inevitable clash of interests of different social groups" must be solved peacefully and mutually beneficially.[16] To assist in reconciling interests between different classes, the Republican Party program outlined a comprehensive social security scheme to be implemented by the state, including rights to education, housing, and health insurance, guarantees to fair pay, a minimum *hourly* wage, and minimum benefits for children, students, the disabled, and senior citizens. The Republican program, however, also outlined a list of rights and laws that must be implemented to protect the entrepreneur. As one delegate at the founding congress later tried to explain, "They ask us: are you going to cultivate business entrepreneurs first and then protect workers from them? Exactly. We are going to tackle this two-pronged task."[17]

Regarding issues of the Union and the state more generally, the Republican Party was one of the first political organizations to propose an alternative structure of relations between republics. In its political program, the Republicans called for the abolition of the USSR Congress of People's Deputies, the replacement of "the federal government with an inter-republican committee, whose members will be delegated directly by the republics," the termination of the USSR constitution, and the drafting of a federal treaty. To put relations among republics on a different basis, the Republican Party helped create the "democratic congress" in January 1991, a coalition of more than forty democratic parties and movements from twelve republics.[18] The Republican Party was a leading advocate of creating a commonwealth of former republics of the Soviet Union based on the structure of the democratic congress.[19] Republican Party leaders were also instrumental in creating the Inter-Republic Parliamentary Group, a coalition of people's deputies from most of the former Soviet republics. Finally, in December 1991, Vladimir Lysenko helped found the Congress of Democratic Forces in the Autonomous Regions, a coalition of democratic movements from different autonomous regions in the Russian Federation.

Tactically, the Republican Party firmly asserted its commitment to pursuing change through parliamentary means.[20] As the program stated, "We are convinced opponents of totalitarianism, but we also oppose its removal by force. We suggest the path not of confrontation, but of political dialogue, reasonable compromise and a peaceful replacement of old administer-by-command structures with new market-based democratic relations." Regarding cooperation with other parties and movements, the Republican Party program declared that "we are prepared to pool our efforts with all democratic forces proceeding from the inadmissibility of a civil war, regardless of how different our views may be." Consequently, the Republican Party continued to participate in the Democratic Russia bloc, becoming one of the bloc's three leading party partners.[21] Moreover, the founding congress passed a resolution that advocated the merger of the Republican Party with the Social-Democratic Party of Russia. In the Russian parliament, the Republican Party formed a faction with the Social Democrats to occupy the leftist-centrist position and agitate against far-left radicalism.[22]

The founding congress elected RSFSR people's deputy Vladimir Lysenko, Vyacheslav Shostakovsky, former director of the Moscow Higher Party School, and USSR people's deputy Stepan Sulakshin as the Republican Party's cochairmen. Almost immediately after the founding congress, however, sharp disagreements emerged within the leadership and the party more generally. The most contentious issue involved the issue of unification with the Social-Democratic Party of Russia. As two of the leading parties, with similar ideological platforms and methods of political action, at the time of the founding RPR congress, advocates for unification in both parties argued that a single party had a more viable chance of challenging the CPSU than two separate entities.[23] Moreover, the two parties complemented each other's weaknesses. As former members of the CPSU, the Republicans would bring greater organization into a unified party, while the Social Democrats would contribute a comprehensive political program and a solid intellectual core.[24] The majority of Republican Party members supported the merger, but the leadership's opinion was mixed.[25] Igor Chubais was the main force for unity, while Vyacheslav Shostakovsky and Stepan Sulakshin, two of three members of the Presidium, opposed the merger.[26] The third Presidium member, Vladimir Lysenko, remained a cautious advocate of unification.[27]

Despite leadership clashes, the two parties began merging from below almost immediately after the Republican Party's creation. On January 19, 1991, the Moscow branches of both parties held a joint conference at which a resolution urging unification was passed.[28] Soon thereafter, more than a dozen city branches of the two parties merged. In the Russian parliament, the activities of the RPR-SDPR faction were more closely coordinated after the turn to the right of the Soviet government in December 1990.[29] The leadership of the two parties in Moscow, however, refused to risk their positions by pursing complete unification.

The issue of joining forces with the Social-Democratic Party gradually faded as opposing ideological positions within the Republican Party became more clearly articulated. Over the course of the party's first year of existence, Vyacheslav Shostakovsky, a one-time advocate of cooperation with the liberal wing of the CPSU, joined Stepan Sulakshin in a further drift to the right (in Western terms), asserting that the party needed to reorient toward Russia's new proprietors, not to the nonexistent middle class.[30] A minority faction, however, remained committed to the social-democratic principles on which the party was originally founded. In January 1992, this faction, led by Vladimir Filin, quit the party and joined a new coalition with the Social-Democratic Party and the Russian People's Party, thus ending the debate about merging the Republican Party with the SDPR.[31]

These tensions and the lack of a clearly defined political platform greatly hampered the Republican Party's growth during its first year. Whereas individuals from the Republican Party played high-profile roles in the Russian parliament, in Yeltsin's election campaign, and in Democratic Russia, the party itself declined in numbers in 1991.

After the August putsch, the Republican Party worked closely with both the People's Party for a Free Russia (Rutskoi's party) and the Movement for Democratic Reform to form a new coalition of former Communist Party members now dedicated to radical economic reform.[32] Several Republican Party leaders were elected to the Coordinating Council of the Movement for Democratic Reform, while Vyacheslav Shostakovsky was elected one of the movement's six cochairmen at the its inaugural congress in December 1991.[33] As the only political party capable of interacting with almost all parties and movements within the democratic spectrum, the Republican Party has tried to position itself as the force for genuine cooperation between all democratic forces.[34]

Vladimir Lysenko

Born in 1956, Lysenko received his Ph.D. in history from Moscow State University. Thereafter, he lectured in the Department of Scientific Socialism at the Moscow Aviation Institute. Since 1987, Lysenko has helped found some of the most important and influential political movements in the history of the Russian democratic movement, including Memorial, the Moscow Party club, Democratic Platform, Democratic Russia, the Republican Party, the Democratic Congress of the USSR, and the Democratic Congress of the Russian Federation. In June 1991, Lysenko served as one of Yeltsin's main campaign managers (*doverenoe litso*). In August, Yeltsin sent Lysenko with several other people's deputies to liberate Mikhail Gorbachev from his Crimean captivity. As a member of the Russian parliament, Lysenko has served on the Committee for Mass Media and Public Relations. In the new Russian government that was created after the putsch, Lysenko was appointed deputy minister for nationalities, although he retained his seat in parliament. He also is a member of the Coordinating Council of Democratic Russia, a cochairman of the Congress of Democratic Forces from the former Soviet Union, and cochairman of the Congress of Democratic Forces of the Autonomous Regions of the Russian Federation.

Interview with
Vladimir Lysenko (June 1991)
· ·

How did you enter politics?
During the 1970s, when I was a student at the historical faculty of the Moscow
State University and then when I was doing my postgraduate course in scientific
communism at the university, I actually supported the official dogma. I did not
read Sakharov or Solzhenitsyn. I only knew about them from the official Soviet
press. In my dissertation, which I defended in 1982, I analyzed the activities of
Communist parties in Eastern Europe and the Soviet Union from a very orthodox
viewpoint common at the time.

Shifts in the conscience began in 1985, after the Twenty-second World Youth
and Student Festival, where I was working as a scientific consultant to the Soviet
delegation. It was the only center where really free viewpoints were exchanged.
At this tribune, I heard for the first time things nobody had spoke about openly
until then.

Two years later, in 1987, I was one of ten people who founded Memorial,
which later expanded to a national level. At the founding congress, which took
place at my MAI [Moscow Aviation Institute] in 1987, I made the acquaintance
of Andrei Sakharov, Yurii Afanasiev, Yurii Karyakin, and others, many of whose
parents were shot in the 1930s. I came to know a huge abundance of new
information that drastically changed my outlook, demonstrating to me that we
lived in a different world than I had perceived earlier. We had simply been
deceived.

My next major political activity after Memorial began in 1989, when Igor
Chubais and myself founded the Democratic Platform in the CPSU. Last year
[1990] at the Twenty-eighth CPSU Congress we left the Party altogether and
founded our own Republican Party of Russia. In the spring of 1990, I was elected
people's deputy of the Russian Federation, and in January 1991 I was elected
chairman of the Democratic Congress—a broad association of parties and movements of different republics. Now I am, or was until yesterday, an accredited
representative of Boris Yeltsin in the election campaign.[35]

**During your early years of political activity, you were familiar with the activities of the
Democratic Union and its leaders Victor Kuzin, Valeriya Novodvorskaya, and others. Why
have these people disappeared from politics? Why have dissidents in general disappeared from active political life?**
Though I was not a member, I regularly participated in the discussions organized

by the club Democratic Perestroika. I was on good terms with Vladimir Kardail-sky, Oleg Rumyantsev, Mikhail Miliutin, and many others. By the way, it was at a meeting of Democratic Perestroika when I met Uris Odoyev for the first time, who informed me about a group that had the idea of establishing a memorial to the victims of Stalin's repressions. That was in September 1987. He invited me to the home of Yurii Skubko, where ten people—Skubko, Victor Kuzin, Yurii Samodurov, Vyacheslav Igrunov, Arkadii Vaksberg, Lev Ponomarev, Dmitrii Yurasov, and a few others whom I cannot remember right now—held the first meeting of Memorial. After that, there were a number of meetings in the art studio of Skubko's father in which we decided that we should go out onto the streets with posters for the first time. We decided to hold our first demonstration on November 14, 1987. Among those who went to Arbat Street to protest were Kuzin and Skubko, the most fearless people of us all, and another two or three persons. I came to the Arbat after the end of my institute hours, only forty minutes after the beginning of the demonstration, to find nobody there. I phoned our lads to find our that they were arrested immediately. Dima Leonov was the person who conceived of our next action.

We held our second activity near the House of Artists opposite the Park of Culture. There, Leonov, Kuzin, and perhaps Skubko again stood with posters while the rest of us stood guard. When the militia came to arrest them, we approached them as witnesses and demanded that they be freed. The militia took the posters and let the lads go.

Later, in December of that same year, I was chairman of a political club at the culture center of the Moscow Aviation Institute. We convened an evening discussion called "The 1930s: Heroic and Tragic Aspects," to which a number of well-known people had been invited, including Dmitrii Yurasov, authors, and Memorial activists. We went through terrible pains to get the permission to convene this event. When they started speaking about the crimes of Stalinism, a part of the audience began to whistle, shout, and protest, especially our elder tutors, who saw these statements as blackening our heroic history. At the end of the program, we circulated a Memorial petition. The next morning, my deputy Party committee secretary for ideology approached me and asked, "What sort of an anti-Soviet declaration were you signing yesterday?" I told him that it was not anti-Soviet, that Memorial participated in the organization of this gathering, and gave him the text of the address. The following day this same secretary came running up to me with the institute's KGB man and said, "You know, the KGB is asking to be shown what you had there; they'll photograph it." They took all the materials from us and went speedily to make photocopies for themselves. At first, the Party committee contained itself for a week. They asserted that the meeting was on the whole a democratic one; there were some extremes, but generally the position was normal. The district committee of the CPSU, however, began exerting pressure on them. The district committee then approached the city committee, which in turn brought the matter to the attention of the Organizational Department of the CPSU Central Committee headed by Yegor Ligachev. These people decided to reprimand us. This was in December 1987.

After this episode, people at the institute who had initially supported me now sat with downcast eyes at Party committee meetings. For organizational and political faults in conducting the gathering, I was severely reprimanded by the Party. Every year thereafter, I received new reprimands for subsequent meetings.

As for the dissident movement and the Democratic Union, which consisted largely of dissidents, they have fulfilled their role by widening the boundaries of the freedom of speech and the boundaries of the possible. Their demonstrations on Pushkin Square were instrumental in pushing these boundaries. But gradually, when it became possible to conduct meetings and demonstrations without permission, the Democratic Union became lost in this new climate. There is no sense in the Democratic Union persisting to exist in the same quality as before.

As for the former dissidents, they have come to occupy different positions. Some of them—Arsenii Raginsky, for example—perform very active research functions in Memorial, and we are very grateful to them. As it happened, all Memorial activists went into politics to head some movement or party, while the people left in Memorial are lovers of history who strive to tell people the truth about what really happened.

Others went another way. For example, Sergei Kovalev now heads the Committee on Human Rights of our parliament and carries out major work in connection with the observance of human rights. He has found his job, and he is presently one of the most interesting persons in our political movement.

Speaking more generally, however, I think that the dissident movement was largely a movement of moral protest. The participants in this movement continue to uphold a similar attitude. They realize that they are not politicians, and they have no wish to go into politics because politics is a complicated and sometimes dirty business. Therefore they try to take their stand somewhere above the political movement. I have all respect for them and believe that their approach is quite understandable.

Could you explain the main stages in the development of the Democratic Platform and then the Republican Party of Russia?

After the Nineteenth Party Conference, which took place in 1988, the Communists saw very vividly that the CPSU was becoming a major obstacle to the economic reforms and that the Party was not capable of reforming itself. That is why there arose from the ranks different Party clubs and conferences of Party secretaries although they were not officially approved. As early as January 1990, there was already a powerful opposition movement growing within the Party, which, during January 27–28, 1990, officially proclaimed itself to be the Democratic Platform. Initially, this movement united some fifty thousand Communists from more than one hundred cities across the Soviet Union. It was an all-Union and not a republican phenomenon. Although initiated by Party clubs like our Moscow Party Club, the movement soon was headed by people of the highest authority at the time, including Yeltsin, Yurii Afanasiev, Gavriil Popov, Nikolai Travkin, Gdlyan and Ivanov, Vyacheslav Shostakovsky, Gennadii Burbulis, and quite a number of other important people who now are all leaders of the democratic movement.

At about the same time, the Russian Communist Party held its founding congress in Leningrad, demonstrating that the CPSU as a monolithic organization was becoming stratified and polarized in a most natural manner. At the time, it seemed that we would be able to agree to divide this party by the twenty-eighth congress.

Does that mean that, in January 1990, you already had it in mind to divide the party? Or did you still hope to reorient it?

The initial idea, and the documents of the Democratic Platform testify to the fact, was to turn the CPSU into a party of the social-democratic type. That was the essence of it—to drastically reform the CPSU, turning it into a parliamentary, democratic party. Many people expressed doubts that it was possible, but initially slogans calling for splitting or disbanding the CPSU would have proved counter-productive. In Moscow we could see this better than anywhere. To put forward the idea of a schism inside the CPSU or leaving the CPSU altogether was completely out of the question as such stances would have frightened away a huge number of Communists who were really supporting the Democratic Platform.

As it turned out, Gorbachev decided against starting a dialogue with the Democratic Platform, a proposition we had proposed at our founding meeting in January. Actually, all our proposals concerning the democratization of the CPSU were ignored, including our proposals for electing delegates to the [Twenty-eighth CPSU] Congress. While polls showed that 40 percent of Party members supported the Democratic Platform, our representatives constituted only 1 percent of the delegates to the Twenty-eighth CPSU Congress.

Did you ever meet with Gorbachev to discuss your alternative platform?

No, the only thing that was done was that Vasilii Shakhnovsky, one of the leaders of the Democratic Platform, and myself were invited to the plenum of the CPSU Central Committee in March. But they did not even give us the possibility of speaking at the plenum, as the domineering conservative and reactionary factions within the Party declared that they did not want listen to the Democratic Platform. Consequently, no dialogue took place. We arrived at the congress with our alternative documents on all issues, but we had no opportunity to debate them. Aside from the speeches by Yeltsin and Shostakovsky, the voice of the Democratic Platform was not heard at the congress. As a result, first Yeltsin, then Afanasiev, Popov, and Sobchak and finally twenty-four delegates altogether from our Democratic Platform announced they were leaving the CPSU at the congress.

Retrospectively, in trying to determine why we were not successful in inducing a schism within the CPSU (and later even within the Democratic Platform, which unfortunately did not become a mass political party but consisted of only around twenty thousand members at the founding congress of the Republican Party in November 1990), there exist two different viewpoints. On the one hand, Igor Chubais affirms that if we had left the CPSU before the congress, we would number over seven million today. In other words, he assumes that the 40 percent of the Party members who supported us in the spring would have joined our new party had we left earlier. But this is exactly what Nikolai Travkin did. On the eve of the [Twenty-eighth CPSU] Congress, he left the Democratic Platform and informed us that "we are creating our own party outside the CPSU, come to us!" But now, Travkin [and the Democratic Party of Russia] has only thirty thousand people, not seven million.

On the other hand, today's new faction within the CPSU, Communists for Democracy, argues that we acted too hastily in leaving the Party. Rather, they argue that we should have waited and continued to help decompose the Party from inside, thereby making the Party much weaker than it is.

Personally, I think that what we did was the only logically correct action; we had led this movement to the culmination in its development to the twenty-eighth congress. We had been telling Communists that the congress would be the ultimate battle, that the congress is the highest organ of the Party, and it is there that the question of splitting the Party should be raised. When we saw that it was not being decided, it was simply morally impossible for us to remain in the Party. Our comrades in the democratic movement would simply stop talking to us and would consider us traitors if, after all those dirty tricks that the CPSU continued to play after the twenty-eighth congress, we would stay in its ranks. Therefore those of us who were the most active left the Democratic Platform immediately after the congress.

Speaking about the principal reason why the attempts to break the CPSU then were futile—and I am sure Rutskoi will not be any more successful now— the heart of the matter is that the Party is totalitarian.[36] It is not even a party but a power machine, an apparat system, which may be broken only if the schism shall progress from the top downward, that is, if it happens in the Politburo, in the Central Committee, in regional and urban committees, and in primary cells. Then and now, divergences of opinions have taken place only on the lowest level; only the primary cells declare that they support the Democratic Platform. Not a single regional, urban, or district CPSU committee did support or is now supporting the democratic movement. Today's Politburo is completely monolithic, and even at that time, despite all the efforts, we could not influence the democratically oriented CPSU leaders.

In particular, before the congress, there was a unique historic moment. After the founding congress of the Russian Communist Party, when all the conservatives sharply criticized Gorbachev and began calling for his resignation, [Alexander] Yakovlev was terrified.[37] He came to us and said, "Lads, we should act quickly to save Mikhail Sergeevich [Gorbachev]. If we do not do something, he will be freed of his duties at the twenty-eighth congress and perestroika shall be over!" We then said to Yakovlev, "Let Gorbachev declare officially that he shall be only the president and shall vacate the post of the general secretary. We will then nominate you to be our candidate from the Democratic Platform for general secretary, and the right wing is then sure to nominate Ligachev as their alternative to our candidate." And in this scenario, the schism was inevitable, with the Party broken roughly in two halves, as Yakovlev's prestige at the time was tremendous. Yakovlev's success would have been secured if Gorbachev had resigned officially and let it be known that he supported the nomination of Yakovlev. Unfortunately, Gorbachev decided not to establish direct contacts with the Democratic Platform, while Yakovlev, with whom we met, did not resolve himself to make this step [of fomenting a split in the Party]. He explained to us that he entered this Party in 1943, during the war years, and that all his life is connected with this Party. And therefore he could not bring himself to betray this Party, to drop it, even though it is evidently no good.

But I think that the decisive argument was his devotion to Gorbachev. Inasmuch as Gorbachev remained at the post of general secretary, Yakovlev could not think of being nominated as an alternative candidate. Quite recently, I met again with Alexander Nikolaevich [Yakovlev] and he told me a very interesting episode. Evidently, after the congress of the Russian Communist Party, Gorbachev made a decision that he was ready to unite directly with the democratic forces. According to Alexander Nikolaevich, Gorbachev was ready to raise the problem [of internal discord within the CPSU] at the congress. Gorbachev even considered submitting his resignation [as general secretary of the CPSU]. But two days before the congress, one of the democratic newspapers published a very critical article by Yurii Afanasiev. Upon reading the article, Gorbachev came with this newspaper to Yakovlev and said, "Look! You say that I have to take counsel with democrats, and here is what they write of me! How can one cooperate with them at all!"

Upon hearing this story, I said to Yakovlev, "But, Alexander Nikolaevich, the democratic movement does not consist of Afanasiev and his position alone! It is not good to be guided by personal emotions in politics."

Yakovlev replied, "What can one do? Mikhail Sergeevich is a man who is extremely sensitive and averse to criticism and attacks directed at him. For him that was a decisive argument."

Therefore, Gorbachev went to the congress already decided that he would not act in unity with the democrats. Such was the situation. As a result, the democrats [who left the Party at the congress] were not followed by the top or middle people but only by the lower echelons. Moreover, this lower strata of the Party saw that Yeltsin, Popov, and Sobchak, who announced that they were leaving the Party, also announce that they were not going to establish a new party.

I think that this was not the best variant. If they had proclaimed that the departing Democratic Platform was going to form a new party, I am certain that they would have been backed by three million people, three million people who are now lost. A powerful opposition party could have come into existence.

Why did people like Yeltsin, Popov, and Sobchak leave the Democratic Platform?

The problem lies in the fact that it is one thing to exist inside the CPSU or in some other movement, keeping one's membership card and a certain degree of loyalty with respect to this organization, and quite a different matter to create an opposition organization generally hostile to the CPSU. Moreover, Yeltsin's position within the Russian parliament at that time was very unstable. If you remember, he had been elected chairman [of the Supreme Soviet] by only four votes. This factor played the decisive role in his decision not to form a new party. He thought that if he openly joined a party hostile to the CPSU, the Communists in the Russian parliament might demand that he be recalled.

Once Yeltsin stated his position, a similar position was taken by Popov and Sobchak. When they saw that Yeltsin was for departicization [sic], they decided that they also should take this stand. In doing so, however, we missed two unique historic opportunities—on the one hand, electing Yakovlev as general secretary and, on the other, creating an opposition party headed by Yeltsin, Popov, and Sobchak.

Speaking about the present-day idea by Shevardnadze and Yakovlev of creating some kind of a social-democratic party,[38] we look at this proposal with a measure of irony because they have missed their opportunity. When they had the apparat in their hands, when they had the financial resources of the CPSU, we could have really created in a very short time a most powerful party. Today these people are not in power; today they have lost the prestige they had both in the CPSU and with the population. I treat them with deep respect and still have the highest esteem for Yakovlev. A short time ago, he and I led talks with the leadership of Democratic Russia on the possibility of cooperation. But at the same time I think that the idea of creating a mass, million-people party based on these names is utopian. Today all the political niches are occupied. All the available activists have long been working in those movements that already exist. Perhaps some sort of elite and prestigious Moscow group could formulate their opinion and thereby influence political events, but I do not think that a political party can be established.

Let us turn now to the Republican Party of Russia. After we left the CPSU, we had three real options of development. First, the Democratic Party of Russia in the person of Travkin enticed us to join the DPR, promising a multitude of advantages. Second, on the left, there was the Social-Democratic Party of Russia, with whom we had very good and friendly relations at the time. However, the third and decisive argument was this: as we were leaving the CPSU, we still hoped that we might be the logical successor to the CPSU. We hoped that we could absorb those people who were leaving the Party at an ever-increasing rate.

Therefore we decided not to fuse with anybody in the short term but rather to form our own post–Communist Party in order to attract as our base those people who had left the CPSU. However, though we have a very good group of activists, this strategy did not work. Today the Republican Party is second in numbers among the opposition parties in the Russian Federation, but our strength has decreased since November 1990 by ten thousand members. Earlier supporters of the Democratic Platform developed hesitations when the registration of party cards began.

At the same time, however, during the election campaign of Boris Yeltsin, I visited many Russian cities and noticed that our local structures do have in many cases rather strong party organizations. Our positions are fairly good in urban and district soviets.[39] Even at village soviets there are complete organizations of the RPR, with their own press publications issued at local centers and in Moscow. We also have a very good faction in the Russian parliament united with the Social Democrats. In sum, I think that our party already has established firm positions and will be progressively accruing its influence in the future.

At the same time, during the last six months, I personally have been actively supporting the trend toward rapprochement and ultimate unification with the SDPR, as in reality as well as in program clauses we indeed support very similar positions. Our parties actually occupy the same political niche, and in the near future, we may be hindering each other if we continue to compete.

Regrettably, the tendency [toward unity with the Social-Democratic Party of Russia] has been weakening. The farther from our founding congress at which a resolution was adopted endorsing the unification process, the worse the general state of affairs for fostering unity. There has been opposition from our leadership, including from my fellow cochairmen Stepan Sulakshin and Vyacheslav Shostakovsky, who are categorically against unification, and from a large part of our local cells, who have spoken out against being united with the Social-Democratic Party of Russia.

Analyzing the situation retrospectively, it seems that Sulakshin and Shostakovsky might have felt themselves in an alien atmosphere in a united party, as they would have been out of their element. But many including myself have had long-standing relations with Rumyantsev, as we were in the informal movement together. It is also possible that a part of our leading personnel at local centers, having just succeeded in registering, establishing working premises, and thus winning a degree of recognition, felt discomfort at the idea of uniting with a new party with unknown consequences for themselves and their local organizations. Finally, in some cities, relations between our party and the local Social Democrats are bad, though such places are few. But there are also reasons of a more general nature.

We have now entered a stage of political development in which a process of differentiation is under way. Now, every moment something new emerges that further splits the democratic movement. As yet, there is not a single instance in which something unites our forces. This process will continue for some time to come. In order to unite different parties, it is necessary that at least one of these parties be headed by a political figure occupying an important government post and highly popular among the people. With this figure in view, both the constituent halves would forget their current discords and unite. Today, unfortunately, neither we nor the Social Democrats have a leader of stature such as Yeltsin. And in this connection, despite my certain influence within the party, my prestige is not sufficient to convince the rest of the party to unite with the Social Democrats.

What kind of relations do you have with Democratic Russia?

I was one of the supporters in creating the Democratic Russia movement, and I take an active part in its activities as a member of the Coordinating Council. Until the CPSU goes into opposition, Democratic Russia will be the main opposition force in the Russian Federation. Therefore I think that all parties who are not only after their own narrow advantage and profit but also interested in the good of Russia should put a major stake in Democratic Russia and help it in any way. Therefore when Travkin says that the Democratic Party of Russia (DPR) is higher than Democratic Russia, or some other parties begin to say that this movement has grown obsolete, I cannot support them. The experience of countries in Eastern Europe has convinced me that it is precisely a movement without strict discipline or strict obligations that is capable of leading millions of people. Right now, Democratic Russia has about one million activists in its ranks.

At the same time, today's Democratic Russia as a coalition of political parties is living through difficult times. On the one hand, a serious contradiction is growing between the radicals and the moderates in the movement. The radicals are led by the group of Telman Gdlyan, which is now called the People's Party of Russia. To a certain degree, these [radical] positions are also shared in considerable part by the former MOI [Moscow Association of Voters] activists—Lev Shemaev, Vera Kriger, Vladimir Boxer, and, in some measure, Leonid Batkin and Yurii Afanasiev. They believe that by supporting a universal political strike and civil disobedience campaigns, we could interrupt economic links and break down the entire system, and then we could throw away at last the hated group at the top. We then would replace these people with democrats who would initiate their reforms without any hindrance.

On the other hand, the moderates argue that if the entire economic system collapses, neither democrats nor other parties would be in power. Instead, this situation would lead to dictatorship and martial law. This would be a devastating line for the democratic movement.

This was the first contradiction, but now it has subsided momentarily as

Yeltsin's victory is quite evident and the radicals have been obliged to keep silent for the time being. But I think these tensions will continue. These divisions were clearly manifested at the inaugural Democratic Congress meeting in Kharkov in January 1991, when Travkin did not sign the documents of the congress, citing the violations of human rights in certain republics as his reason for not joining the movement.[40] It was a very good stand, and we all supported it at the congress. In my speech to the congress, I stated that we all were concerned with the processes in the Baltic region and in Georgia because everything that goes on in these places is far from democratic. But being realistic, we thought that we needed to form a coalition of movements and fronts from all republics to try to influence events in places in the right direction.

Travkin rejected this categorically, referring to the fact that human rights, especially the rights of the Russian-speaking minorities, are not universally observed in these republics. Six months later, Travkin adopted a rather different position. Together with the Christian Democrats,[41] he now supports the idea that the Union should be preserved in any form. The main thing is simply to cleanse the Union of Communists. The only problem that exists for them is to replace the communist leadership and communist center with an anticommunist center. The central structures, however, which infused hatred from the non-Russian republics, are considered to be quite legitimate. In this connection, Travkin has put forward the idea of an all-Union Democratic Party, an idea that has shocked all the other movements. Travkin has traveled throughout Central Asia. In Tajikistan, he appeared at a congress of Central Asian republics at which I was also present. He purposely addressed the most politically backward republics and painstakingly tried to convince them to form an all-Union Democratic Party. Almost everybody rejected the idea with the exception of Turkmenistan and Tajikistan, who said that they were not going to establish a general party but were prepared to enter into a coalition with the DPR. As a result of these actions, five parties have denounced the Democratic Party, stating that they would leave the Democratic Congress if the DPR joined. So there is a serious contradiction.

I have a suspicion that Nikolai Ilich [Travkin] is preparing himself for nomination for the president of the Soviet Union. My bet, however, is that we will never have such an election. In the best-case scenario, we will not have a federative system but some kind of intermediate federative-confederative mix. In this new system, I believe we will not have a Union parliament or a Union president but rather something like a council of the federation consisting of presidents of the republics who would then assign Gorbachev speaker's functions. But I highly doubt that we will have elections for a president of the Union to be elected after the president of Russia. It is incongruous. People will not vote for any kind of president. Therefore, I think Travkin—who is a very clever and well-known person—is wasting his time organizing a Union campaign.

Travkin's position [regarding the Union] is very dangerous. At the last meeting of the interparliamentary conference (an association of parliamentarians from all the republics created by the Democratic Congress), our adherents of the Great Russia idea began speaking out. Ivan Drach, a leader of Rukh (in Ukraine), responded by saying that "if Russian Social Democrats take such a stand, I have no business remaining in this hall." If Drach, who generally has a sympathetic attitude toward Russia and is a stabilizing force in Ukraine, cannot tolerate these Russian nationalist positions, and we other Russian democrats start to waver on these issues, we simply will spoil our good relations with the democratic movement in other republics. This will be a tragedy for us all.

What is your attitude to the movement Communists for Democracy?

On election day, June 12, 1991, we conducted a very important roundtable between the Republican Party of Russia and the movement Communists for Democracy. The subject was "Is a Schism within the CPSU Possible?" In this discussion, we spoke critically of the CPSU. This roundtable was due to air on Russian television on June 13, but a threatening call from the CPSU Central Committee to the chairman of Russian television, Oleg Poptsov, canceled the program. This shows you how democratic Russian television is.

On the whole, we support and welcome their movement [Communists for Democracy], though I do not believe that they will succeed in breaking up the CPSU. Maybe they will manage to break away yet another chunk. Lately, for the Yeltsin campaign, I have been traveling extensively throughout the Russian provinces, and I have been noticing that there are many people still in the CPSU who did not join our party but who behave in an active manner. I say to them, "Lads, come on, create party clubs, work with the Communists for Democracy. They are a normal bunch of guys."

Additionally, I think good relations between Democratic Russia and the democratically minded Communists are especially important today. Unfortunately, some within Democratic Russia adhere to a primitive, stone-age anticommunism. For them, if a person is a Communist or former Communist, having any relations with this person is out of the question. I am dead against this approach and believe that most rank-and-file Communists in the CPSU support us. Therefore, we should cooperate with them.

But at the same time, I have my personal doubts regarding Vice-President Rutskoi, who is the present leader of the movement Communists for Democracy. I believe that he will soon leave the movement. He is a peculiar personality, with arbitrary trends and little prestige with the intelligentsia. There is a definite problem here. If, however, Rutskoi devotes his full attention to the affairs of the state, the movement [Communists for Democracy] could benefit from his absence. Besides Rutskoi, the movement has some very sensible and efficient people.

Leonid Batkin recently stated at a conference of Democratic Russia that Democratic Russia was dead because it has become wholly subordinated to Yeltsin. What is your view on future relations between Democratic Russia and the new Russian government?

This question is very complicated, both concerning relations between Yeltsin and Democratic Russia and relations between Yeltsin and the Republican Party of Russia. At the latest plenum of the Republican Party we had a very serious conversation about our relationship with Yeltsin. Gennadii Burbulis, Yeltsin's chief adviser [and now deputy prime minister] attended this meeting to hear our complaints and concerns about Boris Nikolaevich [Yeltsin] and his team. In particular, we stated that we supported Yeltsin, but we were not prepared to follow him blindly. It is very important that Yeltsin consider himself to be in partnership with Democratic Russia. Yeltsin has adopted quite a number of very important decisions without consulting at all the movement that brought him to power and that today provides massive support in small provincial centers. In particular, the 9 + 1 declaration came as a complete surprise to us.[42] Democratic Russia was very near to opposing this declaration. So one would wish that contact between Democratic Russia and the government authorities was more tight and direct. I also think that the Democratic Russia movement and our parties could be of use in forming the new cabinet of ministers of the Russian Federation. I would very much like to see this new cabinet be a multiparty affair.

How does the Republican Party of Russia (RPR) differ from other parties?

If we speak in classical terms, the Republican Party can be said to be left of center, as it rests, on the one hand, on the values of social democracy (and here we are very close ideologically with the Social-Democratic Party of Russia), and, on the other, we attach great importance to the free business ideas, the ideas of political and economic freedom, and the more general concept of liberalism. Currently, we think that the values of freedom are above all else. Since we have little to distribute or redistribute now in the Soviet Union, it is most essential to create a new system of market relations in the economy. Only after these new economic relations are created can we tackle secondary issues. Therefore, in contrast to the Social Democrats, we have a double-sighted orientation toward the values of liberalism and social democracy.

At the same time, we realize that presently all our parties have a largely temporal, transitional character. Although our party and everything around it exist today, we realize that they may not exist until the very end. I believe that most parties still lack a social base. Our social base is only beginning to take shape. We are starting to work very actively with state office workers and existing commercial enterprises, as we consider these people to be our proper social base.

Could you say a few words about the Democratic Congress?

The idea of uniting democratic movements from different republics appeared long ago, at the time of the origination of the democratic movement in the Russian Federation and other republics. The prime mover was Yurii Afanasiev. Marina Salye was also very active in this campaign.[43] But as a rule these associations were formed one day and folded the next. Besides, they were always joined by some scandalous organizations who compromised the movements almost immediately. You must have some critical mass, some objective preconditions for a mechanism of organization to start functioning. This is what happened in January 1991 when the ideas and the movements themselves sprang up. Democratic Russia was only founded in October 1990. Before then, there had existed in Russia only small, disjointed political parties. The events in the Baltic states in January 1991 were another uniting factor. When blood was spilled there, the democrats at last realized that it was impossible to achieve freedom in a single isolated state. We either had to all unite and eliminate this totalitarian system, or it would stifle us all, one after another. By January, when the Baltic people felt that they were on the brink of destruction, they stopped being hostile toward the Russian democratic movements and informed us that they would participate in these interrepublic associations. Soon thereafter we managed to convene the Democratic Congress in Kharkov. Presently, the Democratic Congress embraces nearly fifty political parties and movements from twelve republics. So far, we lack representation from Georgia, Moldova, and Kazakhstan, although the Azat movement from Kazakhstan has submitted its request to join our union at our next meeting this month. We also have preliminary requests to join the congress from a number of democratic parties in Moldova, the Patriotic Front notwithstanding. As for Georgia, the regime of Zviad Gamsakhurdia is compromising democratic forces in all other republics. The official Party press media of the CPSU says, "Your democrats have come to power, and look at what is happening to people from South Ossetia, Abkhazia, and the opposition!" Democrats from the Union republics and all over the world must take a more definite position with respect to the events in Georgia. Violations of human rights (as far as I know, there are already about seventy political prisoners there) should be made public, and public opinion should demand that those persons be freed and the rights declared in the constitution and the declaration of human rights be observed.

If we do not take a stand regarding events in Georgia, there is a danger that similar regimes may spring up in other republics. It is better to act together against this regime now than to have to fight in the future ten or fifteen anticommunist regimes no less cruel or bloodthirsty than the one totalitarian communist regime we are fighting now.

Postcoup Reflections (December 1991)

Where were you during the coup attempt?

On August 19, I was having a holiday at the seaside with my family. Having heard on the radio the reports of the State Emergency Committee [SEC], my colleague Anatoly Lysenko and I went to Krasnodar. By 7:00 P.M., we were in the White House. This whole day and the following ones, I was at one parliamentary committee helping to spread information to mass media and to different regions that were calling us all the time. On August 20, I addressed the meeting from the balcony of the Moscow City Soviet. On August 21, I flew to the Crimea as part of the Russian delegation to free President Gorbachev. On coming back to Moscow I began work on the commission regarding CPSU property.

What did the Republican Party do during the coup?

The Republican Party headquarters was set up at the Minsk Hotel—the location of the headquarters for the Movement for Democratic Reform—with the purpose of coordinating the efforts of our organizations for putting up resistance to the SEC. Our representatives came to the Moscow City Soviet as early as 8:00 A.M. on August 19. The main centers of our work were at the Minsk Hotel, at the Moscow City Soviet, at the Rossiya Hotel, and in the White House. Republicans worked quite actively in the regions, too, especially in the regions of Krasnoyarsk, Tomsk, Omsk, Sverdlovsk, and Rostov-on-the-Don. Members of the Republican Party also participated in sealing up the Central Committee CPSU building.

Did the Republican Party's policies change after the putsch?

Right after the putsch, when Russia's leadership position was uncertain and its actions were indecisive, we criticized the leadership of Russia and Moscow. But after Yeltsin made up his mind about the reforms, we were one of the first groups to support the course of sweeping reforms. The main efforts of the RPR were aimed at creating a centrist coalition of democratic forces as a political basis for carrying out serious economic reforms.

Documents

. . . .

The following passage is the preamble of the political program of the Republican Party of Russia approved at its founding congress in November 1990. Whereas the entire program is much longer and more detailed, this preamble outlines the basic tenets of the party. The program of the Social-Democratic Party is much more comprehensive, but we have included this shorter document as an example of a platform from a left-of-center party.

Statement by the Founding Congress of the Republican Party of Russia

We, delegates from fifty republics and regions in the Russian Federation, resolved to struggle for its genuine sovereignty and democratic development, declare the formation of a Russian Republican Party as an independent parliamentary party of the peoples of the Russian Federation.

Declaration of the Republican Party of Russia

After the constituent congress of the Russian Communist Party and Twenty-eighth Congress of the Soviet Communist Party, perestroika, as an attempt to bring about a "revolution from above," has ended. With it, the seventy-three-year-old experiment conducted on one-sixth of the planet's surface under Communist Party guidance finished as well. The Soviet Communist Party, with all its ideological currents and leaders, both blatantly die-hard and moderately progressive, finally lost the political initiative and has fallen back to the rearguard of social progress.

The restructuring of totalitarianism is being replaced with efforts to revive universally shared values and civilized forms of public life in Russia.

Dragged along by historical inertia and clinging to the survivals of communist dogmas, the federal government, however, seeks to carry out yet another unheard-of experiment before its inevitable resignation and cross-breed the administer-by-command system with a "market regulated by it," which will inexorably wreak national chaos and touch off an explosion. Home-bred national socialism—a fusion of partocratic and great-power imperial tendencies—is emerging and gaining weight on the basis of revulsion against "new thinking."

We believe that no political or ideological values can exonerate mass deaths among compatriots, hunger, and economic dislocation. We see the principal danger in the possibility of wholesale violence and the transition to a dictatorship in Russia.

In this critical situation, we declare the formation of a new parliamentary party in the Russian Federation.

We are a party for restoring Russia's true sovereignty and achieving civic and ethnic harmony in this republic. To this end, we are prepared to pool our efforts with all democratic forces proceeding from the inadmissibility of a civil war, regardless of how different our views may be. We are convinced opponents of totalitarianism, but we also oppose its removal by force.

We suggest the path not of confrontation but of political dialogue, reasonable compromise, and a peaceful replacement of old administer-by-command structures with new market-based democratic relations.

Our party's ideal is a civil society of free workers ensuring worthy living standards with their knowledge, industry, enterprise, and initiative, a society open to all achievements of world civilization and prioritizing freedom and mercy. Our task is to turn the unavoidable collision of interests of different social groups into a civilized competition of ideas. This is done through the cultivation in the party of two basic concepts expressing the deep inner contradictoriness of the primary values of a democratic society—freedom and progress, on the one hand, and justice and solidarity, on the other.

The awareness that man is born free and worthy of a civilized life is the supreme achievement of humanist thinking. Advocating social security for all, we are strongly against equality in misery, a cult of dependence, and envy at prosperity gained by work and talent.

The party is evolving an economic concept for the transition to a market, based on the right of everyone to own a part of state property.

Relying on broad sections of the population sharing our objectives, our party opposes, on the one hand, the monopoly *diktat* of the elite and, on the other, lumpen extremism.

We stand for filling Russian sovereignty with real contents, protecting it, and restoring Russia's sovereignty as a democratic republic ensuring the rights and liberties of all citizens in keeping with the U.N. Declaration of Human Rights. We favor a commonwealth with other sovereign states that are bound with Russia by a common history.

We are convinced that it will be possible to revive the friendship of peoples inhabiting Russia only in the event of success in forming a free union of sovereign ethnic-state entities and on the basis of an all-Russia market of goods, capital, and manpower. This will set the stage for a broad-based alliance of political forces, based on the priority of human rights, nonviolence, and the renunciation of a monopoly on truth. We do not accept an alliance only with forces acting from the positions of ethnic or class supremacy, totalitarianism, and violence.

Created as a parliamentary party, our party sees its political mission in winning seats on bodies of power at every level in fair competition with other parties. Being in opposition to the Soviet Communist Party, to the Russian Communist Party's Central Committee, and other conservative organizations, the new party will be active in the Democratic Russia movement, closely cooperating with the Russian Social-Democratic Party, the Russian Democratic Party, and other democratic parties advocating constructive views. The new party is based on the generally shared democratic principles of elections, complete public openness, replacement of those serving on steering agencies, and guarantees for the rights of minorities, including the freedom to set up factions and groups. It is based on federalism and organized on the territorial principle. It is a party movement that comprises, in addition to individual and collective members, sympathizers supporting it during elections and other political activities. It is a party that is prepared to enter into voluntary alliances with other parliamentary parties professing similar convictions in sovereign constituent republics.

Our party is being created as a party of political realism, which sets itself attainable tasks at every stage of social development.

We favor a careful attitude to cultural, scientific, and moral values created by mankind, as well as to the natural environment.

We shall seek

1. Support for the key planks of the Russian government's economic platform and its translation into reality

2. The dissolution of the USSR Supreme Soviet and the termination of the powers of USSR people's deputies

3. The replacement of the federal government with an interrepublic committee whose members will be delegated directly by the republics

4. The resolution of ethnic conflicts exclusively by political means

5. The departicization of (removal of Party cells from) the armed forces, the KGB, the Interior Ministry, and other law enforcement services and the deideologization of scientific, cultural, and educational institutions

Democracy in Russia has no future without strong and responsible parliamentary parties enjoying grass roots support.

We are establishing such a party!

chapter seven

The Russian Christian-Democratic Movement (RXDD)[1]

The impetus for the Russian Christian-Democratic Movement originated with the publication of the journal *Vybor* (Choice), which began in September 1987.[2] Published by Victor Aksiuchits and Gleb Anishchenko, the journal soon attracted religious activists in Russia and abroad, including such well-known dissidents as Father Gleb Yakunin in Russia and Alexander Solzhenitsyn in the United States. The publishers of *Vybor* expanded their activities to include restoring Russian Orthodox churches, financing Christian schools, and publishing other religious materials. After the repeal of Article Six of the Soviet constitution in February 1990, the movement decided to form a political party.

During April 7–9, 1990, the RXDD held its constituent congress, at which it elected its Duma (the steering committee of the movement) and approved a charter. Victor Aksiuchits, Father Vyacheslav Polosin, and Gleb Anishchenko were elected cochairmen; such prominent figures as Father Gleb Yakunin and Valerii Borshchov were elected members of the Duma.[3]

Initially, the RXDD program was distinguished from other political movements and parties by its emphasis on traditional Russian Orthodox values.[4] Because seventy years of atheist rule have destroyed Russia's Christian heritage, the RXDD's most immediate task is restoring the Russian Orthodox church and promulgating religious freedoms more generally.[5] In pursuit of these objectives, the RXDD has actively assisted the Russian Orthodox church in repatriating property, and RSFSR people's deputies Aksiuchits, Polosin, and Yakunin have written new Russian laws protecting freedom of religious practices.

Like Christian-democratic parties in the West, the RXDD political program underscores the importance of individual freedoms, placing special emphasis on the natural right to own property.[6] Additionally, the RXDD program stresses the importance of the family, culture, and tradition in reviving the Russian state and economy. To realize these changes, the first RXDD program called for convening an all-Russian constituent assembly to draft the basic government structures of a new Russian state.[7]

Since its founding congress, the RXDD has grown increasingly nationalistic and patriotic, alienating many of its former allies in the democratic movement.[8] Patriotism is valued by the RXDD as a positive and necessary element of Russia's rebirth, not to be confused with national socialism.[9] Although vehemently denouncing communism,[10] RXDD leader Victor Aksiuchits has often sided with the conservative Rossiya faction in the Russian parliament concerning debates on preserving the Union and the Russian Federation.[11]

These RXDD nationalist positions often clashed with the more radical activists in Russia's democratic movement. The RXDD agreed to join Democratic Russia in October 1990 but only after affirming each party's right to maintain its unique ideological identity and platform.[12] RXDD participation in Democratic Russia, however, was short lived. In the spring of 1991, the movement joined the Democratic Party of Russia and the Constitutional Democratic Party (Astafiev) to form Narodnoe Soglasie (Popular Accord). Narodnoe Soglasie left Democratic Russia in November 1991, after which Father Gleb Yakunin and Valerii Borshchov quit the RXDD to protest its nationalistic tendencies.[13] In addition to its new enemies in Democratic Russia, the Russian Christian-Democratic Movement has maintained a vicious rivalry with the other Christian-democratic movements and parties.[14] The oldest and most challenging opponent is the Christian-Democratic Union, headed by Victor Ogorodnikov.[15] Ogorodnikov, who spent several years in prison in the 1970s owing to his religious practices, founded his union August 4–7, 1989.[16] Although the union initially combined several dozen religious organizations and movements, leadership splits have weakened the organization, and several regional branches eventually joined the more prominent RXDD. Nonetheless, the Christian-Democratic Union has several representatives in the Moscow City Council and continues to compete with the Russian Christian-Democratic Movement as the political leader of Russia's newly burgeoning Christian population.[17]

After the collapse of the Soviet Union in December 1992, Victor Aksiuchits and the Russian Christian-Democratic Movement moved even further to the right, leaving Narodnoe Soglasie in favor of more strident patriots. In February 1992, Aksiuchits participated in the formation of a bloc of nationalist, monarchist, and patriotic forces called the Congress of Patriotic Forces, which convened on February 8, 1992.[18] This congress resulted in the formation of the Russian People's

Assembly (Rossiiskoe Narodnoe Sobranie), which combined former leaders of Narodnoe Soglasie, Aksiuchits and Astafiev, with former Communists turned nationalists Nikolai Pavlov and Sergei Baburin (cochairmen of the Russian All-People's Union) and militant noncommunist nationalists such as Nikolai Lysenko, chairman of the National Republican Party of Russia (NRPR).[19] Upon its foundation, this coalition championed the civil rights of Russians living outside of Russia in the former republics of the Soviet Union.[20] In fact, this group has refused to recognize the Russian Federation's current borders, claiming that these Leninist-Stalinist demarcations artificially divide Russian populations.[21]

The RXDD and the Russian People's Assembly as a whole have joined forces with new communist parties and movements in signing a "Declaration about Creating United Opposition."[22] In parliament, Aksiuchits also united with former Communists to form the antigovernmental bloc Rossiiskoe Edinstvo (Russian Unity).[23] During the Sixth Congress of People's Deputies in April 1992, this bloc spearheaded the assault against Yeltsin's government. To widen its social base, leaders of the Russian National Assembly and Rossiiskoe Edinstvo organized the All-Russian Labor Consultation, in which former official trade unions, workers' collectives, strike committees, and other organizations from more than fifty regions of Russia participated. Although Aksiuchits and his supporters in the RXDD were originally anticommunist and promarket, the consultation advocated state control for some prices, abolishing the law on bankruptcy, limits on trade (and banning "speculation"), indexing all wages, credits for state enterprises, and abandoning the present models of privatization.[24]

Since the coup several other movements and parties have formed that espouse nationalistic slogans similar to those of Victor Aksiuchits, the RXDD, and the Russian People's Assembly.[25] Of these *new* organizations, the Russkii Natsio-nal'nii Sobor (Russian National Synod), headed by former KGB general Alexander Sterligov, represents the Russian People's Assembly's greatest rival.[26] Founded in February 1992 in Nizhny Novgorod, the Sobor has echoed the assembly in vowing to arrest the dissolution of the Russian Federation and the robbery of the Russian people.[27] The Sobor also advocates the reconstruction of a strong Russian national army, including the restoration of Cossack divisions now forming independently throughout southern Russia.[28]

As economic and political chaos continues to worsen, these nationalist forces already have begun preparing to seize power.[29] Although their visible public support during the course of several demonstrations has not increased significantly since the collapse of the Soviet Union, more and more people nonetheless think that groups such as the Russian People's Assembly or the Russian National Synod will assume power if Yeltsin's team collapses.[30] If this scenario does unfold, Victor Aksiuchits and his RXDD could play a leading role in the next Russian government.

Victor Aksiuchits

Born in 1949, Victor Aksiuchits entered the Philosophy Department at Moscow State University but was expelled for quitting the Komsomol. He worked as a construction worker and laborer until founding the journal *Vybor* in 1987. Soon thereafter, he created the cooperative Perspektiva, which led to a successful business career. Aksiuchits, in fact, may have been the first wealthy private individual to have entered public life.

Elected as an RSFSR people's deputy in March 1990, Aksiuchits is chairman of the Subcommittee on Religious Freedom. Before quitting in November 1991, Aksiuchits was a member of the Coordinating Council of Democratic Russia. He currently serves as a cochairman of the RXDD Duma and as chairman of the movement's political council. He was the main organizer of the opposition bloc Rossiiskoe Edinstvo (Russian Unity), the Congress of Civil and Patriotic Forces, and the subsequent Russian People's Assembly.

Interview with
Victor Aksiuchits (May 1991)

· ·

Can you first explain your different titles and positions?
I am a cochairman of the Duma and chairman of the political council of the
Russian Christian-Democratic Movement (RXDD), a people's deputy of the
Russian Federation (Supreme Soviet), chairman of the Subcommittee for Ties
with Foreign Religious Organizations, and chairman of the Committee for Free-
dom of Conscience and Charity.

Regarding our Christian-Democratic Movement, we are one of the few parties
in opposition, and we take pride in our having implemented [into law] several
tenets of our program. In particular, our political program includes a clause,
"religion and freedom of conscience," which says that our party aims to set up a
committee for denomination at the Supreme Soviet of the Russian Federation.
This committee already has been formed. Its formation took many efforts, as the
atheist communist regime opposed it. However, we managed to do so, and,
moreover, having formed the committee, we now head it. A member of our
Duma, Father Vyacheslav Polosin, is chairman of the committee and, consequently, is a member of the Presidium of the Supreme Soviet of the Russian
Federation. His deputy, Father Gleb Yakunin, is a member of our Duma and a
well-known figure of the human rights movement.

Our program also includes the following: "to create new legislation on
religion." We have prepared a draft law on religion using as its basis the work
done by our other cochairman of our Duma, Gleb A. Anishchenko. We have
worked out this draft legislation and are working for its adoption. The law on
freedom of denomination is very democratic and progressive. In general, restoration of religious organizations in the USSR became possible due to adoption of
this law. Our program also includes the following: "to abolish the Councils for
Religion at all levels." You probably know what a Council for Religion is: it is a
body, set up by Stalin and Beria in 1943 and virtually an affiliate of the KGB,
which aims to eliminate religion and destroy all religious organizations in this
country. We managed to disband the Council for Religion of the Russian Federation and pressured its Union counterpart to make a radical change in its status;
it has ceased to be a plenipotentiary body that can take decisions and instead has
become a council of experts. Officials of these councils are no longer represented
in all territorial organizations. Moreover, we managed to improve the Union's
legislation through our [Russian Federation] Soviet. We sent letters to [Anatoly]

Lukyanov, appealed to the public, and criticized the draft Union treaty so that improvements were made which now concur with our variant.[31]

Besides these accomplishments, we have achieved the declaration of religious holidays beginning with Christmas. This is one of our successes. Currently we are preparing a draft law to transfer the ownership of all churches and cathedrals back to religious organizations.

I must admit that all these struggles have been very difficult, as we are being opposed by all structures of this regime. We fail to find support from democrats, as they are convinced atheists. For most democrats, Christianity is a utopia and all Christians are clerics. For example, [Sergei] Shakhrai and [Oleg] Poptsov believe that we are clerics because they are absolutely incompetent in religious matters and Christianity in particular.[32] They believe Christians are uneducated people who want to establish priests' power and the power of the church, which is out of the question. This is why our activities face many difficulties. However, if you analyze our yearly activity since we formed last April [1990], you will find that the political activity of our movement has achieved feasible results.

How did your party form and how did you become involved in politics?
I am a Christian philosopher by training and vocation. I graduated from the Philosophy Department at Moscow State University. I come from a family of peasants who were Christians. I was baptized and attended services in church. I come from the western part of Byelorussia. My youth was typical for a Soviet citizen: I was an Octobrist, a Pioneer, and later joined the Komsomol [Young Communist League].[33] At the time, I was a convinced atheist, and when I was in the navy, I joined the Communist Party. I was a real Communist, a "true believer." However, I believed communism in this country was being built in a wrong way and so it was necessary to study communist theory to build it correctly. That is why I went to Moscow State University: to study the theory and practice of communism. My aim was to become general secretary of the Communist Party of the Soviet Union so as to implement all my ideas.

In Moscow, I came across Christian, religious, and political literature published abroad by Russian emigrants, which we were deprived of in Byelorussia. Through this experience, I shifted from Marxism to idealism rather quickly and progressed further on to Christianity and Russian Orthodoxy. By my third year of university, I had become a [Christian] believer. After graduation, I became a graduate student. Both my diploma [an undergraduate thesis] and my postgraduate thesis were on pure religious issues. My diploma thesis was "The Problem of Correlation of Philosophy and Theology in Paul Tillich's Neo-Protestantism," and my graduate thesis was called "The Problem of Man in the Works by Paul Tillich and Nikolai Berdaev."

However, the KGB had been after me since my first year at the university. They searched my room and confiscated my home library. When I tried to convince them that I needed these books for scientific research, being a postgraduate student, I was expelled from the university. At the same time, I canceled my membership in the Communist Party. As a result, I could not find a job in my specialty and had to work as a seasonal construction worker in the countryside.

All the years before perestroika began, I had been working as a construction worker, while studying, reading, and writing in my spare time. My works were first published in the West in 1981 or so. At first they were published by Russian emigrants and later in foreign languages. However, none of my works were published in my native country, which is quite typical. After all these years, I have become a professional political scientist, publicist, sovietologist, and philosopher of Christianity. I specialize in Russian-Christian philosophy of the twentieth century. Naturally, I was oppressed during all these years. My apartment was searched several times, my case was investigated, and some of my friends were sentenced. I too expected to be imprisoned; however, perestroika rescued me.

In 1987, I started publishing a literary and philosophical magazine called *Vybor* [Choice], which propagated Russian-Christian culture. Previously it had been published illegally, but, in 1987, we published *Vybor* openly. The magazine became an intellectual center for the reunion of historians, poets, and writers. Subsequently, we broke all the traditions of samizdat [unofficial] press; we did not type several copies on a typewriter but made up one thousand copies on a Xerox machine. This kind of production had no precedent. The magazine itself eventually became a hardcover book. All this needed money; an illegally published magazine is not self-financing. So I began doing business and got involved in commercial activity. I became deputy chairman of a cooperative in Moscow. Presently I am vice-president of the Soviet-Italian print shop Sirin and a board member of the U.S.-Soviet joint venture Pacific Union Investment Corporation. These business activities were necessary for me to earn my living and finance our publishing activity. I began publishing a fashionable samizdat magazine on political and Christian issues. We were the first to begin selling the Paris-published magazine *Russkaya Misl'* (Russian Thought) and the magazine *Posev* in considerable quantities on the streets of Moscow. However, in this peculiar period of history, our society proved unable to comprehend the ideas these magazines propagated.

The history of our movement is rather interesting. When we began to acquire money, we also found people who needed help. We helped reconstruct churches, set up public libraries and various charity societies, and promoted various Christian initiatives. These various groups united to form the Russian Christian-Democratic Movement in April 1990. These organizations grouped around the party of the Russian Christian-Democratic Movement. This is how the party was formed.

What is the difference between your party and other Christian-democratic unions and parties?

The main difference is that our party exists while the others do not. This is a fact. We have established organizations in 140 Soviet cities and towns. We have people's deputies at all levels of government from our party. We are proud of the achievements that I told you about. We visited the patriarch today, and I must say that we reached an agreement on certain interesting and promising aspects of Christian policy. We render assistance to our church. This is a concrete achievement. The Christian-Democratic Union never achieved anything of that kind.[34]

The story [of the division between the two organizations] is the following. Two years ago, representatives of the International of Christian Democracy, located in Brussels, came to visit us. They met with Moscow's clerical leaders, telling everyone the same thing: "Let's form a Christian-democratic party as soon as possible and we'll find supporters." Father Gleb Yakunin, myself, and some other leaders responded that we could not become utopians and create an artificial organization. I told them that the course of events will lead to the formation of a party, but it should emerge organically. At that time, an inner formation had been taking place and the delivery was to come soon. So I said, "Let's wait."

It has happened just as I said. I participated in all these events and saw that sooner or later growing initiatives of opposition would challenge the regime. My wife is an art director of the Christian theater Kovcheg [Ark]. In 1988 [the year of the millennium of Russia's baptism], under perestroika and glasnost we organized a program at her theater dedicated to the baptism of Russia. [There were] no politics, just history and religious studies. It was a theoretical Christian conference. The KGB broke it up, the theater was closed, and the company was virtually thrown out into the street without any place to perform. To sum it up, all religious and cultural initiatives were stopped short by the existing regime. [To change the regime] we faced the necessity of forming an organization. I knew that it would come to this. I said, "Wait, it will be formed soon."

In response to it,[35] [Alexander] Ogorodnikov gathered five people the next day and formed the Christian-Democratic Union. It was an adventure, a utopia, and the results prove it. Three deputies at the Moscow City Council represent their interests. They had to recruit these deputies. Ogorodnikov misled them by saying that he was the only person to represent the Christian-Democratic Union and the entire Christian democracy. However, we have five deputies representing our interests there [at the Moscow City Council] too. In addition to the fact that the Christian-Democratic Union was initially weak, it suffered several splits because its structure was inorganic from the beginning. On the whole, Ogorodnikov can neither become a political leader nor be a political figure. All he is capable of is giving press conferences and using his background story of a "prisoner of conscience no more." As a result, in order to keep some momentum, he must constantly support his own authority by scheming against his colleagues and humiliating them. Naturally, all groups have drifted away from his leadership. Now, all these groups have joined our movement. The Christian-Democratic

Unions of Saint Petersburg, Konigsberg [Kaliningrad], and Moscow, the Youth Christian-Democratic Movement, organizations in Volgograd, Krasnoyarsk, and other cities—all of them have now joined our movement. However, the paradox is that when they reject Ogorodnikov, he finds another five persons to set up a party and claims all other members expelled. This is an infinite process. As a result, the leadership of the International of Christian Democracy is investigating this problem.

What is the difference between your party and other parties and their programs?

The three basic tenets of our political program are the following: First, we emphasize the priority of Christian values and, naturally, the promulgation of Christian ideals into political life. Second, [we are] fundamental anti-Communists, as we consider communism to be the most radical anti-Christian doctrine and power in world history. Nevertheless, the first tenet combines with the second. As the New Testament puts it, we do not curse flesh and blood, as we do not oppose living creatures but evil spirits. In Sovietspeak, we oppose the ideology and the regime. Our position produces feasible results because, on the one hand, it enables us to see all contemporary forms of the social evil and, on the other hand, it provides for a free dialogue with various other forces. We prompted the formation of this [Christian] bloc, and we invite other parties into discussion even if they cannot cooperate with us directly. Our third tenet is what we call *educated patriotism*, as we understand Christianity within the context of centuries of Russian and Orthodox culture. We are all specialists in Russian history and culture, and we realize that our society and rulers have proven to be absolutely incompetent regarding the history of our national culture. Our democrats are absolutely unaware of the greatest achievement of liberal thought under Alexander II: his reforms, Stolypin's reforms, the experience of the monarchy under the Duma, and the experience of zemstvo [elective district councils]. They are also unaware of the great achievements of Russian political, economic, philosophical, and religious thought of the twentieth century. Until recently, these works have not been published in this country. Censorship deals mainly with these aspects, [i.e.,] the spheres that may generate the greatest of all perils to the regime, the sphere of Christian culture as such. And I mean Christian culture not as a clerical culture but Christian ideas understood universally, including politics, economics, and so on. Even now these spheres are restricted. It is all but natural that my works are not published, as well as those of my colleagues.

The position of educated patriotism implies that we should base our activity in the best traditions of liberal democracy, as well as our culture and history. We want our society to have access to these traditions. Besides, educated patriotism means renouncing all forms of national extremity and chauvinism. Just as communist internationalism destroys patriotism, chauvinism destroys patriotism. We are patriots; we love our motherland and our culture. However, we are patriots open to Western history and culture. The synthesis of Russian national and Western thought was embodied in a genius constellation of Russian philosophers, political scientists, and scholars of the twentieth century who were driven abroad by the socialist revolution. They lived in various countries in Europe and the Americas. They knew Western culture, wrote their works in foreign languages, and amassed experience. The synthesis of their experience with Russian tradition is of paramount importance for the present day. For example, the name of Ivan Ilyin, a political scholar, is barely known to our society. He wrote the draft constitution of Russia. Does anybody know of this draft constitution? I am sure that nobody does. Russia is one of the most wealthy countries in terms of resources, both natural and spiritual. However, Russia cannot make full use of these resources, having been deprived of them for so long. We aim to gain open access to these resources for everybody.

We consider the events currently taking place in Russia to be a mental illness. Some time ago, Dostoyevsky called it the evil power, and Solzhenitsyn calls it a virus of communism. This mental illness resulted in the loss of our historical memory and public consciousness. Our goal is to restore this memory and consciousness. We realize that, like any living body, this national organism cannot revive its memory and consciousness in a short time. We understand that this process will take a long time, patience, and fortitude. We must become therapists. We realize that the process is fraught with relapse. Whenever consciousness is regained, periods of clear states of mind will alternate with periods of failures and delirium. We should distinguish between these two states. We should find the cause of the illness and its bearer, make a correct diagnosis, and estimate the capacities of the sick organism to counter the illness. This is our goal. This is why we reject projecting utopian ideas and new programs onto our society. Being pragmatic politicians, we aim to provide conditions so that society can make a free and deliberate political choice. In this sense, we differ from all other political parties. Unlike us, the others do a lot of utopian projecting. Their mentality is still limited to provisions made by Stalin. We, on the other hand, try to be realists. We understand that of all political parties we have the most comprehensive plans, but the shortest way of reaching our goals requires making a thousand steps, not a single leap. That is why we renounce all radical measures. Violence, revolutionary actions, strikes, and the like will only take a heavy toll of lives without helping to reach the objective. This is why we combine contradictory principles, being radical in our opinions but moderate in our political activity.

However, you have joined Democratic Russia, which is considered by many to be a radical organization.

We joined Democratic Russia to become its right wing. Initially, we played the part of a deterrent, a brake of a kind, because we deem ourselves to be therapists and treatment requires our presence in this political struggle. We see that certain democrats are too distracted to have true objectives demonstrated to them. We have to deal with this. But on certain occasions, we have managed to do a lot.

Sometimes we lose. Such things happen in politics. For example, at the first congress of Democratic Russia we achieved a tremendous success. Despite the fact that the Russian Christian-Democratic Movement is a small group, we managed to have approved our principal position: to include in the charter an article saying that Democratic Russia is a political coalition of groups of various political orientations, aiming to achieve the single objective of dismantling the communist regime. Besides that single goal, though, groups within Democratic Russia differ by nature. This was our position, we supported it, and we managed to achieve our objective despite all difficulties. However, we achieved it not by having a majority of votes but due to our expertise in the problem. This is very important because all the rest is a utopia. The idea to transform Democratic Russia into a superparty is utopian: a superparty combining opposite ideologies cannot exist by nature. If you take a comprehensive approach to the objectives of Democratic Russia, you will see that these objectives are in transition. As soon as Democratic Russia achieves its objective of dismantling the communist regime, it will cease to exist. It will have prepared all the prerequisites for the activity of classical political parties. We aim to achieve this goal. Certain people and powers intend to transform Democratic Russia into a superparty. These are the reactionary forces that we combat. That is why we believe that within the framework of Democratic Russia various political orientations organically cooperate.

As a result of pressure from left-wing radicals, we formed Popular Accord [Narodnoe Soglasie]; it unites Travkin's party, the constitutional democrats, and our party.[36] We set this bloc up within Democratic Russia and announced that our intention was not to leave Democratic Russia but rather to form a counterbalance to left-wing radicalism that claimed to represent the entire organization. If I submit a draft resolution for consideration of Democratic Russia, it is consciously a compromise position and not my own. But when socialists or social democrats submit their draft resolutions, they are definitely trying to thrust their program on Democratic Russia.

What is your viewpoint on Russia's sovereignty and the Union treaty?
The main difference separating us from all other democratic parties is the problem of the future national and state system. The majority of our democrats proceed from the assumption that the USSR is the successor of the Russian Empire, which means that the Russian people are bearers of power in this empire, occupants and imperialists. Therefore, it is necessary to combat Russian settlers [in non-Russian territories]. Russian people should repent and leave. The popular slogan is the following (I'm exaggerating, but the essence is the same): "You are imperialists and occupants, you should repent but still vote in our favor." This is not a productive position. As a result, they may lose Russia defending such a utopian position.

Therefore, Russian democrats face the necessity of destroying the "evil empire," i.e., the Russian Empire. The easiest way to do this would be to divide it in as many states as possible, fifty to sixty states being the optimal number. In our opinion, such an approach is absolutely utopian. History has proven that this is not the Russian Empire but an ideological, international communist empire. The rulers are not the Russian people but an international *lumpenproletariat*, the antisocial denationalized element of all peoples populating this country, united by selfish interests and communist dogmas. Therefore, Russian people are captive like all other nations but to a larger extent, as Russia hosted the epicenter of this empire. Pressure is not so great in the outlying areas, which suffered less captivation and destruction. Consequently, it is not Russian but communist occupants that should be thwarted. All captive peoples and all their democratic forces should unite to oppose the communist regime and the communist system. The communist regime and communist ideology should be driven out of this state without destroying the latter because the state is our home. Only a strong democratic state can guarantee individual rights and freedoms. Considering the aforementioned, all problems including those of national self-determination should be resolved under normal conditions. At present, we live under the communist regime, which is fishing in troubled waters, guided by the principle "divide and rule." Democrats, being guided by utopianism, proclaim fictitious objectives and struggle for fictitious sovereignty without taking account of the communist regime. This loss of orientation strengthens the communist regime and weakens the democrats. In our opinion, a pressing necessity arose to unite all democratic forces of this country for democratization of feasible structures. Only under this condition shall we be able to implement economic reforms and at last resolve the problems of national self-determination by means of democratic procedures and a territorial plebiscite. If the current position of the democrats takes over, it will be fraught with disaster, like any attempt to implement a utopia.

The main reason for conflict in the Caucasus, besides the interference of the Union authorities, is the attempt to create new states based on artificial borders and artificial territorial divisions. If this attempt is repeated anywhere in this vast country, the results will be the same. The events in the Caucasus are a fateful warning to all of us. If Rukh in Ukraine achieves its goal of making the republic independent, this will mean civil war in the eastern regions of the republic and especially the Crimea. Rukh intends to make Russians living in these territories (80 percent of the Crimean population) speak only Ukrainian. If Kazakhstan becomes an independent state, Cossacks in Siberia and the Urals will be separated and begin a civil war for reunification. They will have no alternative.

We base our assumptions [regarding nationality issues] on the fact that all interrepublic borders were set administratively by two dictators: Stalin and Lenin. They were drawn as administrative borders and cannot be used in the new state system. The borders of Ukraine, as well as those of the Russian Federation, are artificial administrative divisions. Before, we never had a state on the territory now called the *Russian Soviet Federative Socialist Republic* so we cannot call it

Russia now. Russia has yet to emerge. We are neither imperialists nor chauvinists, but we want our society to help Russia emerge and independently realize political self-determination. In this regard, we intend to support Yeltsin as long as he does not set up a sovereign Russian state on the artificially fixed territory of the Russian Federation or destroy the newly forming Union. Instead, he should use all his powers to dismantle the communist regime. This is why we have the slogan New Elections for a New Union State, which has been proclaimed jointly on all territories where citizens support joining the new Union treaty. On this issue, we are more consistent than the other democrats. At our first congress, I said that we must painfully create new forms of a state system, combining the principles of autonomy, federation, and confederation. I also said at the congress that no one should be kept in the new state by force. This is not a creative approach. Our major separatist is Gorbachev. If he had not been trying to keep the Baltic states in the Union by force, they would not have been so adamant about leaving.

All those willing to leave the Union should be given an opportunity to do so. However, all those willing to stay in the Union should also have an opportunity to do so. This is a principled democratic approach to the problem. As politicians, we should not thrust our decisions on society but create conditions under which society could make a choice.

What kinds of people join your party?

Mainly intellectuals. This is both our strength and weakness. Our party has a considerable intellectual potential, as many Soviet scientists, especially scholars in the liberal arts, have been attracted to religion and Christianity. They either participate in our movement or sympathize with it, considering themselves Christian democrats. This is why our program is the strongest of all oppositional parties, far superior to the program of the Democratic Party of Russia. At the same time, we cannot boast a mass organization like the Democratic Party of Russia. We are not very influential among workers or farmers. However, we do feel that we are the party of tomorrow. The Democratic Party of Russia is a transitional party as its main objectives are based on contemporary issues. Right now, we shall render all our support to this party. Any real bloc [referring to the bloc of Popular Accord] implies mutual benefit for all joining parties. We combine their large strength with our intellectual potential. I believe that Christian democracy is Russia's tomorrow. It is the party that seeks to revive traditional values.

Currently, one of our goals is sponsor political and religious education in our society. Therefore, unlike other organizations, we place a high priority on publishing. Our newspaper is of a rather high intellectual level. For example, we have articles by such thinkers as Alexander Tsipko published in our newspaper. Our strength is in these people. However, we do realize the necessity of working to influence the workers' movement to a greater extent.

We also consider ourselves to be the followers of Solzhenitsyn, both the writer and the political thinker. We know the fundamental ideas of his works. We used to publish his works illegally, and now we publish them openly. He is aware of our work, supervising our activity and making rather complimentary remarks about us. We received a letter from him and published it in our magazine. This letter was like a Nobel Prize to us. It happened in 1987, and it was quite an event in Moscow. We also have had long-standing ties with many foreign countries since we were involved in religious and human rights movements with the circles of Russian emigrants. In Paris, *Russkaya Misl'* used to issue our magazine, which made us known to many people. Later we began visiting Western countries and made acquaintances with certain religious figures and later with Western politicians. As of now, we have established close contacts and cooperation with the International of Christian Democrats. They could have admitted us long ago, but we were overly cautious. We are more right wing than the [Russian] Christian-Democratic Union, and various revolutionary theologies seemed dangerous to us, as did the influence of left-wing Christian-democratic unions of Latin America, Africa, and Asia. We have been considering the problem for a long time. For example, we believe that we are closer to the European Democratic Union. However, the International [of Christian Democrats] began publishing our programs, and close cooperation was established. We have applied for admission and will be officially admitted to the organization this July.

The Communist Party of the Soviet Union has lost the battle for people's minds; its ideology is absolutely unpopular. However, it still preserves the power, monopolizing the nation's material resources. The Communist Party has monopolized real estate, finance, land, mass media, newsprint, and print shops. The monopolization is carried out in different ways: formal and informal, legal and illegal [the shadow economy]. This Party preserves its monopoly by carrying out privatization in the interests of the Communist Party, which has accumulated initial capital through its structures, apparatchiks, and top Party officials. All this creates dreadful conditions for our activity. We have our publications registered and have all legal support; however, we cannot do anything feasible. To date our party has not acquired a single square meter of office space for its headquarters. This is why we need outside assistance to help our party establish its own mass media. In 1917, the Bolsheviks received large sums of money from the German General Staff. They did not import weapons but began publishing more literature than all other parties combined. This literature inundated the country and everything collapsed. If we had the opportunity to spread our ideas in society, a society that is already welcoming our ideas now, the country would change. This is why we are being censored. Last week, our publishing group was virtually thrown out into the street. Thank God, Travkin made room for our publishers at his office.

The United States and other Western countries place their bets on Gorbachev as the only democratic leader in this country. They are, in fact, supporting the leader of the Party, which is the most destructive power in the Soviet Union. But the United States is not helping to create an open society in this country. The new democratic forces could support Gorbachev if he dared to begin reforms. In this way, the United States is helping to destroy Gorbachev without realizing it. Without outside assistance, the Polish Solidarity would never have come to power. If we enjoyed assistance, Russia would be a different country. I visited the United States Congress and met some wonderful people in the Republican party's committee for assistance to democratic forces in communist states. They told me, "We help everybody but the Russian Federation. We cannot help you as our president prohibits our doing so because he is placing his bet on Gorbachev." That's absurd! He is at the very epicenter of the world communist empire. If Russia becomes free, this guarantees freedom to America, Europe, and Poland, to everyone, because this country is the epicenter of the world communist regime. Tactics and strategy of political struggle demand that the epicenter be hit first. I cannot understand why the West fails to realize this.

If we received aid to propagate our ideas, ideas organic to our society that originate from a centuries-old culture, our society would change rapidly. Society is ready. Despite having virtually no organizations, Christian democrats won everywhere in the last elections; I won in Moscow, Father Gleb Yakunin won in the Moscow oblast' [county or region], and Father Vyacheslav Polosin was victorious in the provinces. What does it mean? This means that society is ready to accept our ideas. We can recruit society to join the only correct route of struggle.

We should aim to acquire power in the Kremlin but not erect new Kremlins next to the old one. What really is required is the democratization of this power at the Kremlin. As an objective, this would be a most radical step, but it is also an objective that can be achieved by moderate, constitutional, and legitimate methods. This is the step to be taken by neoconservatism and Christian democracy.

Postcoup Reflections (November 1991)

How did RXDD react to the putsch and how did it act at that time?
We, the leaders, naturally spent three days and three nights in the White House. We used all our means to distribute appeals and decrees of the president of Russia and to organize the defense of the White House. We also tried to transfer our printing presses and other units underground.

How did RXDD take part in the resistance in the provinces?
In the provinces we mostly distributed the president's decrees. We decided that they were adequate to the situation, exact and complete. That is why we did not make up anything of our own. Only in Moscow we managed to print about 100,000 leaflets and special editions of the newspaper *Put'*. We distributed these materials in railway stations and airports. Information channels were cut off, and it was vital to let the society know the standpoint of the Russian leadership. Our

activists took part in holding different actions in regions where authorities did not support GKChP [the leaders of the putsch].

In Moscow we were in the hottest spots. Lieutenant Colonel Yushenkov, who is also a people's deputy of the RSFSR Supreme Soviet, and myself negotiated with Major Evdokimov and convinced him to negotiate with Vice-President Rutskoi. After that, a momentous event took place: a tank unit went over to our side to defend the Russian parliament. This event led to further developments. Soon thereafter, I joined some others to hold negotiations with other military units. I think that the people's deputies played a remarkable role; they convinced practically all units stationed in Moscow not to attack and formed the cordon of people defending the White House.

In what regions of Russia did you act most successfully?

We were most active in Obninsk, where local authorities took a very constructive stand. From this city, we were able to distribute the president's decrees to adjoining regions. All documents and decrees were faxed from my office to the Obninsk City Soviet. We were also successful in Tzaritsin [Volgograd], Sverdlovsk, Voronezh, Orel, Siberia, and Ukraine, though Ukraine was a peculiar situation.

Since the coup attempt, the situation in Russia has changed dramatically. How would you describe this new situation and what are your new objectives?

As always happens in revolutions, some social forces won the struggle, but different forces have come to power, reaping the fruits of the victory. I think that the spiritual, revolutionary, and patriotic impulses of young people and society as a whole brought about the victory. There was no longer the fear that had consolidated the totalitarian regime and bound the society. But the forces that have since seized power come from the liberal wing of the CPSU, that is the liberal Communists. This generation of politicians has retained a certain continuity of power and has had some experience ruling the state. This is to their credit. But, on the other hand, they have numerous drawbacks. They are limited by the communist regime and ideology. Their narrow-mindedness makes them regard only themselves as democrats, while they look upon alternative viewpoints as extremist. The democratic monopoly that they have declared will lead to the self-destruction of democracy itself. We face a situation in which the CPSU monopoly on power is transferred quickly into the monopoly of liberal Communists in all spheres of life. Economic reforms have been declared but not implemented, while the plundering of state and public property continues. Now, a new nomenklatura is engaged in these activities. The liberal Communists have a monopoly on the mass media as well. Views of centrists and our party can hardly find their way to the central mass media.

For instance, we have experienced great difficulty in solving the problems of religion. Everything that was taken by force seventy years ago by the Communists should be returned into possession of the church—churches, temples, land, icons, property. Otherwise civil society can not be revived. The liberal democrats, including Minister of Culture Gubenko, are more opposed to this proposal than the Communists.

The same happens in politics. There is no plurality and no authentic multi-party system. The following example can illustrate this. Within two days after the putsch, all equipment and real estate of the CPSU were nationalized. Presently, these resources are controlled by the Russian Supreme Soviet, the Council of Ministers, the city hall [Popov's office], and the Movement for Democratic Reform, of which many heads of the above-mentioned organizations are members. Moreover, Democratic Russia does not exist legally as it is not registered. It also does not exist in reality because it is only a union of the new nomenklatura that is not supported by any social forces. Parties that really and legally exist did not get anything. This is an impressive example of monopolization. The same is true about the CPSU printing presses, mass media, paper, and so on.

It is very bad situation because reforms are not being carried out, which further aggravates the situation in the country. Yeltsin has to pursue a course of presidential authoritarianism. It is justified to a certain extent because only an enlightened, authoritarian regime can carry out drastic, unpopular reforms. But if the authoritarian regime is not counterbalanced by a real multiparty system, an independent parliament, and social and political democratic structures, it will inevitably degenerate into a populist dictatorship. This danger seriously threatens us. If events take such a course, it will be extremely difficult to exist and struggle in such a situation.

The other major area of contention concerns the nation and the state. The communist empire has collapsed. It was embodied mainly in Soviet Union structures monopolized by the CPSU. These structures have crashed down, but the Party nomenklatura has now changed its tactics. It is trying to keep its influence by upholding the sovereignty of its boyar estate. In different regions and republics, the nomenklatura is forming an alliance with local nationalist forces to seize power. It acts under the pretense of a national liberation movement struggling for democracy. It is a real disaster because everything that might have made it possible to carry out reforms is being destroyed. An insane policy is being pursued by the Ukrainian leadership. It will result in nothing less than war between Ukraine and Russia. To prevent such developments, it is necessary to change course as soon as possible. We are trying to be realists and realize that it is impossible to build a new and safe state within the arbitrary, fantastic boundaries of all territories, autonomies, and Union republics. These borders will always be revised in the course of history. But there are only two ways to revise boundaries—peacefully or nonpeacefully. The military clashes in the Caucasus and Yugoslavia show what happens when nonpeaceful methods are attempted. The peaceful way of solving this problem presupposes that each republic that seeks to leave the Union should hold a democratic referendum, abide by all democratic legislation, and hear out all alternative opinions. Besides referendums in republics, we also must conduct public opinion polls in disputed territories so that their populations can express their desires about which state they want to belong to. This is the only way to stabilize the situation. Everything else is a gamble, tyranny. Of course these developments can be ignored, but it will undermine these processes; the longer the solution of territorial disputes is postponed, the greater the explosion will be.

What is your attitude toward the territories with Russian-speaking populations in the Baltics?

The Russian Federation should not lay any claims on the Baltics, but it should react to the initiative expressed by the population of certain territories. Estonia, for example, has made some territorial claims. I think that we should hold a referendum in those disputed territories—in Pskov region and Narva—to settle the problem.

Many have commented that you have much in common with the Party of Revival and the Russian All-National Union. The recently formed Russian All-People's Union is headed by Sergei Baburin.[37] The Party of Revival unites the Russian People's Front, headed by Valerii Skurlatov, leaders of Soyuz, such as Victor Alksnis, and several others.

As for Alksnis and Skurlatov, we have nothing in common with them. Our opponents lay claim to a monopoly on democracy. They think that a different viewpoint is antidemocratic. They refuse to enter into open polemics with us in the mass media. Instead, they are trying to muddle our ideology and prevent us from stating it. For example, they are claiming that we have entered into an alliance with these people and the nonexistent organizations that they allegedly have formed. All this is absurdity and misinformation. We tried to refute these insinuations in the *Independent Newspaper* [Nezavisimaya Gazeta], but the paper has taken a very vague stand. As for the groups Rossiya and Soyuz, we always have been democratic federalists, state-oriented from the very beginning. We draw together with those who share our position, be they from the right or the left. The group Rossiya is growing more democratically oriented. They are forgetting about communist utopias. This brings us together. We are separated by our original orientations—they used to be procommunist, while we were always anticommunist. Thus, we have begun to have more in common as they rid themselves of communist fiction. This is quite natural. We do not have political enemies, only political opponents. We are not fighting with people but with the ideology of the system and regime. We always have been ready to cooperate with all constructive forces. This principle is put down in our program and we proceed from it. Thus we back actions of the people's deputies group, Rossiya. We support their constructive actions and oppose their senseless ones.

As for the group Soyuz, we do not cooperate directly with them in parliament; we do not have a common field for work, and so the problem of working together just never arose.[38] On the other hand, as detached observers, we can see that the same processes taking place within Rossiya are also happening in the group Soyuz. Commitments to communist utopias are vanishing, and they are taking a more pragmatic stand, though they are still far from recovery according to our standards. We are ready to discuss common problems with them as soon as they reason sensibly.

What is the attitude of your movement to possible emergency powers of the president of Russia?

First of all, it is necessary to realize that the president is to inform us about the program for which he needs emergency powers to implement. It should be stated clearly without any ambiguity. To our disappointment, he is far from it. We do not know what Yeltsin plans to suggest or how he plans to implement his program. It is a pity that our leadership, government, and parliament activities are declarative.

We are for a more reasonable approach. Our party is practically the only organization proceeding from a thousand-year-old history of Russian statehood culture. We are trying to use all the positive achievements in this history. The RXDD takes a more realistic stand than other parties that prefer utopias. They do not know Russian history and therefore do not understand the only basis on which the Russian state can build.

On the other hand our party is open to the most constructive tradition in Western politics—Christian democracy. The combination of these two factors means that Christian democracy has a historic chance in Russia. There is a very favorable perspective. On the other hand, it depends on us, whether we manage to use this chance.

chapter eight

The Democratic Russia Movement

Although the core elements of this united front had formed much earlier, the idea for Democratic Russia, or DemRossiya, first surfaced at a meeting of democratic political movements and organizations January 21–22, 1990. At this meeting, Russia's top democratic leaders convened to consolidate their ranks for the March 1990 elections of people's deputies at all levels of government. Thereafter, the Democratic Russia bloc established a campaign headquarters run principally by the core organizers of the disbanded Moscow People's Front and the Moscow Association of Voters. During the campaign, Democratic Russia called on candidates to submit their credentials for review. If approved by a review committee at the campaign headquarters, DemRossiya would include the names of unknown candidates on posters and leaflets with more familiar figures like Yeltsin, Popov, and Stankevich.[1] In addition to campaign slates, the future constituent organizations of Democratic Russia coordinated two massive demonstrations in February 1990 in cities throughout the Soviet Union, initiating a new tradition of mass political rallies in Russia that would continue until the coup attempt in August 1991.[2]

This campaign strategy proved tremendously effective, establishing a near majority of DemRossiya deputies in the Russian parliament and pluralities in the Leningrad City Soviet, the Moscow City Soviet, and a handful of other city councils. Radical organizations on the left (Democratic Union) and right (Pamyat') that did not join the DemRossiya coalition fared miserably at the ballot box.

The newly elected deputies then formed DemRossiya factions in their respective parliaments to combat the more organized and disciplined communist blocs. After a postelection lull, the core organizers of the Democratic Russia campaign regrouped behind the idea of a Democratic Russia movement. In July 1990, an organizational committee chaired by Arkadii Murashev began making preparations for a founding congress October 20–21, 1991, in Moscow.[3]

At the founding congress, seventeen hundred representatives from more than fifty organizations joined with people's deputies and prominent independent leaders of the democratic movement to form Democratic Russia. Although DemRossiya represented a wide spectrum of political ideologies and tactical approaches, the group was united behind one basic concept: "the coordinating of democratic forces, opposition to the state-political Communist Party monopoly, holding of a joint election campaign, parliamentary activity and other actions for the common purpose of creating a civil society."[4] Beyond such general statements, Democratic Russia never adopted a political program.

Because DemRossiya aspired to unite all leaders and movements in opposition to the Communist Party, the structure of the movement had to be ultrarepresentative and decentralized. First, three USSR people's deputies—Gavriil Popov, Arkadii Murashev, and Yurii Afanasiev—and three RSFSR people's deputies—Victor Dmitriev, Lev Ponomarev, and Father Gleb Yakunin—were elected cochairmen. Second, a Coordinating Council of forty-eight representatives from independent parties and organizations as well as prominent, independently elected democratic figures was also formed. The Coordinating Council then set up sixteen working groups to address specific issue areas.[5] Finally, the Council of Representatives (243 members) was created, which, in addition to party representatives, people's deputies, and independents, also included regional representatives of Democratic Russia branches throughout Russia.

Top-heavy with egotistical leaders unaccustomed to being one among equals, early DemRossiya events resembled giant debating chambers for Moscow's most bombastic. Military action against Lithuania and Latvia in January 1991, however, solidified DemRossiya into an effective opposition capable of mobilizing an already radical populace.[6] The numbers attending DemRossiya functions grew from tens of thousands at the demonstration to protest the Baltic massacres in January to hundreds of thousands at the rallies in support of the striking miners in February and against the Union referendum in March.[7] Democratic Russia quickly opened branches throughout the Russian Federation as well as cells in workplaces and apartment complexes.[8] Finally, and most dramatically, hundreds of thousands took to the streets on March 28, 1991, to support Yeltsin, who, at the time, was being threatened by a communist initiative to remove him from his post as chairman of the RSFSR Congress of People's Deputies. This rally, declared illegal by Gorbachev, precipitated a major standoff between Red Army soldiers and Russian citizens, the first ever in the Soviet capital. Fearing that a direct confrontation between troops and the masses might end in bloodshed, Dem-Rossiya coordinators rerouted the columns of demonstrators and conducted the meeting at a different location.[9] But the demonstration was held despite Gorbachev's decree, which dealt a major blow to the Soviet regime.[10] Democratic Russia's leadership considered the successful demonstration the beginning of the end for Soviet communism.[11] The following month, DemRossiya called for a roundtable to create a new government of representatives from the old regime and the Union's new democratic forces.[12]

Momentum rolled through the spring and into the June elections; Democratic Russia played a leading role in organizing Yeltsin's campaign for president and Gavriil Popov's campaign for mayor of Moscow. The resounding victories of both candidates only reaffirmed the retreat of the old CPSU guard. Even Gorbachev, beginning with the 9 + 1 agreement in April, seemed reconciled to dealing with Yeltsin and an increasingly independent Russian republic.

Conservatives in the CPSU and Soviet government, however, made one last stand in orchestrating the August putsch, forcing DemRossiya to mobilize once again. As explained by Victor Dmitriev in the interview in this chapter, DemRossiya headquarters in the Moscow City Council served as an information center for all Russia during the coup. Using their phone networks, Democratic Russia organized the two massive demonstrations against the putsch at the Moscow City Council and the Russian parliament building.[13] In the euphoric aftermath, DemRossiya activists organized the removal of communist statues and the seizing of the CPSU Central Committee buildings.

After the coup, however, Democratic Russia's future remained uncertain. As a mass movement of anticommunist forces, Democratic Russia had performed the role that Solidarity played in Poland or Civic Forum in Czechoslovakia. Without the communist enemy, however, the coalition began to crumble. Democratic Russia managed to maintain a veneer of unity until its second congress on November 9, 1991, which was attended by 1,298 delegates from seventy-four regions. Tensions between party leaders and nonpartisan DemRossiya activists had been a constant feature of the movement.[14] At the congress, however, and soon thereafter, cracks in the movement began to widen.

First, the rivalry between Democratic Russia and the parties became acute. As a movement of several million, not tens of thousands like the other parties, insinuations that Democratic Russia's leaders planned to transform the movement into a party threatened those other parties.[15] After the coup, those insinuations became actual proposals, alienating many *party* leaders within the movement, despite pleas for unity.[16] Party leaders were especially critical of "monopolization tactics" undertaken by the DemRossiya Coordinating Council.[17]

Second, ideological and tactical divisions that had been suppressed in the name of anticommunist solidarity emerged with the disappearance of a common enemy. Divisions about preserving first the Union and then the Russian Federation severely damaged the coalition. The Democratic Party, the Russian Christian-Democratic Movement, and the Constitutional Democratic Party (Astafiev) had always been critical of Democratic Russia's promoting the dissolution of the Soviet Union and the Russian Federation. When speakers at the second congress of Democratic Russia, especially Gavriil Popov, spoke in favor of independence for autonomous regions within the Russian Federation, the National Accord bloc quit Democratic Russia altogether.[18]

Another division developed between the founders of the Movement for Democratic Reform and Democratic Russia's leaders when Popov, a former cochairman of DemRossiya, began criticizing the organization's populist and confrontational tactics after several DemRossiya members in the Moscow City Council joined an anti-Popov coalition in October 1991.[19] Popov urged Democratic Russia members to join his Movement for Democratic Reform. Other Democratic Russia activists, however, especially those based in Moscow, have criticized the Movement for Democratic Reform as a party of the nomenklatura bent on exploiting Democratic Russia's grass roots organization for the movement's own political gain.[20]

Another consequential split erupted in February when the "liberals"—led by Yurii Afanasiev and Leonid Batkin—clashed with the radical democrats—led by Lev Ponomarev, Father Gleb Yakunin, Mikhail Schneider, and Vladimir Boxer—over the issue of support for the Yeltsin government; the liberals have been critical of Yeltsin, whereas the radical democrats believe that the government must be supported.

In addition to these splits, Democratic Russia's leadership has been decimated by new government appointments and the chores of governing in a postcommunist Russia. As mentioned, Popov has the monumental task of governing Moscow. Arkadii Murashev, another cochairman, was appointed Moscow's chief of police after the coup, while Victor Dmitriev, a third cochairman, was appointed by Yeltsin to head a new Russian commission on relations with the World Bank. Dozens of other members of DemRossiya's Coordinating Council have also assumed government appointments, leaving little time for or interest in movement activity.

Despite these obstacles, Democratic Russia has begun to define its new niche in postcommunist Russia. In December 1991, Democratic Russia created the Committees for Economic Reform. By reconstituting Democratic Russia branches as these Committees for Economic Reform, the movement's leaders have sought to establish nongovernmental political groups that will work within *society* to support *government* economic policies.[21] Although the future of these committees remains uncertain, their mere appearance demonstrates that Democratic Russia, however renamed or reorganized, will continue to play a role in the Russian transition.

Mikhail Schneider

As a young technical assistant in a Moscow research institute with no political experience until his involvement with the "informals," Mikhail Schneider is typical of the person who joined Democratic Russia. As he explains in the following interview, Schneider's introduction to political organizations was Lingua, an apolitical social group. When the Moscow People's Front formed, however, Schneider represented Lingua in the coalition, thereby taking the first steps to politicize his group. Although others in Lingua retreated to address social and cultural issues, Schneider became increasingly involved in political matters and soon emerged as one of the principal organizers of the Moscow Popular Front. With Sergei Stankevich, Schneider published several documents explaining tactics and strategies for democrats during elections. During the 1989 elections for USSR people's deputies, he organized Stankevich's successful campaign.

In the summer of 1989, Schneider helped cofound the Moscow Association of Voters (MOI), a coalition of voters' clubs that had coalesced around democratic candidates during the 1989 elections. MOI's objective was to prepare candidates and the population for the next elections.[22] Consequently, MOI became the leading organizer of political demonstrations in the Soviet capital, including the series of rallies held at Luzhniki during the summer and fall of 1989 and the two massive anticommunist demonstrations in February 1990. Schneider played a critical role in organizing all these events, earning a reputation as a logistic expert for demonstrations and political campaigns.[23]

At the end of 1989, Schneider became one of the original members of the organizational committee for Democratic Russia. Again, along with Vladimir Boxer and Vera Kriger, he played an instrumental role in organizing Democratic Russia's campaign. After the founding congress of the Democratic Russia movement, Schneider was elected to the Coordinating Council and as chairman of the Organizational Committee. During the tumultuous months of 1991, in which massive demonstrations were convened almost biweekly, Schneider's new office in the Moscow City Council served as the headquarters for all DemRossiya activities.[24] During the August putsch, his office served a similar role.

Schneider's interview focuses on the history of informal movements leading up to the creation of Democratic Russia. The interview with Victor Dmitriev focuses on the history of Democratic Russia, from its creation in October 1990 to the August 1991 coup.

Interview with
Mikhail Schneider (*April/May 1991*)

. . . .

When did you decide to take part in politics? What was the stimulus?
I had a natural desire to change something in my life because I was not pleased
with my life, not only my job, but my entire life-style. I attempted to do something
about my situation, but it was to no avail because it is practically impossible to
do something positive through the official establishment. But then Gorbachev
appeared. His first speeches and appearances on television made it clear that this
was a man who was trying to implement some kind of reforms. I believed in him
at once and began looking for people who thought along the same lines as myself.
That was in 1985 or maybe even earlier, even before Andropov. But the closest
I could come to the dissidents themselves were groups that assisted the dissidents.
Those were people who gathered clothing, shoes, food parcels, and money for
the families of jailed dissidents. I worked with these people, but I wanted more.
I wanted to contact more serious organizations and attempt somehow to find a
way out of the whole situation.

   The year 1985 provided an extra impetus for my search, but it was only in
1987, when I was monitoring newspaper ads, that I read about a sociopolitical
association called Lingua. Lingua was established under the Committee of Youth
Organizations with the aim of establishing contacts with social organizations
abroad. The organization was divided into three groups—one dealing with languages, another with culture, and a third focusing on sociopolitical workshops.
I joined the latter and assumed the functions of a coordinator. We drafted a work
plan and conducted several joint activities, but I could not persuade other members
to take more serious actions like picketing or other protests. They were afraid; it
was December 1987.

   One of my colleagues in Lingua told me about another informal organization
that was founded to discuss the problem of the Arbat pedestrian precinct. So I
went to this group seeking new contacts and met a young man from Club
Perestroika, whose remarks stood out for their logic. I asked him where they
were based and later came to a club meeting. I then began going to their meetings
regularly but continued to be active in Lingua. Club Perestroika was largely a
theoretical discussion club, which in January 1988 split into Perestroika 88 and
Democratic Perestroika. I stayed with the latter group. They created democratic
mandate documents—various appeals, leaflets, and addresses.

   At one of those meetings I became acquainted with people from Memorial.

I later helped them collect signatures for the election of Yurii Karyakin and Vitaly Korotich to the Nineteenth Communist Party Conference. This was my first experience with friction with the police. Soon thereafter, I learned that several groups planned to unite and form a popular front. This idea really appealed to me.

Why was it called a popular front?

It is a term borrowed from France in 1936, meaning an association of people from different organizations and with different political views, with the sole aim of resisting a totalitarian regime. This is why it is a front. It is popular because it is based on the grass roots. I attended a meeting in late May or early June 1988 at which we decided to set up an organizing committee to create the Popular Front. Originally, the project involved twelve Moscow clubs, including Democratic Perestroika, Memorial, Socialist Initiative, and others. Each club was represented in the organizing committee. I took part in that work and even suggested some changes to the democratic mandate, which we later adopted. As an observer from Lingua, I attended the first two or three meetings of the organizing committee. I then talked to the Lingua people, suggesting that, perhaps, we should join the organizing committee, and they told me, "Go ahead." So, I joined the committee to organize the Popular Front as a representative from Lingua, and that was, as a matter of fact, how it all started. I had to work a lot, mostly organizing various meetings and discussing various documents.

Did you have a program?

No, the Popular Front only had organizing principles. These principles declared that the Popular Front movement should unite progressive forces within the Communist Party and the people in order to build a democratic-socialist society, that is, the Popular Front united groups favoring democratic socialism, largely modeled after the Swedish model—mostly public property, the property of worker collectives, and no private property. Our slogans included All Power to the Soviets, Factories to the Workers, and Land to the Peasants, similar to those championed in 1917. At that time, the first years of the Soviet system of government were still idealized. The notion was that the ideals of socialism were distorted in the late 1920s, and it was vital to return to the true sources of socialism.

Did people believe this?

Yes. They united around these principles. In addition to these programmatic bits, our documents focused mostly on organizing principles. We declared that membership in the Popular Front can be either collective or individual and that you are not bound to implement decisions if you have not voted for them. But you have to comply with them if you have voted for them.

Two organizations played a large role in the Popular Front organizing committee—Democratic Perestroika with Oleg Rumyantsev, Leonid Volkov, and Pavel Kudiukin and Socialist Initiative, with Mikhail Maliutin and Boris Kagarlitsky. There were also many Communists, although the Democratic Platform within the Party did not exist as yet. These were Communists who supported Gorbachev but who were taking more radical positions than the general secretary. The attitude toward Gorbachev then was very similar to our attitude toward Yeltsin now; people looked to Gorbachev, believing that he was leading the country to change, and therefore must be helped and at times even pulled along to counter the conservative forces getting in his way. The attitude toward Yeltsin now is much the same.

The Popular Front was formally established at a constituent congress held in the fall. This same congress also established the Moscow Popular Front and the Coordinating Council. The Popular Front fared pretty well during elections to the Moscow City Council and the federal Supreme Soviet. It was one of our primary tasks. Some people were liaisons with worker collectives, others were responsible for contacts with youth organizations, and I was the coordinator concerned with elections. We mounted a campaign in Moscow, and in most of the city's twenty-six constituencies we managed to secure the election of democratically minded candidates who later formed the core of the Interregional Group at the Congress of People's Deputies. Only Sergei Stankevich, however, was a candidate directly from the Popular Front. In the Kuntsevo borough, we backed Roy Medvedev, as we did not know then what positions he would later take. In the Timiryazev borough, our candidate was Arkadii Murashev. In this way, Popular Front activists either identified democratically minded candidates or themselves initiated the nomination of such people and gave them support. Those candidates then had self-organized groups of supporters who helped their campaigns.

At the time, were you confident that democratically minded candidates would succeed?
Not at all. We acted largely by hunch. We first prepared an appeal, which I personally posted in many subway cars. The appeal said something like this: "Muscovites, who will come to power in the country depends on you. We do not need the old-style candidates—the Communist Party apparatchiks. The Popular Front supports a worthy life in worthy conditions and wants every working person to be the master of the products of his labor." It also said that the Popular Front had organized campaign staffs in every borough and mentioned telephone numbers. One of the three was mine. It so happened, however, that two of the three telephones were out of order most of the time and only mine worked. People who wanted to start campaigns and help the Popular Front would call me, and I would give them the telephone numbers of our coordinators in other boroughs. That was how local teams came into being.

Did these structures remain after the elections?
Of course. The Popular Front grew very markedly after the elections. Whereas previously we did not have any borough structures at all, after the elections we were left with fairly large borough organizations. Previously, the Popular Front consisted of about fifty people and the Coordinating Council had eight to ten members. After the elections, it was much larger. Each of the Popular Front

activists had some one hundred to three hundred supporters. Those teams that had worked as campaign staffs during the elections became the Popular Front borough organizations. After this initial structure had been formed and all of our candidates had become known, each borough staff acted independently, producing their own campaign leaflets. There was no centralized direction over them.

I conducted one such autonomous campaign in the Cheremushkinskii borough where Stankevich was running.[25] Our borough organization had only five members, but we had to gather five hundred people in order to nominate him. We filed a petition with the Cheremushkinskii borough council saying that we wanted to nominate Stankevich. They allowed us to hold a nomination meeting in a movie theater. To assemble the required five hundred people, we visited every five-story apartment complex around the Cheremushkinskii theater. Tenants in those small Khrushchevite apartments are the underprivileged who have nothing to lose and who are especially discontented with life. We knocked on literally every door, saying that we had an excellent candidate in order to persuade people to come to nominate him at this meeting. On the day of the meeting, we staged a picket outside the local subway station with posters saying, in large letters, that a meeting would take place in the Cheremushkinskii borough that evening to nominate a candidate from the Popular Front. We also used loudspeakers to invite people to the movie house. All in all, some six hundred showed up at the nominating meeting, a big achievement as there were six or seven other candidates in the city district.

However, we still ran the risk that our nomination would be ruled illegitimate for some far-fetched reason. So we decided to try and nominate Stankevich also through worker collectives, Young Communist League committees, and labor union locals. I called them all up, saying that we had a very good candidate and that they could judge him for themselves if they invited him to speak at a general meeting. Two or three institutes agreed, including the Institute of Higher Neurological Activity. Stankevich spoke there, and they liked him so much that they voted for him unanimously and signed the nomination protocol. The people who attended that meeting also joined our team, which now numbered around 150 people. By the end of the election, our campaign staff had grown to some three hundred people. We took down their addresses and telephone numbers and gave them various assignments. Some people were to post leaflets, while others were to duplicate them.

Did you have duplicating or printing equipment?
We had some access to a printing house. At the end of the campaign, we were helped by all sorts of people. We would sit in my apartment, which served as the campaign headquarters, and suddenly a man would ring the doorbell and say, "Come on, let's unload the stuff." We would go down and see a car full of stacks of leaflets. We had no time to find out who the man was; we only looked to see if they were the materials we needed. We met with Stankevich once a day to

outline a work plan for the next couple of days. We would also look over the leaflets delivered to us by well-wishers to decide whether they were usable or whether they might offend someone. In that way we also exercised psychological supervision and became very good at it. We produced leaflets in printing offices, photocopied, and distributed them. And we won.

Were you surprised that Stankevich won?

No, I was sure of victory. Our people stood outside all the subway stations in our borough and campaigned for Stankevich every day. Western correspondents also attended Popular Front meetings. They got so carried away with the campaign that they began to help us, writing posters, bringing felt-tip pens, standing with us in pickets, and even arguing for Stankevich as did some Japanese journalists. Everyone knew where the Popular Front picketing site was. There were some altercations with Pamyat', which nearly escalated into fighting.

During the campaign, I would accompany Stankevich on meet-the-voter outings to supermarkets. We had about twenty in the city district. At each supermarket, Stankevich would speak for five minutes, followed by a twenty-five-minute question-and-answer session. We would then go to another super-market, where people would be already waiting, and so on for the whole day. Televised debates, held separately for each borough, were also very useful. In the end, four main candidates were left. But after the televised debates, people understood that Stankevich was the best candidate. My daughter, twelve years old then, persuaded her entire class to support Stankevich as well. Walking down the street during that time, one could often hear kids from the first or second grade, playing in the courtyards, shout to one another, "Are you for Stankevich or Lemeshev?"

We began taking public opinion polls approximately three weeks before the elections. Our assistants included two schoolgirls in the tenth grade who came to us after the Cheremushkinskii meeting saying they wanted to help us. I gave questionnaires to them and asked them to poll one hundred different people, fifty men and fifty women, at six different subway stations in the borough from four until eight in the evening. They would bring back the questionnaires at nine or ten every night. There were four candidates, including Stankevich, and we knew how people would vote at every subway station. We had charts illustrating the dynamics of popular preferences every day. And every day, the polls showed increased support for Stankevich, especially after the televised debates.

His main rival was Professor Lemeshev, an ecologist, economist, and United Nations expert on the environment. His ratings slipped, however, when he mentioned Pamyat' at a rally as one of the organizations he supported. We always would remember this and tell people that he was backed by Pamyat', with whom we had a confrontation during canvassing on Pushkin Square even before the elections.

Stankevich won 41 percent of the votes in the first round of polling, and the period leading to the runoff elections was marked by some very rough campaigning. To help him win, we dug up some old works by Lemeshev, written by him a year before the elections. We then made up posters comparing his quotes from then with now. Now he was an environmentalist opposed to the construction of nuclear power stations, while two years before he had argued for the need to build them as our only means of survival. We had a whole selection of such quotes.

We also had a poster that asked: "Who is supported by the press?" The democratic press did not exist at the time, and for everybody the word *press* was associated with *Pravda*, *Moskovskaya Pravda*, and the like. The poster gave just two names—Stankevich and Lemeshev. Under the latter, there was a long column of articles supporting him in many magazines, statements on the radio, and so on. Under Stankevich's name there were just one or two similar articles, making it clear who was supported by the press. Anyone who had seen that poster knew that he should vote for the one not backed by the press.

The house newspaper of the University of People's Friendship [Patrice Lumumba] carried an article by Nikolai Krotov, an instructor from the Cheremushkinskii Raikom Communist Party Committee, in which he asserted that Stankevich supplied the committee with information about independent mass movements. Our opponents began to play this up. We racked our brains for a long time about what to do. I finally wrote a statement on behalf of the Popular Front saying that a smear campaign had been mounted against our candidate. The Coordinating Council of the Moscow Popular Front knew, however, that Stankevich had supplied that kind of information. This project [of supplying information to the Communist Party] had been on our own initiative because we believed that the Party committee's staff [in this district] were sensible and included some aboveboard Communists who had long supported our movement. We also believed that rank-and-file Communists should not be identified with the nomenklatura. In short, the statement said that we had known it all along, that it had been done at our request, and that there was nothing wrong with it. Following the article by Krotov, Stankevich's popularity dropped by 10 percent. But after our address, it rose again. We were able, thanks to our daily polls, to predict the results of the vote with an accuracy of 1.5 percent.

As for our political campaigning for the Moscow Popular Front, I became active on Pushkin Square in late May 1988 as soon as we had the draft of the democratic mandate ready for the Nineteenth Communist Party Conference. People would gather in the public garden on Pushkin Square every day. I would come there with a friend after work every day and tell people about the Popular Front. The Democratic Union and Pamyat' also conducted their demonstrations there. Many people from other parts of the Soviet Union congregated there simply because they knew it was a meeting place of independent organizations. Many would approach us. We would hand them leaflets, write down their addresses, and give them our telephone numbers. Most of these people later became Democratic Russia's regional coordinators throughout Russia.

How were your relations with the Democratic Union and Pamyat'?
We had all-out confrontations with Pamyat' as we have nothing in common. We were also at odds with the Democratic Union, believing that they were provocateurs. But we still had some points of contact with them because our programs have much in common, only they are for private ownership and we are for collective ownership. Moreover, we differed fundamentally in that they refused to recognize the existing system of power and as such held unauthorized rallies, while we acted in the framework of existing laws and held mostly authorized rallies.

[At Pushkin Square] we used to come in contact with Democratic Union leaders such as Sasha [Alexandr] Eliovich, Andrei Gryaznov, Valeriya Novodvorskaya, and Victor Kuzin from the social-democratic faction [of the Democratic Union]. We used to argue with them and with Pamyat' supporters. The Popular Front held its first rally on July 30, 1988. *Izvestiya* even wrote an article about it. It was attended by some one thousand people, whereas previous rallies had not drawn more than one hundred to two hundred people. The first of these rallies at Pushkin Square was held in late May by Obshchina [Community] and Civil Dignity, which were also members of the Popular Front. Only the Democratic Union was not a member of any alliance and still is not, remaining as a kind of sect to this day and, consequently, failing to grow.

There had been a slump in activity after the elections [in the spring of 1988], but things began humming again in May, when preparations were under way for the first congress and our deputies, members of the future Interregional Group, became very active. Stankevich, Murashev, Afanasiev, Popov, and others began gathering even before the congress. The center of activity shifted to the Academy of Sciences, where a voter club was formed at the time, including Zhenya Sevostyanov and Dmitrii Katayev.[26]

Originally, the nascent Interregional Group was based in the House of Scientists. Then, after the first congress had opened, Memorial and the Popular Front filed requests, independent of each other, to hold rallies at Luzhniki. The Moscow City Council allowed us to stage the rallies, after reaching a compromise between ourselves. We agreed that the rallies would be jointly staged by the Popular Front and Memorial; we simply alternated the chair. Attendance at those meetings exceeded 100,000.

During the congress, people gathered at Luzhniki from 6 P.M. till 9 P.M. First, everyone would stand, listening to live radio coverage of the congress. Then a rally would start immediately after the end of congressional proceedings. About thirty minutes later, progressive deputies would arrive—Yeltsin, Afanasiev, Korotich, Popov, Stankevich, and Andrei Sakharov—and give their personal reports on the events that day at the congress.

It was at these rallies that the Moscow Association of Voters [MOI] was born. New activists emerged who were members of neither the Popular Front nor Memorial nor any other organization whatsoever. They began forming alternative groups and voter clubs. During the rallies, random people would proclaim, "A city voters' club has been formed in Moscow. Whoever is for Yeltsin or for our deputies, here is our telephone number. Call to join." They siphoned off so many people from the Popular Front that we suspected these proliferating clubs were the work of the KGB. We had a serious problem on our hands as people stopped joining the Popular Front and Memorial.

To remedy this situation, leaders of both organizations got together and decided that we should set up an organization with a neutral name because the Popular Front and Memorial had names that were too politicized, and people were still afraid to join them. So, Oleg Orlov, the current chairman of the Moscow City Council's commission on social organizations and movements, drew up a charter for the Moscow Association of Voters. We held several activist conferences and established an organizing committee.

In this manner, we managed to defeat self-organized voter clubs. Some of them perhaps were good, while others perhaps were bad, but we decided not to distinguish between them because there definitely were some that had been created by the KGB. This was why we decided to take voter organizations under our own control and set up the Moscow Association of Voters. We formed locals in every borough based on Popular Front groups. So, effectively, the Moscow Association of Voters was a renamed Popular Front, the backbone of which were Popular Front groups numbering 100 to 120 people in every borough, as well as the teams that had acted as deputies' campaign staffs. The Moscow Association of Voters held a founding conference in October 1989 after which we began advertising subsequent rallies not solely as activities of the Popular Front or Memorial but as events sponsored by the Moscow Association of Voters, the Popular Front, and Memorial. In this way, we mentioned organizations that were part of the Moscow Association of Voters as if they had been independent organizations, while in fact, they were all the same.

The Popular Front's constituent congress took place in the livestock farming pavilion at the National Exhibition of Economic Achievements in Moscow in March 1989 following the elections. Despite all our previous activities, it was the first Popular Front congress. It was then that we were joined by Lieutenant Colonel Urazhtsev, who formed the Shchit organization the following winter.[27] So the umbrella then included the Moscow Association of Voters, Shchit, and the Popular Front.

Did the Moscow Association of Voters have a political program?
No, it was just an association of voters to ensure the democratic course of candidate nominations and elections. When the 1990 campaign started, we decided to establish a headquarters and a campaign staff and to work more seriously

than during the previous elections because the coming local and republic polls were very important. We summoned activists from Memorial and future parties, including, for instance, Oleg Rumyantsev of the social-democratic association. Almost all democratic organizations joined us except the Democratic Union, which refused to take part in the elections. We named ten people to run our headquarters, but, in fact, all work was done by three of us—me, Volodya Boxer, and Vera Kriger. We were later called "the bloody clique."

We were at the central headquarters while other local campaign staffs had their own activists. Lyuda Stebenkova worked very well in the Lyublino borough. In the Cheremushkinskii borough, the five people originally supporting Stankevich during the elections formed the basis of a powerful borough group called the People Power Association, which numbered several hundred people. There were campaign staff in all Moscow boroughs.

In the Moscow region, districts for people's deputies to the Russian parliament were divided into six large national-territorial constituencies and fifty-nine smaller territorial constituencies. So sixty-five deputies were to be elected in Moscow. Correspondingly, we set up one central headquarters (consisting of the three of us), six campaign staffs for the national-territorial constituencies, and more staff in each of the thirty-three boroughs. We decided to nominate very well-known candidates in each of the six national-territorial constituencies. We called them *locomotives*.

We also involved journalists closely in that campaign and held a conference with them where we told them that if they chose to sit on the fence, we would lose the campaign. We told them they should run as candidates because they were well known, could speak well, and should help us. In addition, we called the Unions of Moviemakers, Writers (through the April club), and Composers (enlisting Dashkevich). We held conferences with all cultural workers' unions, insisting that their representatives join the race. *Argumenti and Fakti* editor Vladislav Starkov, who was very popular in Moscow at the time, agreed to run in a national-territorial constituency. We also persuaded Lev Ponomarev, Sakharov's close campaign aide, to run in another, and he built his own campaign on the fact that he was Sakharov's closest comrade-in-arms.

There were twenty more of our candidates in the race for the Moscow City Council, and each was followed by ten to fifteen candidates for borough councils. It was like a tree, with the trunk giving off branches and the branches giving off leaves. It was that kind of vertical arrangement. We issued a single list of candidates from the Moscow Association of Voters in the city. It read: "National-territorial constituency No. 1—Starkov, territorial constituency No. 2—say, Ivanov, Petrov, Sidorov." Sometimes, we had several candidates running from the democratic forces. We attempted to prevent it, but this was not possible. These candidates did not care that running against one another might result in the loss of the seat. These people had political ambitions.

We produced candidate lists down to the level of the Moscow City Council. Our whole campaign strategy boiled down to the signatures at the bottom of these lists—signatures from people like Popov, Travkin, Stankevich, and Afanasiev. These signatories were Union deputies, members of the Interregional Group who were very popular in Moscow. A total of ten thousand large leaflets were produced for each borough and were posted literally at every corner. There were also small leaflets, six thousand per candidate for the Moscow City Council, which were issued to the nominees, and they distributed them partly among their own constituents and partly among candidates for the borough council supported by them, so that the latter could insert their names in those leaflets and distribute them in their constituencies. There was a terrible fight to get onto those lists. We were accused of making mistakes as to whom we included on these lists.

During the campaign, we held several conferences with Yeltsin and Popov. Using Popular Front and Memorial contacts, we summoned people from all over Russia to Moscow at the end of 1989, held a meeting, and established a Democratic Russia bloc of candidates. It was before the elections, and all leaflets and candidate lists later were issued not on behalf of the Moscow Association of Voters, but in the name of Democratic Russia. Democratically minded candidates were now under a common umbrella—Democratic Russia. The attending candidates then returned to their regions and cities as the bloc's nominees.

In the election, we won a majority in the Moscow City Council. When the Russian parliament convened after the elections, Democratic Russia deputies formed a faction there. The Moscow Association of Voters and scattered voter clubs at the local level remained, but they were idle again after the elections. It was Volodya Kamchatov who said, "Let's get together. We have to do something." Several of us, including Arkadii Murashev and Victor Dmitriev, then got together and decided to create the Democratic Russia movement. This was in July 1990. Vladimir Boxer and I were opposed to creating a party and most others were of the same view, and we told this to Ponomarev and Vera Kriger. But Lev Ponomarev and Vera Kriger were of a different view; they kept wasting their time with Travkin.[28] We told them that the people were sick and tired of the word *party* because they associated it with the Communist Party and therefore would not join a new party.

Nonetheless, they formed an organizing committee [for the first congress of the Democratic Party of Russia]. To prevent them from regaining the initiative, we decided to form our own organizing committee to which we gradually lured both Ponomarev and Vera Kriger over, while Murashev belonged to both. We then elected Murashev, a well-known person, to be the organizing committee chairman, and Ponomarev was made his deputy. I became the Democratic Russia organizing committee's executive secretary. I began preparing newsletters right away.

At first, there were ten to twelve of us, and we agreed to meet once a week.

Then, there were about thirty of us in the organizing committee. Initially, we did not pay attention to which parties were represented, but then we began inviting members of different parties to send representatives to our organizing committee. Representatives from the Christian Democrats, Memorial, and the Social Democrats all participated. When we distributed our first newsletter to all our voter clubs, we urged them to prepare regional Democratic Russia conferences. We advised them to work with news organizations, intellectuals, and working-class movements because now that the nation was in crisis, a mass democratic movement was needed. We roughly described what kind of movement was needed. The newsletter was signed by Murashev as the organizing committee chairman and me as executive secretary.

We then decided to register the organizing committee with the Moscow City Council so that it would have the status of a legal entity. Victor Dmitriev wrote the organizing committee's charter and we quickly registered it with the Moscow City Council. That was important purely in terms of discipline: we knew that we were no longer an informal club but an organization registered with the Moscow City Council. We sent out the announcement to all our affiliated organizations that the organizing committee had been registered with the Moscow City Council and that they were dealing with a lawful organization. We then began preparing a constituent congress, which took place in Moscow October 20–21, 1990. It was then that the real work began.

The statement [claiming that Lev Ponomarev was a KGB agent] by People's Deputy Sergei Belozertsev came as a complete surprise to us.[29] If we had not done something, we would have lost the congress: either the congress would be split or the entire congress would have followed Oleg Kalugin and Telman Gdlyan.[30] I do not know whose idea it was, but we decided to call up Yelena Bonner, Sakharov's widow, who knew Ponomarev very well. I told her, "Yelena Georgievna, a catastrophic situation has developed at the congress because Belozertsev accused Ponomarev of being connected with the KGB." Yelena Bonner arrived, and I took her to the hall immediately. Sakharov's prestige is unparalleled, and the house stood up to greet her. Bonner told them that she knew Ponomarev long before any of them had emerged, that he visited Sakharov in exile, something only a very few dared to do. In short, the congress was saved after we brought her there. And if we hadn't done so, it would have been a different history.

Postcoup Reflections (October 1991)

What role did Democratic Russia play during the putsch?

In short, Democratic Russia acted as one of the headquarters to organize the people who came to the White House. Democratic Russia used its resources to organize mass meetings and demonstrations. We formally reacted at once. At

9:35 A.M., we made a statement that called on Muscovites to back Yeltsin's appeal to start a political strike. We organized propaganda and distributed it to servicemen in tanks, cars, armored troop carriers and among people in the streets and at metro stations. Leaflets were distributed exhorting people to go to protect the White House. On Tuesday, the second day, there were two massive demonstrations. We held a big meeting near the White House and simultaneously held a meeting near the Moscow City Council.

What is the situation within Democratic Russia now? How have your objectives changed since the putsch?

Our main objective as stated in our regulations, the struggle against the CPSU monopoly of power, only has been achieved in Moscow, Saint Petersburg, and other big cities. In the provinces everything remains practically the same. Although activities of CPSU organizational structures have been suspended, in reality the majority of soviets in the territories and regions consists of Communists. In these regions everything is the same. The power remains in the hands of the same nomenklatura, leaders of enterprises, and party officials at middle and lower levels. Now, they are doing everything they can to hinder land reforms.

It is difficult to describe the status of privatization. Because they began to do it themselves, it has taken a wild, spontaneous course. The objective of breaking the CPSU has not been achieved yet. A new goal that has emerged since the putsch concerns the direct participation of Democratic Russia in government bodies. We are working out constructive programs for the participation of Democratic Russia in the development of the economy and culture.

We also have several immediate tasks. First, we must support immediate elections of local government authorities and new elections for the local soviets in order to dispose of the nomenklatura that now occupies most of the soviets. It seems to me that the latter task is more important than elections for local administrative leaders. If we elect only the former officials and keep old soviets, we will wind up in the situation we have now in the Moscow City Soviet. It has practically turned into a reactionary force that hinders development.

In the provinces it would be even worse if these soviets are not dissolved and new deputies are not elected. Moreover, this system should be changed. Large soviets should be substituted for small municipalities of thirty to forty people at most. We also need a constituent assembly because the Supreme Soviet of Russia and the Russian parliament are mostly communist, which gives rise to friction with the president's power that in the future will become more serious. That is why it is urgent to convene a constituent assembly to solve the crucial issues: will Russia be a parliamentary republic or a presidential republic? will we have a union of republics or an economic or political union? will we preserve Soviet power or will soviets be eliminated? All these issues must be decided.

As for organizational issues, the structure of Democratic Russia that had developed, a coalition of parties and a mass of nonparty members, does not satisfy us any longer. This structure was efficient before the putsch, but now, when we have to create constructive programs as fast as possible, it is no longer efficient. To take part in management, we need to be a party in the American sense of having a firm structure with a great variety of opinions. It means that if we face opposition of parties—it is internal opposition now, and Travkin's party can serve as an example of it—these parties will simply step aside. Thus, it will not mean the disintegration of Democratic Russia as only these parties will step aside. The majority of Democratic Russia will remain. Perhaps we will call it the Union of Democratic Russia as Afanasiev proposed. It will be a party in the American sense but by no means a party in the West European or Soviet sense.

Victor Dmitriev

Like Mikhail Schneider, Victor Dmitriev had no experience in politics before becoming active in the election process in 1989. Dmitriev detested the communist system and the CPSU much more than did Schneider or the majority of Democratic Russia leaders and, as such, had little faith in all reform measures. In 1989, however, Dmitriev decided to oppose the communist nominations to the USSR Congress of People's Deputies and run his own campaign for the Russian parliament. A former sports hero from a small town outside Leningrad, Dmitriev easily defeated his communist and democratic rivals. On moving to Moscow, Dmitriev emerged as an outspoken critic of the communist system. When a Democratic Russia faction formed in parliament, his colleagues elected him as one of its cocoordinators. After the formation of the Democratic Russia movement, he was also elected as one of its cochairmen. A stocky, authoritative figure, Dmitriev frequently served as master of ceremonies for DemRossiya demonstrations, including the rally of tens of thousands of people at the Russian parliament building that took place on the second day of the coup.

After the coup, Dmitriev worked with Arkadii Murashev and Garry Kasparov to found the Liberal Union, a coalition of political groups and individuals that espouses radical and rapid economic reform. In the fall of 1991, Gorbachev, on Yeltsin's recommendation, appointed Dmitriev to head a new commission on relations with the World Bank.[31] After the dissolution of the Soviet Union, Dmitriev's commission became a Russian governmental entity.

Interview with
Victor Dmitriev (*June 1991*)

· ·

How, when, and why did you go into politics?
Within Democratic Russia's framework or in general?
Let's start from the very beginning.
Above all, it was a physiological urge. I have never believed in the idea of social
justice and social equality simply because I am, by nature, healthy and physically
strong. As a result, people around me always believed that I should work more
than everyone else because I was hefty and fit. Why? [In the Soviet system] we
get equal wages and everything is shared equally, but we put in different work-
loads. This is why I have not believed in the general theory of social equality
since my childhood. I had first doubts way back in the technical school when
they forced me to join the Young Communist League. I was an excellent student,
but I was told that if I did not join I would be denied a bonus scholarship given
to those with exceptional academic records. They threatened to take it away.
Why? Because an excellent student is entitled to a bonus scholarship only if he
is a member of the Young Communist League. The bonus scholarship is not for
knowledge but for Young Communist League membership. So I joined the league;
it would have been a pity to lose the money. But I protested inside, and those
inner protests have accumulated.

My real understanding of what is what came when I began reading philosophy
and the classics. The final straw, however, was when I began reading dissident
literature.
When was that?
I started reading this literature when I was finishing at the institute and starting
to work at the Izhorskii factory. But I was not at all active politically then.
Generally, I am very active by nature and have a knack for organizing. I did it
well in my regular job, and I have been managing well now within the democratic
movement. But I did not undertake to organize any movements at the time [that
I began to become politicized] because I was not yet sure if I had the inner
conviction. I was aware that there were some movements, but I saw how weak
they were and I saw why. But I believed then that it would be pointless to argue
with those people because, for them, it was important to start and not important
how. The most important thing was to get started and to begin working. Organization was a secondary matter.
Why were they weak?

To understand this, you must take into account the situation at that time. Here everyone was afraid [of political organization]. Most organizing actually was done across the border. Abroad, they had literature, communications, telephones, while here, in this country, we had nothing. Nonetheless, it was essential to set up those organizations here, inside the country, using any legal forms possible.

Some people, however, who I knew, took the view that legal forms were not needed. Rather, it was vital to preserve purity. This is the attitude that the Democratic Union now upholds. I do not agree with this approach because I think that legal forms must be used in order to prevent bloodshed. It is clear that socialism is a utopia and that it is doomed, but I do not think it's right to wait until it all explodes by itself. We need to try and bring about a smooth transition if it is possible at all.

Because of this attitude, I only started my principal activities and organizing efforts during the election campaign in 1990 [for the USSR Congress of People's Deputies]. In our constituency, the candidates included then Leningrad mayor Vladimir Khodyrev. He was a tough Party apparatchik, a man right from the nomenklatura, from the elite. But when other candidates were nominated, I joined [the opposition movement] and began campaigning at the factory in Leningrad where I worked. I began talking to people in various shops, departments, and services, reasoning with them, helping establish canvassing cells, looking for aides, and going on the local radio to recruit supporters. We eventually were able to nominate our own candidate from the shops. But the partyocracy [sic] then was still strong, and it managed to railroad through its man [Khodyrev] at the factory nomination meeting. Nonetheless, we responded with another nomination through a neighborhood meeting. It was a veritable war. In the end, we were able to prevent Khodyrev from being elected to parliament. In the runoff elections, we nominated a candidate, Lesha Levashov, who later became a member of the Interregional Group of [People's] Deputies.

During the nomination process, I decided for myself that I would not run for the federal parliament even though I had several hundred campaign aides who could have worked for me throughout my constituency [located just outside of Leningrad]. In principle, I could have enlisted all those people to assist in my campaign as they had offered to assist me. But I decided to wait and run for the Russian parliament because I decided that its members eventually would be more important than those in the Union parliament. Everything augured this because debates on republic sovereignty and independence were under way even then, and the main force that could change our situation was the division of the Union into republics in order to weaken our centralized system and the center, which is hated by all republics. The only fundamental way it could be crushed was by parting company so that later those who wanted to create a normal new Union could get together again and do so. So I decided that Russia and its MPs [members of parliament] would mean more, and so I became a Russian parliamentarian.

How were you elected?

Very simply. I had no doubts about succeeding, thanks to the federal campaign elections. I knew that my name was better known than those of other candidates. So I knew that I did not have any strong rivals.

How did you become so well known? Was it during your campaign work during the first elections or earlier?

My name was known much earlier because I have always been active as the captain of various sport and recreational teams at the factory. And still earlier, I was a successful athlete so the local press would write fairly often about me.

I did have competitors including democrats with whom I worked to defeat the conservative nominees to the federal parliament. I put in a lot of effort stumping at practically every corner and talking to many people. I did not rest on my laurels; I worked.

Did you join Democratic Russia before or after the elections?

Democratically minded candidates first formed a bloc before the elections. It included both regional and local candidates to the Russian parliament. It was a very long list of names. Everyone was asked: "Are you with us or not?"

There was a congress before the elections [in January 1990]. After the elections, we organized a meeting in March attended by Russian MPs supporting Democratic Russia's ideas. There were many of us, about two hundred people, from all over Russia. For this meeting, we sent out invitations to deputies backing Democratic Russia. During that meeting, we adopted some documents and became organized. We also mapped out guidelines for our work at the forthcoming congress [of people's deputies] because we knew that very much depended on it. Either our opponents, the Communists, would succeed in making it as lackluster, sour, and unexciting as the federal congresses, or we would turn the tables on them. I think that our preparations for this congress were the beginning of Democratic Russia proper. Thereafter, we kept up our activities as a unit in commissions preparing for the congress. It was then, as I see it, that Vitalii Vorotnikov and his supporters made their big blunder. They wanted to appear to be democratic to the commissions preparing for the congress so they invited new people to participate. [Unknown to them], these people from various regions had fresh, new ideas that they brought to these preparatory commissions, ideas that infected many diehard Communists and many of those undecided. At this moment, we won many supporters. The preparatory commissions gave a powerful boost to the congress because they prepared a sound agenda that included draft resolutions on the declaration of sovereignty as well as the decree on power and drafts of the constitution. In other words, we put in a great deal of work. Working procedures had also been hammered out in advance, which is very important as well because without clear-cut procedures it is very difficult to fight for the desired congressional decisions.

And you also voted in Yeltsin as chairman of the Supreme Soviet?

We had nominated Yeltsin to the post of chairman even before the congress at that meeting in late May, which brought together the Democratic Russia deputies' bloc, or the Democratic Russia bloc of people's deputies of the Russian Federation, as we called it.

In our bloc, we do not have a chairman. Our people are very wary of authoritarianism. A Russian saying goes, "The burnt child dreads the fire." This is why people here do not want to participate in parties, and many do not see a single person as the party's leader. At that meeting, too, nobody wanted to see a single chairman. Several cochairmen were elected to lead the bloc. They were called bloc coordinators. I am one of the Democratic Russia bloc coordinators.

Which members were elected cochairmen?

The list is changing all the time because after we were elected committee chairmen everything had to be reshuffled. But at the very beginning, the following people were elected: Oleg Rumyantsev, Mikhail Bocharov, Yevgenii Kim, Anatoly Monokhin, Sergei Filatov, and myself.

How did Democratic Russia become a mass political movement?

It became clear during the first Russian congress that without grass roots support and voter backing, it was going to be very rough for us. But hundreds of thousands of telegrams came to the congress, and great numbers of Muscovites would come to meet deputies all the time, demanding that either Boris Yeltsin be elected or that the decree on power or the declaration of sovereignty be adopted. It was powerful support, and it became clear that if we chose to be a purely parliamentary group, we would not be able to achieve much. Consequently, we drew up a statement of intent at the time, which we published and sent out to the regions and invited comments. Right after the congress [of people's deputies], we set up an organizing committee to form the Democratic Russia movement.

At the first organizing committee, we had Misha Schneider, Volodya Komchatov, Zhenya Kim, Monokhin, Zhenya Sevostyanov, Lev Ponomarev, and Arkadii Murashev. We agreed that we would create an organization and divided up tasks. I wrote the charter for the Democratic Russia movement because I have a talent for organizational and structural issues. We decided that Democratic Russia would consist of three components: first, political parties; second, members of governing councils at every level, including village, district, regional, and republic (they are all members of Democratic Russia's factions and make up the main vertical); and third, other vertical groups consisting of regional committees, social organizations, and independents throughout Russia. This last group turned out the most numerous and the most active as it unites nonparty people and regional committees. They have their own difficulties and complications, but the most important thing is that people do not sit idle but attempt to do something in a concerted way. We have our clashes, but we still forge ahead in the same direction.

So this is the structure we have. It is important to note that as I worked on the charter, I visualized how the movement would be the seed for a future multiparty system in Russia.

So that idea was already in the air?

With respect to the seed, no. It was my own idea that no one had aired before me. But I believe that it was a quite obvious idea. I thought that small parties in the future would grow as Democratic Russia activists joined them. But, alas, that did not happen. And the reason is that our small parties became so engrossed in political activities in the Russian parliament and the federal parliament that they paid too little attention to party building.

The only one who has gotten ahead in this respect is Nikolai Travkin, but even in his case, this is truer of form than substance. It is more like a facade. But then, what are the criteria? How do you determine what is a party? In our condition, regrettably, a facade is better than nothing, and the criteria used in the West do not fit here. We are so used to a strict party, to discipline, to a rigid party structure, and to orderly party functioning that for us a poorly disciplined group calling itself a party is not at all a party but something else. Although in the West it probably would be considered a party. I like, for instance, how parties function in America, and I do not like tight discipline. There, people determine their own priorities. They choose a candidate to project these priorities, they vote for him, and he defends their interests. They do not have to hold report-and-election meetings and similar nonsense all the time.

Travkin has something very much like the Communist Party in form: preparations, responsibilities, record keeping, stringent accountability, punishments, tough discipline, all the trappings of party. It resembles a Bolshevik party. This is why he is called a Bolshevik: not because he shares Bolshevik views but because he wants to create a party like the one established by Grandfather Lenin. After all, he graduated from the Higher [Communist] Party School. In my mind, he has this Communist Party mentality.

When was Democratic Russia, the movement, founded?

The Democratic Russia movement was formed in October [1990]. After having set up the organizing committee, we contacted many Russian regions, and practically all of them responded—from the Baltics to the Sakhalin Islands in the Pacific—Novgorod, Pskov, Kamchatka, and Vladivostok. They all joined in, and we knew that it was time to convene a founding convention. A special group was formed to prepare the convention. I was busy writing the charter, somebody else was looking for addresses, others were concerned with correspondence, and still others worked on other documents. Finally, the Democratic Russia movement held its founding convention October 20–21, 1990. Very many people came to attend. The Rossiya theater hall was packed to capacity, and it did not go smoothly.

Why? What issues were discussed?

The toughest part was not the issues. The toughest task was to decide the primary objectives of the movement. The overall thrust was easy to determine—opposition to the Communist Party and to its state-political monopoly. We were able to agree pretty quickly on that. But that was only the foreground. There also was the background, and there we ran into some wide disagreements within the movement.

Within the movement, we have the right wing, represented by the Russian Christian-Democratic Movement, the Cadets [Constitutional Democrats], and the Free Labor Party. But Democratic Russia also includes the Social Democrats and the former Democratic Platform in the Communist Party, which is now the Republican Party. They have totally different views on the future of the Soviet Union and how it should be built. The only thing that keeps Democratic Russia together is its anticommunism. This is why, at the time when we were organizing the Democratic Russia movement and writing its charter, we initially attempted to unite all anti-Communists. Then, after the downfall of communism in this country, we will take different positions in the political arena. But it was important—and I still think so—that we should have, even if only a little, a common history. It is important that we have developed some traditions of discussing things together and that we evolve a mechanism to work out decisions that are acceptable to all, that is, a mechanism for joint decision making. It is important that we in Democratic Russia work out some inner ethics, which will then, after the collapse of communism, catch on and spread across the entire political spectrum in Russia. Because when we have a multiparty system here, it is important initially that we do not drift too far apart. If we remember our common history all the time, this will help a lot.

Arguments at the convention October 20–21 centered precisely on this: are we a new superparty or are we a movement? My point of view is that this is a movement and must not be turned into a superparty, although functionally we already have a superparty.

Who supports the idea of a superparty?
It is those who advocate a purely organizational structure, those who emphasize organization in the movement above all else. But because the movement is now loosely organized, this organizing group is replacing those people who supply ideas—theorists and thinkers—because it will have all the means of communications and will decide itself what is to be done. Theorizing may still continue, but this organizational team will see to it that everything goes the way they like. I do not like this because the dominant role in the movement will then be played by technical personnel. These people will be the gray cardinals who do not write articles themselves, are not known anywhere, and cannot do anything practical to develop political thinking and political acting in Russia, but they will still run the show within the democratic movement. This is why I repeat that I favor Democratic Russia's being a movement.

I want Democratic Russia to be a movement based on two components: first, coordination, which will depend on communications, and, second, the mechanisms of ethical norms and of reaching agreement within the movement. These are delicate mechanisms, but they should be there. Woven together, these small traditions form an environment that you get so used to that you find it practically impossible to do without it later. I felt this, incidentally, in America, when I would ask legislators in a state congress, "Do you have a state charter and working procedures?" They responded, "Yes, we have." I then asked to see them after which a little confusion would ensue because nobody would know who had a copy. In principle, they must be somewhere around, but nobody had read them for a long time because people had become accustomed to practicing these small, fine traditions. People there know how different factions reach agreement, how people make statements, how they discuss an idea and how they argue. The people are accustomed to all this, and they can now even do without having a charter and working procedures always at hand. I hope, that as we fight the Communists, the Democratic Russia movement can develop such traditions as well. These traditions need to be learned by the different parties within Democratic Russia because they will dominate Russia's political scene in the near future.

I do not think that radical parties like Ubozhko's or Zhirinovsky's will put up any strong competition or opposition.[32] For the most part, the Russian political arena will be taken over by forces that have already manifested themselves—the Democratic Party, the Republican Party, the Social-Democratic Party, and the Christian-Democratic Movement. I think that there will also be a liberal-democratic party—not Zhirinovsky's group—but a true liberal-conservative party.

Will this be your party?

Maybe, because I am a liberal. In general, in America I identified myself as an extreme-right Republican. My views are very close to those of Arkadii Murashev, Garry Kasparov, Larissa Piyasheva, and Academician Tikhonov.[33] I think that others will join in too because, seriously speaking, there are three forces that determine the political spectrum in various countries. They are the social democrats, the liberals, and the Christian democrats [Western-style]. This country today is an atheist nation, but the yearning for spirituality and the restoration of lost traditions is very strong, and I believe that the Christian-Democratic Movement will become very popular. The restoration of our Orthodox traditions will later make an impact in that people will gravitate more toward such parties as the Russian Christian-Democratic Movement.

What kind of people join the Democratic Russia movement? Why have such different people as Lysenko and Aksiuchits joined in one organization?

For those who would like to actively counter communism in this country, there was no way out other than getting together. This is why no matter how different the views of Lysenko and Aksiuchits may be, they were brought together by a more serious matter, a more important goal, namely, that of resisting the Communist Party's state and political monopoly. Although the constitution has already been amended and Article Six dropped, the changes were only on paper, while in real life the Communist Party still wields enormous power and carries enormous weight. They continue to rule because they have first-rate communications, including closed-circuit telephone networks, closed-access teletype facilities, a good courier service, and lots of other dependable, fail-safe communications. If we cut this ground from under their feet, they will crumble to pieces in no time.

They are also united by the tremendous material resources they still have. Now they are busy investing these resources in business and also are involved in usury and lending money for profit because they have a great deal of money. They even have set up various banks by proxy. Nonetheless, they are afraid of creating real market conditions because this will take the wind out of their sails. On the one hand, they lend money in order to line their pockets, and, on the other, they are afraid lest the money give an impulse to real production development. Opposition to this was the powerful force that united Lysenko and Aksiuchits.

I believe that it is very important that such people as Lysenko, Aksiuchits, Rumyantsev, Afanasiev, Murashev, Ponomarev, and Travkin should learn to talk to one another and discuss things together. This is because in the future there inevitably will be clashes among us for various reasons, and perhaps some of these leaders will drift so widely apart that nothing will be able to reconcile them. So it is extremely important for us to have a common history, to sit in the same room, drink tea, and discuss all the details of the future system of Russia. This will help us to reconcile disagreements and avoid conflict later.

Why did Yeltsin not join Democratic Russia?

Yeltsin did much more; he quit the Communist Party. That was, to my mind, an outstanding step. I saw how he hesitated. I saw how his friends and associates urged him to do it. I myself suggested to Boris Nikolaevich that he withdraw from the Communist Party. But it was, of course, a very hard step for him to take. He believed that the Party could still be revived, pushed off the fallacious road of Marxism-Leninism, led from such idiotic positions as class-based hatred, the dictatorship of the proletariat, democratic centralism, and all that kind of stuff and made into a normal and strong social-democratic party. But the Communists here are so dyed-in-the-wool that they fail to foresee their future. They believe that any concession is the end for them, although every time they fail to make a compromise, it brings their end closer.

Yeltsin quit the Communist Party but did not join Democratic Russia for precisely the same reason that he cited when leaving the Communist Party: "I promised that if I were elected, I would be neutral because I should accommodate all sides and tread the middle of the road." In my view, Yeltsin now represents this kind of center in Russia, succeeding where Mikhail Gorbachev has failed. Gorbachev only declares that he is a centrist, while he is not. He is, in principle, like a boat in an ice hole [*sic*], drifting first in one direction and then in another.

Yeltsin was right not to join Democratic Russia. He should not be a leader of Democratic Russia because he is the effective head of state. After living under the Communist Party for seventy years, people here would not understand it if Yeltsin joined another party, Democratic Russia, after just having left the Communist Party. No, Yeltsin did everything right; he took up a position in the center. He is a very wise politician, and I will tell you frankly that before I became acquainted with him, I had underestimated him. Then, I came to know him at the Democratic Russia bloc meetings before the congress. I realized that Yeltsin may have a number of shortcomings, he smiles rarely, and he looks like a tyrant, a rude, stern despot. But he is an ordinary, kind man, a workaholic who wants those around him to put in as much work and show initiative. He does not appreciate dummies who only pretend to be working hard. When you talk to him, he never interrupts you. He will hear you out and then will possibly formulate his objections, but he will never say, "It's trash, you can't be right. Get out, because you're wrong." This never happens, and this is indicative. He is a real politician and is aware that people have to be respected.

What is Yeltsin's relationship with Democratic Russia?

It is very good. Today we support Boris Nikolaevich, and he knows it. Most of his following and his aides are from Democratic Russia. So far we have been united—and, I think, will continue to be united—with Boris Nikolaevich by common ideas about democratic principles. But I do not rule out the possibility that when he becomes president and our positions are no longer as shaky as now, it will be possible to talk to Yeltsin not as an ally but as the key figure in Russia and criticize him without pulling any punches if we disagree with some of his positions. For example, we were critical of his 9 + 1 agreement.

We, Democratic Russia, have drafted some very good documents, but so many have been spoiled because of the need to reach some kind of compromise with the Communists. Take even the idea of an executive presidency. We have to fix everything with the Communists, we have to coordinate everything, and while we do this, the documents lose their quality. But you have to look at everything in perspective. If we fail to agree on something with them now and then try to deceive them at the congress, for instance, the decision may go through and it will seem as if we have won. But, in fact, this will prompt a backlash from them and compel them to dig in their heels. We can do more a step at a time, drawing them into the democratic process.

Postcoup Reflections (October 1991)

Where were you during the coup?

I was in the Hotel Rossiya when I heard the news. Immediately I looked out onto Red Square from my window and saw that it was occupied by military vehicles. I immediately called the headquarters of Democratic Russia. I heard them saying, "At last, one of the cochairmen." I was the first DemRossiya cochairman to appear as Yurii Afanasiev and Arkadii Murashev were abroad at that time and Lev

Ponomarev was in Sochi. As I was leaving my room, I turned on the television and heard the announcement of the state of emergency and the establishment of the Emergency Committee with Yanaev as its acting president. Well, from that moment on, everything was as clear as daylight.

Various ideas came to my mind as to what should be done. I raced to the Moscow City Council, where activists of Democratic Russia used to gather. We met in [Mikhail] Schneider's office. Democratic Russia, in fact, was the first to raise the alarm. In Moscow we phoned all our offices and activists, suggesting that everybody should head for the White House and the Moscow City Council, arrange meetings at their plants and factories, and in general create a certain atmosphere of disobedience and not submit to this Emergency Committee. Later, when I arrived the White House, there were already a lot of people there.

The situation was critical. People began talking about the necessity of erecting barricades. Yeltsin by that time was already in the White House. I met a lot of acquaintances there, and they all were unanimous as to what measures should be taken. The decision was taken to resist in every possible way.

How did you come to this decision to resist actively?

Everyone I talked with at that moment was of the same opinion. No one hesitated. This shared attitude led to quick action—to defend the White House with barricades.

I should like to point out that there really was no putsch, as nobody intended, in the final analysis, to violate the constitution grossly. Yes, infringements took place. Setting up the Emergency Committee, removing the president, and depriving him of the possibility to perform his functions—all these are acts that violated the constitution. But I would argue that this is our constant practice, our habit, our world. Our apparatchiks always were accustomed to violating the laws written by themselves.

Those who decided to participate in the Emergency Committee just abused their official status. They believed that they did not need to notify everyone, that they did not need to prepare any special documents in advance, or get together at secret places and prepare for armed action. Because they all were holding office, they believed that it was enough just to raise the telephone receiver as people in our centralized state are used to obeying the orders from above regardless of what the constitution says is legal.

I have noticed that foreigners cannot understand this. They have become accustomed to respecting the law. As for us, the practice has been that people always have looked for a boss and a protector, never abiding by the constitution and laws. We have never possessed private property. Therefore, people deprived of property always try to find a protector, whereas people owning property always try to make laws guarding their property. This is where our psychology is rooted. Yanaev, Yazov, Kryuchkov, and the others [leaders of the coup] were very well aware of this. They themselves have been brought up in our system. They knew, or thought they knew, that a phone call, giving their names and instructions to do such and such things, would suffice, even though the one who received the instruction knew that it was a breach of the constitution. He would nevertheless carry it out because the order was given from a authority at the top. As for the constitution, to hell with it. No one has ever read it.

Why didn't the coup leaders disconnect all the information lines?

They trusted that their authority would be enough. Judge for yourself: they were the prime minister, the minister of defense, the head of the KGB, and the minister of internal affairs. What other authority do you need in order to exercise power over the state? Yes, the president should be there too. For some time, the president [Gorbachev] had been trying to balance these forces. For their part, they [the coup leaders] had been trying hard to attract him to their side. Not infrequently, they presented Gorbachev with a fait accompli as in T'bilisi and the Baltic states, where they provoked bloodshed, skirmishes, and murder. Later President Gorbachev did all he could to vindicate them. He said that they would find those to blame and start investigations. However, the necessary investigations were not carried out and nobody was punished, though, of course, there were certain people who had issued orders to move tanks into the city and open fire.

The coup leaders thought that Gorbachev would endorse their general decision to introduce the state of emergency and martial law. It was a matter of primary importance for the Emergency Committee that the USSR Supreme Soviet recognize its actions as constitutional, to get endorsement from the highest legislative body. I am quite sure that if no resistance movement had been organized immediately at the White House, the USSR Supreme Soviet would have approved the actions of the Emergency Committee by a majority of votes. By that time [Anatoly] Lukyanov, a shrewd rogue, had completely tamed the Supreme Soviet, driving away quite a lot of democrats from the composition of various commissions by means of voting procedures.[34] Therefore, the approval of the Supreme Soviet would have been received, and Yeltsin, Silayev, the whole Russian parliament, and all Democratic Russia activists could have been arrested. Special lists had been drawn up enumerating the persons to be detained temporarily. After their detainment, they [the coup leaders] would have violated the constitution and human rights to their hearts' content, and nobody in the Supreme Soviet would ever say anything.

As to the White House, the majority of us realized that things would take exactly this course, so our main task was to resist. We had no other way out. If we look at the matter in a detached spirit, the actions of the Emergency Committee were called a *coup*, in fact, thanks to the measures undertaken by those in the White House. If we had not shown resistance, disseminated Yeltsin's decrees and other information, and erected barricades to provide for a long-standing, all-around defense, they could have obtained the desired approval [from the USSR parliament] or could have put into effect their unconstitutional moves only through bloodshed.

They expected complacency even on the part of Yeltsin. But Yeltsin is a good muzhik [Russian peasant]; he feels his finest when fighting is going on. He is a man of strong willpower. His weak point sometimes is the lack of a program. But his decrees, in which he cited the unconstitutional character of the Emergency Committee's actions and called for its arrest, were of paramount importance. These decrees explained much to the people. Otherwise, our fellow citizens might have thought, "Well, those people [the Emergency Committee] represent power, they are ministers, they have decided to act, so they must be right." People in our country have grown accustomed to obey. It was extremely significant that people could read Yeltsin's decrees in which these people were called criminals. These documents had a strong emotional impact. I watched people reading these decrees eagerly in Moscow streets. It was like fresh air. In those three days, some forty decrees were issued. I myself participated in preparing many of them.

How did you organize the demonstrations?

To my mind, Popov and Yeltsin made a mistake on this issue, as they did not take the intentions of the Emergency Committee members seriously enough. It was hard to believe that they would deliberately go against their own people, would open fire, and so on. Therefore, it was decided to hold a mass rally on August 20 on Manezh Square.[35] However, the square was surrounded by the troops and tanks, so it was next to impossible to arrange a rally there. I am sure though that some people would have managed to struggle through somehow. I saw people gathering including deputies of the Moscow City Council. All together, there were only two or three thousand people. Some of them were making speeches, standing on trucks with megaphones. Military vehicles were not too numerous at that time, but many more appeared. It was clear that they wanted to frighten the people. But when a person is put under strong pressure, he may take action in the heat of the moment, thinking "I may die but I will act against them." In moments like these, people are ready to sacrifice their lives in order to prove that they are worth something. So under these circumstances, I considered it unreasonable to hold the rally on Manezh Square.

Therefore, that night I met with Lev Ponomarev and we agreed we should not hold a demonstration there, as it might result in provocation, bloodshed, and murder. Instead, we came to the conclusion that the rally should be held at the White House. We had nothing to defend on Manezh Square. Instead, we needed to arrange defenses. Common people could block the access to the White House. So we called the Moscow City Council, informing our people there to redirect people to the White House.

Yeltsin himself was against this. He was afraid of possible bloodshed near the White House. Though scanty, we had obtained information about a raid on the White House planned for a certain hour. Yeltsin read this information—describing the order to open fire, to crush the glass windows of the ground and the first floors with grenade dischargers—and suspected the worst. We also thought that as soon as Yeltsin appeared to speak at the rally, he might be killed then and there. However, if we held the meeting here [at the White House], Yeltsin could not abstain from participating. He would never forgive himself, for he is no coward and could not respect himself if he did not address the people in person.

As it happened, a lot of people turned up. Near the Moscow City Council the number of people was approximately 150,000. Here, they estimated the numbers to be around 300,000. Ilya Zaslavsky was the first to speak at the meeting. As everyone else was engaged in other activities at the time, I asked him to take his time. Then I spoke, stressing that the rally was not just a meeting but an action to defend the White House as a symbol and a stronghold of the legitimately elected power of the president and parliament. We were unanimous in our thinking. Gleb Yakunin, who is very much loved in Moscow, appeared a little later. He managed to create an upbeat atmosphere. The meeting lasted about four hours. Around forty-five people spoke.

Most strikingly, a lot of young people were present. Here I saw with my own eyes that the future of our Russia, the young, had come to defend their freedom; this was a first in our history. The three young boys that died had attended the rally and listened to what was being said. I feel guilty for urging the people to be eager for battle because after the meeting people were ready to fight with their bare hands. And it really was that, as these boys dashed against the tanks with bare hands. On the other hand, it was the first time in a thousand years of Russian history that people gave up their lives for personal liberty. They did not die so that Boris Yeltsin could stay in office or for the sake of the parliament. Yeltsin and parliament simply represented to them personal liberty.

When did it become clear that you had won?

To me, it was clear when I saw the enormous number of military vehicles that were assembled to intimidate us. But we were not intimidated. It was then that I drew the conclusion that they had lost. It was on August 20. All the RSFSR people's deputies who were at the White House moved around Moscow, meeting the troops and talking with the servicemen. The reactions of the troops were diverse. Some servicemen read the president's decrees and eagerly conversed with us. Some stayed neutral. Others avoided any contact and strictly carried out orders. However, it was after I talked with the servicemen that I realized that the putsch would not be supported.

During the night of August 20–21, at about 5:00 A.M., I had a strong feeling that the Emergency Committee would fail to do anything.[36] They counted on strict execution of their orders, but it so happened that the Alfa unit, a KGB division, and many other servicemen refused to carry out their orders. Tank columns were moving toward the White House, but they never attacked as ordered. They just occupied positions around the White House as if to keep order. One could even notice that these military machines were linked with ropes just to show that they had a full complement. But one could also see that they either had an idle engine or that some other part was out of order. To some extent, these were deliberate malfunctions; it looked like window dressing. So by the early hours of the twenty-first, I realized that the whole thing was over. Later in the day, a session of the Russian parliament was convened, which was a very correct thing to do—to hold this session before the Union parliament met. The new Russian flag was hoisted in place of the red Soviet flag.

During the coup, together with other Russian deputies, I visited the troops based on Tushino airfield [the Tamanskaya Tank Division and the airborne regiment of the Kantemirovskaya Division]. In our delegation, we had two people's deputies who were colonels in the military—one a tank man and the other a commando. They did a good job working with the troops. The commando went to talk to the soldiers from the Kantemirovskaya Division, but they put him under arrest and took him to the tent of the regiment commander. But even there he tried to talk with them and persuade them to take our side.

The regiment had received the order to start moving in the direction of the White House at 12:00 P.M. [August 20]. When we visited them the second time, all their vehicles and equipment were ready to move; all the engines had been started and every piece of equipment was in operation. I wandered among the tanks, but nobody paid any attention to me as everyone was busy with his own job. Occasionally I did manage to engage a soldier in conversation. These conversations usually ended with them taking me to their commander, who would doggedly say, "Now we are going to carry out our orders." Then I would hand him Yeltsin's decrees. He would read them and then inquire, "Which punishment will be less severe: that for not fulfilling the commander's or that for not obeying the president's decrees? Whose orders shall I execute?"

Of course, I would answer, "Certainly, you should follow the president's decree." "Why?" "Because we have the Criminal Code of the Russian Federation. And if you violate the decree of the Russian president it means that you will be punished accordingly. But if you do not fulfill the commander's order, it is not exactly clear by what code you will be punished." "Well, I will think it over."

When I returned to the airport in Tushino that night, I met our man, who had stood on alert there watching and informing the White House all night long about which type and number of military vehicles were leaving. Based on his reports and others, it seemed to us that they could have defeated us very easily that night [the nineteenth]. All of our barricades were made of debris, and a tank would not even lose speed breaking through such a rickety barricade. Late in the evening of the nineteenth, when we knew that the order to storm the White House had been given, deep in our hearts we were preparing for the last fight in our life. When it did not occur on the nineteenth, we expected it on the twentieth. But on the twentieth, after the rally, some fifty thousand people stayed around the White House in a very dense circle and kept an all-night vigil.

Who organized the defense?

Both Democratic Russia and the military, operating under the command of the defense headquarters, organized the defense. The defense circle consisted of several lines of people. There was no direct corridor by which one could get to the White House. You had to go through a zigzag-type labyrinth before you could enter. And every time you entered you had to pass personnel control so that you could not bring inside a tommy gun, a light machine gun, or anything else of the kind. All your things were checked and you were searched.

On the twentieth, it would have taken a thousand times more bloodshed to storm the White House than on the nineteenth. On the nineteenth, only those inside the White House would have died. On the twentieth, many thousands of people standing around the building would also have died. Again, most of these people were young and energetic—thousands of people like Komar, Usov, and Krichevsky.[37] These people had come to defend their future, their personal liberty; it was no time for fear. Therefore, August 20 was the most anxious day. We dreaded provocations. When this did not happen, in the early hours of the twenty-first we captured the military vehicles positioned around us. Everyone climbed on these vehicles—boys, girls, clergymen, and others. And with tricolor flags, they were driven behind the barricades, their barrels turned in the opposite direction. It was at this particular moment that I realized that what we dreaded most was over.

chapter nine

Strike Committees and the Independent Union of Miners

Although it proclaimed to be a workers' paradise ruled by a "proletarian dicta-torship," the Soviet Union repressed all independent workers' strike and union activities, including slaughtering workers in Temir-Tau, Kazakhstan, in October 1959 and in Novocherkassk, Russia, in June 1962.[1] On July 10, 1989, however, three hundred miners in the Kuzbass defied these historical precedents by orga-nizing a successful strike. Spontaneously, the strike spread first throughout the Kuzbass and then to other mining regions of the Donbass (Ukraine) and Vorkuta (Siberia). Within a week, 177,000 miners from 158 enterprises had joined the strike, making it the largest organized "work stoppage" in Soviet history.[2]

Initially, strikers' demands were limited to improvements in their standard of living, that is, increased salaries, better food supplies, and soap.[3] Demands, however, quickly proliferated to include everything from a ban on all Communist Party activity during work hours to the writing of a new Soviet constitution.[4] The scope of the strike combined with the miners' absolute refusal to deal with local officials forced Gorbachev to become involved in its resolution. On July 16, 1989, the Soviet president appointed a task force, headed by Politburo member Nikolai Slyunkov, to investigate the miners' grievances and negotiate with the strike committees. Less than week later, the commission had signed an agreement with the strike committees in the Kuzbass that guaranteed among other things increased pay, increased supplies of consumer goods, and greater autonomy for the mines in managing their operations. Agreements were signed with strike committees in the Donbass and Vorkuta shortly thereafter. In August, the government's promises were consolidated in Resolution 608. The failure to implement Resolution 608 would become one of the bases for a second wave of strikes in 1991.

In the aftermath of the strike, the strike committees' leaders worked to develop permanent institutions to defend miners' interests. On May 1, 1990, the Confederation of Labor was founded to act as a coordinating council of all worker activities and as a liaison with political movements and parties. The leaders of the Confederation of Labor hoped that the organization would eventually develop into a massive workers' movement along the lines of Solidarity.[5] As the founding charter of the confederation stated,

> Labor unions and political organizations of workers will, perhaps, act separately in the future. But today, it is vital to pool all our forces. We need unity for mutual enhancement, mutual assistance, and joint actions of solidarity. We need to become united both to push for our economic interests and to make sure that the peaceful revolutionary democratic movement gain in scope, gather momentum, and triumph in the USSR.
>
> This is why our newly founded organization is a broad alliance of labor unions, social and sociopolitical organizations of factory workers, and all working people.[6]

The coalition, however, never coalesced, as divisions among the workers, intellectuals who wanted to "help" the workers, and leaders from Moscow-based political parties and movements stymied the confederation's development.[7]

Soon thereafter, the Independent Union of Miners (Nezavisimii Profsoyuz Gornyakov, hereafter, NPG) was created at the second congress of miners in Donetsk October 22–25, 1990.[8] NPG leaders reorganized the dormant strike committees into trade union cells, which became the basis of this new organization. The goal of the NPG was straightforward: to create an independent union that would defend the interests of the miners instead of the interests of the state.

At the founding congress of the NPG, Pavel Shuspanov, who would become the first chairman of the Independent Union of Miners, presented the draft of the General Model Tariff Agreement (*General'noe Tipovoe Tarifnoe Soglashenie*, or GTTS). This document outlined a new basis for all contractual relations between the miners' union and the management at the mines, be it private owners or the Soviet, Russian, or Ukrainian governments. Most important, the document demanded that miners be paid an hourly wage according to qualification and indexed on the cost of a bundle of consumer goods. The tariff also stated that administration officials should be paid according to the profits of the enterprise, extending the responsibility of productivity and profitability beyond that of the workers.

Armed with this document, the NPG sought to negotiate new working relations for miners and to demand that the promises made in 1989 be fulfilled.[9]

Its efforts were quickly frustrated by the stonewalling of the new conservative Soviet government. Prime Minister [Valentin] Pavlov ignored the miners' demands and refused to meet with the NPG representatives.

Seeing no other option, the miners went on strike again on March 1, 1991, first in Donetsk and then in the Kuzbass, Vorkuta, Sakhalin, the Urals, and other places. Unlike the wildcat strikes of 1989, this effort was organized and coordinated, but the miners made several tactical errors. First, the timing was poor. Prime Minister Pavlov had planned price hikes for April 2, 1991. If the miners had started their strike after these price hikes, they might have been joined by workers from other industries.[10] Second, the demands of the strikers quickly escalated to unrealistic levels, thereby clouding the important issues on which the strike had originally focused. In particular, demands for the Union government's resignation, including that of Mikhail Gorbachev, shifted the focus of the strike to the battle between the USSR and Russia. Late in the strike, the striking miners even proposed that a new governmental structure be created—"an interrepublic parliamentary group composed of representatives of the Council of [Republic] Ministers, the strike committees, and political forces that have mass support, for the coordination of interrepublic actions in the conditions of the paralysis of the Union power."[11] Meanwhile, disputes about terms of the GTTS agreement, the original impetus for the strike, were forgotten.

The strike ended in April after Gorbachev and Yeltsin signed the $9+1$ agreement, which established a new framework for negotiating a Union treaty. Although the agreement was heralded by most as a major victory for Yeltsin, the miners, and the democratic movement as a whole, the direct benefits for the striking miners were unclear. The settlement transferred jurisdiction over the mines from the Union to the Russian and Ukrainian governments and increased wages for coal miners.[12] But the majority of striking miners were dissatisfied with the final outcome.[13]

The mixed outcome of the 1991 strikes, however, only slightly impeded the development of the Independent Union of Miners. Although supporting the transition to the market, miners realize that they have to defend their interests, whatever the state of the economy.[14] Since 1991, the Independent Union of Miners has established representation at virtually every coal mine in Russia and Ukraine, making the miners' union one of the only political organizations organized on a well-defined social base. The union has raised the specter of a strike to pressure the Yeltsin government to increase wages, but, in general, miners have worked closely with enterprise directors and new government officials to privatize the coal mining industry.[15]

Other Independent Trade Unions

Although the miners have been the most active in establishing an independent trade union, other forms of organized labor have also appeared.[16] At the level of the enterprise, several thousand workers' collectives have formed throughout Russia and the other states of the new commonwealth.[17] More broadly, Sotsprof (Socialist Trade Union) was founded on April 1, 1989.[18] Unlike the Independent Union of Miners or workers' collectives, Sotsprof was not founded as an organization for workers of a particular enterprise or industry. Rather, this union seeks to "create conditions under which one can work, not serve or subserve" for all working people in Russia.[19] Like the Confederation of Labor, Sotsprof also aimed to unite workers' movements with other anticommunist political associations, parties, and fronts.[20] Finally, after the August 1991 putsch, many official trade unions formerly subservient to the Communist Party have been reconstituted as "independent trade unions." For instance, the Moscow Federation of Trade Unions has preserved its former structures while also working closely with new labor organizations such as the Socialist Party, KAS-KOR (the Information Center for Trade Union and Workers' Movements), and the Party of Labor.[21] In the fall of 1991 and winter of 1992, the Party of Labor organized a series of demonstrations protesting the market reforms, but the new organization failed to carry out the all-city strikes planned in response to the price hikes in January 1992. It remains to be seen what kind of role these old trade unions will play in the new political and economic situation in the country.

Anatoly Malykhin

Anatoly Malykhin was born in 1957 and worked in the coal mines all his adult life until becoming politically active in 1989. During the 1989 coal mine strikes, Malykhin helped organize his strike committee at the Isakievskaya coal mine. During the second wave of strikes, Malykhin served as chairman of the Strike Committee at the Isakievskaya coal mine, as a member of the Kuzbass Workers' Committee, as a member of the Novokuznetsk City Workers' Committee, and as chairman of the Interregional Group of the Council of Workers' Strike Committees. As chairman of this last organization, Malykhin negotiated in Moscow with the Union and Russian governments on behalf of the striking miners.

Although nationally recognized as a leader of the striking miners, Malykhin's credibility was seriously undermined by the outcome of the 1991 strikes, when many of his fellow miners accused him of becoming too attached to Moscow's political limelight. Through his Moscow negotiations, however, Malykhin developed close relations with Boris Yeltsin and, during Yeltsin's campaign, served as Yeltsin's representative in the Kuzbass region. In July 1991, Yeltsin appointed Malykhin as his representative in the Kemerovo region.

Interview with
Anatoly Malykhin (May 1991)

· ·

When and why did you decide to take part in politics?
It was in 1989. Mezhdurechensk [miners] went on strike, and their actions were soon supported in other towns. That night, when I finished my day shift, the night shift did not go to work. We then organized a strike committee at our coal mine. Our coal mines are scattered and separated, so nobody knew the state of affairs at our coal mine. My team where I work proposed that I become a member of our coal mine Strike Committee. Then we went to Mezhdurechensk, and on the way there we visited a number of other coal mines inviting their representatives to come with us. In Mezhdurechensk we learned what was happening at other mines throughout the region. On our return home, we again visited all the mines with proper information about the activities of the miners. Thus the strike began.

How would you describe the stages of development to date of the workers' movement?
The workers' movement is a rather serious force today. For the last two years, it was assigned a gladiator mode of existence: those who could not endure fell to the wayside. But people have changed over the course of two years. We agitated and people changed. Many have quit [the workers' movement] because of a sheer loss of strength. But a basic skeleton of three to five persons in each town has remained. They keep hold of the situation and they are held in respect.

What can you say about the structure of the working movement?
At the outset, the workers' movement was based on strike committees. Later, on the basis of the strike committees, we formed the Independent Union of Miners [NPG]. For the time being, it is still very small, but we hope it will continue to grow. These new trade union structures should be reinforced. The fact is that the guys with the greater abilities for organizational work must remain at the mines directly, while here in Moscow we have people who are dispensable at the mines. I only managed to come to Moscow eight days into the strike, and the only way I could come is because I have left behind me a mighty working committee.[22]

Are there any alternatives to strikes?
For the time being, we live in an abnormal country. You see, trade unions here are extremely politicized. In addition, on account of their respect and authority, the workers' committees are compelled to deal with a multitude of different issues, including, for instance, economics. In this strike, we have succeeded in transferring ownership of the coal mines to the republics—in other words, to a change in the form of property.

This strike exposed a vast technological chain of interdependencies between different branches of industry. As a consequence, we have forced several metallurgical plants to support republic legislation that supports our political demands. Whether voluntarily or involuntarily, they were obliged to accept our terms.

But, in other regions and industries, the workers' movement is still poorly developed.

Why this differentiation?

First, the country is enormous. Second, there is a lack of people with initiative. In the Kuzbass, we have a particularly rigid structure of the workers' movement. At each enterprise there is a workers' committee, and in every town or city there is a city workers' committee. Two persons are taken from every city to make up the Council of Workers' Committees of the Kuzbass. The council outlines a program for each week. On Wednesdays, its members go to their cities and coal mines to fulfill these programs. We are constantly exchanging information regarding the state of affairs at the coal mines.

How did the demands of the striking miners become political? And how do you evaluate the 9 + 1 agreement between Gorbachev and Yeltsin?

The political demands emerged as a result of our struggle for economic demands that were included in the minutes of Resolution 608. There were forty-two separate demands that have been elaborated for a long time. The government, having signed this document with us, has undertaken an obligation to fulfill them. But they did not do this, and they did not want to do that. To be more precise, they are unable to do this and that because it is a weak government. It has so happened, Russia, with the exception of Peter the Great, has always had weak leaders. When the strike commenced, the miners' demands were limited to economic concerns— the doubling of wages. But then we realized that this government is not capable of fulfilling this demand. We then made the realization that under this government, under this system, none of our economic demands can be fulfilled. Consequently, we put forward the political demands and called on coal miners of other regions to do the same. It was on March 10, 1991, when our Coordination Committee started to work. We gathered here in Moscow and collected all the demands into one whole.

In the long run, we moved beyond economic demands. In a week, it was clear that we were supported by lads from other regions, for example, from the Donbass.

As to the 9 + 1 agreement between Yeltsin and Gorbachev, we have accepted it without any hysterics, in contrast to some of our Russian people's deputies of the extreme, leftist, democratic orientation and also in distinction to a number of organizations that were calling Yeltsin a traitor and blaming him for political duplicity. As for us, we simply brought Yeltsin to the Kuzbass for an explanation. We gathered 623 representatives from the striking coal mines, and they asked him questions. He answered them, and, moreover, he was understood. On the whole, the position of the Russian government and Yeltsin suits us perfectly well as it coincides with our intentions. Therefore, we do not view 9 + 1 as something awful.

As a confirmation of our good relations with Yeltsin, one can consider our nomination of Yeltsin to run for president of Russia. One year ago we signed an agreement with the Russian government regarding our intentions. We do not, however, outline our future plans based on a certain personality. Today most of our positions coincide with Yeltsin's. So we support him. But if Yeltsin alters his position, then our attitude toward him is likely to change as well.

As for relations between Yeltsin and Gorbachev, everyone has been saying for some time, "When are they going to get together? When are they finally going to stop blaming each other?" Maybe they are too hysterical. Hysteria is, perhaps, a normal state of being for those who are inclined to think in categories of either passionate love or passionate hatred. But a person participating in the political arena should be able to behave with composure and calm. Without compromise there is no politics.

What are the most important goals before the miners today?

There should not be any ultimate objectives aside from the ordinary human desire to change this system and to build a normal economy. Why are the miners active in these aspirations? It is a matter of history. Perhaps, it is a product of our collective labor. In the mine, everyone bears a responsibility for the other as we work under hard conditions. Almost every miner, at least once every ten years, is compelled to participate in cleaning up the remains of one of his comrades who was either smashed or broken into pieces in the mine. These experiences form a particular kind of core in a man that is apt to disclose itself when times are difficult.

Your situation in the country is unique. In most of the world, the workers struggle with those who advocate the market. But with you it is the opposite. How did this occur?

Under ordinary market relations, trade unions demand the improvement of labor conditions and the increase of wages. But here, in this country, we all are slaves of the state, the entire bulk of people are slaves. The whole country is under the command of a small group of people who are exploiting the laborers. If a worker in the USA gets 70 percent of his labor's worth or even more, in the USSR we get only 5–10 percent. The differences in the standard of living [between workers and administrators] is very easy to see, as a miner earns about 300–400 rubles a month, whereas the one sitting in the administrative office gets 600–700 rubles.

You want to change the system. Do you want to establish a system that is similar to the one in the United States or the one in Germany?

For a great many years, we have been brought up in a peculiar way. A so-called homo-Soveticus [new Soviet man] has infected our people; he is not inclined to earn his wages but merely likes to get a salary. In this system, a good boss is the one who pays nicely!

I do not think that this system is wanted by people. It is a matter of normal existence in a natural community. There is a no other road. We need a normal, ordinary economy. If before, Brezhnev was feeding us food purchased with petroleum dollars, today nothing of this kind remains. Everything is sold out at fantastically cheap prices by the way. Nothing is left to lull us into further sleep. Whether we are eager to have a market or not, we have no choice. It cannot be otherwise. The Bolsheviks wanted to rid the country of the rich. Well they have succeeded. Now, all the people in our country have become poor. It is time to reverse this situation.

What kind of relations do you have with other political movements and parties?

With the CPSU, we decided everything a year ago. This Party is not respected by any of the miners. To be more exact, the miners have a very negative attitude toward the CPSU. Party meetings are not attended by anyone. When a secretary of a district Party committee appears at the coal mine, he will undoubtedly be called obscene words.

As for the other emerging democratic movements, we collaborate with them but with caution, for there are too many people [in their ranks] who do nothing. They do not wish to go through a thorny bush. They intend to bustle through the crowd very hastily in order to be at the head of the movement. This will not do. Here again is our communist essence. They say that the entire reforms are executed from the top. They consider themselves to be fairly educated in the sphere of both knowledge and politics. And we are supposed to listen to them and implicitly follow their directions and wishes.

But ours is an absolutely independent workers' movement. We collaborate with Democratic Russia and with the other democratic parties, but within the workers' movement we do not have party cells or divisions. Miners are not inclined to create a sort of social-democratic or Travkin party, for example, although in Democratic Russia there are a sufficient number of rather sensible people with whom we cooperate. But that movement is also not devoid of all kinds of scum, both in Moscow and in other places. When these new organizations were created they could not, as a rule, become very numerous, for people joining the ranks of those organizations were not aware of things they ought to do. A great many of them were seeking a leader to guide them. Consequently, those organizations are filled with plenty of insolent people.

What about your international relations. In particular, what kind of relations do you have with the AFL-CIO?

We have collaborated with the AFL-CIO for a number of years. This winter our delegation went to America to take courses in trade union training. During the strike, we (including me personally) appealed to them with a request for a moratorium on the delivery of coal. We have signed a memorandum of mutual cooperation with them. In fact, the AFL-CIO has a delegation here right now. Very soon, we also will host an American delegation of coal mine specialists who will visit our major coal basins and give us their ideas pertaining to the problems involved in making the transition to the market. They also will attempt to estimate our economic potential. The delegation includes representatives from private coal mining companies, trade unions, and the U.S. State Department.

What kind of ownership should there be at the coal mines? Should the mines belong to the Russian government, to the workers' collectives, or to private owners?

We now are of the opinion that all sorts of property should be developed including the private sector. But here in our country we have never lived under conditions of private property. In other countries, miners do not live too badly under private property. The miners there can negotiate and stipulate the terms of their work and wages with the owner of the mine. They are organized into trade unions, and they conduct negotiations, while the owners promote the development of their enterprises. With development of that sort, everyone ultimately gains including the workers.

How do you see the workers' movement developing in the near future?

One can mention now two fairly serious amalgamations: the Confederation of Labor and the Independent Trade Union of Miners. Although the confederation still has greater legitimization, it has not been very active lately. As for the Independent Trade Union of Miners, it is intended to function as a trade union that will struggle to achieve economic demands. Unfortunately, right now it is impossible to escape from politics. In the future, however, when things settle down, a majority of miners will plunge into trade union activity.

We want to strive for the ordinary development of a normal system with economic vitality. This is the objective we are pursuing. At the present moment the workers' movement is the most organized and the most advanced detachment of the forces striving to achieve this end. It looks like we have imposed a responsibility on ourselves; there is no way out of that. If we wish to exist as human beings, we must struggle with that system that has turned us into slaves. Therefore, political demands are prevailing now, although we are, naturally, interested in economics first of all.

Postcoup Reflections (November 1991)

What did the coup signify for the workers' movement?

It could have been a great leap backward, a suspension of the whole set of elaborated reforms. We have been busy for a couple of years working out economic reforms. By the way, our program, "Provisions about the Zone of Free Entrepreneurship," won a prize from the European Economic Community amounting to $1,300,000 for its practical approach to creating a market structure. That prize means a recognition of our way to the market economy; it denotes fresh credits and the aid of experts, first and foremost, in the sphere of new technologies and improvements in the use of natural resources. Besides threatening the economic reform, a victory for the putschists might have led to the actual physical elimination of activists.

Where were you during the coup?

Well, on August 19 I was here in Moscow. The news about the coup came to me at 6:00 A.M. I immediately contacted the White House. Then, together with Kislyuk [Mikhail Kislyuk, the head of the Kemerovo regional administration], I went to the White House. There we were present at the morning session of the RSFSR Presidium of the Supreme Soviet at which they discussed the appeal of Yeltsin, [Ivan] Silayev, and [Ruslan] Khasbulatov.[23] Soon thereafter, Silayev approached me and asked to lead a strike by the miners. At 1400, Yeltsin read his appeal from the tank near the White House and made a speech in front of the crowd gathered in the square. While standing on the tank, Yeltsin noticed me and later came up to me and asked, "What about the miners? Are they going to support us?" I answered that they should begin their strike at midnight. But Yeltsin responded, "You must start it earlier!"

From the very beginning, on August 19, the people's volunteer corps had begun their formation. The head of the militia had declared that he should follow only the orders of Russia's leadership. We were preparing the dispatch of five aircraft, each with three hundred miners, to participate in the defense of the White House. On the twentieth of August, the first group of one hundred miners arrived in Moscow. We were behind Yeltsin all the way.

In what way was the strike supported? How many mines participated in the strike during the coup?

Forty-two out of 117. To launch a strike, one needs a whole week to prepare for purely technical reasons. The flooding of mines needs to be prevented. Precautions against explosions also should be taken. But all the mines declared that they planned to enter the strike.

How has the situation changed for the workers' movement since the putsch?

The workers' movement has significantly strengthened its positions. For instance, truthful information during the coup reached different regions of the country in large measure only through the structures of the workers' movement.

Pavel Shuspanov

Pavel Shuspanov has worked in the coal mines for seventeen years. In 1989, he organized one of the first strike committees, eventually becoming chairman of the regional strike committee in the Donbass. The following year he was elected first chairman of the Executive Committee of the Independent Union of Miners (NPG). That union played an active role in organizing the 1991 strikes at coal mines in the Donbass, Kuzbass, and Vorkuta, but financial scandals plagued the organization after the strike, forcing Shuspanov to resign at the end of the year.

Interview with
Pavel Shuspanov (*June 1991*)

. . . .

Why were there strikes in the mines this year?

This strike was provoked by the center and the republics. The fact of the matter is that we are entering into the market. But we must struggle for ourselves in these new market relations. To make the market work, they need to achieve a surplus of labor power. They are trying to achieve this by closing unprofitable enterprises. In Tula, they just flooded the mine, meaning that 330 workers were out of a job. And the government is not going to preoccupy itself with making new working places for these people.

In order to become a real independent trade union, we need economic freedom. At our congress of representatives, we approved the working plan of the executive bureau. I liked the speech of a guy from the Kuzbass who made a concrete proposal that we establish our own bank, insurance company, information center, and communication network. We are working now in this direction. We already have created an information center, but we need an apartment for it. But our native "democrats" fail us. In order to acquire an apartment for the information agency, our Russian government fleeced us for 70,000 rubles even though, according to the law on trade unions, they were supposed to grant us an accommodation for free.

We are also setting up an insurance company that will offer both personal and collective insurance for enterprises. But unlike the official All-Union Central Council of Trade Unions [VCSPS], we will not provide social welfare, as they deceive us when they take money from the people and then the trade union delivers the money back to the people and tells them that it is the trade union that does everything for them. They buy people's accommodations on the money that people gave the union in the first place. And where does the huge sum of money go—the trillions that the VCSPS has for social insurance? You can guess where. It may be spent on drink or on creation of a bank. Who knows? It is also necessary to have our own "miners" bank, financed through our economic programs with branches opened in all our regions.

The strike, nevertheless, produced results. Economically, everything in this country is stolen not by us but by the nomenklatura. Everything goes to them, and we get nothing in return. But we won politically with this strike. You will remember that we made five political demands, including the resignation of the president [Gorbachev]. We reached a deadlock. Finally, the Russian parliament founded an interrepublic parliamentary group charged with issuing documents related to a new Union treaty. Working with this group of deputies from the Supreme Soviet were representatives from the workers' movement, our trade unions, and democratic parties. Our leaders [Gorbachev's government], seeing the people begin to work out our problems without them, quickly put together the 9 + 1 agreement. If the details are worked out, this agreement will be profitable for the republics and the center, but we do not know if it will be profitable for us. Unfortunately, they are working out this treaty behind closed doors. Nevertheless, we forced them to sit together because we are bored with all these national strifes. Just look at what is happening in the Baltic states, Kazakhstan, and the southern republics. They want us to bark at each other like malicious dogs, want Russians to go against Ukrainians, Byelorussians against Tatars, and so on. They want to see interethnic slaughter.

And in this situation, our [government] leaders ask the West for millions for a stabilization program. Yesterday, when we met with the American ambassador [Matlock], we warned that if the United States gives trillions to this government, the money will go in the sand. These trillions should be given to specific programs.

Returning to our situation, I would like to stress that it is not prestigious now to work at the mines and factories. The best men leave the mines. So who will stay to manage the mines? All they give us is a piece of bread—our salary. The state will not preoccupy itself with improving our living conditions if we do not do it ourselves. We ourselves must develop our economic independence. You know that the general agreement [GTTS] includes changes in the structure of government and industry. The general agreement offers the possibility of forming budgets of local soviets from the bottom up. This means that independence starts at the lowest levels of government, moving from the rural soviets up to the Supreme Soviet. It also means that we are moving toward the construction of a new state that does not exist yet. It takes time. That is why these guys with the 9 + 1 idea gathered quickly in order to not let it [the new formation of government structures] happen without them. I am sure that they will sign the 9 + 1 agreement quickly because we know our parliaments in the Ukraine, Byelorussia, and Russia.

Let's return now to the structure of our trade union. Frankly speaking, we have cells but we do not have a trade union yet. A trade union is a harmonious structure. We have horizontal structures, which means everyone is on the same level. The salary of trade union leaders will depend on membership dues only. Furthermore, I am against the division of our trade union into national departments. This would kill us at once because if we divide along national lines, it will be easier to struggle with us. There are different laws, however slight, in Byelorussia, Ukraine, and Russia. These differences will hurt our pockets. What shall we do? We should struggle for a unique structure with which we would be able to fight for improving our rights. Laws should be aimed only at improving our rights. What is the difference between a miner in the Rostov region and a miner from the Urals? Labor conditions and living standards are the same. We have different levels of structure in the trade union on the local level, the regional level, and the [coal] basin as a whole. If economic discipline is constructed on such a structure, then workers consider joining our ranks. We now also have our strike fund. When pilots and air traffic controllers announced their plans for a strike, we quickly sent them some hundreds of thousands of rubles as a sign of our solidarity. And [as a result of this act] we were noticed. Our rulers take into consideration those who have money.

The NPG Executive Bureau includes ten men, of which only four are full-time workers and the other six are still at the mine. This indicates that even in the executive bureau, not everyone believes that we have the chance to succeed.

The strike helped push some new laws into place. For example, the law on privatization will finally produce an owner. He will supervise his own industry, but he will have to follow the terms of our agreement [GTTS] and pay us by the hour.

In order to pay us by the hour, it is necessary to change the whole system of wages in this country. But to change these laws, we must create our own lobby in the parliaments of both the Union and the republics. In Russia and Ukraine, such work is already in process, but it has been more difficult at the Union level. We are not well versed with laws and lawmaking, but we have to pressure them to adopt laws that are beneficial to us. We also need our own newspaper. Information bulletins will be issued one of these days and will be sent to the regions.

Regarding the American delegation here, we have signed a preliminary agreement with them.[24] They are meeting with our minister of labor and then flying to the Donbass and Kuzbass. Our main task in working with them is to improve our contracts and receive assistance in making the transition of our coal industry to the market. Then we would like to develop American forms in the mining industry. We have consulted with them and decided to organize an economic and political study of trade union activity. But it is impossible to do everything at once; we must do things little by little. It is necessary to work on forming our cells and working with the bottom structures.

How did you become a politician?

I have worked at the mine for seventeen years. I began working in Lugansk in the Donbass region. In 1979, I moved to the western Donbass, where I was a brigade leader, a unit leader, a combine man and thus passed through all the working structures. This was all before the strike. I have two general technical educations and an unfinished degree in the humanities. Before my military service, I finished a machine-building technical school and then finished a two-year management course in 1989. I was also a student of journalism for three years at Rostov University.

I entered politics when our strike began. At first, our strike was spontaneous and at only one mine as all connections [between mines] were closed. Then our guys passed through the police and GAI [the State Auto Inspection] posts—all the roads were closed then—and united all the mines. From June 17 to 26, 1989, all the mines in the western Donbass were on strike. We organized a strike committee and I was elected chairman. Then we began to establish a union. With the other strike committees, we created the RSCD [Regional Strike Committee of Donbass] based on four regions. There were four representatives elected from every region. We went to Moscow to register the RSCD as a public organization, but we failed. They just inspected and reinspected our regulations and then told us that only the Supreme Soviet [of the Soviet Union] had the authority to approve our agreement. But the Supreme Soviet was not in session, and, besides, this was out of its competence.

Then the strike committee promoted me to participate in trade union activity. I was nominated to become chairman of the trade union committee, but I was not elected. All the mines approved my candidacy and voted for me, but we have a branch trade union that included everybody from salesmen to the administration. These kinds of people did not vote for me. So I continued my work with the strike committee.

According to Resolution 608, five of us were nominated to organize a central commission with the task of registering the RSCD. When we filed to register the RSCD, we started to gather representatives from every strike committee in the region. The commission was invited to attend the congress of trade unions in March of last year [1990].[25] At this congress, we realized that nobody would fight for the interests of miners. So we decided to hold our own congress with the objective of creating our own independent trade union. That was in April [1990].

A bit earlier the Confederation of Labor was created. We set up a commission that made preparations for the congress; Filenko and I and representatives from the strike committees of Donetsk, Kuzbass, and Donbass helped. At the first congress, a resolution was adopted demanding that our Ministry of Mining finance the second congress. An organizational committee began to prepare for the second congress. Beginning in July 1990, I started working on the tariff agreement [GTTS], though I did not know what I was doing.[26] I just began to read documents on our legislation and wrote it. To prepare this document, I investigated Russian legislation, collective contracts and agreements from the United States, Brazil, Germany, Spain, and all the records of the Conciliatory Commission of 1989. In October it was approved by all the strike committees, and it was approved by the commission too.

At the second congress, the Executive Bureau of the Independent Union of Miners was elected, which was made responsible for organizational activity— setting up the cells—and the creation of the general tariff agreement [GTTS]. The first task has been accomplished, but the second—the general tariff agreement—is a difficult and long problem. I already have said that it is necessary to change all the ruling structures gradually. This is why we started with the political struggle, which includes separation from the center and acquiring independence, including economic independence. It is clear that to do anything, it is necessary to construct a new state in which legislative structures would be determined precisely and in which executive and judicial branches of government would be independent.

Pavel Anatolevich, the Confederation of Labor was organized in May 1990. At the same time, an organizational commission on creating the Independent Union of Miners was also established. What is the difference between these two organizations?

The Confederation of Labor refers to those who wanted to go the way of Solidarity—to unite all the parties with all the branches and streams of the workers' movements as well as others in the fight against totalitarianism. But you cannot compare Poland's Solidarity with us because we differ from Poland in many political, geographic, ethnographic, and economic ways. The only thing that united Poland was the fight against Moscow, against occupation. I have tried to show people how our regime is also occupational, but they do not see it. So the Confederation of Labor failed, but people in this organization—people like Mikhail Sobol'—understood that they have to go and create trade unions and that people would be united through them.[27]

We did not have any quarrels with the strike committees as we ourselves are from them. We just thought in a different way. They wanted to unite everybody in a "collective farm" and then go with a banner against the Kremlin, the Communists, and the totalitarian regime. But it is not right. Everybody will not go. Only a profession can unite people. [In a trade union based on a profession], we always know what unites us. It necessary to unite those who have similar hard working conditions. We need to start with them. Those who have more comfortable conditions do not understand us yet. But those who live in difficulties will try to find a comparison, and we will give them an opportunity to join us. We have the same aims: better working conditions of our members. Our demands are first and foremost economic. So it is necessary to unite and fight to change our labor legislation.

What are the main problems in changing the current labor legislation?

We need to have laws respecting the importance of the collective contract. We need laws regarding a minimum wage, the work of women, the work of youth, the length of a working day, and a state insurance. Other problems should be addressed in collective contracts. There is a state and there are workers, but the second side with which we should sign a contract does not exist yet. We have yet to create a class of owners. The state also should protect its interests regarding relations between the owner and the hired worker. But our state is a monopoly, and it will not sign any agreements against itself. It is nonsense.

What are the relations now between local branches of the NPG and the strike committees?

They vary from place to place. For the most part, strike committees have been reorganized into trade union structures. The strike committees are extraordinary and provisional bodies. In new conditions they must reorganize into trade unions.

How are relations between NPG and Democratic Russia?

Do such relations exist? We have no relations. They play their own game.

Do you support any political movement?

Yes. We support Yeltsin's program because it is more radical.

What kind of relations do you have with the Federation of Independent Trade Unions (the FNPR)?

I would like to tell you that I will not have any relations with them because they robbed the Vorkuta miners.[28]

How did that happen?

During the strike, in order to avoid hunger and starvation among the miners, we founded a commodities and raw materials exchange. We signed an agreement in accordance with Pavlov's decree by which the miners were given the right to sell 5–7 percent of the planned coal production. Our exchange was given the right to sell this coal, and the Vorkuta miners were to receive 50 million rubles in advance from the sale of their coal. But our exchange was not registered on an all-Union level. So Yeltsin recognizes only the FNPR and does not understand the workers' movement as it truly exists. The Russian government and the FNPR signed an agreement. In the agreement, the FNPR said that it gave the 50 million rubles to the NPG of Vorkuta, but it took 9 million for its own pocket. What kind of relations should I have with such an organization? It is the same insurance company as VCSPS; it deceives people with this state insurance. But they went even further, for those factories that have established FNPR branches are given special tax privileges. But what about the others? We can see that the FNPR is the same old structure, just a bit more to the left.

What kind of a relationship do you have with Russia's leaders?

We do not have any kind of a relationship. We must work out an arrangement under which we could sign the tariff agreement [GTTS] with the Russian government. But now they do not see us as a partner. When [Lane] Kirkland, the president of the AFL-CIO, visited here, he asked Yeltsin, "What do you think about the new trade unions?" Yeltsin answers, "Yes, we have signed an agreement . . ." Kirkland interrupts, "Oh, no, I do not mean the VCSPS. I mean the new movement." Yeltsin continues, "Yes, we signed an agreement, we see that trade unions are a force." Kirkland responds, "But I mean the new trade unions." But Yeltsin does not acknowledge them. He says, "Excuse me, there is a congress."

But he knows us very well. We have met. But he is an old apparat member. He profits from FNPR because that structure works on behalf of the state and has signed agreements that do not improve our life. The Russian government does not want independent structures.

So there is an attempt to ignore independent and free trade unions?

Well, this is their approach. But honestly speaking, workers' committees and our trade union organized this entire strike. And we in our work are guided only by our regulations and our rights. We submit only to the decisions of our members. Is this profitable for the state? Of course not.

What is your attitude toward privatization?

We have a very normal attitude [toward privatization]. According to our general agreement [GTTS], there must be two sides of any negotiation. But the second side will appear only after privatization.

Who should be an owner and what is the best method of privatization?

There should be all forms of ownership—collective, private, and joint-stock companies. But I personally think that joint-stock companies are the best.

What is your attitude toward Gorbachev?

What kind of an attitude can one have to a man if he is president. He is not a friend or an enemy but the president. He also does not want us.

But the miners' strike supported Yeltsin; didn't it pull the mining industry from Gorbachev to Yeltsin, from the Union to Russia?

No, that is nonsense. We never tried to go from Gorbachev to Yeltsin, from Gorbachev to Fokin, or from Gorbachev to Nazarbayev. We just asserted that every republic should have its sovereignty. If the central structures move into the republics and obstruct development, there will not be any sovereignty.

What are the main problems facing miners and the Independent Union of Miners?

The most important new problem new is the wage and changes in it.

Are you seeking higher wages or changes in the principles of allocating wages?

We want changes in the principles. We do not make anything up. We just remember how it was before the revolution, how it was during the NEP [New Economic Policy], and how it was during the crisis of the 1930s. We simply argue that the wage should be based on a consumer's basket.

Many workers are now demanding an hourly wage.

That is exactly right because right now the wage does not depend on the miner or his capabilities. I have a sixth category qualification. I can earn 30 rubles a shift according to old rates. But my wage does not depend on my qualification. It depends on such things as whether or not we will have electric energy. Will they give us strengthening material or not? Everything depends on such things, on the organization, on the work process. Unfortunately, centralization does not give us any control over these matters. This is why we favor privatization. Why should we be against privatization when we will have direct contracts, obligations, and a person before us who will take responsibility for everything? Why should we go against it? We should fight for it and greet it.

What are the main obstacles to the further development of the NPG?

We need to construct a lawful state. But this does not depend on the NPG. For instance, in order to change the wage system, it is necessary to change everything, to construct a law-based state.

Now we are uniting. We are planning to hold a congress of independent trade unions and working movements from all over the country in order to create a trade union structure based on professions. Pilots, aviation controllers, fishermen, the Confederation of Labor, miners, the trade union of free businessmen, and the trade union of cooperators will all participate. The doors are open to everybody.

Who are your main allies from the new movements and organizations in constructing a lawful state?

New movements and new parties speak about it, including first of all the Christian Democrats and the Party of Free Labor. But there is no real party besides the Communist Party. Travkin's party has no authority now. Democratic Russia has even less.

What kinds of workers are you hoping to attract to your trade union? I mean, who first of all takes part in your activities?

Not everyone has joined us. Some did not come because they did not realize what a trade union is. They know what a strike committee is. But what is a trade union? Those who did come to us are active people who live and work in bad conditions. Where there are strike committees, there are strong trade unions.

Do you have white-collar workers such as engineers in the trade union?

We have very few. This is because an engineer is connected strongly with the old system. He is blocked. Although we have abolished discipline regulations, nevertheless an engineer's salary depends on the director and the administration. We tell them, "Guys, unite together at every mine. We will accept you." Their interests needed to be protected by a trade union. The construction of a lawful state requires three structures of trade unions: trade unions for hired workers, trade unions for employers, and trade unions for state employers.

You have had some contacts with the AFL-CIO. How do they help you?

They are teaching us how to use seven new computers. And if they see that the working movement develops further and unites several trade unions, they will help us in this sphere [i.e., organizing a coalition of trade unions]. But we do not rely on Western help. Our own happiness depends on us.

Documents

· ·

The following documents give the flavor of the kinds of demands the strikes were based on and the kinds of issues facing the development of the Independent Union of Miners. The first document is the protocol that ended the 1989 strikes in the Donbass region. Because of space limitations, this abridged version does not include all forty-seven demands. The second document is a statement of general principles issued by the striking miners of the Kuzbass region. The resolutions adopted at the founding congress of the Independent Union of Miners are the third set of documents. The fourth document is the list of demands from the 1991 strikes. Finally, the fifth document is the agreement that ended the 1991 strikes.

Document 1: Protocol on agreed measures between the miners' strike committee of the city of Donetsk and the Commission of the USSR Council of Ministers and the All-Union Central Council of Trade Unions

July 20–22, 1989, Donetsk

The strike committee and the Commission of the USSR Council of Ministers and the All-Union Central Council of Trade Unions note that the socioeconomic situation in Donbass has deteriorated as a result of social services and amenities remaining inadequate for a long time. This came as a consequence of the dictates and arbitrary actions of ministries and economic agencies, the connivance of the local Communist Party, government, and economic bodies, and worsened supplies of foodstuffs and basic necessities for the population.

As a result, a spontaneous strike ensued, starting at individual mines of the Makeyevugol production amalgamation and spreading to pits in Kuzbass.

Having considered the demands of striking mines, the strike committee, the Commission of the USSR Council of Ministers, and the All-Union Council of Trade Unions have come to the following agreement:

1. To grant complete economic and legal independence to mines, enterprises, and organizations of the coal-mining industry in Donbass upon demands by their worker collectives and in accordance with the USSR Law on State Enterprises [Amalgamations]. . . .

2. To instruct the USSR Ministry of the Coal-Mining Industry to draw

up, within a month, proposals on the size of state orders for coal-mining enterprises, with a view to making it possible for an enterprise to supply products over and above the state order as it sees fit at negotiated prices. . . .

3. To instruct the USSR Committee on Prices and the USSR Ministry of the Coal-Mining Industry to make provisions in the draft decision on wholesale price reform for increasing prices on coal in keeping with the actual costs of mining. . . .

4. To bind the USSR Ministry of the Coal-Mining Industry to prepare, within a week, and submit to the USSR Council of Ministers proposals for changing the normative correlations of the growth of pay and labor productivity, proceeding from the need to furnish more favorable conditions for Donbass enterprises to stimulate their employees. . . .

5. To introduce, from July 1, 1989, pay raises for coal-mining personnel for work during night and evening shifts, amounting respectively to 40 and 20 percent of the wage rate [salary rate]. . . .

6. To introduce payment, as of August 1, for workers permanently employed on underground jobs (including section foremen) for the time it takes them to travel from the shaft to the working and back, amounting to 100 percent of the wage rate [salary rate].

7. To instruct the USSR Ministry of Public Health, the USSR Ministry of the Coal-Mining Industry, and the USSR State Committee on Labor jointly. . . .

8. To establish a differentiated scale for determining the size of pensions, bearing in mind that with a record of twenty-five years of work underground a pension should amount to 70 percent of one's average earnings and with a ten-year length of service underground, to 50 percent of one's average earnings. . . .

17. To demand that the All-Union Central Council of Trade Unions and the Central Committee of the Union of Workers in the Coal-Mining Industry increase the number of places available to miners, in the first place those convalescing after injuries or chronic patients at rest homes, sanatoriums, and guest houses. . . .

To bind the All-Union Central Council of Trade Unions to return to miners the sanatoriums that earlier belonged to the USSR Ministry of the Coal-Mining Industry by January 1, 1990. . . .

If a miner is killed on the job, to grant his family a one-time allowance amounting to his yearly earnings, by decision of the respective worker collective council.

To provide the bereaved family, if need be, with a well-appointed apartment within the next three to six months. . . .

19. To guarantee the immunity of all strikers and members of the strike committee.

After the strike, to organize, under the guidance of strike committees, new elections to worker collective councils and, jointly with labor union organizations, those to the labor union committees of mines and enterprises of the coal-mining industry. To instruct the new worker collective councils to decide, at general meetings, the issue of new elections to the posts of enterprise directors and mine managers. In order to conduct this work, members of the miners' strike committee will be relieved for two weeks of their regular jobs, while continuing to draw their average pay. The strike committee will select the time for preparing and holding the elections as it sees fit.

20. In the opinion of the strike committee of the city of Donetsk, the Donetskugol city administration is a redundant managerial link, and it is expedient to abolish it, while donating its building to the social security system for use by orphans, the disabled, and so on.

To call on strike committees in other cities to back this demand.

21. To demand that the USSR Council of Ministers not withdraw more than 30 percent of profits earned by worker collectives.

To consider it expedient to cancel compulsory contributions to the Ministry of the Coal-Mining Industry. To establish that as of January 1, 1990, contributions to the ministry's centralized fund should be made voluntarily by the decision of worker collective councils for specific sectoral programs in which the worker collectives would like to take part.

22. To instruct the USSR State Committee on Labor and the All-Union Central Council of Trade Unions to stipulate, when drafting a bill on pensions, and propose to the USSR Council of Ministers and the USSR Supreme Soviet that preferential term pensions earlier granted to retirees in the coal-mining industry should be increased in keeping with new pension legislation.

23. To grant, as of August 1, 1989, worker collective councils the right to declare common days off on Sundays.

24. To instruct the USSR Ministry of the Coal-Mining Industry in keeping with the USSR Law on State Enterprises [Amalgamations] to conduct preparations for introducing a common day off on Sundays for working people at Donbass coal-mining enterprises not later than the second quarter of 1990.

25. To instruct the USSR State Committee on Labor to submit to the USSR Council of Ministers, by the end of 1989, amendments to the draft law on taxes on the population that would provide for exempting one-time length-of-service bonuses from income taxes.

To ask the USSR Supreme Soviet to envision in the new USSR law on taxes on the population that one-time length-of-service bonuses to workers in the coal-mining industry be exempted from taxes. (To make the proposal to the USSR Supreme Soviet before October 1, 1989.)

26. To rule out the denial of one-time length-of-service bonuses to anyone for any reason. To regard length-of-service bonuses as immutable.

27. To ask the USSR Council of Ministers and the Ukrainian Council of Ministers to resolve the issue of supplying coal-mining enterprises, starting from 1990, with construction materials for individual builders and for repairs of old housing. . . .

43. To instruct the USSR Ministry of the Coal-Mining Industry and the Central Committee of the Union of the Workers in the Coal-Mining Industry to establish a supply quota for toilet soap for workers in the Donbass coal-mining industry at 800 grams a month, starting from August 1989.

44. To issue miners, by decision of worker collective councils, soap over and above the existing norms at the expense of the social development fund. . . .

46. To recognize the need, in view of the strike (from its beginning till July 22, 1989, including the night shift), to adjust coal production plans for mines without reducing the wage fund. To compensate workers involved in the strike for this period with payment according to their wage rates, as an exception.

47. The standing strike committee, whose representatives should be involved in discussing miners' demands at every level, is the guarantor of the fulfillment of the miners' demands.

L. D. Ryabev,   A.D. Bokarev,
Deputy Chairman,   *Chairman,*
USSR Council of Ministers   *Strike Committee*

V.A. Masol,   P.I. Poberezhny,
Chairman,   *Deputy Chairman,*
Ukrainian Council   *Strike Committee*
of Ministers

V.N. Makeyev,   V.I. Shcherbakov,
Secretary,   *Chairman,*
All-Union Central Council   *USSR State Committee*
of Trade Unions   *on Labor and Social Issues*

A.P. Fisun,
First Deputy Minister
of the Coal-Mining Industry

*Document 2: Policy-setting statement by
the Alliance of Working People of Kuzbass
(Adopted by the 4th Conference of the Alliance of
Working People of Kuzbass on November 19–20, 1989)*

Having achieved after the October 1917 revolution, as everyone knows, great successes in creating an independent economy, ensuring victory over nazism, breaking through into space, and tackling a number of social tasks, Soviet society over recent years has been gripped by severe economic, political, and ideological crises.

The economic crisis is marked by declining production growth, which often hits zero level, disappearing incentives for scientific and technological progress, lack of individual motivation to increase efficiency, worsening social problems, soaring inflation, and plummeting living standards.

In the sphere of power, the crisis is reflected in the replacement of the socialist government of the people and for the people by the authority of a narrow circle of persons representing the bureaucratic upper crust and in the underdevelopment of society's democratic institutions.

In the political and ideological fields, the crisis manifests itself in the ideology of communism having become discredited in the eyes of broad popular masses and in the absence of political and legal institutions that would guarantee the openness of society and essential freedoms for its citizens.

The order of the day includes the task of the revolutionary transformation of the economic and political systems of socialism and the overhaul of the structures of power and administration. The proclaimed course of perestroika and the methods it has involved so far have been conciliatory rather than reformist in nature. The policy pursued so far has been one of isolated, partial, and unduly slow changes that have been exceptionally painful for working people. The revolution started by the Communist Party from above may suffer defeat if not supported from below. It is this function that is being assumed by the Alliance of Working People of Kuzbass, founded as a sociopolitical organization.

The Alliance of Working People of Kuzbass, while proclaiming socialist ideals as its own, will at the same time wholly rely on universally shared values.

Economic Platform.   . . . The Alliance of Working People of Kuzbass sees its fundamental task as dismantling the bureaucratic command system in the economy and the transfer of the right to manage wealth to those who create it. The alliance recognizes the equality of all forms of ownership possible under socialism— public, state, republican, municipal, collective, cooperative, work-related private, joint stock, mixed, personal, and others. . . .

The Alliance of Working People of Kuzbass proclaims the maximum satisfaction of people's material and cultural requirements and their all-round development to be the priority goal of economic progress. It is free time, life expectancy, the people's physical and moral health, and their cultural development level rather than gross national product that should be the yardstick for economic success.

. . . Efforts to realign economic machinery should focus on cost accounting, which presupposes the real independence of production units, their moral responsibility to one another, and mutual benefits in relations. The principle of cost accounting has been declared in our economy for many decades, but there is no profit-and-loss accounting at our enterprises even today. The bureaucratic command system of economic management tenaciously holds the line even after worker strikes, prompted mostly by demands to adopt the pay-your-own-way system.

The Alliance of Working People of Kuzbass makes this challenging problem the centerpiece of its activities in the economic sphere. . . .

Market relations are an invaluable experience of human civilization, and the absence of a market harms the Soviet economy. Combined with planning, an invention of the twentieth century, the market should become the primary form of enterprises' relations among themselves and consumers. Regulation should be done only by economic levers—taxes, investment policies, preferential crediting, subsidies, price limits. . . .

Worker collectives should have real opportunities to choose any form of ownership and economic management, including opportunities to lease factories, workshops, stores, and other projects or buy them out from the state. In this way, an enterprise may be state owned but leased, public, collective, cooperative, individual [private], or mixed.

The Alliance of Working People of Kuzbass rejects the use of private property based on the exploitation of man by man but accepts work-related private property based on individual or family labor. . . .

The Alliance of Working People of Kuzbass will press, through local governing councils, for uniform ecological policies concerning the use of nature and for the transfer of full power in these issues to the councils. The alliance also believes it essential to facilitate the creation of a Shora National Park.

Political Platform.

1. The Alliance of Working People of Kuzbass, representing and protecting popular interests, will proceed in its activities from the fact that in the USSR there is not and cannot be any other system of power than that of soviets of People's Deputies. . . .

3. People power can be achieved only by democratizing the electoral system. The Alliance of Working People of Kuzbass will press for direct elections to the Supreme Soviet of the USSR and the Russian Federation,

direct elections of the chairman of the USSR Supreme Soviet and the chairmen of governing councils at every level. [The alliance also supports] a ban on membership in any two governing councils at the same time, the abolition of elections to government councils from social organizations without polls in constituencies, the abrogation of district electoral meetings, and guaranteed possibilities for citizens and social organizations to monitor all stages in election procedures and protest in court all cases of violations of legislation on elections.

The alliance supports the creation of party, social, scientific, and organizational structures of the Russian Federation. . . .

The alliance is prepared to cooperate with religious organizations in educating people on spiritual and moral ideals.

Consistently upholding the interests of working people, the alliance will show unfailing concern for the education and promotion of its leaders to be able to take an active part in all election campaigns and for their nomination as candidates to serve on governing councils. The alliance will act through them to project its goals and tasks and uphold the interests and ideology of working people. . . .

6. The Alliance of Working People of Kuzbass is clearly aware that the continued democratization of society is impossible without radical political reform. Possible related measures could include granting Soviet nationals the right to freely form sociopolitical, social, professional, and youth organizations acting within the framework of federal laws, ensuring the possibility of referendums on major issues of public life, giving citizens free access to any information that is not a state secret, realizing people's right to freely buy duplicating equipment and use it for legitimate purposes, giving organizations the right and opportunity to publish newspapers and magazines, and putting an end to the imposition of stereotypes in culture.

7. It is a reality that the Communist Party remains the nucleus of the political system in the USSR. The alliance considers it its duty to openly formulate its attitude to the Party's guiding role in society, which is sealed in the USSR constitution. The Communist Party has covered a long path strewn with heroic accomplishments and tragedies. It is entitled to claim the guiding role in society. But this role must be won by one's prestige rather than be forced on society through legislative acts. Therefore, we shall press for scrapping Article Six of the constitution.

The long existence of a single party has caused our society great harm because this institutionalized its monopoly on working out the strategy and tactics of economic and political development. Any monopoly leads to stagnation. The alliance supports the existing opinion about the possibility and expediency of a multiparty system in the USSR. But the Alliance of Working People of Kuzbass does not claim the role of a party. . . .

9. The Alliance of Working People of Kuzbass will exert great efforts to fight red tape, administrative outrages, formalism, and disregard for worker needs. Bureaucratism has grown to dangerous proportions, becoming a chronic social ill and the principal brake on society's development. We see a remedy for this ill in establishing the full power of the people and for the people, in fulfilling the tasks of radical economic reform, reorganizing administrative agencies along democratic principles, increasing public openness in society, and making all state and social institutions readily accessible to the people. . . .

Joining the mass movement supporting perestroika, the Alliance of Working People of Kuzbass assumes full responsibility for the results of its activities in pursuing its objectives.

Document 3: Resolutions of the First Congress of Miners, the city of Donetsk, June 1990

Resolution of the First Congress of Miners on the socioeconomic situation, the fulfillment of USSR Council of Ministers' Resolution No. 608, and outlook for the transition to a market. Having discussed the social and economic position of miners, the implementation of USSR Council of Ministers' Resolution No. 608, and prospects for the coal-mining industry's work in a market environment, the First Congress of Miners of the USSR notes that our principal problems are the same that confront the overwhelming majority of working people. All of us live under the administer-by-command system. The monopoly of state property that is characteristic of it, and the absence of a market and of competition, doom the economy to stagnation and backwardness and the people to misery. This country is poor because all our economy is improperly organized.

The nation's top leaders have promised to rectify the situation.

But life demonstrates that they do not pursue reform in real earnest and that the social and economic situation in the country is at breaking point. In the latest government program we do not see, once again, any concrete proposals, save price hikes. The top priority is to form a government that would be competent and resolute enough to do away with the monopoly of state property and the effective monopoly of the Soviet Communist Party in politics and effect a real transition to a market and democracy.

The last few months have demonstrated that the incumbent cabinet is unable to do this. This is why we demand its resignation. . . .

This is our main demand, and we believe that it expresses not only our own interests but also the interests of the vast majority of working people.

Demanding the formation of a government that would ensure the switchover to a market economy and guaranteed democracy, we believe that such a transition must not be too painful for the majority of people and should involve mechanisms for social protection. It is especially significant to work out measures concerning job placement and unemployment. . . . The closure of loss-making enterprises should be allowed only if their staffs refuse to take these enterprises into their collective ownership for free. The gratis transfer of basic assets should also be widely used in other cases of the changeover to collective, joint-stock, and individual ownership.

Decisive cuts in military spending and in aid to other countries, in particular, to totalitarian regimes, may also be very important to facilitating the transition to a market. We believe that it is only under these conditions that the working people will give the government the credit of trust that is indispensable to reform.

Should our prime demand—the government's resignation—remain unfulfilled, all responsibility for the deterioration of the political situation in the country will be with the USSR Supreme Soviet and Congress of People's Deputies.

Resolution of the First Congress of Miners of the USSR on relations with the Soviet Communist Party. The First Congress of Miners of the USSR, reflecting the will of its delegates, stresses the complete independence of worker organizations in the coal and mining industries from any political associations. Independent working-class movements and organizations of working people are subordinate only to the will of their members and take the view that no political forces and parties may guide them. Our desire for independence determines our attitude to the Soviet Communist Party. Although the Communist Party is living through a deep crisis, it still attempts, through its steering bodies, to retain its monopoly on power, claiming that only that Party could consolidate society. We strongly disagree with this. It is true that five years ago some leaders of the Party launched the perestroika drive. But today, the Communist Party hampers reform in society to a greater extent than it facilitates it. The more conservative forces have been gaining in strength and becoming organized in the Communist Party over recent months. The Party leadership and apparatus are losing their prestige. The grass roots response to government proposals attests to the lack of trust not only in the cabinet but also in the ruling Party. The Communist Party asserts that it remains a party of the working class and its vanguard. We are workers as well, but we do not regard the Communist Party, in its present form, as our party. Preparations for its 28th Congress do not offer any serious hopes that the Communist Party is capable of decisive renewal. This is why we treat with understanding the mass exodus from the Party.

We demand that the Communist Party be deprived of its privileged position at our enterprises and in our organizations right away. Communist Party committees and Young Communist League locals must be withdrawn from the enterprises.

Privileged length-of-service arrangements for full-time Communist Party and Young Communist League functionaries must be abolished. We believe that as a multiparty system emerges, the Communist Party's property created by the people should be nationalized and real possibilities created for the activities of other parties.

Document 4: Statement by plenipotentiary representatives of striking enterprises that took part in talks with the USSR Cabinet of Ministers and president on April 2–3, 1991, (April 4, 1991, Moscow)

The USSR Cabinet of Ministers' resolutions and ordinances issued as a result of the talks do not meet fully even the demands of the agreed protocols of 1989. Failing to provide either for the complete preferential pension list [one profession was excluded from it] or for the indexation of wages in view of the overall growth of the price index since July 1989, they suggest instead phased pay increases by 25 percent a quarter, whereas prices have already more than doubled since July 1989.

Most dangerously, the talks did not produce an agreement on a mechanism for halting the strike, and, therefore, the striking enterprises are not only unable to take advantage of the above pay raises but are also complete bankrupts and do not have the money needed to resume work.

These developments demonstrate the true intentions of the Cabinet of Ministers and president—the entire system of power: to put an end to the strike at all costs, split the miners' movement, and doom the striking enterprises to closures and their collectives to hunger and poverty.

The response can be only one, the fulfillment of all demands made by the ongoing strike:

1. Resignation of the federal president, who does not have the mandate of popular trust and wages an offensive against his own people

2. Dissolution of the USSR Supreme Soviet and Congress of People's Deputies as having failed to justify the trust of the people

3. Resignation of the federal Cabinet of Ministers, which does not have a program to go out of the crisis

4. Transfer of supreme authority to the federation council of sovereign states, their parliaments and governments

5. Conclusion of the standard general wage-rate agreement adopted by the Second Congress of Miners throughout the coal-mining industry, and similar agreements providing for fair working conditions and pay in other industries, as desired by their working people

We urge all miners and all working people to join the strike.

Document 5: Resolution of a joint conference of the Interregional Coordinating Council of Worker [Strike] Committees and the Independent Union of Miners, May 14, 1991

Having discussed the political and economic situation at the local level resulting from the spring strike of 1991, the Interregional Coordinating Council of Worker [Strike] Committees and the Independent Union of Miners declare that despite the basic political demands—an immediate resignation of the president and disbandment of the USSR Congress of People's Deputies—remaining unfulfilled, the strike has

- Greatly expedited the realization by most strikers and others that real improvements in the social and economic position of working people are impossible without dismantling the existing totalitarian state and political system and ending the Communist Party's monopoly on power from top to bottom—from federal to factory levels
- Helped reveal who among statesmen, political leaders, and sociopolitical organizations and movements really are allies of working people and who are only capable of sloganeering
- Facilitated deliverance from "paternalism" and from faith in a "good" czar, president, and like saviors of the fatherland and people

As a result of the walkouts

- An interrepublic parliamentary group has been created that worked out a mechanism for realizing the strike's political demands
- The practical and irreversible process of devolution of power from the center to the republics has picked up on the basis of enterprises' withdrawal from federal control to go under republic jurisdiction
- The strikers' economic demands have been partially satisfied, and republic governments and the federal Cabinet of Ministers recognized the need for a wage-rate agreement
- The exodus of working people from state-sponsored labor unions to join the independent miners' union has quickened

The strike has helped the working-class movement to strengthen its unity and transcend the bounds of the coal-mining industry.

Connections and cooperation between worker [strike] committees, the Independent Union of Miners, democratic labor unions, and sociopolitical movements and organizations have become closer.

P. Shushpanov,   A. Malykhin,
Chairman,   *Chairman,*
Executive Bureau,   *Interregional Coordinating Council*
Independent Union of Miners   *of Worker [Strike] Committees*

chapter ten

The Neo-Communists

Under Gorbachev, different ideological factions within the monolithic Communist Party of the Soviet Union began to splinter into independent political organizations, first as factions, later as platforms, and finally as new political parties.[1] The Democratic Platform, Communists for Democracy, the Republican Party of Russia, the People's Party for a Free Russia (Rutskoi), and the Movement for Democratic Reform all grew out of the liberal wing of the Communist Party. From the right, though less well known, several political platforms, fronts, and parties also proliferated as the authority of the CPSU centrist leader, Mikhail Gorbachev, began to wane.

Although struggles between liberals and conservatives[2] had polarized much earlier behind Gorbachev and Yegor Ligachev, the first significant neocommunist formation materialized in 1989 with the founding of the United Workers' Front (OFT).[3] OFT was founded July 15–16, 1989, in Leningrad on an all-Union basis, but its more substantive manifestation occurred when the Russian United Workers' Front was founded September 8–9, 1989, in Sverdlovsk.[4] According to the OFT's own count, the congress was attended by 110 delegates from twenty-nine Russian cities as well as guest representatives from Russian minorities living outside the Russian Federation. Organizers of OFT included Venyamin Yarin, a USSR people's deputy later appointed to Gorbachev's Presidential Council, CPSU Central Committee members Alexei Sergeyev, Igor Malyarov, Victor Anpilov, Richard Kosolapov, and communist philosopher Vladimir Yakushev.[5] Groups such as Nina Andreeva's Stalinist front Edinstvo and the Marxist Platform of the CPSU also sent representatives to attend the inaugural congresses.[6] Despite its name, however, the OFT attracted few workers to either the Union or the Russian founding congresses. The core of the organization, in fact, consisted of institute and university instructors from scientific socialism faculties who had organized an association of communist instructors some months before the creation of OFT.

Ideologically, OFT promoted classic communist causes. Leaders of the front called on workers to resist all market reforms, defend Russia from becoming a Western colony, liquidate speculation of cooperatives, and support the struggle against bourgeois nationalists. To guarantee that workers' interests prevail, OFT argued that people's deputies to soviets should represent workplaces rather than residential districts.[7] Finally, OFT leaders argued that Russia needs to rekindle the idea of a dictatorship of the proletariat struggling against the emerging capitalist and bureaucratic dictatorship.[8]

Despite initial fears of a neocommunist renaissance, candidates affiliated with the United Workers' Front fared poorly in the 1989 and 1990 elections.[9] Again, in the June 1991 presidential elections, the United Workers' Front ticket of General Albert Makashov and Aleksei Sergeyev garnered less than 2 percent of the vote.[10] OFT was supported by the CPSU's apparatus but only on the lowest levels, as official CPSU policy (as determined by General Secretary Gorbachev) considered the OFT to be a renegade organization.

Communist Initiative and the Russian Communist Party

Despite the lack of popular support, the United Workers' Front served as the nucleus for the formation of several other neocommunist organizations.[11] Most important, the Communist Initiative Movement was created at the second OFT congress in January 1990 in Leningrad.[12] Based on classic communist principles, this initiative aimed to create a Russian Communist Party, an objective realized June 19–20, 1990. More than twenty-five hundred delegates attended this founding conference at which Ivan Polozkov was elected first secretary of the Central Committee of the new Russian Communist Party.[13]

Initially, the Russian Communist Party claimed to represent the true interests of true Communists as opposed to the revisionist agenda of the liberal CPSU. However, Alexander Rutskoi, the future Russian vice-president, still served on the Central Committee of the Russian Communist Party when he formed the Communists for Democracy faction in the Russian parliament. When Rutskoi's parliamentary faction began preparing to create a new party, now called the People's Party for a Free Russia (Narodnaya Partiya Svobodnoi Rossii), the

Russian Communist Party threatened to expel it.[14] At this stage, the Russian Communist Party represented the most conservative forces in the CPSU.

Postcommunism Communism

Relations between liberal and conservative wings within the Soviet and Russian Communist parties became a moot issue after all Communist parties were banned in the wake of the August putsch, when the conservative Communists went underground. By the fall of 1991, however, they had reorganized their ranks under new political party headings. Victor Anpilov, Richard Kosolapov, and others from the Moscow branch of the United Workers' Front created Trudovaya Moskva (Working Moscow) and later Trudovaya Rossiya (Working Russia), united fronts of new communist clubs, organizations, and parties that formed after the dissolution of the CPSU. Neocommunist groups that sprouted after the coup included the Workers' Soviets, the Union of Communists, the Working Party of Communists, the Socialist Workers' Party, the Marxist Workers' Party, the Independent Trade Union of Workers' Defense (Nezavisimii Profsoyuz Rabochikh 'Zachita'), the Russian Communist Workers' Party (Ekaterinburg), the movement Nashi, the Party of Popular Prosperity, the Federation of Communists Movement, the All-Union Communist Party of Bolsheviks, the Worker-Peasant Socialist Party, and a new Komsomol.[15]

After the putsch these organizations joined together to organize several antigovernment demonstrations, first to recognize the October revolution, then to protest the collapse of the Soviet Union and the Russian Federation, and finally to protest the Yeltsin economic reform.[16] These neo-Communists have been keen to highlight the unlawful acts of the "dictatorship" of the Russian government, especially the disregard for the results of the March 17, 1991, referendum in which a majority voted for the preservation of the USSR.[17] Their slogans have become increasingly nationalistic and patriotic and less dogmatically Marxist in an effort to attract nationalists and Fascists to their demonstrations.[18] A demonstration February 23, 1992—formerly the Day of the Soviet Army—ended in a bloody clash between Moscow militia and communist demonstrators.[19]

The actual number of supporters attending neocommunist demonstrations has not increased significantly over the course of their almost biweekly demonstrations throughout the winter and spring of 1992. These organizations have, however, succeeded in several campaigns, creating the impression of a growing neocommunist movement. Most important, these neocommunist organizations conducted daily demonstrations outside the television station Ostankino from June 12 to June 22, 1992, to demand access to that government entity.[20] Eventually, Russian special forces violently dispersed these pickets, but the government did grant the opposition movements a weekly television program on which to air their views. Neocommunist leaders considered the Ostankino campaign a major victory.[21]

Whether these neocommunist organizations will threaten the stability of the new Russian state or subside to become a marginal nuisance remains to be seen. Working with former local leaders of the CPSU, the Russian Communist Workers' Party, the All-Union Communist Party of Bolsheviks, and the more moderate Socialist Workers' Party have already established local cells in almost every region and main city in Russia.[22] Trudovaya Rossiya and its local affiliates have also been successful in coordinating simultaneous demonstrations throughout the Russian Federation, giving these forces an organizational structure rivaled by few groups on the democratic ledger.[23] Violent wars on Russia's borders, a worsening economic situation, evidence of government corruption, and the threat of a disintegrating Russian Federation give these neocommunist organizations issues around which to mobilize popular support.[24] If executed in alliance with patriotic organizations, a persistent antigovernment campaign launched by these groups could undermine Yeltsin's regime.

The communist banner, however, mobilizes mostly older generations longing for the stability of the past. Communism as an idea has been thoroughly discredited in Russia, making a communist revival in the spirit of the CPSU legacy remote. However, political instability coupled with further economic collapse will continue to offer opportunities to all extremists from both the left and the right. In this context, these neocommunist groups, especially in alliance with extremist organizations on the right, still have a political future—a future that threatens both Yeltsin's government and Russia's democratic prospects more generally.

Richard Kosolapov

Born in 1930, Richard Kosolapov has been a leading communist philosopher and a loyal CPSU functionary for most of his adult life. After receiving his Ph.D. from the Philosophy Department at Moscow State University, Kosolapov worked as a lecturer first for the Komsomol and later for the Central Committee of the CPSU. He eventually became a member of the CPSU Central Committee and worked for its apparat. From 1976 until 1986, he was the chief editor of *Kommunist*, the main theoretical journal for the Communist Party. In the early 1980s, Kosolapov was a close adviser to Yurii Andropov. In 1986, Kosolapov retired from active CPSU activity and became a professor at Moscow State University. However, the new political climate created by perestroika and glasnost' drew Kosolapov back into active political life. Beginning in 1988, Kosolapov helped organize several communist movements and parties independent of the Communist Party of the Soviet Union, including the Association of Scientific Communism, the United Workers' Front, the Communist Initiative Movement, and the Russian Communist Party. Since the August 1991 coup attempt, Kosolapov has actively participated in almost every new neocommunist organization, including Trudovaya Moskva and Trudovaya Rossiya.

Interview with
Richard Kosolapov (April 1991)
· ·

How did you first become involved in politics?
My involvement dates back many years, well before this new stage of politics. I am old. My generation is the war generation. The war [World War II] started when I was eleven years old. This war raised the consciousness of the population. First, we all became patriots as a result of our common misery, but we were oriented toward the collective as a way of emerging from this disaster. So when I was fifteen or sixteen, I accepted this orientation and was in love with all humanity.

However, my attitude toward politics was also shaped by my father's repression. My father participated in the war, but when he was forty-six, he was imprisoned for six years [after the war]. Stalin was still alive. I was sixteen years old.

In connection with my father's fate, my Komsomol career was delayed. After graduation from the university, I did work with the Komsomol. The place [the Komsomol] was rotten, and I had no desire to work there at that time because I only thought of my scientific future. But I resigned myself to this destiny. I then parted with Komsomol work forever but kept with me the experience of formality gained from those callow youth who tried to maintain their bureaucratic leadership. After that, I was busy for a very long period with my scientific research. I returned to politics in the mid-1960s, when I was invited to work in the Central Committee of the CPSU apparatus. My scientific research, however, was never that far removed from politics.

What position did you occupy in the Komsomol?
I was an instructor and leader of a lecture group on a regional committee. Then, in 1966, I came to the Central Committee as a lecturer. A year later, I became a consultant, and two years after that I was appointed the chief of the Central Committee's lecture group. At the end of my formal Party activity [before retiring], I was the editor of the journal *Kommunist* and a member of the Central Committee of the CPSU and the Supreme Soviet of the USSR. I was particularly active during the time when Andropov was general secretary of the Central Committee of the CPSU. After this period, I received a very good retirement and began working at my native university [Moscow State].

All these Party posts, however, are only formal appointments. I always felt that I had a duty to carry out an idea without respect to which position I occupied.

This is why I have not simply reverted back to the academic routine now but continue to work to save the communist movement in our country. I think that the communist idea is immortal, notwithstanding any tragedy of this idea or the tragedy of its bearers. In politics, it can be said that I was born in politics and will die in politics. But in what politics? That is the question. I think [Mikhail] Sholokhov excellently expressed one of the features of the real Communist—this is the communist disinterestedness. So I look on my former friends and colleagues with sorrow as they betray the truth of the ideals of their youth.

What role are you playing in the new political structures today?

Well, the new political structures have not consolidated yet but are in the process of forming. I am a devotee to the CPSU's fate. But I see within the Party now that a social-democratic, better to say a social-liberal, deviation is predominating thanks to initiatives from above. So, I prefer to belong to the left wing. I try to counteract these deviations and not conceal my opinion. The Initiative Movement of the Russian Communists exists now. It declared its all-Union status in April [1991]. In Russia, three million people support this movement. The process of developing this movement is beginning now. We will not permit them to destroy the communist movement or the Communist Party. We do not conceive the communist movement in the dogmatic, bureaucratic variant. We use classical sources and regard communism as real humanism in the spirit of Marx's early works. Communism is the most democratic system for the masses. We recognize the democracy of the workers and reject the democracy of the propertied classes. We return to the classical axioms that the liberty slogan is always false if it contradicts the liberation of work from capital. Only wage-earning people are the social basis of our movement. Changes in the social structure are leading to the crisis of the working masses who are suffering greatly from the present perestroika process. People are becoming destitute due to the economic measures of this year, including the intelligentsia, which does not belong to the elite, that is, the engineers, teachers, doctors, the technicians, the designers, and some parts of the scientific community.

Over half the people supporting and participating in the Communist Initiative come from the intelligentsia. The main body comprises people from the social sciences. We also have many engineers. Perhaps it is people who deal with concrete issues who can solve our problems.

The group of workers is not so large. This is because of the following facts. First, the CPSU has not been addressing the needs of the workers for several years. Now, in the midst of economic disaster, which the workers played no role in creating, the Party has been operating again in a crude manner. The local Party committees fulfill directives from above without going to the workers [for their assessments or recommendations]. Consequently, this year we have heard demands to expel the Party committees from enterprises. Nevertheless, the number of workers in the whole country is very large. These are good people; they provide good conditions for our movement.

The Initiative Movement has its own structures without compulsory discipline or regulations. Participation is based on disinterestedness and voluntary companionship. This is very good. We are working within CPSU regulations, although we are on the verge of being broken; that is a fact. The right-wing faction of the CPSU is already organized. Formed in January 1990, it is called the Democratic Platform. It seems to me that it was sanctioned by the highest Party leaders. Some within the Democratic Platform left the CPSU in order to draw people away from the Party. Others stayed within the Party in order to lead the Party toward this right-wing political orientation.

We must realize that our present situation is forcing people to take sides and change their behavior. Our communist movement is being transformed, but it does not lose its old traditions, the roots of which date back to even before the great French revolution to the age of Enlightenment. Marxism will live and develop once we throw away the husk of dogmatism.

We have an organizational bureau within the Communist Initiative Movement consisting of one hundred members. All members are equal. Nikolai Polovodov is the chairman, but there is no structure behind him. Traditionally we have as the chairman of the Communist Initiative congress Victor Tyulkin, who is the secretary of the Party committee of the enterprise Vanguard in Leningrad. Then there is the Central Committee, which is chaired by Vladimir Karyakin.

Our movement has two main goals. First, we seek to pressure, from below, our central Party organs while also influencing social opinion to support the founding of the Russian Communist Party. If there is no such movement from below, Gorbachev will not take this step independently. Second, we are preparing our own variant for the CPSU program. Knowing the spirit of the current CPSU program being prepared by Ivashko's working group, we feel obliged to submit an alternative program that can consolidate the Party's healthy strength and prevent the current disintegration. We can see the tendencies promoting the dissolution [of the CPSU] now. We want our party to start with a clean slate. Naturally we accept the whole historical process and do not reject what the Party had before. But it seems to me that we have deviated since the Eleventh Party Congress, the last in which Lenin participated. We begin from the premise that the Second Party Program has yet to be realized in its full scope. Of course this document must be revised, but its basic tenets can be realized now.

What the future holds is hard to say. I fear that the faction at the top of the Party may instigate a split of the Party into different party trends. Naturally, political succession will remain with us. As for the status of the Party's property, its distribution will depend on the political activity of the people. But this does not upset me. I am happy to be among the honest people who aspire to neither glory nor position, but simply think about the destiny of their fatherland.

Perestroika may bring about the disintegration of our country. This will happen because of the strong influence of Western capital, which has not arrived yet, but could burst into the country soon. The weakness of our protective mechanisms may lead to colonization. Its form will not require the total destruction of our sovereignty, but this neocolonialism will delay our development for decades. Our resources will be pumped out without any benefit to our territory. Our cheap working wages and incomes will precipitate an invasion of Western owners akin to the gold rush on the Klondike. There were some protective mechanisms, but they are now being removed.

So we regard our movement as internationalist and patriotic. Some people do not understand how aspects [of our policy] are connected to the necessity of preserving the Russian political system. We base our analysis on the world historical process and Russian history.

What are you tactics for educating people about this situation and turning them toward communism?

We are working very actively now, but our main difficulty is access to the popular press. Most of the press now belongs to the opposition. Our regional Party committees are subsidizing the anticommunist press. What about the content of the Komsomol newspapers or the leading communist newspaper *Pravda*? *Sovetskaya Rossiya* is maintaining a true Party position as is *Glasnost* to a certain extent. [Gaining access to the popular press] is the first thing we need to do.

The numerous other parties that exist today do not really function in reality. They have an untrue existence. Those parties that represent the frank interests of capital will strengthen. The new middle class is growing along with the upper bourgeoisie. And the party that represents their interests will grow too. I see a strengthening of forces of those who want to liquidate all the achievements made after the October revolution [1917]. Unfortunately, our CPSU has no goal-oriented, ideological program [to address these challenges].

What is the Communist Initiative Movement doing?

We began as a very small organization consisting primarily of scientists.[25] Although even at the beginning of perestroika it was clear which direction our country was going, we did not organize immediately. We did form an association in October 1988 that attempted to formulate new models of development. It began as a seminar. We produced the demand to create a Russian Communist Party. The founding of the United Workers' Front was an intermediate stage. Although we were an member of the front, our association was not identical to the United Workers' Front. The United Workers' Front [UWF] appeared when we began having these discussions about the socioeconomic situation in the country. The front assumed formal structures in Leningrad in June 1989. This event sparked a similar formation in Moscow two weeks later, and then the process spread. We had the first all-Union UWF congress in June 1989 in Leningrad and the first Russian congress in September 1989 in Sverdlovsk. Oddly, a delegation from the

Interregional Group came to Sverdlovsk during our congress. Andrei Sakharov, who was among them, called for the crowd [at our meeting] to disperse. Travkin also came and called for people to disperse but achieved no result. Soon thereafter, UWF organizations appeared in several cities. Starting in Kuibyshev in November [1989] cities began holding conferences in connection with the formation of the Russian Communist Party.

In January 1990 at the second congress of the United Workers' Front in Leningrad, which corresponded with the founding congress of the Democratic Platform in Moscow, Communists gathered there took the decision to organize the Communist Initiative congress. The first stage of the congress in April 1990 coincided with preparations for the Twenty-eighth CPSU Congress. Our goal was to create an integrated Communist Party organization in Russia. We campaigned persistently and received the attention of the CPSU's upper strata. I think that Gorbachev was eager to limit this process. The Russian Bureau of the Central Committee of the CPSU was organized. It was a bureaucratic organ that did not want to resolve any questions. This Central Committee fixed a conference [to discuss Russian Communist Party issues] for June 15.[26] We then called the second stage of our congress to convene June 9–10, several days before the Central Committee's conference. In this manner, we were able to organize and influence the situation so that the creation of a Russian Communist Party became inevitable.

The Initiative group participated, without announcement, in the drafting of a special platform at the Twenty-eighth CPSU Congress. The Initiative also participated in the constituent congress of the Russian Communist Party. The third stage of the Initiative congress was held in October [1990], at which we discussed reports about the fulfillment of our main program directives and questions about our future party program. This June [1991], we will hold a another congress where we will discuss a new program and the work of Communists who are involved with the workers' movement.

Why, so far, has the workers' movement supported the transition to the market?

It is very simple. There is no alternative position articulated in the mass media. There is intensive brainwashing going on. Moreover, people do not understand what the market is. For a person who is searching for basic necessities and is suffering from high prices, the market means full markets and shops. People do not know anything about the realities of criminal capitalism. They see the beautiful pictures from Western life on television all the time.

We have the opposite view of capitalism. I have visited many countries—both highly developed and weakly developed—around the world. I know perfectly well their living standards. Our people are convinced that everybody in these countries lives very well, not sowing or reaping but only eating the pies. Our people are driven to such a state that it makes no difference to them who provides the bread, be it the Communists, the Mafia, or the capitalists. So people yield to the unrestrained market propaganda. They are being forced [to accept the market] by life's circumstances. My comrades and I are not opposed to the market in general. We believe that we need a varied market of goods and services. But why must we pay for this market with unemployment? Why must we have 100 million people who live below the poverty line? They say that there is no alternative to the market. They say that we will have an abundance of goods under the market. But by the end of this year production will have fallen by one-third. The science of economics asserts that production is primary. The market is derivative, secondary, and can operate only after production is secured. So the talk about the market right now is self-deception and conscious lies.

What economic model in the world today does your Initiative Movement support?
There is no such model right now. When I speak about the planned economy, people accuse me of holding a conservative position. But this is not accurate. The planned economy, as envisaged by Marx, Engels, and Lenin, was never realized in our country. In recent years, I think that the United States, Japan, and some small European countries even may have gone farther toward realizing this model than we did in our country. This is a paradox. Capitalism is turning to planned production based on an assessment of human requirements. In our country, planned production was connected to human requirements only during Lenin's rule. Thereafter, these human requirements were met only in an elemental way during the process of extensive growth in which we had no contemporary branches of production. We had no automobile industry, so we had to create one. We had no aviation industry, so we had to develop one. The requirements of our defense industry were covered by special investments. But after we created a complex national economy, what did we do? We should have incorporated into the plan society's requirements, which could be assessed from sociological research done periodically around the whole country. But we did not. Instead we centralized the plan. When somebody says that we need to plan twenty-six million jobs, that is, all forms of production from one industry, I think that this is either demagogy or stupidity. We can have hierarchy in the plan with the center steering it in strategic directions, but the rest of plan should be left to the competencies of the republics, oblasts, and districts. Our science in this field [economic planning] has been very passive and played a cruel joke with the socialist economy. We would not have had such sharp deficits [in goods production] if we had taken into account people's requirements and needs regarding consumer goods. But now we have deficits in everything from cheese to diamond rings. Basic goods, which should be secured automatically, are not fixed in any plan. As a result, we have discredited the planned economy. Lenin understood that central planning had as its minimum the provision of basic goods. In our time, nobody has followed this basic rule. As a result, we have witnessed the complete collapse of the planned bureaucratic-administrative economy.

The market, on the other hand, will also not achieve the necessary results because the market is a very difficult mechanism, which forms after dozens of years. How will we be able to manage the transition to capitalism that took the West two hundred years to accomplish? The only way is if someone forms the market for us. But if this happens, we will become a market for the West, which will not be very favorable to our own interests. I think that it will only be through the rebirth of the planned economy based on consumer interests that will produce large results.

What other political formations in this country support your ideas? Who are your allies?
The agrarian union may be our logical ally. We are also looking attentively at the Socialist Party. Moreover, there are many patriotic organizations such as Otechestvo, which may share our views, but there are differences because the patriotic groups are being organized by different motives. Feeling that the country is in danger, they have assembled under the slogan of rebirth for the national-patriotic movement. Some of these people, however, pursue Stalin's ideals. We have to be careful in our association with them. It is necessary to cooperate but not without discrimination.

Who are your opponents?
First and foremost, it is the wide bloc of anticommunist forces. People know very little about us because of their information blockade against us.

What is your attitude toward Gorbachev and Yeltsin?
From a socioeconomic point of analysis, they are the same kind of people. The only difference is one is in a hurry, while the other is thinking more.

Igor Malyarov

Born in 1965, Igor Malyarov has established himself as one of the leading figures in the Russian neocommunist movement. Educated as an economist at Moscow State University, Malyarov has taught in the Economics Department there since 1987. He was one of the original organizers of the United Workers' Front in 1989. He then created the youth wing of Communist Initiative. Since the August 1991 putsch, Malyarov has been a leading organizer of combined neocommunist and nationalist demonstrations against Yeltsin, including the demonstration on February 23, 1992, that ended in bloody clashes between protesters and the Moscow city police. Although the Komsomol disbanded after the coup, Malyarov reconstituted the communist youth organization in February 1992.

Interview with
Igor Malyarov (*April 1991*)

· ·

How and why did you become involved in politics?
I got involved in politics in 1989, when I was one of the initiators of the United Workers' Front in an attempt to resist those aspects of perestroika that aimed to transfer full power to the nascent bourgeoisie. Since then I have been fairly active in politics. Since the fall of 1990, I have been mostly concerned with the communist youth movement.

Can you describe the landmarks in the history of your movement?
The United Workers' Front became the first organization in the foundation of what I would describe as an independent communist movement. The Edinstvo [Unity] society, which rallied around Nina Andreeva, was founded at about the same time, but it is smaller and pro-Stalinist, something the front does not support. The front later formed the nucleus for various other organizations with different functional tasks. They include the Communist Initiative Movement in Russia, which grew out of the front and which has important positions in the Russian Communist Party, the Women's Movement for the Socialist Future of Children, and, to a large extent, the Communist Initiative Youth Movement, although our members include both supporters of the Marxist Platform in the Communist Party and young people from Moscow's more moderate Edinstvo society. Many of those who formed the core of the United Workers' Front were originally with the Marxist Workers' Party of the Dictatorship of the Proletariat, especially its Moscow branch, which later became the Marxist Workers' Party. The first stage of our history was the formation of independent groups, and the second was the emergence of organizations that have already begun to win influence in the Komsomol, the Communist Party of the Soviet Union, and the women's movement.

How was the first stage distinguished from the second?
The first initiative congress for creating the Russian Communist Party took place in the spring of 1990. It was then that the United Workers' Front began rallying Communists inside the Party because it had become obvious that far from all Party members were real Communists and that many were effectively anti-Communists.

Members of the independent neocommunist movement include people from the extreme left to those further on the right. The extreme left flank is occupied by Nina Andreeva's Edinstvo society and its more moderate Moscow branch, which, as far as I know, has withdrawn from the national Edinstvo society. Then we have the Marxist Workers' Party and the Dictatorship of the Proletariat Party, which were once a single party with some popular backing but later split into these two parties with two centers—the Marxist Workers' Party in Moscow and the Russian Party of the Dictatorship of the Proletariat in Samara. Next comes the United Workers' Front, which is more closely intertwined with supporters of the Initiative Congress of Russian Communists, the Women's Movement for the Socialist Future of Children, the Communist Initiative Movement, and the Marxist Platform in the Communist Party of the USSR. Many members of the Marxist Platform attended the Initiative Congress and vice versa. This bloc of the United Workers' Front, the Marxist Workers' Platform, the Initiative bloc, and the youth and women's division are very closely intertwined, even at an individual level.

Where is the Russian Communist Party in the spectrum?

It is more correct to speak of the Russian Communist Party's Central Committee and the forces rallying around it. From our point of view, they are more communist in nature than the forces grouping around Gorbachev's Soviet Communist Party Central Committee. However, it would be wrong to say that it is a uniform movement, First, there are differences in the positions of Russian Central Committee leaders. Second, Rutskoi is also a member of the Russian Communist Party Central Committee. That he is in the same movement with Gennadii Zyuganov makes no sense.[27] The Russian Communist Party is not yet a uniform whole, and the forces rallying around its Central Committee are fairly heterogeneous. So it would be more correct to distinguish the informal, unofficial, neocommunist structures leading up to the Initiative Congress from the official communist structures.

Apart from ideological differences, there are also functional differences between, for instance, the United Workers' Front and the Initiative Congress of Russian Communists. One is an independent movement targeting worker collectives that does not seek to become a party but aims to suggest ideas and unite workers and arm them theoretically. The Initiative Congress, in contrast, seeks ideological leadership within the Communist Party. The same can be said about the youth movement as well. Our task is to form a communist youth organization based on Leninist principles that seeks to acquire the Party's support and thereby to consolidate young forces within the Komsomol.

What are the distinctive features of the Marxist Workers' Party and the Russian Party of the Dictatorship of the Proletariat?

The Russian Party of the Dictatorship of the Proletariat, which is based in Samara, is strongly oriented toward workers. They admit as members only workers and support only working-class representation in elected governing councils. The Marxist Workers' Party is less rigid in this respect, and this is not surprising because they include more intellectuals and have a more developed theory. They are led by Yurii Leonov and Nizami Dezgen.

Why did they split?

Both share the view that during the transitional period we need to establish a dictatorship of the proletariat. Their split was simply the result of leadership ambitions. Both groups, however, are not very large. Regrettably, none of these groups or parties are mass movements yet.

What is the total membership in all the neocommunist organizations?

I can give you a very rough estimate. Edinstvo has perhaps one thousand members across the Soviet Union. The Marxist Workers' Party and the Russian Party of the Dictatorship of the Proletariat are even smaller. They have a total of two hundred activists, some one hundred in each. The United Workers' Front has approximately four thousand to five thousand members throughout Russia. The United Workers' Front also includes intermovements in the Baltics, but their tasks are somewhat different, and it would be wrong to automatically count them as well. Then there is the Initiative Congress. Many official Party structures are closely connected with it. Its influence in the Party is rather extensive, which can be seen even from the fact that a number of its leaders have been elected members of the Russian Communist Party Central Committee. The last congress was attended by 850 delegates representing nearly all Russian regions. So this movement is the most powerful among all self-organized communist groups, though its membership is hard to estimate. The Communist Initiative youth movement has another several hundred people with local branches in twenty Russian cities. Finally, the Marxist Platform has six hundred to seven hundred members. It stresses, however, that it is a federal, not a Russian-based, party.

Which cities or districts have the strongest branches?

The most influential locals are in central Russia. We also are well represented in major cities like Leningrad, Moscow, Nizhnii Novgorod, and perhaps Samara. In terms of individual enterprises, we have strong representation at the Skorokhod amalgamation in Leningrad, the Moscow-based ZIL auto factory, and the car factory in Togliatti.

Could you give more details about the youth movements?

The first groups of the Communist Initiative youth movement originated last fall [1990]. We had two preparatory meetings in Nizhnii Novgorod and then the founding congress December 15–16 in Moscow, which was attended by some 170 delegates from twenty-eight regions. Some forty Russian cities were represented at the congress. Our tasks include protecting the social interests of working youth and working to make the Komsomol a truly communist alliance of young people guided by a Communist Party updated along Leninist principles. We focus on propaganda and theoretical issues and hold theoretical seminars. Members of our group even initiated the drawing up of two drafts of the party program. We also concentrate on political campaigning. We actively campaigned before the referendum on the future of the Soviet Union [March 17, 1991] and are now doing the same in connection with the [Russian] presidential election campaign. We also conduct practical work at enterprises, concentrating on such issues as the social protection of workers. We sponsored a meeting of young people from industrial projects and worked out a number of specific proposals. We are an umbrella for a wide circle of people, starting from Edinstvo sympathizers and ending with those gravitating toward social-democratic ideas. So far we have coexisted without conflicts.

What is the social basis of the bloc as a whole and of its member organizations?

We are oriented primarily toward the working class interpreted broadly, not only factory workers but other kinds of laborers as well. Workers, however, are not a majority in any of the neocommunist movements. In the United Workers' Front they make up one-third of the membership, but our youth movement includes just a handful of workers. Our members are mostly college students, young researchers, and high school students, while young workers are few and far between. Edinstvo has a few workers. Workers form the larger part of the Russian Party of the Dictatorship of the Proletariat. But its membership is very small, just some one hundred people.

What is the relationship between your neocommunist organizations and Communist Party cells at the enterprise and local level?

Everything depends on the specific nature of these CPSU committees. I can speak in greater detail about the Komsomol. In Ryazan, for example, the Komsomol organization is very close to us. Similarly, the regional Komsomol organization in Kursk decided at its plenum to support the Communist Initiative youth movement. On the other hand, in Chelyabinsk, our local chapter has been engaged in a fairly tough confrontation with the regional Komsomol committee regarding ideological issues. In Volgograd, the Komsomol district organization backs us, while the regional committee does not. The same can be said of our relations with the Communist Party; everything depends on specific people. There is hardly any Communist Party committee directly supportive of the Marxist Workers' Party or the Edinstvo society, but the Initiative Congress of Russian Communists is very involved and influential in existing Party structures. Its [Initiative's] last congress was attended by six regional committee secretaries of the CPSU, some seventeen leaders of district committees, and fifty or sixty secretaries of Party locals. This gives an idea of the contacts maintained by the Initiative Congress.

Who are your allies and who are your enemies?

Our allies are, first, official Communist Party structures and, second, new left-wing organizations such as the Socialists, the Anarcho-Syndicalists, and the Social Democrats, who are potential left wingers. The Green Party also belongs here.

One of our main problems is that we have not yet been able to establish any effective contacts with the miners, although I personally attended the Confederation of Labor's congress and formed contacts with many delegates.

Our main opponents are the forces in Democratic Russia, which reflect the interests of the new bourgeoisie.

You, naturally, then are opposed to privatization?
Yes. Privatization should be distinguished from denationalization and broader self-management. We oppose privatization if it means simply the transfer of enterprises into private ownership. We speak of the possibility of work-related private property, that is, property based on one's own labor. A number of groups from our communist movement do not object to private ownership with the use of hired labor on a limited scale. But the number of hired workers should be limited, and the private sector also should be strictly limited.

What is your attitude toward Gorbachev?
Practically all these neocommunist movements have a negative attitude toward him because he is leading the country toward capitalism. Calling a spade a spade, we must state that his policies will change workers from the masters of production into hired labor without any rights. He does it very subtly; while continuing to talk about socialism, he pursues antisocialist policies, making him especially destructive.

What is your attitude toward Yeltsin?
Everyone has a sharply negative attitude toward him.

What is your attitude toward Lenin?
It is unequivocally positive on the part of practically everyone, although with certain reservations.

What is your attitude toward Stalin?
Attitudes differ on Stalin, ranging from the unambiguous support of all Stalinist views of the Edinstvo society to their downright rejection in the right wing of the Marxist Platform. There are some Stalinists in the United Workers' Front, but they do not play a leading role there, while Communist Initiative does not have any Stalinists.

Stalin suppressed democracy and worker self-management, which undoubtedly dealt a hard blow at the communist movement.

What is your attitude toward Khrushchev and Brezhnev?
Positions regarding these people differ all the way from categoric rejection to justification. Edinstvo believes that the bourgeois restoration period started with Khrushchev's ascent to power, while the United Workers' Front says it began with the 1965 reforms. I believe that the Brezhnev period did great harm to the Communist Party and the development of socialism in this country. The restoration of an exploiter class got under way precisely under Brezhnev.

What is your attitude toward Russian nationalism?
Russian nationalists fail to see that not only Russians live in this country. A more accurate term is the people of Russia. As soon as we attempt to separate the Russians from other ethnic groups living in this country, we will land ourselves in a blind alley because everything is so mixed and intertwined, including territorial borders. Regarding the territorial issue, the nationalists claim without batting an eye that the Russian Federation is the same as Russia. But what then

is the northern Caucasus, where the population consists of 90 percent Russians? What about the eastern Ukraine? In general, we all existed as a single, multinational family, which was knit together not by Stalin's regime or Nicholas's empire but by some unique conditions of living on vast expanses of land where people and ethnic groups mixed. This is why my attitude to nationalism is negative, and this applies not only to Russian nationalism but to any other as well.

When I say that we should rely on our history, I mean not only the history of the Russian people alone. I mean that each country has its special path of development. This includes both the special path of Japan and the special path of West European nations. There, the current trend is toward closer integration, and they indeed are very close. There is also the special path of Africa. In any case, every country has powerful roots stemming from its history that determine the distinctive features of its current economic structures. Collectivism, the community spirit, and the primacy of spiritual values always have been part of Russian traditions. In general terms, I believe that the philosophy of Western liberalism is totally unacceptable and will not take root on our soil.

Does this mean that Yeltsin will fail in his desire to build a liberal Western society here?
Of course he will fail. At best, he will only be able to create some enclaves in the form of free economic zones, which will operate at the expense of other regions or economic branches.

It is already happening. When we say that we are moving toward a market and capitalism, we tend to forget that we already have cooperatives, self-financing arrangements, joint-stock companies, and other factors disrupting existing economic links. I believe that we will not be able to build this kind of capitalist society, while the cost of the mistake will be popular suffering.

Are you suggesting that the new bourgeoisie will not dominate your society?
The new bourgeoisie is merged with the state and shows signs of the feudal, Asian means of production. Speaking of these people personally, they have already won and are prevailing now. The interests of this social class now are coming to power. They will not create some American type of welfare society but instead will erect some brutal, criminal, partocratic system that will combine features of feudalism and capitalism at an early stage of capital accumulation. This is not the Western economic model. It will be closer to some Latin American type of economy and state.

What are the main problems impeding the development of the communist alternative?
First of all, we need influential leaders who can win people over to our side. And we also need, of course, access to leading news organizations because *Komsomolskaya Pravda* and *Izvestiya* are now, effectively, the newspapers of our opponents, while only *Sovetskaya Rossiya* can be considered our supporter. Second, it is essential to develop closer ties with the working-class movement. Without relations with the workers, we shall never become a real force.

Document

. . . .

The Motherland Is Sick. How Can She Be Aided?
Platform of the United Workers' Front

Compatriots, Comrades, People living by honest work, People knowing what poverty is and not despising it, People not allowing themselves to get rich by arrogating others' property, People who want to work honestly in accordance with their abilities rather than get along by all manner of tricks, PAY ATTENTION TO THE UNITED WORKERS' FRONT! Its representatives that are risking standing at elections intend to stress the following priorities.

1. In the economy:

• The well-being of all and everyone primarily thanks to the elimination of humiliating shortages of basic necessities. Efforts to saturate the market with consumer goods and prevent the restoration of a market of capital and manpower, that is, of the omnipotence of wealth and the exploitation of labor.

• No to attempts to abolish plan-based economic management! The abolition of the bureaucratic system of planning, the decisive subordination of the planned economy to the needs and requirements of the working family. Plan-based guarantees against shortages. The implementation of Lenin's behest: "I see centralism as a minimum ensuring the material security of the working masses." Plans should serve the material and cultural needs of the individual.

• The possibility for working people to earn adequate money first of all at socialist enterprises. Cuts in wage rates and job prices should be suspended for two or three years from the start of the 13th five-year plan period regardless of increases in labor productivity as a result of modernization. Working people should be treated not merely as wage earners but as multifaceted personalities. High productivity and quality labor and creative attitudes to work should be stimulated by providing more advanced equipment, promoting workers to positions of greater responsibility, and rewarding them with more time for leisure.

• The fulfillment of planned targets should be judged not by profits but by the choice and quality of products. The situation at present is abnormal: as a worker, a person is interested in raising prices on his products, while as a consumer, he is interested in reducing these prices. This contradiction should be removed by taking advantage of ideas worked out by United Workers' Front economists. Cuts in retail prices should be made one of the major sources of improvements in living standards.

• The "shadow economy," which drains social production of its life-giving juices, should no longer be concealed, and all its conduits of supplies should be cut off. The antisocialist alliance of underground capital with the bureaucracy should be exposed. It should be finally understood that the capitalist sector is able even today to begin buying out state-owned factories. Corrupt bureaucrats facilitating the bourgeois degeneration of the state should be brought to account.

• With a view to confiscating stolen wealth, a campaign should be waged for the change of banknotes at a rate of 1:1 for sums under 10,000 rubles upon the presentation of a passport and for sums exceeding 10,000 rubles without any restrictions upon the presentation of a document certifying the work-based origin of the savings.

• Vigorous action to protect the public ownership of the means of production and opposition to its transformation into private ownership under the guise of individual, family, group, cooperative, joint-stock, and other forms of ownership. The private ownership of the means of production means that hired workers have no rights to them. This is nothing other than their estrangement, automatically meaning the abolition of the right to work. It should not be forgotten that the issue of replacing private property with public property was decided by the people not in parliamentary debates but in the course of battles during the civil war. Therefore, the issue of ownership in the USSR may only be decided now through a nationwide referendum. Work-related private property under clearly defined conditions can facilitate the building of socialism, but the latter's strategy and destiny is connected with public property.

• An optimum model of a "civilized" socialist cooperative should be worked out and the cooperative movement developed extensively on its basis. The money grubber's bourgeois-cooperative slant in economic policy must be righted. Cooperative prices should not exceed state prices.

• Agriculture should be provided with the full range of required modern machinery and mechanisms in accordance with soil and climatic conditions. An organic technological link should be established and strengthened between farming and industry, and a network of enterprises for the on-site storage and processing of farming produce should be set up. The free development of both state and collective farms and family farms should be ensured without any administrative pressure and bureaucratic regimentation and with the clear understanding that, according to Lenin, we shall not be

able to overcome poverty by relying on small farms alone. The conditions of life in the countryside should be on a par with those in the city.
• All channels for the distribution of food and manufactured goods should be under the independent collective control of working people. Practices should be promoted whereby consumer goods will be marketed by enterprises producing them. The retail trading and public catering networks should be extended and updated. Honest and considerate workers in the trading industry should be rewarded with high pay and general respect! Shame and a war should be declared on the Mafia in the trading industry, those abusing their positions to supply themselves, bribers, those provoking artificial shortages, and black marketeers cashing in on public needs.
• Socialist society should set itself the long-term aim of completely ecologizing production.
• The power industry should be deatomized. The best scientific and engineering forces should be concentrated on mastering cheap and safe energy sources—solar, wind, tidal, thermal, and biological sources of energy as the basis of the power industry of the future.
• The creation of a network of modern roads and well-developed supply lines and communications across the country, especially in Russia.
• No to the sellout of national territory and riches and to the encouragement of capitalist monopolies to cut up this country and exploit its cheap manpower! No to the transformation of the Soviet land into a dump heap for nuclear and other noxious wastes and to the deployment here of polluting Western production operations!

2. In social policies:

• Genuine distribution according to one's work. Not egalitarianism that equalizes the hard working and the lazy, not the theft of public property, but equality in work. No restrictions on wages earned by honest work! No indulgence to unscrupulous tricksters getting rich by foul means.
• Underlying principles for socialist income policies should be worked out and put to a popular vote. The notions of "a socialist source of income" and "a nonsocialist source of income" should be introduced into legislation
• The right of inheritance should be limited and regulated in order to prevent the exploitation of the poor by the rich, of living labor by dead labor, and in order to prevent the legalized parasitism of the heirs of wealthy relatives.
• Equal economic and cultural starting opportunities should be ensured for young people irrespective of their social origins, place of residence, sex, and ethnic backgrounds. No privileges must be allowed in acquiring education, and the feeling of being an "elite" must not be encouraged in

any way. Equal possibilities should be ensured for all to reveal their aptitudes and talents.

• Most favorable conditions should be ensured for free medical services. The pay and public prestige of medical workers, especially in state clinics, should be increased and the latter's equipment upgraded to meet world standards.

• Independent public control should be established over the building, quality, and distribution of housing.

• Workplaces should be humanized, the comfort levels of production raised, and the standard of amenities (canteens, locker rooms, showers, medical stations, hairdressers, boutiques, etc.) in production drastically improved.

• Public catering should be upgraded to exemplary standards. The network of canteens, cafes, and restaurants should be widened so that any woman and any family can be relieved of cooking chores either temporarily or completely.

• Mental and physical work, organizing and executive work, creative and monotonous work, work in industry and in agriculture, and work in material production and in culture should be brought consistently closer together.

• Lenin's policy of restricting and getting rid of exploiter elements, eliminating differences between classes, and building a classless society of working people should be reaffirmed.

3. In politics:

(a) Human Rights:

• To life and personal security guaranteed by the state
• To work and material security in keeping with one's personal contribution to public property
• To housing
• To protection from exploitation and disinformation
• To change one's place of residence, including emigration from the country
• To take part in running production and society and in electing representative governing councils
• Freedom of speech, assembly, and association into social organizations
• Other rights and liberties envisaged by the USSR constitution and international legal acts

(b) The Soviet System:

• Consistent democratization targeting not the upper crust but the entire mass of the population and proceeding from the shop floor. The people in a country of wholesale literacy do not need political guardians that arrogate the monopoly to govern them. The people include specialists in administration and law who are called upon to conscientiously fulfill their professional and civic duty but do not give away popular sovereignty. All working people without exception should be involved in administration at different levels of society. Every adult—from senior-grade high school students to pensioners—should go through this school of practical politics.

• The bodies of direct democracy—work team, plant and factory councils, general meetings at the workplace, house, block, and street committees, and neighborhood meetings—should be activated and developed as a matter of priority. The bodies of direct democracy should be directly linked to the lower-level organs of representative democracy—soviets of people's deputies at village, settlement, district, borough, and city levels.

• Direct and equal elections to all soviets of people's deputies by secret ballot, with no limitations on the nomination of candidates. Abstract interpretations of the All Power to the Soviets slogan should be mistrusted. Lenin in 1917 argued now for advocating this slogan and now for withdrawing it, depending on the social and individual makeup of the soviets. The masses should be reminded of the lesson all the time, as the soviets, especially at the local level, can be seized by agents of "shadow capital," profiteering cooperatives, and even simply by members of the Mafia, who, unlike working people, have enough free time, money, and vast connections.

• A campaign should be waged for the organic combination of elections in production constituencies and territorial constituencies and for the proper representation of worker collectives in the soviets of people's deputies. Voters' rights to recall deputies that have failed to justify their trust, that violate civil and universal morals, and that have compromised themselves by connections with antisocial elements should be implemented in practice, and assistance should be given toward the elaboration of respective legal norms.

• Administrative staff workers should be systematically replaced in keeping with established regulations or by citizens' demands. The circle of voluntary activists helping the soviets of people's deputies should be broadened and turned into a continuously renewed reserve of administrative personnel who will, in the meantime, continue in their regular jobs.

• Greater democracy should be achieved in production management. Cooperative principles should be boldly introduced, and Lenin's idea of making society into a network of self-administered producer-and-consumer communes implemented.

• Assistance should be given to efforts to work out a model for democratizing the armed forces, completely overcoming hazing, and improving the moral climate in the ranks and among the officers. The baiting of the Soviet armed forces, state security service, and militia must be stopped! Attempts to ridicule the glory and traditions of our predecessors, who gave their lives and shed their blood for the freedom of the motherland, must be strongly rejected! Shame on those who, while jeering at "the curse of strength," intend to foist on us a "curse of weakness"! The proposal to replace the popular armed forces, manned in accordance with the USSR constitution, by a professional hired army is undemocratic from beginning to end. An army raised from among the people fights for the people rather than against them, while mercenaries do not care. The democratically minded public should strengthen relations with the armed forces as the guarantee of protection for society and the individual.

• The supremacy of the law should be ensured both by all the possibilities of a democratic law-governed state and by all democratic public forces.

(c) The Party:

• Lenin's behest to increase the number of workers in the Communist Party Central Committee should be fulfilled and workers should be elected to the Politburo. The United Workers' Front believes that collective farmers and rank-and-file office workers that do not occupy any administrative positions should be treated on equal terms as workers, as regards the demand to elect more workers to the steering bodies of the Communist Party. This category of people should account for at least one-third of the Central Committee and the Politburo.

• Ex officio membership in steering Party bodies should be ended.

• Communist Party committees at district, region, republic, and national levels, as well as delegates to Communist Party congresses and national conferences, should be elected by all Communists directly in primary Party organizations in direct and competitive elections by secret ballot.

• It should be made certain that the post of the Communist Party Central Committee general secretary should not be occupied by one and the same person for life. The term of office in this post should be limited to the period between two congresses, although the incumbent should have the right to stand in elections to serve for the second term on condition that there will be other candidates and the minimum required for him to win the election will be raised. Other measures should be developed to prevent a cult of personality, Bonapartism, and authoritarianism.

• A control commission, elected along with the Central Committee by congress, should be reinstated and have the power to check the work of all party organs from the bottom to the top and of any functionary, including the general secretary.

• The principle whereby a decision may be freely discussed before being passed but must be fulfilled after being passed by all Party members, including those disagreeing with it, must be observed unswervingly. There should be exercised the freedom of intra-Party discussions on any theoretical or political issue. Organizationally isolated factions in the Party are inadmissible, while it is desirable that either individual Communists or groups of Communists suggest different ideological-political platforms and options for solving these or other pressing problems.

• A Communist should have the right to criticize any Party body and official; the statutory protection of Communists against harassment for criticism should be ensured.

• Party members and Party functionaries should enjoy no privileges.

• Party members committing unseemly deeds should be punished for them strictly and publicly.

• Communists should have the right to freely leave the Party.

• There should be greater influence by non-Party masses on intra-Party affairs. A worker collective should have the right to recommend a member to the Party or recall him from the Party.

• The Russian Communist Party should be reestablished as a condition of ensuring the motherland's integrity and independence, perfecting the socialist system, and strengthening the communist movement in the country.

4. In ideology:

• Complete and general public openness. Nobody may be allowed to monopolize the mass media.

• The freedom to form a personal outlook and disseminate it, freedom of conscience for both believers and atheists.

• Freedom of scientific and artistic creativity and freedom to publicly criticize its results.

• Active support for humanist and freedom-loving, democratic and realistic traditions in cultural life, their continuation and development. The United Workers' Front openly stands on positions of the dialectic-materialistic philosophy and scientific communism but is prepared for dialogue with all other currents of social thinking without any manifestation of intolerance.

• Any manifestations of "elitist" seclusion, cliquishness, corporatism, and egoistic isolation from the working masses should be opposed, and efforts should be made to promote an enduring alliance of "representatives of science, the proletariat, and technology," whom, in Lenin's words, "no dark horse can resist." Our motto is Labor, Science and Democracy.

• The intellectual fleecing of our country, the "brain drain," and the theft of inventions should be strongly countered. Works of art created fifty and more years ago must be banned, while the import of cultural and historical values into the USSR should be encouraged in every way.

• The melodic environment of society should be made healthier. The monopoly of deafening, numbing, and politically and morally dubious rock [music] should be ended. Priority should be ensured for folk music that corresponds to the national psychology and for classical, universally appreciated music. The understanding should be spread that the prevalent musical culture can either ennoble individuals or cause their degradation.

• Government concern should be shown, and a mass social movement maintained, for preserving and restoring historical and cultural monuments. The demolition of buildings and structures erected one hundred and more years ago without prior expert examination should be banned. The list of holidays and commemorative dates should be reviewed, and a National Remembrance Day on January 22 (which was observed before the war as a day of honoring the memory of Lenin and the victims of January 9, 1905) and a Moscow Liberation Day in November (to mark the anniversary of the city's liberation from the Polish interventionists in 1612 and Napoleon's forces in 1812) should be instituted.

• The full truth should be revealed about the past and present of our motherland in all its drama and contradictoriness. Efforts to discredit the Russian and Soviet state and uncritically transfer conclusions and judgments by emigrants and so-called experts on Soviet affairs onto the pages of the Soviet press should be rebuffed. Attempts to blacken and denigrate the path traversed by the land of Soviets after 1917, the building of socialism, the Great Patriotic War, and the activities of Marxist-Leninists must be repulsed. The inferiority complex that is now being inculcated in the Soviet people is a delayed-action mine. A people deprived of a feeling of dignity and used only to repenting cannot accomplish anything great. The national pride of Russians and their Slavic brothers—Ukrainians and Byelorussians and all Soviet people—can, in the opinion of the United Workers' Front, become one of the mighty moral and political motivating forces of perestroika. Neither antipatriotism nor nationalism can be its banner.

• The ideas of people's fraternity and consistent internationalism should be affirmed, as should be the complete equality of working people of all nationalities and the free development of ethnic languages and cultures. The discrimination of citizens on the basis of ethnic origins, native language, or the length of living in a given locality is inadmissible, illegitimate, and immoral. The civil rights and dignity should be ensured of both small ethnic groups in the Russian Federation and the Russian-speaking population in other constituent republics. The nationalism and chauvinism of both big and small ethnic groups should be opposed. "Shadow economy" dealers' covert but active role in aggravating ethnic relations in the USSR should be exposed.

It goes without saying that everything said above can be enriched and actualized in the course of later events, depending on where and when they take place. This is why this document should be seen only as the starting point for thinking and analysis.

Common working people—factory workers, blue-collar workers, the factory and humanitarian intelligentsia, and white-collar workers of mass trades—are the category of the population that has been neglected in the largest measure during the years of perestroika. Moreover, they began to be treated as the lowest-grade human resources, "lunar landscape" personnel, "Sharikov's children," and so on. The "elite"—the country's top leadership and "progressively minded" scholars, cultural personalities, and news organizations—were declared to be the motivating force of perestroika. This is why the spontaneous upsurge of workplace democracy enraged those who, as it seemed to them, had already assured themselves of success. The "illegitimate" intrusion by the vibrant masses into politics disrupted the chesslike logic of professional "political scientists."

The United Workers' Front comes under a hail of libel, slander, and defamation. It has hardly been able to make its first timid steps as it was branded as

- An invention of the apparatus (which is very suspicious of the front)
- A tool for rescuing the bureaucracy (with which the front wages a resolute struggle)
- An anti-intellectual force (though socialist and patriotically minded intellectuals are most closely involved in the front)
- Even a fascist-type organization (although the consistently democratic, antidictatorial stand of the front is known to all)

The United Workers' Front considers it beneath itself to deny these allegations or to respond to abuse with abuse. When there have been no grounds for the accusations, there is no reason to look for excuses. The people themselves will see where the truth is and where the lie is.

The United Workers' Front puts a high value on the noble traditions of advanced social thinking and relies in its activities on such historic documents as

- The American Declaration of Independence (1776)
- The French Declaration of Human and Civil Rights (1793)

- *Russkaya Pravda* (Russian Truth), by P.I. Pestel (1824)
- The Communist Manifesto (1848)
- Lenin's Declaration of the Rights of Working and Exploited People (1918)
- The Program of the Russian Communist Party (Bolshevik) (1919)
- The U.N. Universal Declaration on Human Rights (1948)

Comrades, do not believe demagogues shouting about communist ideals being incompatible with universally shared and democratic values. Both communist ideals and universally shared and democratic values are incompatible with the views and conduct of formal holders of Communist Party cards who have never been Communists in fact but have only sneaked into their ranks for careerist considerations and personal enrichment and of the advocates of the restoration of capitalism. Under the cover of "left-wing radical," pseudo-democratic, and other phraseology, people who have nothing but a yearning for power or, bluntly speaking, the desire to get ahead at your expense without working themselves are attempting to force themselves on you as rulers. Check all new-minted "leaders" and "idols" on their attitude to whom they disdainfully call plebeians. Power in the country should belong to you, not to self-styled "gods," "czars," and "foremen." It is only you that can reasonably use power.

Manual and mental workers of all nationalities, unite!

Indifference to the suffering of the socialist motherland may invite an irreparable misfortune!

Moscow, December 1989

chapter eleven

Soyuz

Soyuz (the Russian word for union) was founded on February 14, 1990, as a faction within the USSR Congress of People's Deputies dedicated to the preservation of the territorial integrity of the Soviet Union. At the time of its creation, Soyuz was a small collection of people's deputies consisting predominantly of Russian deputies from republics other than Russia. By the time of its constituent congress, December 1–2, 1990, Soyuz had grown to include 350 people's deputies from thirteen different republics, including 175 from the USSR Supreme Soviet. Only six months later, Soyuz claimed to have more than five hundred members in the Union parliament alone.

Soyuz founders included Colonels Victor Alksnis and Nikolai Petrushenko as well as Yevgenii Kogan, Yurii Blokhin, Georgii Komarov, and Venyamin Yarin. Sometime later, former Politburo member Yegor Ligachev joined the organization. Although internally split over a market economy and multiparty democracy, Soyuz was united by the goal of preserving the Soviet Union at whatever cost. To this end, Soyuz leaders orchestrated a successful campaign to oust Soviet foreign minister Shevardnadze from office in December 1990, asserting that he had jeopardized Soviet state security by "giving up" Eastern Europe to the West.[1] After Gorbachev's swing to the right in the fall of 1990, and the military interventions in the Baltics in January 1991, Soyuz leader Victor Alksnis assumed a high profile as the leader of the conservative forces in the USSR Supreme Soviet who had forced Gorbachev's change of heart. As early as February

1991, Soyuz leaders called on the Soviet government to issue a state of emergency to restore law and order.[2]

When Gorbachev began negotiations with Yeltsin in the spring of 1991 concerning a new Union treaty, Soyuz once again attacked the Soviet president, calling for his resignation in June 1991. Although the parliamentary challenge to Gorbachev's rule was aborted (though Soyuz claimed they had the votes to oust him), Soyuz openly opposed the president and urged his removal.

Soyuz as an organization did not officially support the August putsch. Victor Alksnis appeared on American television on the second day of the coup supporting the principles of the coup but criticizing its illegal form.[3] The failure of the coup, however, had devastating consequences for Soyuz, as the USSR Supreme Soviet was subsequently abolished. Three months later, the Soviet Union was dissolved.

After several weeks incognito, Soyuz leaders joined with the leaders of the parliamentary faction Rossiya (led by Sergei Baburin) to create the Russian All-People's Union, a conservative movement in defense of the territorial integrity of the Russian Federation. The group held its founding congress on December 21, 1991, at which Victor Alksnis was elected to its Coordinating Council.[4] This new movement combined with other nationalist and neocommunist movements to stage antigovernment demonstrations during the winter and summer of 1992. Victor Alksnis was also one of the organizers of the Congress of Patriotic Forces, held on February 8, 1992, another attempt to unite old Communists with nationalist and patriotic organizations.

On March 17, 1992, Soyuz leaders tried to resurrect the dissolved USSR by convening the abolished USSR Congress of People's Deputies.[5] The organizers of this event had hoped that more than a thousand deputies would participate, but only two hundred attended. The failure of the congress appeared to mark the end of the Soyuz movement as a political organization. However, border disputes between the former republics, referendums for independence in autonomous regions within the Russian Federation, and a disgruntled Soviet Red Army provide fertile issues for patriotic leaders such as Victor Alksnis.

Colonel Victor Alksnis

Born in 1951 in Latvia, Colonel Victor Alksnis began his political career by joining the Latvian Popular Front in 1988. When the Popular Front began advocating independence, Alksnis helped create Interfront, a movement dedicated to preserving Latvia's membership in the USSR. Alksnis was subsequently elected to the USSR Congress of People's Deputies and the Latvian parliament.

Although an adamant and outspoken supporter of the USSR, Alksnis has not championed orthodox views about either communism (he supports the market) or nationalism (as a Latvian, he is not a Russian nationalist). He maintains cordial ties with such extremists as Vladimir Zhirinovsky, but Alksnis also communicates openly and regularly with members of the Russian democratic movement. Within the military, Alksnis has remained popular. A poll conducted at the All-Army Officers' Assembly in Moscow on January 17, 1992, showed that 29 percent of the officers rated Colonel Alksnis most favorably as a political leader, compared with 36 percent for Alexander Rutskoi and only 21 percent for Boris Yeltsin.[6] With the disintegration of the Soviet Union, the colonel's political future remains uncertain but certainly not over.

Interview with
Colonel Victor Alksnis (June 1991)

· ·

When and why did you get involved in politics?
I have been engaged in politics since 1988, when the Latvian Popular Front was being set up in my home republic of Latvia. The organization had a rather attractive program. At that time, there were no divisions between natives and the nonindigenous population. It was, in principle, a generally democratic organization that united everybody—Letts, Russians, Jews, Byelorussians, Ukrainians, and so on.

But later these general democratic principles were gradually pushed into the background, while the idea of national superiority and the priority of the indigenous ethic group came to the forefront. The first congress of the Popular Front in October 1988 gave me great concern. Until that time, I had been a passionate supporter of the front. But when downright racist and fascist statements were made at the congress to the effect that there are guests and hosts [in the republic] and that the guests should be sent away from Latvia, I was very disappointed. Thereafter, I began to oppose the Latvian Popular Front.

In what ways did you participate in the Popular Front?
I took part in the first organizational meetings and in the first political demonstrations. I was not among the leading activists in the front, but I sympathized with this movement and tried to render my assistance as far as possible. Then, in November 1988, I wrote an article titled "It Is High Time to Gather Stones." It was the first in a series of articles about the dangerous processes that were developing in the Latvian Popular Front. The article invoked great interest and discussion in the republic.

Ever since then, I have been in politics officially. Soon thereafter, I participated in organizing the Latvian International Front, but this group did not satisfy me either because it was too orthodox and conservative. Although I was one of the founding organizers of the International Front, I resigned at the first congress for the following reasons. First, I am a serviceman and think that if the army divided into supporters of the International Front and the Popular Front, we would split the army. I recommended that servicemen, workers in the KGB, and officers in the public prosecutor's office must not participate in either organization.

Later, in January 1989, I was nominated as a candidate to the Union parliament by the college where I studied in the 1970s. I had four competitors but won in the second round. I also became a people's deputy of the Latvian Supreme Soviet from this same electoral district.

When was Soyuz created?

Soyuz was created in the autumn of 1989 in this [the Moscow] Hotel in Deputy Kogan's room by five people.[7] For the most part, we were people from the Baltic republics who already understood the dangerous processes happening in our country. We initially talked about the necessity of uniting a wide circle of deputies, a group that would look beyond ideology to push the idea of a state system into the forefront of the political agenda. After several months of little activity [after the initial meeting], I took the initiative and worked out a draft of a platform for Soyuz, which I then circulated among other deputies.

What were the main principles of this declaration?

To defend human rights throughout the entire territory of the USSR irrespective of a person's nationality and, as a means of observing human rights, to preserve the united, federal state. I started to receive answers to my appeal immediately, and by the end of 1989 I already had received about a hundred letters from other deputies consenting to join. Deputy Kim made an official announcement of the existence of our group at the Supreme Soviet session in February 1990. At this moment of registration, we had 114 deputies. Soon thereafter, our membership started to grow rapidly. By December 1990, one year later, we had 460 members and were continuing to grow. At present, Soyuz has 563 members at the Congress [of People's Deputies of the USSR], but we have 200 more applications for membership, making our total around 750 people.

What kinds of people join Soyuz?

Our opponents claim that we represent only the military-industrial complex, but I must tell you that of the eighty military deputies present at the congress, only about twenty are in Soyuz. That is, out of 750 deputies in our organization only 20 are servicemen. Out of 2,250 deputies in the congress only 80 are servicemen, so the proportion of servicemen [in Soyuz] is being observed.

Among our members, we have many office and industrial workers.

What kind of a relationship does Soyuz have with the Union leadership?

At first, we were on good terms with Lukyanov [the Speaker of the USSR Supreme Soviet]. He supported the idea of setting up such a group. But over the last six months, we have been in serious disagreement regarding our radical stance toward Gorbachev. Lukyanov is upset with our stance, and so we are on rather cool terms.

As for relations with Gorbachev, they used to be quite good. We backed his nomination for the USSR presidency. Initially, Soyuz was planning to nominate Ryzhkov. But at a meeting before the congress [which eventually elected Gorbachev] some people asked, "Why are we supporting only Ryzhkov? Why not Gorbachev?" Another said, "I prefer Bakatin!" So as to not split our organization, we nominated three candidates. In doing so, we were, of course, suffering from the child's disease of democracy.

We backed Gorbachev until 1990, though my attitude toward him was skeptical from the very beginning. But after events in Lithuania [in January 1990] and after March 11, 1990, when Gorbachev refused to carry out the decisions of the Third Congress [of the USSR People's Deputies] regarding Lithuania, our group began to oppose Gorbachev.

What have been his major mistakes?

All his actions concerning the preservation of the Union have been erroneous. He did not take a single correct move during the last two years. Every one of his actions only aggravated the situation. Let us take, for example, his idea of self-financing for the Baltic republics. It failed. His policy of appeasement in Lithuania also failed. Because the country is on the verge of ruin as a result of his errors, we of course understand that he must go.

Who is to replace him?

At the least, a person who has political will. Gorbachev lacks political will. I have had personal contacts with him. Thus, I can say that he is a nice person, he can speak, he knows how to behave, he can compromise. But he totally lacks will. This trouble is common for all people from the apparat; they are absolutely incapable of working in extraordinary situations. They had grown accustomed to "telephone law," when it was enough for an official to give an order and the apparat would then carry it out in no time down through the lower floors of the pyramid. He did not have to do anything—just give an order. But now when he gives an order and the order is not fulfilled, it is necessary to get the order fulfilled using force if necessary. He does not know how to do this. He is at a loss. The tragedy is that Gorbachev hates to use violence. As he said at the army Party conference, "I will never use violence. I rule out using violence ahead of time." Such a person can follow the teachings of Lev Tolstoy, but he cannot be engaged in politics. Real human lives are behind his policy of nonviolence against evil. And no matter what he says, during the last two years more than two thousand people have been killed in interethnic clashes. Moreover, we have hundreds of thousands of refugees.[8] All the world comes to the rescue of Kurdish refugees, but we have hundreds of thousands of the same refugees all over the country. We just keep silent about it. And all that Gorbachev has to offer is his conscience. I doubt that President Bush would let people to be driven out of their homes in the United States. Is it a kind policy to pretend that nothing is happening, that everything is all right? This policy, unfortunately, brings about the opposite result.

What kind of leader, then, do you need, and what kind of policy should be pursued?

The major problem today is not even economical; it is political. It would be impossible to carry out economic changes now. For example, suppose Yavlinsky comes out with a "hundred-day program."[9] He needs political stability to carry it out; he needs a mechanism that will make people abide by it. What will happen if miners and oil industry workers go on strike? What if they shout, "Down with Yavlinsky!" I am convinced that Yeltsin will have to restrict democracy in Russia to carry out any economic reforms—that is, to prohibit strikes, meetings, demonstrations. It is inevitable, as democracy has degenerated into chaos in our country.

If Yeltsin suppressed democracy and introduced strict authoritarian structures, would Soyuz support him or defend democracy?
We are for solutions that are within the framework of the [Soviet] Union because Yeltsin will not manage to do it separately in Russia if there is chaos in the rest of the Union. He will fail if he tries to split the Union apart and solve only problems in his republic. But if Yeltsin's actions were aimed at preserving the state, [that is,] the Union as a whole, we would support him.

But today he is driven by ambition. In principle, there is nothing wrong with a desire to have power, but since his ambitions are ruining the state, we oppose him. Do you remember what a noise was made this spring over the joint militia and army patrol? Now that Sobchak has been elected mayor, his first order was to introduce joint patrols in Leningrad. We will not solve the problem of political stability in this country until we have achieved the priority of law over politics. If a republic wishes to secede from the Union, there is a law by which it can do it freely. There is the constitution of the USSR. If you do not like it, let us change it and approve a new one. But while the constitution is valid, let us observe it. It is not all right just to say, "I will not abide by it because it was written by Stalin and Brezhnev." This kind of declaration leads only to chaos.

As a result, we now have a second wave of violating the laws within the Russian Federation. Now Tatarstan is infringing upon the sovereign rights of Russia. It is clear that Tatarstan wants to secede from Russia. These developments were provoked by Boris Nikolaevich [Yeltsin]. He has achieved in his Russia what he was actively promoting in the Union. This is why the number-one question is political stability.

How can political stability be achieved?
Unfortunately today it is impossible to do anything. We will have to wait until everything gets worse because right now illusions are still lingering. The mass media should be blamed for fanning this democratic hysteria. The change of public opinion has not taken place yet, but people already are demanding order. But when things get worse, when industrial enterprises come to a standstill, it will be understood that if we do not start creating democracy and observing laws, there will be only one way out—to declare a state of emergency. I am sure that Yeltsin will have to declare a state of emergency in Russia as well. Kravchuk [in Ukraine], Nazarbayev [in Kazakhstan], all of them will declare a state of emergency. And then we will tell them, "We told you so; we had suggested that you do this long ago." For now, we must wait, but it will happen by the end of the year.

More concretely, we suggest the following way out of this crisis: first establish the market and then democracy. We need to follow the pattern of the postwar development in Japan, when General MacArthur did everything to introduce a market in Japan, or in West Germany, where American occupation troops helped Erhard carry out economic changes, or the way of South Korea or the most offensive example, Chile. The last example is too extreme, as anticonstitutional actions were taken in Chile during the coup. We stand for the solution of our problems by observing the constitution. We want the legally elected authorities to carry out the state of emergency.

How do you regard the growing U.S. influence on the process of reform in the USSR? What is your attitude to "new thinking" in Soviet foreign policy?

"New thinking" is a myth. Contradictions between the USSR and the USA existed before, they exist now, and they will exist in the future, just as contradictions exist between the United States and Japan, the United States and Germany, and the United States and Great Britain. It is inevitable. Now we are told that new thinking is good. But, excuse me! On March 28, 1991, [Secretary of State James] Baker handed over a note from the American administration to Mr. Chetvertakov, the acting chargé d'affaires of the USSR in the United States. This was a very interesting note. As you remember, on March 28 meetings and demonstrations organized to coincide with the opening of the Russian Congress of People's Deputies were prohibited in Moscow. This note included the following interesting phrase, "the American Administration demands that the Soviet Government cancel all restrictions on meetings and demonstrations in Moscow." This is an example of new thinking! Let us suppose that a couple of weeks later, hooligans are discovered in downtown Washington, and therefore the Washington mayor imposes a curfew. How would the United States respond if [Soviet foreign minister] Bessmertnikh handed over to [American ambassador] Matlock a note demanding that the curfew be lifted?

I do not really believe in this new thinking. We are deceiving ourselves and others. Of course, it is necessary to seek mutually acceptable compromises to preserve the balance of interests. The United States, as well as the Soviet Union, has vital interests of its own, and these interests do not always coincide. They can be opposite in some respects, but I am a realist.

Why did the revolutions in Eastern Europe occur?

It all started in 1987. Gorbachev himself told us at a meeting with Soyuz that, until 1987, perestroika was not progressing. He said that attempts were made to carry out economic reforms before 1987, but the people were still fast asleep. So, as Gorbachev put it, they decided to accelerate the restructuring process by beginning political reform from below.

These days, this issue is hushed up, but the Baltic republics, in fact, were chosen as a training ground. They decided to test the situation with the creation of the Latvian Popular Front. Decisions were made by the CPSU Central Committee, and local Party organs were involved in the creation of the Latvian Popular Front. Recently, a former leader of the Latvian Popular Front, Alexander Blinov, the editor of the newspaper *Soviet Youth*, published a portion of his memoirs in the newspaper *Reform* [no. 1, published by the Center of Democratic Initiative] under the headline "I Can Reveal a Little Secret to You." The article describes how Boris Karlovich Pugo, the former first secretary of the Latvian CPSU Central Committee, summoned him and gave him instructions on how to create the Popular Front of Latvia. Disciplined Communists created the front. I remember very well that at that time, in 1988, we had commands to hand in statistical reports on how many people had joined the Latvian Popular Front. These reports were given to Party committees at enterprises and offices. If only a few people joined at a particular enterprise, the Party secretary there was given a dressing-down. Thus, they nurtured a snake in their bosom that later suffocated them.

They failed in the Baltics, but they failed to take this unpleasant experience into account. In Eastern Europe, the same methods were employed. Recently, I talked with one of the former GDR [German Democratic Republic] leaders. He claimed that when Gorbachev visited the GDR for the fortieth anniversary celebration, he demanded that Honecker begin to pursue a policy of restructuring. But in the GDR at the time, everything was frozen. There were no movements. Honecker committed a drastic mistake by making the following statement, "Dear Comrade Gorbachev, the Soviet Union is a big country, but as a result of perestroika, it will split apart in ten years. The GDR is a small country, and therefore we cannot follow the course of perestroika." Gorbachev replied that we will use a different method [in the Soviet Union] then. Recently, a videocassette was brought to me from Sweden that showed how the former GDR leaders Krentz, Modrov, and Shabovsky were working with the Soviet Union. Modrov said, "I had to visit the embassy of the USSR secretly for a while. I used to get into the Lada [a Soviet-made car] out in the countryside and then was driven into the embassy through the back gate." You see, there was a plot against Honecker. Since he did not suit the Soviet leadership, they decided to get rid of him. Shabovsky says that, when the first attempt to remove Honecker failed because Willie Shtoff did not back this idea, Shabovsky called the Soviet ambassador and asked him to summon Shtoff and make him oppose Honecker. The ambassador invited Shtoff to the embassy, gave him instructions on what to do, and the next day, at the Politburo meeting, Shtoff raised the question of Honecker's removal. They voted to remove Honecker. And after this intervention, we claim that we have renounced the Brezhnev doctrine, that we are not going to interfere with home affairs of sovereign states, that we have the policy of new thinking! I do not see any real difference. In 1968 we removed Dubchek with tanks, and in October 1989 we removed Honecker through a plot. The essence of these actions is the same—interference with the internal affairs of a sovereign state, moreover, of an ally. It is not much to our credit. When a leader advocates the ideal of noninterference, of new thinking, on the one hand, and, on the other hand, does such things, he is two-faced. It is very sad.

What is your attitude toward the withdrawal of Soviet troops from Eastern Europe?
Besides ideological and political purposes, any war also has geopolitical aims. Americans, for instance, are interested in maintaining military bases in Western Europe, the Philippines, Okinawa, and so on so as to have an opportunity to influence the situation in these regions in favor of American interests. So for our own state interests, we needed to have our troops in Eastern Europe so that the line of the possible military conflict was far from Soviet territory. We thought just like Americans; war can be waged somewhere far away, like in Vietnam or Afghanistan, but not on the territories of the United States or the Soviet Union. In principle there existed a balance of forces that both sides tried to keep. The world order that took shape under conditions of two superpowers actually suited a lot of people, as it let many countries pursue their own independent policy. If, for instance, the Soviet Union began to pressure some country too persistently, this country could move closer to the United States and thus balance the imperial ambitions of the USSR. The same happened if the USA grew too aggressive. So, many parties capitalized on the balance of power between two superpowers; this situation suited the majority of people.

But now, many are at a loss and do not know what to do or how to behave. Developments that took place in Eastern Europe are very sad. I recently spoke at the Supreme Soviet [of the USSR], where I noted that on April 2 [1991], the day we signed the last two agreements on Germany, the USSR suffered an utter defeat in World War II. And the loss came not from the people who had won the victory in the war but from the politicians fifty years later.

The six years [1985–1991] we are living through now will make our ears burn for a long time. I am afraid that our children and grandchildren will bitterly regret everything that happened during these last six years. I am a realist. I am not interested in *isms*. Socialism, internationalism—all that is secondary. But I know that there are state interests—vital interests of the United States and vital interests of the Soviet Union. And to my deep regret, I have to admit that our interests have been very seriously damaged.

Our withdrawal from Eastern Europe was a failure in foreign policy. Only professionals should be engaged in politics. James Baker is a professional. He was not a Party official who was suddenly nominated as foreign minister by the general secretary. By the time he became secretary of state, he had had fundamental training. When the first secretary of the Georgian CPSU Central Committee [Eduard Shevardnadze] was appointed his counterpart, I could understand why the Americans applauded. When nonprofessionals assume such positions, it is an example of incompetent policy.

You said that you are against *isms*. Does this mean that Soyuz is not against the market?
For God's sake! We stress that we are beyond ideology. We are not interested in

what it will be called—capitalism or socialism. All that is secondary. We are concerned about the state, how to feed the people and provide them with clothes, how to preserve the state and ensure the political stability necessary to carry out market reforms.

You have talked a lot about the failures of reform. Why, then, do you think people support these changes?

The American political system has a great advantage in that it is a two-party system. If a Republican government fails, Democrats come to power and the people then believe that "these guys will make things right." Five years pass, the Democrats have failed, and the people start to believe in the Republicans again. A similar thing is now happening in the USSR. Quite frankly, the Communists compromised themselves. In the United States, however, the change [from one administration to another] is smooth; there are no sudden turns and the political system is not destroyed. In the Soviet Union, however, it was clear that the totalitarian system had compromised itself. But Gorbachev could have salvaged the situation. Gorbachev could have begun political reforms in the Party by dividing it into two parties—Communist and Social-Democratic. [He could have said] Comrades Ligachev and Polozkov, could you please form this party, and Comrades Yakovlev and Shevardnadze, could you please form that party. If Comrades Ligachev and Polozkov failed in government, Comrades Yakovlev and Shevardnadze would take their place. But the change in government would take place smoothly and not ruin the system. But this was not done and so today the chaos begins.

It is only the beginning of the process. The same is true in Eastern Europe. For instance, I am sure that Solidarity will keep power for a while, then fail, and then everybody will say that "times under Jaruzelski were better." It is inevitable.

That is why I think that a two-party system is the best possible variant. At present, the CPSU will have to exit the political scene for five or ten years. New political powers will win elections, then these new powers will fail, and the role and the influence of the CPSU will grow. It might come to power again in five to ten years. Only then will a normal political system start to take shape. The system we have now is not in complete ruin. Only now are we starting to appreciate the advantages we used to have—for example, the absence of unemployment. In this new system, we do not even have a social welfare mechanism. According to the prognoses, we are going to have up to thirty million people unemployed by the end of the year and as many as one million unemployed in Moscow alone. Just think what will happen here on Manezh Square when the democrats demanding further democratization and openness are replaced by the hungry demanding a piece of bread.

I remember very well the stifling atmosphere of the stagnation times [under Brezhnev], when one could speak openly with your wife only in the kitchen with closed doors so that nobody could hear. Now, I have breathed the air of freedom and nothing can drive me back. But I want changes to be within the limits of law. The CPSU is leaving the political scene, but its vacant place must be substituted with something. At present we have no ideology. Our state used to be based on communist ideology and it united us. Now it has collapsed. And the trouble, now, is that we have got nothing to oppose the national idea. Nationalism is very attractive for people of some particular nationality. But it is necessary to oppose it with something. We need a new ideology badly. I think the most promising is the ideology of statehood. But all that lays ahead. First, it is clear that it will be necessary to set up a party.

Have you already taken steps toward setting up a party?

Yes, in principle. This idea was mentioned in a draft declaration, which made the formation of a party contingent on developments in the country.

What is your attitude toward Democratic Russia? Will this movement become your major adversary?

It will be our major political adversary, but it is doomed to failure. This movement used to support actively the process of splitting the Union apart. But now Russia itself has started to collapse. Under these circumstances, I cannot rule out the scenario that Russian president Boris Yeltsin will command airborne troops to capture the Kazan television center.[10] At present, Tatarstan plays the same role for Russia as Lithuania did for the USSR. I had a talk with Vladimir Lopatin [a military officer known for his radical views], who spent a month in Tatarstan. He was telling me with horror what a complicated situation is taking shape there. Nationalism penetrates everything. Separatism has reached the point where people have started demanding to secede not only from Russia but from the USSR. But where can they go—the moon? And this is the case not only with Tatarstan. Last autumn, Yeltsin toured the autonomous republics and suggested to them that they take as much sovereignty as they could afford. They followed his advice. Now he is going to face this situation as his major problem. He has an advantage over Gorbachev because he will not be ashamed to use force to put autonomous republics in their place. But it is going to be difficult. And [in these conditions] the democrats will have to change their slogans and start talking about the one and indivisible Russia and give up the principle of sovereignty. But they will find themselves in a complicated position. How can they reject sovereignty within Russia and back it beyond its borders?

They also will start radical economical changes, and I am sure that real Russian businessmen will appear—not those who seek to snatch millions, commit robbery, escape, and never think of the future—but real old-style Russian businessmen, like the Stroganovs, who were concerned not only about their purse but about the problems of the state as well. As they become more prosperous, they will tell Yeltsin, "We are sorry but we need Baltic ports. Why should we pay customs duty to Lithuania, when the Klaipeda port [in Lithuania] was constructed at Russia's expense. Besides, this Landesbergis [the president of Lithuania] does not let us ship goods there. Do something to get rid of this customs duty." I am sure that economic demands will make those who now cry "Freedom to Lithuania!" start looking to cut the window into Europe again. They will also have to break up Rukh and put [Geogian president] Gamsakhurdia into prison. It is inevitable. I am sure that the living conditions of Russian-speaking populations will be used as a pretext to put autonomous republics in their place.

You said that you are against all *isms*, but it seems to me that Soyuz has formed an alliance with the group Rossiya in the Russian parliament.

The position of the group Rossiya appeals to us much more than that of Democratic Russia because the former backs the state. If Democratic Russia supported statehood, we would have been with them. For the most part, I also have no disagreement with the Interregional Group.[11] I stand for the market and a multiparty system. But I did not join the Interregional Group because of their attitude toward the state. I would not compromise with them on this subject.

Did Soyuz join the Centrist Bloc?

You see, this was my personal mistake. We were seeking to find support from the masses, and then a Centrist Bloc uniting twenty to thirty parties and movements appeared. We fell for the bait. But when we understood the real situation, we quit a month later. It is not a serious movement. The parties in the bloc only have ten to fifteen members each but have high-sounding titles like the Party of Peace and so on. It is not a serious organization.

What about Zhirinovsky, another organizer of the Centrist Bloc?[12]

He is a serious politician. If he stops being so eccentric, he will acquire a reputation by capitalizing on the "Russian problem." He will have a very good position in the future.

***Nezavisimaya Gazeta* (Independent Newspaper) recently analyzed the speeches by Zhirinovsky and discovered many similarities between his rhetoric and that of Hitler.**

We also compared the papers of the Latvian Popular Front with Pamyat' and they coincided. As for nazism, if we read the nazi programs, disengaged from reality, they sound appealing. Now, we know what fascism is and to what it led. But if you do not know the context, it [nazism] sounds quite all right. Nazism's ideas make everything sound nice and attractive. But I do not think that we should call Zhirinovsky a Fascist. It is not so.

How are your relations with the United Workers' Front and Pamyat'?

We are allies in some respects, but we disagree over certain points. The orthodox Communists are rather cautious toward me.

Finally, what can you say about the situation within the military right now?

I spoke about this subject at our last session [of the USSR Supreme Soviet]. In 1814, the Russian army came back from Europe after a victorious campaign against Napoleon and brought home the ideas of the Decembrist uprising of 1825. It was the first action for democracy in Russia against monarchy. What kinds of ideas the Soviet Red Army will bring back after being driven out of Eastern

Europe in disgrace, God only knows. It is a major problem, especially taking into account the ruins of our economy. These people lived there in conditions of developed socialism. Standards of living in East Germany, Czechoslovakia, or Hungary were much better than in the Soviet Union. It was profitable to serve in the armed forces even in terms of salary. Moreover, as they return there is an acute shortage of housing. All these people used to have apartments. They were respected. It was pleasant to serve there. So, to leave there to come to this hellish disorder where there are no apartments, prices are outrageously high, and there is political instability—this is a very serious problem.

What is the future political role of the military?

Its influence will grow. The fact that Yeltsin selected [Colonel] Rutskoi to run as his vice-president, that Ryzhkov chose [General] Gromov, and that [General] Makashov was nominated [as a presidential candidate] demonstrate that despite the antiarmy campaign that was launched in the country, the servicemen's rating is still rather high. We are the least corrupt structure of our society. The army is the only organization that has preserved its centralization and unity. That is why its influence will grow.

chapter twelve

The Liberal-Democratic Party of the USSR

The founding congress of the Liberal-Democratic Party (LDP) of the USSR took place on March 31, 1990.[1] Although only a handful of people participated in that congress, the party's chairman, Vladimir Zhirinovsky, announced shortly thereafter that the Liberal-Democratic Party had more than three thousand registered members.[2]

These inflated membership figures are just one of many mysteries surrounding the LDP. Many, in fact, believe that the party and the charismatic Zhirinovsky were created by the Communist Party and the KGB to discredit and divide the democratic forces.[3] For instance, the LPD program represents a comprehensive strategy for establishing a democratic, capitalist society, as stated in its introduction:

Liberal policies can give an individual the required scope for all-round development, creating social prerequisites for realizing various alternatives. These policies decisively reject bureaucratic and totalitarian restrictions on the development of the assorted aptitudes of an individual.

One distinctive feature of a liberal society is respect for the personal responsibility of citizens and, at the same time, the state's readiness to assume a measure of responsibility where the citizens' possibilities run out.

A liberal society, the building of which is the LDP's goal, is a society that looks for the right solutions to problems confronting it amid ideological, political, and economic competition. It is a society that seeks to avoid a division into enemies and friends in open discussions of alternative programs.[4]

Zhirinovsky's speeches and actions, however, bear little resemblance to the carefully crafted program.[5] As demonstrated in the interview below, Zhirinovsky has espoused the elimination of the CPSU monopoly on political and economic power but also has advocated the preservation of the Union, the strengthening of the military, and the persecution of non-Russian ethnic groups that seek independence.[6] At times Zhirinovsky has called for the construction of a market economy, but on other occasions he has advocated the "quarantine" of privatization and the destruction of the "southern Mafia" (i.e., people from the southern republics of the former Soviet Union) and the "Zionists" that seek to pilfer Russia's assets through privatization schemes.[7]

Russia's democratic forces quickly distanced themselves from the LDP, claiming that the organization was neither liberal nor democratic. But Zhirinovsky's party did find allies within the government and Russian nationalist movements. On June 8, 1990, Zhirinovsky helped found the Centrist Bloc, a coalition of both real and fictitious parties with tacit support from conservative figures in the Soviet government.[8] Soon thereafter, the official Soviet press printed detailed and frequent articles about Zhirinovsky's meetings with top government officials, including KGB chief Kryuchkov, Minister of Defense Yazov, and Minister of the Interior Boris Pugo.[9] Zhirinovsky also frequently traveled to the other republics, where he spoke in defense of Russian minorities.

Besides the Communist Party of the Soviet Union, the Liberal-Democratic Party was the only party to have its own candidate in the Russian presidential election in June 1991. During the campaign, Zhirinovsky promised law and order, a return of Russian greatness, and cheap vodka. Although virtually unknown before the election campaign, Zhirinovsky placed third out of six candidates (behind Yeltsin and Nikolai Ryzhkov), winning six million votes.[10]

Zhirinovsky's success shocked everyone and brought him much attention in the Russian press. The democratic press, although denouncing him as a fool, also compared the Zhirinovsky phenomenon with Hitler's rise to power in Weimar Germany during the 1920s.[11] After the June elections, Zhirinovsky began conferring with several nationalist and patriotic organizations as well as with neocommunist movements about creating a committee for national salvation to save the country from the democrats, who were usurping power and destroying the country.

During the coup, Zhirinovsky and the Liberal-Democratic Party actively supported the Emergency Committee, an action that Zhirinovsky had encouraged since January 1991. Thus, when the putsch collapsed, Zhirinovsky's popularity quickly dissipated. Soon thereafter the special commission investigating the putsch charged Zhirinovsky with conspiring with the KGB and the putschists. Beginning in January 1992, however, Yeltsin's economic reforms again fueled

Zhirinovsky's popular appeal. At antigovernment demonstrations, Zhirinovsky again promised stability, law and order, the end of profiteering by non-Russian nationalities, and the restoration of Russia as a world superpower. Claiming that the dissolution of the Soviet Union was illegal, Zhirinovsky promised to reciprocate by readjusting Russia's borders and making claims on territories in Ukraine, the Baltic states, Kazakhstan, Turkmenistan, and Finland. As for ethnic conflicts in Russia and the other new states of the commonwealth, Zhirinovsky promised to end all wars within seventy-two hours of becoming president. To accomplish this task, Zhirinovsky estimated that 300,000–400,000 lives would be lost.

Zhirinovsky is a charismatic leader of Russia's fascist and neonationalist forces. His future depends on the success or failure of the new Russian government. As Zhirinovsky argues, the worse the economic and political situation in the country, the better his chances are of assuming power.

Vladimir Zhirinovsky

Trained as a Turkish specialist and lawyer at Moscow State University, Vladimir Zhirinovsky worked for Mir publishers and the Soviet Peace Committee as a law consultant and publisher for several years before becoming active in politics.[12] In May 1988, Zhirinovsky appeared unexpectedly at the founding congress of the Democratic Union. After the second day, however, he was expelled from the organization as a provocateur. He surfaced again in October 1989 at the founding congress of the Liberal-Democratic Party, was elected chairman, and has dominated the organization ever since.

Interview with
Vladimir Zhirinovsky (May 1991)

. . . .

When did you first get involved in politics?

In 1967, I sent a letter to the country's leaders pointing out the necessity of reforms in education, economics, and society in general. Thereafter, I used to make speeches at disputes, meetings, and discussions on television. I often appeared on a television discussion club in Ostankino. At the time, I was not oppressed directly. However, I was barred from going abroad and could not get a promotion or study where I wanted. I realized at that time that they would not do much to you if one acted in a mild and law-abiding way. I was not considered a dissident. That is why I was neither sentenced nor sent to a mental hospital by force.

I became most active, however, fours years ago. For many years, I had been thinking about creating an alternative party as I have always supported a multiparty system. In 1971, I wrote a monograph called *Political Parties of Turkey*, so I have always been doing research on multiparty systems as an aspect of my job, as a hobby, and as part of my creed. Practical implementation of my ideas became possible three years ago. In May 1988, my program [for creating a multiparty system in the Soviet Union] was published throughout the West. All tenets of my program are now being implemented: a multiparty system, a mixed economy, a presidential form of government, and changes in foreign policy. All these ideas that are currently being implemented were included in my program.

Didn't you begin your political career as an activist in the Democratic Union?

I attended their founding congress in 1988. The delegates listened to me and promoted me into their leadership. However, the other leaders of the Democratic Union were frightened of me as I was a competitor. [Valeriya] Novodvorskaya [a Democratic Union leader] was frightened then, and Yeltsin is afraid of me today. They are always afraid of me. It is not my fault that I am better or superior to them. In 1988, the leadership of the Democratic Union opposed me from the very beginning, claiming that the congress's decision [to elect me into their leadership] was invalid. They told me that I should become a rank-and-file party member. How could I be rank and file? Did not the congress elect me? So I quit that same day. I understood that they were extremists and today they have proven this. I was right again. Three years have passed and they still have no party. This is a party of arrests, imprisonment, tearing down posters, hunger strikes—that's not my style.

Nonetheless, I continued to be involved in politics. And, at last, in December 1989, my colleagues and I wrote a program for a Liberal-Democratic Party. On December 13, 1989, we held a minicongress in an apartment, coincidently in the same apartment where the first congress of the Democratic Union had been held, at which we approved the party's program. At this minicongress, I outlined the main objectives of the party and was elected leader. In March 1990, we held an all-Union congress of the party, and since March 31, 1990, I have been chairman of the party.

We faced great difficulties publishing our program. It is a large program that covers all aspects of life. No other party has a similar program. We are short of newsprint and financial support because we do not have any Russian DuPonts or Rockefellers. Those that have money are afraid to invest in our party. Black marketeers and dealers are afraid to give us money because the KGB will find out about their contributions. But we have received some help. We have a car, a driver, and money to publish twenty-six thousand brochures. However, this is next to nothing. I need millions to make the party an active force. If I had 100 million rubles, I would win these elections [for the Russian presidency]. I would become president of Russia, and the country would take a new course. So my only problem is finance. I have everything else.

What is the origin of your party's name?

I studied platforms of various European parties and realized that social democrats are too left wing. They have the backing of workers' movements because they offer comprehensive social guarantees and support public ownership. Liberals, on the other hand, are centrists, moderates; they support private ownership, human rights, and a legal state—all in which I believe. Right-wing parties—nationalists, republicans, and Fascists—they are too dangerous. They can lead to dictatorship again. We are a middle variant, somewhere between the Republican and Democratic parties in the United States.

The name of your party includes the words "of the Soviet Union" doesn't it?

Yes, it's called Liberal-Democratic Party of the Soviet Union. I support preserving the whole of this state. Russians live in all parts of the USSR. If we preserve only half of it and decrease the size of the state, then Russians will have to return. That would lead to chaos, severing ties. This is unthinkable today. Besides, many people want to stay where they are now. In Georgia, Abkhazians and Ossetians want to reside in their localities. What should we do? Because of their desire to live in the homelands, Georgians kill Ossetians! Is that democracy? In Georgia, a Yeltsin has come to power. Gamsakhurdia is the Georgian Yeltsin. Now that he is in power it is difficult to know what is next. Landesbergis is the Lithuanian Yeltsin. These are poor variants.

This is why I prefer contacts with Communists. They are harmless. As their party [the CPSU] gradually withdraws, however, they will still have power. Democrats accuse me of working with the Communists. Yes, I deal with the

Communists because it is easier to work with them. The democrats are hungry and impudent fanatics, while these Communists already have calmed down, making it easier to deal with them. I need minimal support and a legal status, and the Communists have power. These are my tactics.

The democrats try to explain to the citizens that I get on too well with the Communists. Well, I am ready to get on with anyone, even these democrats. But they turn their backs on me. I am a competitor so they are afraid of me. They want to break down the Communists and take their positions. There had been Red Bolsheviks, and now there are White Bolsheviks.

My tactics, however, are correct. I am winning. Of all the candidates for the Russian presidency, only two can win, Yeltsin and me. The rest are nothing. Yeltsin has power and money. Give me his money and that will be the end. They will not give it to me because they are afraid.

Do you intend to debate Mr. Yeltsin?

I insist on it, but Yeltsin refuses. He is afraid. On June 10, 1991, central television has invited all candidates to a roundtable discussion. Yeltsin, however, is leaving Moscow and will not return until June 11, 1991. He is leaving because he is a coward, a real coward. Ten days before the elections, I have proposed that we should be debating on television continuously. The others don't want it because they are afraid. What can I do?

I have achieved breakthroughs in certain areas, but it's not enough. People are afraid of me and that makes me feel optimistic. I know I will win. At the Congress [of USSR People's Deputies in the spring of 1991] I got more votes than Yeltsin. He received a four-vote majority while I won a forty-vote majority, ten times more than him.[13] This is why he's afraid of me.

What is the difference between your electoral program and Yeltsin's?

My program differs in four aspects from all other programs. First, the national problem: I support restoring the old administrative divisions. We need to go back to the old tested variant and re-create seventy to one hundred provinces populated with three million people each. They, on the other hand, support some notion of the friendship of peoples, a union of sovereign republic states. This idea is idle talk and will have no result. The Union that was established in 1922 has collapsed. My proposal [for new governmental structures] would be cheaper and safer. This is a radical difference between me and all the others.

Second is foreign policy. Focus on East-West relations has to end. North-South relations should be our focus. Turkey, Iran, Afghanistan, the Middle East: this is where we could become a key figure. And we could do this together with the Americans, Japanese, and Europeans. You [the United States] need oil from the region. Take it. Wherever there is unrest, our troops from the Transcaucasian and middle Asian military districts can carry out a neutralization policy in the region. Because it is in your interests, you will pay for these military operations. Using your own forces requires transporting troops from far away. For us, these regions are only a 100 kilometers away. It would be cheaper for you and we would get the profits. Who will suffer from that? How much have you spent on the gulf war? A hundred billion? We could do it for eighty billion. You will save money and your soldiers can stay home. If we, the whites, the European and North American races govern the world, the world will enjoy peace and order. We need to return to the concept of spheres of influence. [As president] I will withdraw everything from Cuba. We withdraw from there [Cuba], you withdraw from here [states closer to the Soviet Union]. We will have our new spheres of influence in the South. They [the democrats] lack this concept.

Our third difference is related to the national economy. For me, a market means an equal market for all. The Communists also agree; however, they object to private ownership, and they are uncertain about privatization. Democrats are the opposite; they support urgent privatization. I propose a compromise variant: a market economy for all but no foreclosures. If a plant is producing, it should continue to operate. There is no need to sell it at an auction. Let it go bankrupt first, and then someone can purchase it at an auction. The same is true about collective farms. If a farm can operate in the black, let it operate. There is no need to scare anyone about unemployment. Strong individual farms will eventually force weak collective farms to dissolve. Or perhaps a strong collective farm will swallow up new farmers. Let economics decide these questions.

They [Zhirinovsky's opponents] are used to taking administrative decisions. They say, go ahead and do your business even while the criminal code contains an article prohibiting entrepreneurial activity. I am a lawyer. I know English, French, German, and Turkish. I graduated from two departments at Moscow State University, receiving two liberal arts degrees. I graduated from the Institute of Asian and African Studies. We need someone with my background because we are an oriental country. That is my region and I know it well. I have studied these regions for twenty-six years. I have spent half of my life in these [Asian] republics. I know all. They have never been there. They do not know anything. It is like Africa to them. I have never been to the South African republic and know little about it. How could I govern there? They, on the other hand, arrive in Yerevan only to find out upon arriving at the airport that Armenians are Christians. How can you govern such a country, unaware of the religion of the whole republic?

They lack competence. Being Communists, they have a different ideology. They find management difficult today. Communist ideology has to withdraw. It was a mistake, a failed experiment. They, however, cannot change themselves as all of them have been in the Party for over thirty years. The Party gave them everything. That is why they are flying high now. It will not be free elections on June 12, 1991. It is just another seizure of power like the Bolsheviks did on October 25, 1917. I tell them that they should postpone the elections, but they are afraid to do so. The Bolsheviks said the same thing in October [1917]:

yesterday was too early, tomorrow will be too late, power must be seized today. Yeltsin acts in the same manner; yesterday was too early for him, fall will be too late. Therefore, power should be seized on June 12, 1991. They are cowardly politicians. What can I do?

You recently have traveled widely throughout the non-Russian republics. How has your plan for the reorganization of the Soviet Union been received outside Russia?

In Abkhazia, they applauded me. In Lithuania, they welcomed me and supported my concepts. People in Kazakhstan fully support me as the republic is populated mainly with Russians. Another two million Russian people live in Uzbekistan. Wherever Russian people or Russian-speaking ethnic groups live, they support me. They will vote for me. That is why Yeltsin is afraid of me. Gamsakhurdia and Landesbergis hate me. They are afraid that if I become president of Russia, they will have to make radical changes in their policies.

I have been everywhere, from Moldavia to Chukotka. I also have traveled throughout Europe and America. So I know the world. My father studied at the Sorbonne. My family is a family of lawyers. We are a centuries-old family of the intelligentsia. My grandfather was a banker in America. This is a family with high intellect and culture. I am fighting against those from the Red proletariat who are trying to preserve their power. Look at who their candidates are for the post of vice-president: a colonel and a general.[14] Yeltsin's candidate for vice-president is Colonel Rutskoi. What did he do in Afghanistan? He made a lot of fuss and did lot a shooting. He is unstable. What kind of a vice-president will he make? He is not an intellectual but a muzhik from Kursk. Ryzhkov's candidate is another general, Gromov, who is also the first deputy minister for internal affairs. Makashov [another candidate] is a general. Tuleyev is a railroad worker, while his candidate for vice-president is a miner from the Kemerovo region.

Where is the intellect? All of them are no good. Yeltsin pretends to be a radical, claiming that Ryzhkov supports the military-industrial complex, collective farmers, and workers. But you understand that Yeltsin [if elected president] means war for this country. He will carry out a military coup d'état, and then you Americans will have to spend more money to safeguard America from the new radical, semibarbarian regime.

Today you should place your bets on such people as me because I am with you. I tell you openly that you will be safer with me. I will provide you stability so you can spend less on defense. You have spent trillions opposing Red Moscow, trillions between 1945 and 1985. Do you want to spend more billions and trillions until the year 2000? Invite Yeltsin into the European Community of states and that is the end, chaos, destruction. Do you want to repeat the Georgian events all over again here in Russia?

But so far the West has been very cautious toward Yeltsin.

I know what you want. You know that Yeltsin and his team will never make Russia strong and powerful. In principle, your industrialists profit from a weak and dying Russia so that you have no economic rivals. However, Yeltsin's team will pose a tremendous military threat; your manufacturers will win but your generals will lose. I, on the other hand, will create a new scenario so that you will not have to spend so much on defense and your manufacturers will not be afraid of rivals. We shall divide our spheres of influence. You want to do away with the Japanese? I will help you wipe them out so that Japan can no longer compete with you. Western Europe needs something here? No problem, we will not interfere. Each country should have its own sphere of influence. Turkey, Iran, and Afghanistan: that is all we need. I claim these three countries, no more. My troops in the Middle East will defend your interests there. You will get your oil wherever you want it to be delivered. What else do you need? What else do you need, Americans?

However, you prefer to deal with Democratic Russia, with people like Murashev and Afanasiev.[15] They enjoy talking, calling for such things as freedom for the Baltic states. It is like Lenin granting independence to Poland and Finland.

What is your attitude toward Democratic Russia?

I dislike them. They are Bolsheviks. They are fanatics. When I come to their meetings, they do not admit me. They will not let me attend their discussions. They say slanderous things about me and spread dirty rumors. I was ready to cooperate with them, but then they got frightened. Lenin acted similarly, rejecting everyone except for himself and his Party. Democratic Russia is very similar. These are Bolsheviks, the new Whites, fanatics and radicals.

Will you please say a few words about your Centrist Bloc.[16]

We withdrew from it. Since April 18, 1991, we have been an independent force. The bloc became compromised when various organizations within the front promoted the idea of national salvation committees.[17] I, however, stick to the law. The activities of too many organizations [within the Centrist Bloc] do not always coincide with my views and the position of the party. Hence we do not need such dependence right now. We will form a new alliance of political powers later. We would like to unite, for instance, with the Cadets, but, just as in 1917, they are so weak and incapable of doing anything. We also find something in common with the Christian Democrats, but they all were trapped by Yeltsin's policy on nationalities. They do not agree with my views on national issues.

In all likelihood, Soyuz, the Russian National Party, and other large patriotic forces will join us. Currently, Soyuz supports Ryzhkov [for the Russian presidency]. Ryzhkov is their Stalin. They wanted to nominate someone who could oppose Yeltsin. Ryzhkov is well known, so they talked him into running for the presidency. Some people at the meeting [that nominated Ryzhkov] supported my nomination. If Ryzhkov does not compete in the second round of elections, his supporters—Communists, patriots, and Soyuz—will switch over to me.

What are your tactics to attract more people to your party?

We do not organize strikes. Rather, we participate in roundtable discussions and debates. However, we face financial difficulties. If I had a strong headquarters and finance, I could influence public opinion on a massive scale. The Moscow City Council would not give us an office for a headquarters because this body supports Yeltsin. This is sabotage. Because of these impediments, it has been very difficult for me to mobilize people.

That is why we try to participate in all electoral campaigns. By participating in the present campaign, we have been able to tell people about our party.

You have had several meetings with several high-ranking officials. Why do they meet with you and not others?

Yes, I have had meetings with Yazov, Kryuchkov, Laptev, Silayev, Ryzhkov, Nishanov, Oleynik, and Minister Sheadov.[18] I have tried to explain to them the necessity of another policy. [In those meetings], I have seen that many of these senior officials would be glad to support our party, as Democratic Russia is too radical for them. It is more beneficial for Communists to have contact with us, as we consider them to be the ruling party. Although our ideologies clash, we never accuse each other of anything. That is why we can cooperate and manage to preserve our positions.

As for the other parties, who are the Cadets? They are neither seen nor heard. Same for the Christian Democrats. Sometimes you hear about the Social Democrats and the Republican Party. Travkin's party has made a little fuss, but what next? He thought that he would set up a party and have a million members next day. Instead, he has thirty thousand members, that's all, a dead end. He could not even be nominated [for the Russian presidency].

How strong is your party?

To date, we have some seventeen thousand members. By fall, we will have fifty thousand members, and by the end of 1991 we will reach a hundred thousand. We can organize a large party, but money is needed. If we had financial support, we could stir up a lot of agitation.

How do you evaluate Gorbachev's leadership?

He has done the maximum of what he could have done as a Communist. Being a Communist within the Party, he cannot do anything else. People fail to understand this. In general, his tactics were correct initially. He was centrist. But lately, he has been very indecisive. He cannot take final actions. Most recently, he has made another mistake concerning the nationalities problem. The 9 + 1 agreement is a weak treaty. It will last for five to ten years, and then the other republics will begin to play tricks again.

My variant is much more simple: eliminate the republics and create seventy to a hundred provinces with locally elected governors. Let Tatars elect a Tatar governor in Kazan. It is not a republic but a province, so it will never generate the idea to leave the Union. In the United States no state intends to leave. Countries like Canada, France, and Spain have problems similar to ours, but the difference is that our problems will lead to a bloodbath. It is not Gorbachev's fault; it is his Party's fault. This policy was originated by Lenin.

As to his convictions, Gorbachev is no longer a Communist, but he leads a Party that includes a lot of hard-liners and fanatics.

What is the social base of your party?

It is very complicated. We have no businessmen, no merchants, no cultural elite, as the majority of these people are with the CPSU. We do not have real liberals of high intellect or any propertied businessmen. This the crux of the matter; we have neither good people nor money. Consequently, we have to admit all those willing to join.

I am telling you openly that this is our problem. We are a young party, only one year old. We grew out of a totalitarian regime composed of Communists, workers, collective farmers, and no one else. This poses problems. I need thousands of lawyers, entrepreneurs, physicians, merchants, businessmen. Where are they? They are either with the CPSU or with the shadow economy, either afraid or uncertain, so they have yet to come to our party. But we expect them to join us eventually.

Do you have relations with other liberal-democratic parties abroad?

We have excellent relations. I had good contacts with Germany, Switzerland, Belgium, Italy, and the Turkish centrist party. As we promote contacts with liberal parties, I find a common language with them. It is easier than with our workers or collective farmers. They are hostile toward me because they do not understand me. They call us the bourgeoisie. This will take time to change. Western liberal parties formed 150 years ago and were in opposition for 120 years. They have only been in power for the last thirty years. We are only one year old. What can you expect from us?

Postcoup Reflections (November 1991)

What did the putsch mean for you and for your party?

The putsch demonstrated a new stage of the thoroughly thought-out plan in the transition period from the communist Soviet Union or communist Russia to a new variant. We assume that there are international and internal factors in this scenario. The executors of the plan inside the country are of course well known: it is the present leadership. I think that it is a continuation of the January events in the Baltic republics. Besides, the USSR president seeks to reveal all his adversaries and let them fail, having created unfavorable conditions for their activities. All these new separatists—Gorbunovs, Ruytel, Landesbergis, Gamsakhurdia, Snegur, Kravchuk—are protégés of the center.[19] They purposefully inspire anti-Moscow, anti-Russian sentiments that stir up separatism. They behave as if the country was falling into pieces.

In Russia Gorbachev's main opponent is Yeltsin. Attempts to remove him from power through the parliament or make him lose at the elections have failed. So now he has been given the opportunity to change internal policy drastically, especially economic policy, and cause catastrophe, chaos, so that, in the spring, demonstrations, meetings, and strikes will wipe him away. Then, Mikhail Sergeevich [Gorbachev] will become a sole master again, president of the whole country.

I think that a real state of emergency will be declared later. We had only a rehearsal in August, but it demonstrated that a greater part of the population supported the GKChP [the Emergency Committee of Eight that led the coup attempt]. It means that if more worthy people form such a committee and the president himself heads it, it will receive an even more powerful backing. Eighty percent will support him, especially as he will show the population that there is chaos, ruin, civil war, Russians being killed, violence, plunder, fire, blockade, sabotage, paralysis. In these conditions, he will try to restore order. Besides the nomenklatura, people-appointed secretaries and second secretaries of regional committees of the CPSU and regional executive committees of local soviets still remain in power. Certain rearrangements have taken place so that now a former second secretary of the regional CPSU committee has become the head of the local authorities and thus remains in power. All Gorbachev's former councillors are surrounding Yeltsin at present.

On the other hand, there are representatives of Democratic Russia. These people will block Yeltsin and prevent him from acting the way in which he would like. Yeltsin is a resolute person, but they can make him act in favor of their own social politics, so that he becomes a kamikaze, a suicide. The Congress of Russian People's Deputies is a congress of suicides; it may be the last one. Yeltsin will convoke the Supreme Soviet next spring, and it will be the end of them all.

Yeltsin is sure to fail because it is impossible to make such a reform in the hungry and angry Russia of today. This reform is a possible variant but not at present, not in this country. The reform can not help failing and Gorbachev will use it. In the spring, when a real coup will take place, it will be necessary to salute Mikhail Sergeevich [Gorbachev] and restore the validity of the USSR constitution. Gorbachev is the USSR president. He was elected for five years. The term of his office will expire in 1994 so he has some time left.

What are the present objectives of your party? How has your situation changed since the putsch?

Our social basis has been expanding rapidly. After August 19 [the day of the coup] many former Communists, KGB servicemen, policemen, people from the rural areas, collective farmers, and factory workers have been joining us. A big part of the USSR parliament and Russian parliament deputies has come over to us. A bloc of patriotically oriented political parties has been forming from which we only benefit. Our present task is to have Gorbachev come to an agreement with us, so that later we might carry out necessary reforms to create better living conditions for our citizens or act independently. We realize that Gorbachev will not lean on Democratic Russia while our positions can coincide with his. He will seek personal power, but I am young enough; and if other candidates are ready to wait, we will let him have what he wants. His dependence on foreigners, on American capital, is a drawback, of course. To carry out a policy dictated by American business circles and the American leadership is not the best variant. It somewhat hurts patriotic feelings. Gorbachev's plan is to turn the country into an appendage of the American economy. This is very dangerous.

Who are your political allies now and who are your opponents?
Our allies are the group Soyuz, which is the closest to us; deputies of the USSR parliament; the group Rossiya in the Russian parliament; and individual politicians who have taken the most decisive stand against Yeltsin's and Gorbachev's policies.

The All-People's Union of Russia and the Republican People's Party of Russia in Saint Petersburg, where Nikolai Nikolaevich Lysenko is the leader, and the Russian National Party form a bloc of parties that have worked out a common platform and set for themselves the same objectives.[20] They can act together. Deputies, journalists, parties, businessmen, directors of enterprises, and private business—all of them are consolidating into one patriotic-oriented force.

I suppose that our main opponents are the Interregional Group, Democratic Russia, and the Social-Democratic Party of Russia under [Oleg] Rumyantsev. However, we have much in common with the Constitutional Democrats headed by Mikhail Astafiev. I think we can come to an understanding with them. The Russian Christian-Democratic movement headed by Aksiuchits has also taken a stand close to ours. They simply envy me and are therefore angry at me. They used to be extremely anticommunist and resolutely opposed to Gorbachev, but they failed to understand that by backing Yeltsin they helped the Pink to come to power instead of the Red, as the same nomenklatura people have remained in power. In this respect, [Valeriya] Novodvorskaya and the Democratic Union are right when they claim that everything remains the same. But what kind of forces does she represent? Her criticism of the authorities is extremely severe. The same is true about certain leaders of the Pamyat' society. They claim to be working underground, but in fact they do not take any practical steps. It seems to me that all these forces are artificial. We, on the other hand, are prepared to act in the very midst of the masses. We have taken a concrete stand. For that reason I think that we are going to form a bloc with certain parties, deputies, and businessmen. We will have our own candidates, and this will give us a chance to win free elections.

Are you still for private property?
Certainly, but I oppose the privatization being carried out by Yeltsin's team. Agrarians in the Russian parliament have voted against the sale of land, and we backed them. If the project were adopted, land would be bought by the caucasian Mafia, shadow economy representatives, the criminal bourgeoisie, the party

apparatus, and the nomenklatura. This would hurt millions of our electors. Thus it is not reasonable for us to support a handful of rich people who have stolen money under Brezhnev, laundered it under Gorbachev, and are spending it under Yeltsin. But, theoretically, we are for private property and a powerful private sector of the economy. State-run enterprises, however, should be privatized slowly and gradually. Those who carry out this plan should take into account Russia's peculiarities. For instance, the agrarians are against the sale of land because they realize that Russian collective farmers are poor and cannot afford to buy real estate, agricultural implements, or equipment. That is why it is necessary to create favorable conditions for Russians to become owners. At present, Yeltsin's team carries out privatization in favor of forces alien to Russia.

Let us turn to your party's activities during the putsch. What steps did you take and how did you personally react? You have been accused of supporting coup leaders. How accurate are these charges?

I always backed Gorbachev because he is the legally elected president. I realized that these events could not have taken place without his consent. The whole thing was a show. The first act took place in the Baltics in January [1991]. It [the crackdown] started well and was to be continued, but then Gorbachev put a stop to it. I supported him in January [when Soviet troops intervened in Lithuania and Latvia], I supported him in August, and I am going to support him this spring, or else I will carry out this scheme myself if I am elected president.

Yeltsin and Gorbachev are fulfilling my program but in their own way with certain peculiarities. Yeltsin has been appointing local government authorities, which is identical to my program of appointing governors. Gorbachev opposes separatism and is for a united state.

They have to maneuver while I remain in opposition and can speak openly. Unlike them, I am not connected with the communist ideology so it is easier for me. There is nothing to blackmail me with; I am innocent. I did not steal. I never had a country house. I did not write memoirs nor did I receive hard currency. On the whole, I have not made mistakes. I am free and can act openly. More than six million people voted for me because I am honest, open, and have a clean record. If elections were held now, I would receive forty-six million votes, while Yeltsin would win only six [million]. The situation has changed dramatically, and this is their trouble.

On August 22, 1991, the newspaper *Sovetskaya Rossiya* published an article claiming that you supported the putsch. Is this true?

We learned of the program of GKChP [coup leaders] on Monday morning [August 19] and liked it. Stabilization of the economy, restoration of the constitution, struggle against crime, and struggle against separatism—all these points correspond to our program. That is why we supported these ideas. We do not support anticonstitutional actions. But on the morning of August 19, nothing was clear yet. There were people in the Kremlin who had been there before. [Soviet vice-president] Yanaev had been at the Kremlin on the seventeenth and eighteenth. If some general had brought rebellious troops into Moscow and seized the Kremlin, it would have been a different matter. But the people who suggested emergency measures were members of the government. They held key posts. At the time, I supported these measures. But now I am for a certain part of Yeltsin's program. Our party did not take part in these events. It's only my personal standpoint. Members of our party and party structures did not take any steps to support either GKChP or Yeltsin. This is our style. We are not going to support actions that are beyond the limits of the constitution. But we support the program [of the coup leaders].

I still back Gorbachev, but my plan is more pure, it represents the interests of Russia and Russians much better. I would not make concessions to Americans, Germans, or Japanese. But Mikhail Sergeevich sometimes compromises too much and thus undertakes certain obligations that prevent our people from enhancing the prestige of Russia and the Russians. It restrains us, places us in a position of dependence, and makes us even second-rate sometimes. I do not support such tendencies.

Did members of the Liberal-Democratic Party resist the putsch or remain neutral?
Several people were expelled from the party because they were among the defenders of the Locker—this is what we call the White House because it looks like a locker. But on the whole, members of our party did not take any actions to support Yeltsin or the White House's politics.

So why did you expel these people?
We expelled people who defended the White House because their actions did not correspond to party policy. We are against the disintegration of the country. Right after the putsch, practically every republic declared its sovereignty, and this contradicts our program. Separatist activities within Russia also have intensified. This hurts Russia. We realize that GKChP was bad, but it was better than the democrats who rule today. Thus I chose the lesser of two evils.

chapter thirteen

The Movement for Democratic Reform

Divisions between reformers and conservatives in the upper echelons of the Communist Party had polarized several years before their final split.[1] Only Gorbachev's skillful mastery of the center held the Party leadership together. Gorbachev's turn to the right, however, in the fall of 1990, precipitated the final falling out between the two Party factions.[2]

Eduard Shevardnadze began the exodus of the reformers in December 1990, when he resigned as Soviet foreign minister.[3] Although he did not quit the CPSU at that time, he and others who were disaffected by the ascendance of the conservatives began talking about establishing a new liberal communist party. During the spring of the following year, other prominent leaders such as Anatoly Sobchak, Alexander Yakovlev, and Yegor Yakovlev published a series of articles in *Moscow News* calling for the creation of a social-democratic party as an alternative to the Communist Party in a two-party system.[4] Although the Social-Democratic Party of Russia already existed, as did a mass-based, anticommunist coalition (Democratic Russia), the leaders of this new initiative were too senior to join someone else's movement.[5] They wanted to form their own opposition movement to which others would be invited.

After much preliminary fanfare, this group of reform-minded Communists announced the formation of the Movement for Democratic Reform (Dvizhenie Demokraticheskikh Reform, or DDR) on July 1, 1991.[6] Calling their movement a coalition, not a party, the movement's leadership hoped to unite reformers within the CPSU who were dissatisfied with Gorbachev's turn to the right and with all the major democratic parties and movements challenging the CPSU from without.[7] As a cofounder of both Democratic Russia and the new movement, Gavriil Popov was considered the linchpin in forging this coalition. A founding congress was planned for the fall.

In the interim, however, the August putsch dramatically altered the movement's role. In purging the Soviet government of those who supported the coup, Yeltsin and Gorbachev appointed many of the DDR's founding members to ministerial posts. For instance, Vadim Bakatin became head of the KGB, Yegor Yakovlev took over Soviet television, Eduard Shevardnadze and Alexander Yakovlev returned to the Kremlin as advisers to the president, and three of the four members of the committee assigned to run the economy were movement members. When coupled with the fact that Popov was mayor of Moscow, that Sobchak was mayor of Saint Petersburg, and that Alexander Rutskoi was Russia's vice-president, the DDR temporarily became the new ruling party in the wake of the putsch.[8]

The collapse of the Soviet Union, however, undermined the DDR's hegemonic political power almost as fast as the August putsch had created it. First, all those Union posts that DDR leaders had occupied were abolished, and people like Shevardnadze (who had returned to the post of Soviet foreign minister), Yakovlev, and Bakatin were now unemployed.[9] Second, unlike most other political organizations, the DDR had been intentionally created on an all-Union basis. On February 15, 1992, the Russian Movement for Democratic Reform was founded, but the dissolution of the Soviet Union has complicated the position of non-Russian DDR members, including Eduard Shevardnadze.[10]

Nonetheless, the movement has tried to carve a new political position within the Russian democratic camp. Although divisions between social democrats (Yakovlev), liberals (Popov), and neutrals (Shevardnadze) had initially confused the movement's ideological orientation, the DDR's founding congress in December 1991 unequivocally redirected the movement's social base toward the former nomenklatura, which now seeks to privatize and own former Soviet industries.[11] As the head of the Union of Industrialists of Entrepreneurs, a lobby organization for factory managers and directors, Arkadii Volsky's election as a DDR cochairman served to solidify this link between those prominent politicians and the powerful proprietors.[12]

After the Russian economic reform program was initiated on January 2, 1992, movement leaders became increasingly critical of Yeltsin's government. In December 1991 and again in January 1992, Popov threatened to resign as Moscow's mayor, claiming that Yeltsin's laws on privatization were obstructing his more radical plans for Moscow.[13] At the December founding congress, Popov argued that the movement should go into opposition to the Yeltsin government. Sobchak has also criticized the Yeltsin reform plan from the opposite end of the spectrum by asserting that the price hikes and pace of privatization are dangerous and destabilizing.[14]

The staying power of the Movement for Democratic Reform has yet to be established. Although the constellation of movement founders included some of the best-known *Soviet* reformers, the organization has not yet established a presence in the Russian Federation. Because almost everyone in the leadership wears a second hat either in the government, industry, or another party, no one has a firm stake in the movement's success.[15] The resources available to people who wear several hats, however, be it in government, industry, or both, give the movement the potential to be a powerful player in Russia's future.

Eduard Shevardnadze

Born in 1928 in Mamati, Georgia, Eduard Shevardnadze followed a traditional path in the Communist Party for the first forty years of his political career.[16] He joined the Communist Party in 1948 and worked his way up the ranks of the Georgian Party and government to become first secretary of the Central Committee of the Komsomol of Georgia, then first secretary of the district Party committee, then deputy minister of public order, then Georgian minister of internal affairs, then first secretary of the Central Committee of the Communist Party in Georgia. In 1985, he became a member of the Politburo of the Communist Party of the Soviet Union and minister of foreign affairs.

As a close associate of Mikhail Gorbachev's for several years, Shevardnadze was entrusted with shaping Soviet foreign policy. He became one of the principal architects of "new political thinking," a strategy of rapprochement with the West that ultimately ended the cold war.[17] Domestically, Shevardnadze became one of Gorbachev's two closest liberal allies (the other was Alexander Yakovlev) within the leadership of the CPSU. When Shevardnadze resigned as foreign minister in December 1991, the liberal wing of the Communist Party essentially collapsed. On resigning from the Communist Party in July 1992, Shevardnadze began his work as a founder of the Movement for Democratic Reform.

After the putsch, Shevardnadze reassumed the post of Soviet minister until the position was eliminated after the Commonwealth of Independent States was created in December 1991. In addition to his involvement in organizing the Movement for Democratic Reform, Shevardnadze assumed an active role in Georgian politics.[18] Soon after the ouster of Georgian president Zviad Gamsakhurdia in January 1992, Shevardnadze became the interim chairman of the State Committee of Georgia, the de facto head of state in Georgia. In October 1992, he was elected to this position.

Interview with
Eduard Shevardnadze (*November 1991*)
· ·

Eduard Amvrosievich, how did the Movement for Democratic Reform (DDR) begin?
It is a rather complicated story. The idea of a party functioning simultaneously within the CPSU appeared early this year [1991]. Before then, however, the leadership of the CPSU, which was a ruling party then, needed to begin to ensure its political position, take care of reinforcements, develop a constructive and serious theoretical stand, and rethink organizational matters. We discussed this problem on all levels. Unfortunately, this idea did not meet large-scale support then, as it was not easy to speak about such matters at that time.

Early this summer, I stated officially that it was necessary to form a party in opposition to the CPSU. If we speak seriously about building up a legal democratic state, it is impossible to form such a society without an efficient and constructive opposition. It is illustrated by the world historic experience. You know what has been going on in the CPSU.

[Gavriil] Popov, [Alexander] Yakovlev, [Stanislav] Shatalin, [Nikolai] Travkin, [Nikolai] Petrakov, [Arkadii] Volsky, and I met then and discussed how to implement this idea. On the one hand, we realized that the process of faction formation or the creation of the left-centrist wing was under way within the CPSU. Given these developments, some people suggested that we form a social-democratic party.[19] In the long run, we arrived at the conclusion that it was too early to form a party. Rather, we needed to form an organization that would unite all democratic forces. At that time, we were already aware of the mounting danger of a right-wing coup d'état. We realized that it was impossible to form a well-organized party with its own ideology within a rather short period of time. But it was quite possible to form a movement uniting political forces true to democratic ideals. Therefore, we suggested this idea.

Naturally we were concerned about the future of this movement. We regarded it as a political force for the transition period, which would last for five or six years. At the next stage, a party could be formed on the basis of this movement. It will be called democratic or social democratic—the name is not very important—but essentially it will be a party supporting democratic reforms, like the DDR itself.

Another reason we supported the idea of a movement was due to our attitude toward republican and democratic parties and democratic movements. If we remained a movement, we could create a suitable form of cooperation with republic and democratic movements, parties, and so on because they could be represented within the limits of the party; they could be elected delegates to elective organs. Democratic forces in the center are interested in the formation of an integral democratic space all over the country. We are willing to back democratic movements in all republics but without infringement on the sovereign rights and independence of these movements and parties. We feel that we must work with democratic movements in republics on this basis. This kind of cooperation can succeed within the movement. But if we form a party, it will have narrower objectives and a more limited space than the kind we need for large-scale cooperation. It would look like the old CPSU structures, with their democratic centralism, the principle of subordination, and so on. Thus at the present stage we decided to cooperate with movements. This is the history of the matter, and this is where we are now.

Our main task is to form an integral democratic space. It became even more urgent after the putsch. If we take into account that the CPSU is destroyed and is even banned in certain places, a vacuum has appeared in society. It is very important that democratic forces and movements fill this gap. I suppose that our organization corresponds to the present period of development of our society and can fill this vacuum together with other democratic parties. If we are late, it can cost our country a pretty penny. The vacant space can be occupied by Fascists, jingoists, nationalists, and right-wing conservatives.

You have mentioned that discussions took place within the CPSU about ensuring its position. When did this understanding about the vulnerable position of the CPSU come about?

It was discussed three years ago at various levels but only in private. These were no official statements because the ideas were not approved of then. Only a few months ago, I suggested that we form a parallel party, and a Party investigation was ordered. So, as far back as two years ago, we could hardly pronounce the word *plurality*.

Why did the Democratic Platform fail? After all, it had a strategy very similar to the Movement of Democratic Reform—that is, to create an opposition movement within the CPSU.

[It failed] because forces of reformers were comparatively weak while the conservatives were in power. They used corresponding methods of crushing opposite opinions.

Which political forces does the Movement for Democratic Reform regard as allies?

This is a difficult question to answer because all forces that support building up a legal state and a central, democratic space are our allies. But these relations are not always registered officially. We do not always manage to unite within democratic blocs because we are different in character and ideology. But I see nothing tragic in this situation. I am sure that when elections and large-scale actions are held, democratic forces will act together. Just remember the August events.

Nobody asked who represented the democratic movements, who represented the Movement for Democratic Reform, or who represented the republic parties. Everybody was on the barricades and helped create an atmosphere in which every movement's voice was heard. At the meeting [on the second day of the coup] held by Democratic Russia near the Moscow City Soviet, I was persuaded to make a speech. They moved aside their own speakers to give me an opportunity to address the people. They did the same for Yakovlev and representatives of other parties. Nothing separated us. After the putsch, some problems have arisen, but I do not feel like making a tragedy of it. Such developments are normal for democratic movements and parties. Yet I do regard unity as our most urgent task at present. The danger of the right-wing reaction remains.

Which political forces are regarded as opponents by the Movement for Democratic Reform?

[When we first began our activities], high-ranking officials in the CPSU and, first and foremost, within the CPSU Central Committee Secretariat were very hostile toward us. They said that Communists were not to have anything to do with our movement. Communists were forbidden to enter it. Right-wing, conservative parties made similar statements. These people still exist and regard the Movement for Democratic Reform, Democratic Russia, and other democratic organizations with hostility. I need not speak about Fascists; we are natural opponents.

Will the Movement for Democratic Reform develop a particular ideology—let us say liberal or social democratic—or it will be a nonideological movement?

It will most likely be a nonideological movement, open for everybody—all parties, movements, and citizens interested in building up a legal state based on personal freedom for whom human rights and freedom of an individual come first.[20]

What are the major dangers that threaten the Movement for Democratic Reform?

The main danger that threatens not only our democratic movement but the society as a whole is the possibility of a right-wing coup d'état. It remains an ever-mounting threat. This threat, in fact, has grown to become more tangible now than before the August events because social tension and people's resentment are growing. I think that reactionary forces can act much more boldly in such an atmosphere and that their actions will be greeted with a certain support by society. This is the greatest danger. Thus it is vital to accelerate reforms announced by the Russian government. Some elements of this reform are insufficient, so it is necessary to assist Yeltsin's initiative by ensuring their completion. Reforms must be also carried out in other republics and regions and should be done as soon as possible. There is a certain limit to people's patience. It is necessary to act seriously and with great responsibility.

Critics of the Movement for Democratic Reform assert that it is practically the new party in power and that it was formed as a ruling party. In particular they state that, in the provinces and rural areas, the DDR is joined not only by former reform-minded Communists

but by officials from the CPSU apparatus as well. Does the DDR's leadership regard this tendency as dangerous?

I do not think this phenomenon is dangerous because after the August events the president [Gorbachev] and many others suddenly turned to democracy. Thus people that personify democratic processes and changes found themselves in our movement. For that reason we trust them. The society needed everything that has happened. It would be strange if, after the putschists were defeated, the right-wing conservatives, not representatives of democratic movements, occupied key positions. As to former CPSU functionaries, even leaders, it is not so difficult to understand their true value. On the other hand, we should not think that only reactionaries and conservatives used to be Party members. There were also intellectuals. What society can refuse them? For example, I invited many former Party functionaries from the CPSU Central Committee apparatus to our movement to carry out individual tasks, let us say, of national policy. What will happen if we appoint a democrat from the factory [to do this job] who is absolutely ignorant of national policy? Naturally we need a person with a certain intellectual capacity and professional training. That is why Mikhailov, a well-known person who formerly headed a CPSU department, was invited for this position on my initiative. He is a real professional and knows all the problems of national policy. I am acquainted with his outlook, and if he was not successful at his previous post, it happened not because he was bad but because they simply did not pursue national policy in a proper way. I can give you many more examples of people who used to have a different opinion but were among the Party members. On the whole if highly skilled specialists are not appointed to key posts, there will be no movement. Democracy will not be able to win. How can a democratic movement work out economic policy without the assistance of the best economists? We cooperate with Petrakov, Shatalin, Yavlinsky, yet all of them used to be Party members, members of the CPSU Central Committee.[21] Shatalin was expelled from the CPSU. He made his choice [to leave the Party] a month earlier than I did. Should we mistrust him now? I think that it would not be fair. The merit of our movement is that we regard a person according to the forces he represents, his way of thinking, his principles, and his professional skills. If he is committed to democracy and is useful for society, we are ready to cooperate with him.

Our attitude toward conservatives is the same. I do not find conservatism a dangerous phenomenon. Conservative parties and movements exist all over the world. Right-wing conservatism or fascism is a different matter. But we can cooperate with normal conservatives.

Nearly all the leaders of the existing democratic parties were once members of the CPSU.

It was natural. People entered the Young Pioneers organization when they were eight, then they became members of the Young Communist League, and later they entered the CPSU. The majority of Soviet people followed this scheme. As such, I would not divide our society into former Communists and democrats. Everyone can change his stand and join people that are ready to build up a new society.

Some analysts say that the moderate faction within the DDR should unite with the most pragmatic, highly skilled, and democratically oriented part of the former CPSU apparatus. How do you evaluate this proposal?

This is what is happening now. We are working actively with the military-industrial complex. We even have been criticized because there are too many servicemen among us. But I think this criticism is unjust. How can we ignore nearly half the state—I mean the economic and scientific potential of the military-industrial complex? When we made our statement [of the intention to create a new movement], the whole staff of some of the biggest scientific research institutions expressed their interest in joining our movement as collective members. Why did it happen? We never supported them. On the contrary, one of our principal propositions is cutting military expenditures, building a new army, and military reform. Thus, these people were not supposed to support us. But they realized how events are moving in society and that principles enunciated by our movement have good prospects. That is why twenty-seven directors of the biggest enterprises, including munitions factories, supported our movement only two or three days after our formation.

What are the greatest problems that the movement faces?

Strange as it might seem, the most pressing problem is the weak organization of the movement. We enjoy broad support, but we have not learned how to form an organization and run it. Leaders of the movement have their allotted work, which they cannot quit or ignore. Consequently, we have not managed to form a backbone that would be able to organize the movement's action in provinces, republics and establish contact with other parties. It is a serious drawback that prevents us from getting greater support.

When will you consider the work of the Movement for Democratic Reform completed?

In principle, I suppose that the movement has prospects for a long life. Reforms are necessary at all stages of development of society. We will be comparatively satisfied if we manage to achieve objectives enunciated in our founding statement. As for myself, personally I would regard the formation of a democratic space and the observance of human rights as our most urgent tasks. We cannot rest content as long as the danger of right-wing, jingoist, nationalist forces remains in any region or republic. [Under these threats] a person cannot be free. It will take us much time to eliminate this threat. It is certainly impossible to speak about an integral democratic space if we have not built up a legal system, and the problem is more complicated because there are many states within our country.[22] It means that a legal system must be constructed not only in Russia but in other republics as well. If reactionary forces hold key positions in another republic, we cannot remain indifferent. Dictatorship is incompatible with our principles no matter where it appears. We will be happy if at some stage in our social development we are able to say that democratic processes, processes of the integral democratic space formation, have become irreversible and the danger of dictatorship has been eliminated.

Notes

Preface

1. Some of the organizations discussed in this book—including the Democratic Union, the Democratic Platform, the Union of Independent Miners, the United Workers' Front, the Liberal-Democratic Party, and the Movement for Democratic Reform—were founded on an all–Soviet Union basis. This book, however, focuses on their activities in Russia.

2. For such surveys, see M.A. Babkina, *New Parties and Movements in the Soviet Union* (Commack, N.Y.: Nova Science Publishers, 1991); Vladimir Pribylovsky, "Slovar' Oppositsii: Novie Politicheskie Partii i Organizatsii Rossii," *PostFactum Analytical Review*, nos. 4–5 (Moscow) (April 1991); Institut Massovikh Politicheskikh Dvizhenii, *Rossiya: Partii, Assotsiatsii, Soyuzy, Kluby*, tom I, chast 1 and 2 (Moskva: RAU-Press, 1991); *Neformal'naya Rossiya* (Moskva: Molodaya Gvardiya, 1990); and *Neformali: Kto Oni? Kuda Zovut?* (Moskva: Politicheskaya Literatura, 1990).

3. The first draft of this book included interviews and chapters on the Green Party (Anatoly Zheludkov), the Anarcho-Syndicalist Union (Alexander Shubin), the Socialist Party (Boris Kagarlitsky), the Party of Free Labor (Igor Korovikov), the Russian People's Party (Telman Gdlyan), the Christian-Democratic Union (Alexander Ogorodnikov), the Party of Constitutional Democrats (Victor Zolotarev), the Confederation of Labor (Ilya Shablinsky), and the Union of Workers' Collectives (Galina Rakitskaya). Owing to space limitations, however, we did not include full chapters on these parties and organizations but have made reference to them and others in other chapters.

Moreover, again because of space limitations, we have not included the political programs of all parties and movements surveyed in this book. Rather, we have included a select few that represent the full spectrum of ideological positions in the Russian polity.

4. Before 1988, this focus was well placed, as most important political developments in the Soviet Union took place at this level.

Chapter One

1. Portions of the chapter first appeared in Michael McFaul, "Russia's Emerging Political Parties," *Journal of Democracy* 3, no. 1 (January 1992): 25–40.

2. On the importance of political parties to democracies, see Moisei Ostrogorski, *Democracy and the Organization of Political Parties*, vols. 1 and 2 (New Brunswick, N.J.: Transaction Books, 1982); Joseph Schumpeter, *Capitalism, Socialism, and Democracy* (New York: Harper and Row, 1950); and David Robertson, *A Theory of Party Competition* (London: John Wiley and Sons, 1976). Most theoretical work on the role of political parties, however, is based on research in established Western democracies. For studies on the transition to democracy that may be more relevant to the Russian case, see Guillermo O'Donnell and Phillipe Schmitter, *Transitions from Authoritarian Rule: Tentative Conclusions about Uncertain Democracies* (Baltimore, Md.: Johns Hopkins University Press, 1989). Unlike the cases analyzed in these studies, however, Russia is undertaking not only political reform (from dictatorship to democracy) but also economic transformation (from state socialism to market capitalism) and decolonization all at the same time. The large literature on transitions to democracy has been based primarily on case studies from Latin America and southern Europe, where all of the countries reforming already had functioning (albeit with varying degrees of success) capitalist economies. For one of the first analyses looking at the transition to the market and democracy simultaneously, see Adam Przeworski, *Democracy and the Market: Political and Economic Reforms in Eastern Europe and Latin America* (Cambridge, Eng.: Cambridge University Press, 1991). Given the simultaneity of change in both the political and the economic system, the Russian case may be more properly labeled a social revolution analogous to that of France in 1789 or Russia in 1917 rather than simply a transition to democracy. On the definition of revolution, see Sigmund Neumann, "The International Civil War," *World Politics* 1, no. 1 (April 1949): 333–34.

3. Article Six of the constitution of the USSR of 1977.

4. This book deals primarily with Russia, not the Soviet Union as a whole. However, when appropriate or when it is difficult to distinguish between the Soviet Union and the Russian Federation, we make specific reference to the large entity, the USSR. Otherwise, the discussion deals only with Russia.

5. See, for instance, Abraham Brumberg, ed., *In Quest for Justice: Protest and Dissent in the Soviet Union Today* (New York: Praeger, 1970); Vladimir Bukovsky, *To Build a Castle: My Life as a Dissenter* (New York: Viking Press, 1978); Peter Reddaway, ed., *Uncensored Russia: Protest and Dissent in the Soviet Union* (New York: American Heritage, 1972); Joshua Rubenstein, *Soviet Dissidents: Their Struggle for Human Rights* (Boston: Beacon Press, 1980); Rudolf Tokes, *Dissent in the USSR* (Baltimore, Md.: Johns Hopkins University Press, 1975); and Ludmilla Alexeyeva, *Soviet Dissent: Contemporary*

Movements for National, Religious, and Human Rights (Middletown, Conn.: Wesleyan University Press, 1985).

6. For a survey of these positions, see George Breslauer, *Five Images of the Soviet Future: A Critical Review and Synthesis* (Berkeley, Calif.: Institute of International Studies, 1978). Breslauer's view that the Soviet system changed from a totalitarian state under Stalin to an authoritarian welfare state under Brezhnev is outlined in George Breslauer, "On the Adaptability of the Soviet Welfare-State Authoritarianism," in Karl Ryavec, ed., *Soviet Society and the Communist Party* (Amherst: University of Massachusetts Press, 1978).

7. For assessments of Gorbachev's reform agenda, see Archie Brown, "Perestroika and the Political System," in Tsuyoshi Hasegawa and Alex Pravda, eds., *Perestroika: Soviet Domestic and Foreign Policies* (London: Royal Institute of International Affairs, 1990); Jerry Hough, "Gorbachev's Endgame," *World Policy Journal*, Fall 1990; and George Breslauer, "Evaluating Gorbachev as Leader," *Soviet Economy* 5, no. 4 (October—December 1989).

8. Guillermo O'Donnell and Philippe Schmitter refer to such reforms as "liberalized authoritarianism." As they explain, "Authoritarian rulers may tolerate or even promote liberalization in the belief that by opening up certain spaces for individual and group action, they can relieve various pressures and obtain needed information and support *without* altering the structure of authority, that is, without becoming accountable to the citizenry for their actions or subjecting their claim to rule to fair and competitive elections." O'Donnell and Schmitter, *Transitions from Authoritarian Rule*, p. 9. On Gorbachev's conception of democratization, see John Gooding, "Gorbachev and Democracy," *Soviet Studies* 42, no. 2 (April 1990): 195–231.

9. When the pace of political reform began to spin out of Gorbachev's control, he had no qualms about suspending glasnost' or democratization. In his final year as president of the Soviet Union, Gorbachev closed down independent newspapers, censored and then removed popular political television programs, and even ordered fifty thousand soldiers to surround downtown Moscow to prevent a political demonstration.

10. See Victoria Bonnell, "Voluntary Associations," in Alexander Dallin and Gail Lapidus, eds., *The Soviet System in Crisis: A Reader of Western and Soviet Views* (Boulder, Colo.: Westview Press, 1991), pp. 151–60.

11. See Stephen Hanson, "Gorbachev: The Last True Leninist Believer?" in Daniel Chirot, ed., *The Crisis of Leninism and the Decline of the Left: The Revolutions of 1989* (Seattle: University of Washington Press, 1991).

12. On the initial proliferation, see Frederick S. Starr, "The USSR: A Civil Society," *Foreign Policy* 70 (1989).

13. Given the degree of penetration of the Soviet state and the Communist Party into all aspects of society, seemingly apolitical issues were actually packed with political meaning for those participating. Because the Party had tried to control all forms of social association, be it a science club or chess association, any form of independent social activity constituted an implicit protest against the state-Party structures.

14. Two classic examples are Club Lingua, within which formed a political committee

headed by Mikhail Schneider, and Nash Arbat, which assumed an increasingly political profile owing to Mikhail Maliutin.

15. *Neformali* ("the informals") was the term used to describe these political organizations to distinguish them from the formal political organizations of the Communist Party and its affiliates. See *Neformal'naya Rossiya* (Moskva: Molodaya Gvardiya, 1990) and *Neformali: Kto Oni? Kuda Zovut?* (Moskva: Politicheskaya Literatura, 1990).

16. See Vyacheslav Igrunov, "Public Movements: From Protest to Political Self-Consciousness," in Brad Roberts and Nina Belyaeva, eds., *After Perestroika: Democracy in the Soviet Union*, CSIS Significant Issue series, vol. 13, no. 5 (Washington, D.C.: Center for Strategic and International Studies, 1991), pp. 14–31.

17. As cited in Vladimir Brovkin, "Revolution from Below: Informal Political Associations in Russia 1988–1989," *Soviet Studies* 42, no. 2 (April 1990): 239. See also Boris Kagarlitsky, *Farewell Perestroika: A Soviet Chronicle* (London: Verso, 1990), passim. Kagarlitsky was one of the founders of FSOK, the Moscow Popular Front, and the Socialist Party.

18. Groups such as Helsinki Watch, Doverie (Trust), and the Vienna Committee grew out of this political tendency.

19. Because of their differences about methods and tactics, the Democratic Union also split with the human rights organizations.

20. As three prominent Russian sociologists and pollsters concluded, "Until the end of 1988 the very expression of 'multiparty system' had a pronounced negative connotation. However, during the course of the electoral campaign in 1989 a multiparty system came to be accepted with more tolerance as a cultural and political idea. The term began to appear in pre-election programs of some of the most radical candidates for people's deputies of the USSR. By the time the First Congress of People's Deputies drew to a close in June 1989, about 42% of almost 700 surveyed participants said that they were against retaining the one-party system." Their study showed a similar trend within the Russian population more generally. (L.G. Byzov, L.A. Gordon, and I.E. Mintusov, "Reflections of Sociologists on the Political Reforms," *Soviet Sociology* 30, no. 1 ([January-February 1991]: 29–30. This article originally appeared in *Rabochii Klass i Sovremmii Mir*, no. 1 [1990].)

21. Pamyat' (the Russian word for *memory*) is not one organization but has several strands and branches (see chapter 3 for details). Regarding this particular demonstration, led by the most infamous Pamyat' group headed by Dmitrii Vasiliev, critics claimed that the demonstration was officially sanctioned if not orchestrated by right-wing elements in the CPSU. (See Igrunov, "Public Movements," p. 30.) Pamyat' leader Vasiliev, however, firmly denied these assertions, asserting that the "Jewish-conspired" Communist Party has been just as destructive to Russian society as Western capitalism and the "Masons" (see chapter 3).

22. The letter is reprinted in English in Dallin and Lapidus, eds., *The Soviet System in Crisis*, pp. 338–46.

23. Although theoretically an independent social movement, the core founders of the United Workers' Front were all members of the CPSU.

24. Liberals within the Politburo eventually published a response to Nina Andreeva's

letter in *Pravda* on April 5, 1988, thereby confirming that her letter was at least perceived as a manifesto of the conservative wing of the CPSU.

25. This document was then passed on to Yurii Afanasiev after he had been nominated as a delegate to the conference.

26. Campaigns for Yeltsin's inclusion as a delegate were initiated in Sverdlovsk at the giant Uralmash plant, in Moscow by workers' collectives (later consolidated as the Committee of 19), and in Karelia, from which he was eventually elected (authors' interview with Lev Shemaev, cofounder of the Committee of 19, Moscow, May 1991). In Moscow, students at the Historical Archive Institute initiated the campaign for Yurii Afanasiev's candidacy as a delegate. See Kagarlitsky, *Farewell Perestroika*, pp. 3–4.

27. The first demonstration took place on May 28, 1988, recognized by many as the christening of Pushkin Square as Moscow's Hyde Park.

28. To the disappointment of many within the informal movement, however, Afanasiev never publicly presented their recommendations to the conference.

29. The year before, Boris Yeltsin had been removed as a candidate member of the CPSU Politburo and from his position as first secretary of the Moscow City Committee of the Party. At the Party conference, he represented the most radical and maverick wing of the Party. Yegor Ligachev, in contrast, was the senior member of the conservative faction within the Politburo. See Timothy Colton, "Moscow Politics and the El'tsin Affair," *Harriman Institute Forum* 1, no. 6 (June 1988), and Yeltsin's personal account in Boris Yeltsin, *Against the Grain* (New York: Summit Books, 1990), pp. 177–210.

30. Kagarlitsky, *Farewell Perestroika*, p. 21.

31. Unlike most other organizations, the Moscow Popular Front had functioned effectively for several months *before* its founding congress.

32. On Yaroslavl, see Brovkin, "Revolution from Below," p. 236.

33. For details, see Kagarlitsky, *Farewell Perestroika*, pp. 31–38. Toward the end of 1988, Valerii Skurlatov did found the Russian Popular Front. This organization, however, had little to do with the popular fronts based at the city level. On the contrary, the Russian Popular Front had closer ties to Pamyat' organizations than to the reform-oriented popular fronts in Moscow or Leningrad.

    Informal political organization proved to be more difficult in more-rural areas, however, as the local CPSU apparat continued to repress noncommunist political activities. See Brovkin, "Revolution from Below," pp. 236–37.

34. The dispute over the word *socialism* was half ideological and half tactical. Obshchina leader Alexander Asaev and Civil Dignity leader Victor Zolotarev opposed references to socialism for ideological reasons while committed Socialists (not Communists) like Boris Kagarlitsky argued for its inclusion. Pragmatists such as Oleg Rumyantsev from Democratic Perestroika supported the inclusion of socialist rhetoric in the front's documents to appease communist authorities. (Authors' interviews with Boris Kagarlitsky, Alexander Shubin [from Obshchina], and Victor Zolotarev, spring 1991.) See also Kagarlitsky, *Farewell Perestroika*, pp. 9–11, and Igrunov, "Public Movements," pp. 22–24.

35. "Khartiya MNF," *Grazhdanskii Referendum*, no. 1, (Fall 1989): 2.

36. "Koe-Shto ob Ekspluatatsii," *Grazhdanskii Referendum*, no. 1 (August 1989): 17–18; "Khartiya MNF," p. 2.

37. Interviews with two of the original founders of Memorial, Victor Kuzin and Vladimir Lysenko, are included in this book. People of Sakharov's prominence were elected to the governing body in 1988, though the organization was founded the year before. See Andrei Sakharov, "Moscow and Beyond," *Harriman Institute Forum* 3, no. 11 (November 1990): 14–15.

38. For a comprehensive account of Memorial's role in the formation of Soviet civil society, see Kelly Smith, "Coming to Terms with Previous State Repressions: Civic Activism and State Responses in the USSR" (Ph.D. diss., University of California at Berkeley, 1993).

39. Members included Yurii Afanasiev, Andrei Sakharov, Gavriil Popov, Leonid Batkin, Galina Starovoitova, and Tatyana Zaslavskaya. See the interview with Leonid Batkin, "Yeshche ne Probil Chas," *Moskovskii Komsomolets*, March 16, 1991, p. 2.

40. Anatoly Sobchak, *For a New Russia* (New York: Free Press, 1992), pp. 16–17. This book is almost the same book as *Khozhdenie vo Vlast'* but contains some additional information, including that quoted here.

41. Nonetheless, the 1989 electoral process was a vast improvement over past Soviet elections. For a chronicle of the electoral reform process leading up to the 1989 elections, see Peter Lentini, "Reforming the Electoral System: The 1989 Elections to the USSR Congress of People's Deputies," *Journal of Communist Studies* 7, no. 1 (1991): 69–94. For a personal memoir of the election process, see Anatoly Sobchak, *Khozhdenie vo Vlast'* (Moskva: Novosti, 1991), chap. 2.

42. The most famous example concerned Andrei Sakharov's candidacy. Despite the fact that more than fifty academic institutions nominated him, the Presidium of the Academy of Sciences initially did not include Sakharov's name on the list of candidates. After several thousand scientists from various research institutes organized to demand his inclusion, Sakharov finally appeared on the ballot.

43. In Moscow, for instance, four candidates—Mikhail Maliutin, Sergei Stankevich, Rimma Goncharenko, and Sergei Druganov—passed through the first round of the election process. See Kagarlitsky, *Farewell Perestroika*, p. 94.

44. At the time, Stankevich was still a member of the CPSU. For more details on Stankevich's campaign, see the interview with Mikhail Schneider in chapter 8, "The Democratic Russia Movement." Schneider was Stankevich's campaign director for this election.

45. In Leningrad, Yurii Solovev, the first secretary of the Leningrad oblast', ran unopposed but lost by not receiving the required 50 percent. The deputy chairman of the Leningrad Party committee, Aleksei Bol'shakov, and the city Party first secretary, Anatoly Gerasimov, also lost.

46. Unlike any other political event in Soviet history, millions of people were riveted to television and radio to follow the proceedings of the congress. The congress may have been the single most important mobilizing event for future political movements in Russia.

47. See "Luzhniki, Ekho S'ezda," *Moskovskie Novosti*, no. 24 (June 11, 1989): 14.

48. The Supreme Soviet was elected from the larger Congress of People's Deputies.

Whereas the congress met on an ad hoc basis, the Supreme Soviet served as the regular functioning legislative organ of the Soviet government.

49. On the dilemmas of the Interregional Group, see the interview with group member Galina Starovoitova in "Political Reforms in Eastern Europe," *Moscow News*, no. 41 (October 21–30, 1990): 12.

50. The word *democrat* in the Russian political discourse at the time referred to all liberal reformers while the term *Communist* referred to conservative opponents to change.

51. The sheer number of the 1990 elections coupled with the unknown reputation of most of the candidates from the democratic camp allowed dozens of conservatives and antidemocratic candidates to run under the Democratic Russia banner. One of the most notorious cases is that of former KGB major Alexander Tsopov, who was elected to the Moscow City Soviet as a Democratic Russia member even though he was responsible for suppressing political dissidents only several years before. See Julia Wishnevsky, "Russian Gripped by 'Court Fever,'" *RFE/RL Research Report* 1, no. 10 (March 6, 1992): 4.

52. Most of the popular names appearing on DemRossiya posters became famous through their activities in the Interregional Group. Telman Gdlyan became famous for leading an investigation into Party corruption that was subsequently called off by Gorbachev himself.

53. See Dawn Mann, "The RSFSR Elections: The Congress of People's Deputies," *RFE/RL Report on the USSR* 2, no. 15 (April 13, 1990): 11–17. For a detailed study of the Moscow election, see Timothy Colton, "The Politics of Democratization: The Moscow Election of 1990," *Soviet Economy* 6, no. 4 (October–December 1990): 285–344.

54. See Nikolai Travkin, "Speech at the January All-Union Congress of the Democratic Platform," *Demokraticheskaya Platforma*, no. 2 (April 1990): 6.

55. During his election campaign for the position of chairman of the Russian Supreme Soviet, Yeltsin pledged to remain nonpartisan. As Yeltsin only won the election by a majority of four votes, he did not want to risk his position by joining another political party.

56. As political commentator Andrei Fadin summed it up, "Travkin, despite his appeals for democracy, displays the style of a true communist." See Andrei Fadin, "Emerging Political Institutions: From Informals to Multiparty Democracy," in Roberts and Belyaeva, eds., *After Perestroika*, p. 34.

57. Lev Ponomarev, a close associate of Andrei Sakharov, and Marie Salye, a leader of the Leningrad People's Front, left the Democratic Party at the founding congress when Travkin refused to share his chairmanship. Gennadii Burbulis, a personal friend of Yeltsin's from Sverdlovsk, gradually lost interest in party affiliations as he moved closer to Yeltsin's advisory circle. Arkadii Murashev and Garry Kasparov walked out of the Third Democratic Party Congress in the spring of 1991 allegedly because of disagreements with Travkin over the party's stance on the preservation of the Soviet Union. Travkin advocated preserving the USSR, while Murashev and Kasparov supported self-determination for the republics. Murashev and Kasparov later formed the Liberal Union, a coalition of political parties and individuals with a political orientation well to the right of the American Republican Party. For details, see chapter 5.

58. Oleg Rumyantsev, October 29, 1990, cited in Michael McFaul, "The Social Dem-

ocrats and the Republicans Attempt to Merge," *Report on the USSR*, January 18, 1991, p. 11.

59. The Social-Democratic Party (SDPR) joined the Republican Party and handful of independents to form a social-democratic faction of more than fifty members within the Supreme Soviet of the Russian Federation. Moreover, SDPR cochairman Oleg Rumyantsev also chaired the Constitutional Committee of the Supreme Soviet, which drafted a new Russian constitution. Half the committee members were affiliated with the Social-Democratic Party, and most of the committee's staff were SDPR members.

60. The Democratic Union was founded earlier, but this party refused to participate actively in either the 1989 or the 1990 elections.

61. *Soviet*, the Russian word for council, is the basic legislative organ in the governmental system. The Russian Supreme Soviet is now the highest soviet; before it was disbanded, the Supreme Soviet of the USSR was the highest.

62. For an analysis of how this "neutrality" affected the development of Democratic Russia, see the interview with Arkadii Murashev, "Shto s Nami Proiskhodit?" *Nezavisimaya Gazeta*, February 2, 1991, p. 2.

63. For a further discussion, see chapter 5.

64. Of all Russia's political associations, the Union of Independent Miners and the Party of Free Labor have the most clearly defined social bases.

65. Nationalist parties in the other republics, of course, have not encountered this problem. In the postcommunist political climate, parties based on Russian nationalism also will bypass the search for a class-based constituency.

66. For listings, see Institut Massovikh Politicheskikh Dvizhenii, *Rossiya: Partii, Assotsiatsii, Soyuzi, Klubi*, tom 1, chast 1 and 2 (Moskva: RAU-Press, 1991).

67. At their third congress in May 1991, the Social-Democratic Party of Russia considered proposing its own candidate but opted instead to support Yeltsin, while recommending Galina Starovoitova as *its* choice for Yeltsin's running mate. The SDPR also tried, unsuccessfully, to include Pavel Kudiukin on the ballot for Moscow's mayor. Nikolai Travkin, from the Democratic Party of Russia, also considered running against Yeltsin but decided that unity among the democratic forces was more important at that stage. Besides the Communist Party, both the Liberal-Democratic Party and the United Worker's Front had candidates for the presidency. (Candidates from the United Workers' Front, however, were members of the Communist Party as well.)

68. Several by-elections have been held to fill vacated seats. In almost all these elections, however, less than 50 percent of the eligible voters participated. (Fifty percent is the necessary minimum, according to Russian law, to validate an election.)

69. "The Mysterious 'Third Force,'" *Moscow News*, no. 7 (November 17–24, 1990): 9.

70. Chairman Anatoly Sobchak wanted emergency powers, but the city council refused. See Andrei Chernov, "In Favour of 'the Strong Hand': Notes from the Session of the Leningrad City Soviet," *Moscow News*, no 41 (October 21–28, 1990): 4; Anatoly Sobchak, "Municipal Government Needs More Power," *Moscow News*, no. 43 (November 4–11,

1990): 6; and Sergei Shelin, "Peterburg Vibiraet Anatoliya Sobchaka," *Nezavisimaya Gazeta*, June 18, 1991, p. 2.

71. As in Leningrad, the main issue dividing the council was Popov's quest for greater executive power. For details of Popov's reform plan, see his *Shto Delat'* (Moskva: Lanit, November 1990), pp. 12–15.

72. "The Times Are Getting Tougher," interview with Gavriil Popov, *Moscow News*, no. 42 (October 28–November 4, 1990): 7

73. See Sergei Mitrofanov, "Chrezvichainaya Sessiya Mossovieta Nachalas', no Tut Zhe i Konchilas'," *Kommersant'*, no. 48 (December 10–17, 1990): 13.

74. Ilya Zaslavsky, "V Strane Nenuzhnikh Sovietov," *Stolitsa* 10, no. 4 (January 1991): 3; "Chego Khochet Ilya Zaslavsky?" *Moskovskie Vedomosti* 14, no. 2 (January 1991): 13.

75. This situation precipitated the "war of laws" between the Soviet and Russian governments in the fall of 1990. See Lyudmilla Telen, "New Federal and Republic Laws Clash," *Moscow News*, no. 44 (November 11–18, 1990): 7.

76. The soviets that the "democrats" took over in 1990 never had true political power in the old Soviet system because all power was vested in Party structures. The soviets were simply rubber stamps; Party organs controlled all resources. For an analysis of the old system, see Jerry Hough, *The Soviet Prefects* (Cambridge, Mass.: Harvard University Press, 1969). On the struggles between the Party and the democratically controlled soviets, see Jeffrey Hahn, "Local Politics and Political Power in Russia: The Case of Yaroslavl'," *Soviet Economy* 7, no. 4 (1991): 322–41; and Michael McFaul, *All Power to the Soviets? An Assessment of Local Government in the Soviet Union* (Washington: National Democratic Institute, Spring 1991).

77. For descriptions of these groups, see chapter 10.

78. *Nash Sovremenik*, no. 9 (1990), as quoted in *Moscow News*, no. 47 (December 2–9, 1990): 7. On February 27, 1991, a movement called For the Great and Unified Russia was created that included twenty-six patriotic and communist organizations. See "Kommunisti i Patrioti Reshili Spasti Rossiu. Ot Demokratov," *Kommersant'*, no. 9 (February 25–March 4, 1991): 13; and Vladimir Todres, "Soyuz Gosudarstvennogo Spaseniya," *Nezavisimaya Gazeta*, March 2, 1991, p. 2.

79. "New Arms for the Army! Ban the CPSU!" (interview with Colonel Victor Alksnis), *Moscow News*, no. 6 (February 10–17, 1991): 7.

80. Despite its name, the A.D. Sakharov Union had nothing to do with Sakharov himself. His wife, Elena Bonner, was furious that this organization had used his name.

81. See Olga Bychkova, "The Invisible People," *Moscow News*, no. 7 (February 17–24, 1991): 8.

82. The composition of DemRossiya cells outside Moscow, however, varied from city to city. In some places, DemRossiya has coattailed on the activities of political parties, particularly the Democratic Party of Russia. In other areas, a reverse relationship occurs.

83. On the demonstration demanding a Russian television station, see "22 Febralya: Demokrati Poyut i Khotyat Telefira," *Nezavisimaya Gazeta*, February 26, 1991, p. 1. On the Union referendum, see "Kakaya-to Tainaya Tsel'," *Argumenti i Fakti*, no. 10 (March 1991): 3; and "Zayavlenie Koordinatsionnogo Sovieta Dvizheniya "Demokraticheskaya

Rossiya," *Dvizhenie "Demokraticheskaya Rossiya," Informatsionnii Biulleten'*, no. 6 (March 1991): 1. On Democratic Russia's support for the miners, see *Moskovskii Komsomolets*, March 12, 1991, p. 1, and "Pomosh' Moskvi," *Kuranti*, March 13, 1991, p. 2.

84. Many Western observers cynically scoffed at the numbers that turned out at DemRossiya demonstrations, claiming that they did not compare with the larger crowds in Czechoslovakia in 1989 or even in Lithuania in 1990. Calculations about crowd size, however, must be understood in the context of Russian history and culture. First, as Russia's history clearly demonstrates, a handful of organized revolutionaries can orchestrate revolutionary events without millions of supporters. Second, and more important in the contemporary Soviet context, the Russians are *supposed to be* complacent, apathetic, and timid. That anyone showed up to these demonstrations was significant; that tens of thousands assembled regularly was revolutionary.

85. This politicization of demands was not originally intended by the strike committees. The nature of the stalemate between Gorbachev and Yeltsin at the time, however, quickly placed the strike in a political context of national importance. For details, see chapter 9.

86. Again, this was the political discourse of the time. By co-opting the label "Russia," Yeltsin quelled almost all nationalist opponents to his government. Once this bipolar structure broke down after the August coup attempt, however, Yeltsin could no longer maintain the monopoly on Russian nationalism. See the discussion of new nationalist forces below.

87. Interview with Boris Yeltsin published in *Moscow News*, no. 25 (June 23–30, 1991): 5.

88. See the 9 + 1 joint statement in *Izvestiya*, April 24, 1991.

89. This party should not be confused with the Party of Constitutional Democrats headed by Victor Zolotarev, which grew out of Civic Dignity. For descriptions of both Cadet parties, see Vladimir Pribylovsky, "Slovar' Oppositsii: Novie Politicheskie Partii i Organizatsii Rossii," *PostFactum Analytical Review*, nos. 4–5 (April 1991).

90. Authors' interviews with DemRossiya cochairs Lev Ponomarev and Victor Dmitriev and Coordinating Council members Lev Shemaev, Vladimir Boxer, and Mikhail Schneider (spring 1991).

91. When Yeltsin first proposed the notion of a mass party at a DemRossiya congress in March 1991, Afanasiev opposed the idea, perhaps fearing its domination by Yeltsin. Later in the spring, however, Afanasiev began to talk about creating a new party as a means to resist both communist totalitarianism and Yeltsin's authoritarianism. See Boris Yeltsin, "Ya Ne Khochu s Nimi—V Kommunism," *Moskovskii Komsomolets*, March 12, 1991, p. 1, and Afanasiev's remarks in *Demokraticheskaya Rossiya* 7, no. 1 (March 1991): 9.

92. Rutskoi's faction, like many other eventual supporters of the Movement for Democratic Reform, hoped that senior figures like Shevardnadze and Yakovlev would be able usurp control of the democratic opposition from DemRossiya radicals like Yurii Afanasiev.

93. Some argued that a multiparty democracy already existed by this time. See Alexander Meerovich, "The Emergence of Multiparty Politics," *Report on the U.S.S.R.* 2, no. 34 (August 24, 1990): 8–16.

94. Sergei Stankevich, "The USSR's Protracted Crisis," *Journal of Democracy* 2, no. 3 (Summer 1991): 56.

95. On the importance of multiple sovereignty for revolutionary outcomes, see Charles Tilly, *From Mobilization to Revolution* (Reading, Mass.: Addison-Wesley, 1978), chap. 9.

96. Without question, the outcome of the coup would have been vastly different had it taken place in 1988 or even 1990. Analyses that focus only on splits within the military tend to forget that opposing positions within the armed forces would not have crystallized without clearly defined choices as to which political group to support. If, for instance, Yeltsin had been arrested immediately and popular resistance had not taken to the streets to defend the Russian parliament building, who would defecting Soviet military units have supported? For an interpretation focusing on the military and downplaying the role of democratic political movements, see Stephen Miller, "The Soviet Coup and the Benefits of Breakdown," *Orbis*, Winter 1992. On the politicization of the Soviet military, see Stephen Miller, "How the Threat (and the Coup) Collapsed: The Politicization of the Soviet Military," *International Security* 16, no. 3 (Winter 1991/92).

97. According to DemRossiya activists, the fact that they had actual buildings to defend—the White House and the Moscow City Council—was critical to their opposition efforts.

98. A decree from Yeltsin on August 19, 1991, stated that "until the convocation of the special Congress of the USSR people's deputies, all bodies of executive power of the USSR, including the KGB of the USSR, the Ministry of Internal Affairs of the USSR, the Ministry of Defense of the USSR, acting on the territory of the RSFSR, become directly subordinate to the President of the RSFSR, elected by the people. . . . The Committee of State Security of the RSFSR, the Ministry of Internal Affairs of the RSFSR, the RSFSR State Committee of Defense are to fulfill temporarily functions of corresponding organs of the USSR on the territory of the RSFSR. All regional and other bodies of the Ministry of Internal Affairs, KGB, and the Ministry of Defense on the territory of the RSFSR must immediately fulfill decrees and orders of the President of the RSFSR, the RSFSR Council of Ministers, orders of the RSFSR KGB, the RSFSR State Committee of Defense. . . . All bodies, officials, citizens of the USSR are to take urgent measures to prevent implementation of any decisions and orders of the anticonstitutional committee of the state of emergency."

99. Yeltsin, already elected president in June 1991, also appointed himself Russian prime minister. He then appointed three deputy prime ministers, Gennadii Burbulis, Yegor Gaidar, and Alexander Shokin, under which all other branches of government are subordinated.

100. As described above, several ideological factions had formed *within* the Communist Party of the Soviet Union well before the August putsch. When Yeltsin banned the CPSU from the Russian Federation after the coup, these factions then assumed individual party and movement status.

101. Afanasiev later left Democratic Russia over the issue of support for Yeltsin's government (see chapter 7).

102. Michael Parks, "Yeltsin Party Fragments over Russian Unity," *Los Angeles Times*, November 12, 1992.

103. Zhirinovsky has stated that the Union need not be resurrected if the newly independent states of the former Soviet Union return to Russia lands incorporated into other republics under the communist regimes. In his estimate, this includes large portions of Ukraine, all of Kazakhstan and Turkmenistan, and portions of each of the Baltics as well as part of Finland. As for the Russian Federation, Zhirinovsky has argued for the return of the tsarist governor system whereby autonomous regions and republics would be replaced by one hundred administrative units to be established without reference to ethnicity.

104. The Democratic Party of Russia declined to participate.

105. *RFE/RL Research Report* 1, no. 13 (March 27, 1992): 81.

106. The Communist Party of the Soviet Union was banned by Yeltsin several days after the coup.

107. See Grazhdanskii Soyuz, "Dokumenti Foruma Obshchestvennikh Sil" (Moskva, June 21, 1992, Mimeographed).

108. Within Democratic Russia, several positions regarding economic reform have emerged. The most radical position is maintained by the newly formed Liberal Union, a loose coalition of parties, individuals, and associations organized by Victor Dmitriev, Garry Kasparov, Arkadii Murashev, Larissa Piyasheva, Boris Pinsker, Galina Starovoitova, Stepan Sulakshin, and Victor Zolotarev. These self-proclaimed neo-Thatcherites advocate the complete privatization of the entire economy immediately. With less vigor, segments of both the Republican Party and the Movement for Democratic Reform have advocated a similar view. At the other pole within the democratic movement, the Social-Democratic Party of Russia, the People's Party of Russia, and a faction of the Republican Party of Russia have argued that immediate privatization without state intervention will lead to "nomenklatura capitalism" in which the economic managers of the old Soviet system will retain control over their enterprises through clever joint-stock schemes in which the controlling interest in these newly privatized companies is owned by the old management. In their view, this method of privatization will stifle true competition and lead to powerful alliances between new state bureaucrats and the old nomenklatura.

109. Officially, the "committees" have been created on the basis of Yeltsin's campaign cells (during the 1991 election) and thus are independent from Democratic Russia, though in many cities, the vast majority of committee organizers are members of Democratic Russia. In December 1991, the founders of the committees signed an accord with Gennadii Burbulis, then first deputy prime minister of the Russian government, which outlined the terms of cooperation between the civic organization and the government. In agreeing to promote the government economic reforms, the committees gained access to government information, office space, and other infrastructural facilities. Additionally, the committee has published a monthly information bulletin called *Zerkalo* and *Privatizatsiya: Kommentarii v Voprosakh i Otvetakh, Dokumenti i Materiali* (Moskva: Respublika, 1992).

110. "Initsiativnaya Gruppa za Sozdanie Partii Truda," *Obozrevatel': Spetsial'nii Vipusk*, 1991, p. 11.

111. See Mikhail Lashch, "Baburin, Alksnis, Isakov Reshili Ob'edinit'sya so Skurlatovim i Pozvali Zhirinovskogo," *Nezavisimaya Gazeta*, September 23, 1991, p. 1; *Rabochii*, no. 1 (December 1991); "Informatsionnoe Soobshchenie," *Nasha Rossiya*, no. 20 (1991):

2; "Oktyabr'skii Manifest Kommunisticheskikh Dvizhenii," *Nasha Rossiya*, no. 21 (1991): 4; "Uchrezhdena RKPR," *Molniya*, no. 28 (December 1991): 2;" OFT," *Kontrargumenti i Fakti* 10, no. 1 (1992): 3. For further details, see chapter 10.

112. The "pragmatic" wing of Democratic Russia is led by Lev Ponomarev, Gleb Yakunin, and Vladimir Boxer.

113. Gavriil Popov also wanted the Movement for Democratic Reform to formally oppose the Russian government, but his proposal was rejected at the movement's December 1991 conference.

114. For instance, the Social-Democratic Party of Russia claims to have nominated Alexander Shokin as their candidate for minister of labor and later deputy prime minister. However, Shokin is not a formal member of the SDPR.

115. Although tempered and constrained de facto by the Supreme Soviet and the Constitutional Court, this powerful executive is the model deemed necessary by Igor Klyamkin and Adranik Migranyan for the Soviet regime to make a successful economic transition. See articles by Klyamkin, Migranyan, and others commenting on the "iron hand" model in *Sotsializm i Demokratiya: Diskussionnaya Tribuna (Sbornik Statei)* (Moskva: Institut Ekonomiki Mirovoi Sotsialisticheskoi Sistemi, 1989), and *Sotsializm i Demokratiya: Diskussionnaya Tribuna (Sbornik Statei)*, chast 2 (Moskva: Institut Ekonomiki Mirovoi Sotsialisticheskoi Sistemi, 1990).

116. See Larry Diamond, Juan Linz, and Seymour Martin Lipset, *Politics in Developing Countries* (Boulder, Colo.: Lynn Rienner, 1990), p. 9.

Chapter Two

1. Most of the older dissidents refused to participate in any kind of politics, deeming the whole enterprise as morally corrupt.

2. See Michael McFaul, "Last Hurrah for the CPSU," *Report on the USSR* 2, no. 30 (July 27, 1990).

3. Even the founders of the Democratic Union were not optimistic about their chances for survival at the time. (Authors' interviews with Ekaterina Podoltseva, Leningrad, June 1988, one of the founders of the Democratic Union in Leningrad, and Yurii Skubko, Moscow, September 1989.)

4. The platforms of each of these factions are printed in *Demokraticheskii Soyuz: Byulleten' Soveta Partii*, no. 2 (Moskva: April 1990), pp. 6–12.

5. See Vladimir Pribylovsky, "Slovar' Oppositsii: Novie Politicheskie Partie i Organizatsie Rossii," *PostFactum Analytical Review*, nos. 4–5 (Moscow) (April 1991): 10.

6. For instance, several Democratic Union activists who supported the social democratic faction later joined the Social-Democratic Party of Russia.

7. In the fall of 1990, Novodvorskaya called Gorbachev a Fascist and was charged by the state with defamation of the president.

8. "Pis'mo Dvenadtsati," *Voennoe Polozhenie—Kak c Nim Borot'sya?* (Moskva: DS-Inform, 1991), p. 2.

9. Pribylovsky, "Slovar' Oppositsii," p. 10.

10. The Democratic Union as an organization was never a member of the Democratic Russia coalition.

11. In our interviews for this book, Victor Kuzin's name was mentioned by almost everyone as a person honored and respected for his courageous acts and honest politics. Accolades for Kuzin were in sharp contrast to the rabid denunciations accorded to other colleagues in the democratic movement.

12. This position was a minority view in the Democratic Union despite many of its most vocal supporters being from the margins of Soviet society.

13. In the Moscow City Council, Kuzin serves as deputy chairman of the Standing Commission on Justice, Human Rights, Law and Order and chairman of the Human Rights Subcommittee.

14. *Press-Reliz*, Mossoviet, no. 8, November 26, 1990.

15. The crisis of the appointment, however, began in November when the Moscow City Council's Legal Commission recommended that Komissarov replace General Bogdanov as chief of police. When the Legal Commission's review of candidates began in October, Bogdanov indicated that he intended to resign. The council, however, failed to approve Komissarov's candidacy in the fall. Popov and Stankevich spoke out against Komissarov's appointment on the grounds that the position of chief of police should be selected by the chairman of the Executive Committee, Yurii Luzhkov, and not the Legal Commission. Their stance elicited harsh denunciations by radical democrats who claimed that both Popov and Stankevich had succumbed to pressure from Gorbachev to resist Komissarov's appointment. Luzhkov eventually nominated the liberal major general for the post in January, which was then approved by the city council on January 23, 1991. But by then the hard-line Boris Pugo had replaced the liberal Vadim Bakatin as minister of the interior and firmly rejected the Mossoviet's candidate. See Boris Pugo, "Reshenie Kollegii Ministerstva Vnutrennikh Del SSSR," no. Ikm/2, February 4, 1991; Postoyannaya Kommissiya po Zakonnosti, Pravoporyadku i Zashchite Prav Grazhdan, "Reshenie: O Volokite c Izdaniem Prikaza MVD SSSR v Otnoshenii Nachal'nika GUVD Mosgorizpolkoma Komissarova V.C.," no. 53/8–I, February 4, 1991; *Press-Reliz*, Mossoviet, no. 23, January 23, 1991; and Lev Sigal, "Moscow without Police Chief as Union Blocks City's Liberal Appointment," *Kommersant*, February 11, 1991, p. 3.

16. Murashev, a former cochairman of Democratic Russia and USSR people's deputy, is a civilian with no experience in police affairs.

17. Popov's frustration with the city council eventually influenced his decision to resign as mayor during the summer of 1992. (Authors' interview with Sergei Stupar', press secretary for Mayor Popov, June 1992.)

18. The Democratic Union was an all–Soviet Union organization.

19. May 9, commemorating the end of the World War II, was one of the biggest holidays in the Soviet Union.

20. Under the Soviet system of *propiska*, it was illegal to travel to another city without permission.

21. As a people's deputy of the Moscow City Council, Kuzin later became famous for leading hunger strikes for various causes.

22. At the time of this interview, Victor Kuzin was representing Democratic Union leader Valeriya Novodvorskaya, who was being tried for slander of the Soviet president. Novodvorskaya had called Mikhail Gorbachev a Fascist. She was eventually acquitted.

23. The authorities evidently had hoped that people might take aggressive actions against Fascists.

24. Kuzin is referring to an April 1989 demonstration in T'bilisi, Georgia, in which unarmed demonstrators were killed by Georgian government forces.

25. On June 12, 1991, Moscow elected Popov as mayor and Yurii Luzhkov as vice-mayor. The election created a new executive independent from the Moscow City Soviet. Before this election, Popov was the chairman of the Moscow City Soviet, the equivalent of a Speaker in a legislature or parliament. Many Western observers, however, erroneously referred to Popov as the mayor of Moscow during the time that he was chairman of the Moscow City Soviet.

26. The Council for Mutual Economic Assistance was the organization that coordinated economic arrangements between East European countries in the Warsaw Pact. After the revolutions in 1989, the organization collapsed.

27. Soon after the coup, Popov named Arkadii Murashev—a prominent member of the now defunct Interregional Group of People's Deputies of the USSR and a former cochair of Democratic Russia—to become Moscow's chief of police. This appointment was highly controversial as the city council had been struggling with the USSR government for more than nine months to appoint their candidate—General Komissarov—in this position. Kuzin, along with a dozen other people's deputies of the Moscow City Council, went on a hunger strike for this cause in the spring of 1991.

28. Marshal Shaposhnikov, then the head of the Soviet Air Force, is now the new defense minister of the Commonwealth of Independent States. General Kobets was the Russian minister of defense.

29. The "White House" is a nickname for the Russian House of Soviets where the Russian parliament is located. During the putsch, Yeltsin was situated inside the White House.

30. General Komissarov was first nominated for the post of Moscow police chief in November 1991 by the Standing Commission on Justice, Human Rights, and Law and Order of the Moscow City Council. At the time, Kuzin was deputy chairman of this commission.

31. Kuzin is referring to the Movement for Democratic Reform.

Chapter Three

1. Others include Pamyat' National Patriotic Front (headed by N. Filimonov and I. Kvartalov), Pamyat' Orthodox Christian National Patriotic Front, the Popular Orthodox Christian Movement, the Russian Popular Democratic Front–Pamyat' Movement (Igor Sychev), the World Anti-Zionist and Anti-Masonic Pamyat' Front, the Coordinating Council of the Pamyat' Patriotic Movement, the Russian Assembly Pamyat', the Pamyat' Historical Association, the Union of Patriotic Organizations of the Urals and Siberia, the

Russian National Unity, National Social Union, Vened Union, National Democratic Party, the Union for the Revival of Russia, the Republican Popular Party of Russia, the Christian Patriotic Union, and the Union for the Spiritual Revival of the Motherland. For descriptions, see Vladimir Pribylovsky, *Dictionary of New Political Parties and Organizations in Russia* (Moscow: Postfactum, April 1991), pp. 27–28.

2. See for instance, "Protokoli Zionskikh Mudretsov o Zemle i Ekonomike," *Pamyat'*, no. 2 (January 1991): 11; "Im' Nuzhni—Velikiya Potreseniya, Nam' Nuzhna—Velikaya Rossiya!" *Pamyat'*, no. 1 (January 1991): 3.

3. On Rustkoi's involvement with this nationalist organization, see Ilya Kudryavtsev, "Bataliya pod 'Brestom'," *Khronograf*, no. 26 (May 24, 1989): 2–6.

4. Significantly, Rutskoi's party, the Party for a Free Russia, boycotted the meeting. Likewise, Nikolai Travkin and the Democratic Party of Russia also did not participate.

5. See Francis Clines, "Tug of War, with Rallies, Is Played Out in Moscow amid Mood of Discontent," *New York Times*, February 10, 1992.

6. See "Manifest Natsional'no-Patrioticheskogo Fronta "Pamyat" (Moskva), January 12, 1989, reprinted in B. Kobal', ed., *Rossiya Segodnya: Politicheskii Portret, 1985–1990* (Moskva: Mezhdunarodnye Otnosheniya, 1991), pp. 291–94. In lieu of a political program, this manifesto is list of sixty-one demands.

7. At the time, Victor Grishin was the first secretary of the Moscow City Party Committee.

8. Manezh Square later became the central meeting place for Democratic Russia demonstrations in 1990–91.

9. Manezh Square is adjacent to Red Square.

10. Before the interview, Vasiliev's assistant specifically warned us not to ask questions about the organization's membership.

11. Vasiliev is referring to the elections for the Russian presidency held on June 12, 1991.

Chapter Four

1. They later formed the Party of Free Democrats headed by Marina Salye. The party is active in Saint Petersburg but has few followers elsewhere.

2. The identity of the Democratic Party became so intertwined with Travkin that many people referred to the organization as "Travkin's party."

3. Even before this congress, yet another split occurred when Georgii Khatsenkov, the editor of the party's newspaper, *Demokraticheskaya Rossiya*, quit the party, taking his newspaper with him. *Demokraticheskaya Rossiya* subsequently became more closely affiliated with Democratic Russia, while the Democratic Party of Russia began to publish *Demokraticheskaya Gazeta*. See Lev Sigal, "Rossiiskie Predprinimateli Otkazalis' Finansirovat' 'Partiyu Il'icha,'" *Kommersant'*, no. 41 (October 15–22, 1990): 11.

4. The two positions are clearly outlined in statements by Nikolai Travkin and Arkadii Murashev in "Krov'—Kto za Nee Otvetit?" *Demokraticheskaya Rossiya* 18, no. 12 (June 14, 1991): 5.

5. *Platforma Demokraticheskoi Partii Rossii* (Moscow: undated though circulated in April 1991). The official program was published as "Programma Demokraticheskaya Partii Rossii (DPR)," *Demokraticheskaya Gazeta* (Moscow) 9, no. 6 (1991): 10–11.

6. Travkin's supporters asserted that Kasparov and Murashev sought division within the party for their own political careers. See "Kak Garri Kimovich Possorilsya c Nikolaem Il'ichem. I Zachem," *Demokraticheskaya Gazeta* (Moscow) 9, no. 6 (1991): 8–9.

7. Kasparov and Murashev later helped found the Liberal Union, a coalition of parties and individuals advocating radical economic reform. Other prominent members of the Liberal Union included economists Larissa Piyasheva and Boris Pinsker; DemRossiya cochair Victor Dmitriev; Victor Zolotarev, chairman of the Party of Constitutional Democrats; Igor Korovikov, chairman of the Party of Free Labor; Academician Tikhonov, head of the Union of Cooperatives; and RSFSR people's deputy Galina Starovoitova.

8. Fodorov, one of the financial supporters of the Democratic Party, was named businessman of the year by *Moscow Magazine* in 1991. See Paul Hoffheinz, "The Pied-Piper of Capitalism," *Moscow Magazine*, December 1991–January 1992, pp. 50–51.

9. See *Moscow News*, no. 42 (October 28–November 4, 1990): 2.

10. *Deklaratsiya Konstruktivno–Demokraticheskogo Bloka "Narodnoe Soglasie"* (Moskva: April 19, 1991).

11. Quoted in Michael Parks, "Yeltsin Party Fragments over Russian Unity," *Los Angeles Times*, November 12, 1992.

12. See the communiqué issued only a few days before the Minsk agreement at the Third DPR Congress, "Obrashchenie III S'ezda DPR k Narodnim Deputatam RSFSR" (mimeo, undated but released at the third congress on December 3, 1991).

13. Authors' interview with Alexander Terekhov, Moscow, January 16, 1992. This meeting also catalyzed the formation of the "liberal faction" within the party, which opposed Democratic Party participation in such events. See "Zayavlenie Soveta Liberal'noi Fraktsii DPR" (Saint Petersburg, February 8, 1992).

14. Yurii Bondarenko, "Prosti, raspyataya Rossiya!" *Obozrevatel'*, nos. 2–3 (February 1992): 2.; see also insert, pp. 1–20 (materials of the congress).

15. *RFE/RL Daily Report*, no. 85 (May 5, 1992): 1.

16. Grazhdanskii Soyuz, *Dokumenti Foruma Obshchestvennikh Sil* (Moskva, June 21, 1992). In addition to Shumeiko, Deputy Prime Ministers Georgii Khizha and Viktor Chernomyrdin also are very close to this new coalition. See Evgenii Yanaev, "Pravitel'svto Preodenut v Grazhdanskoe'," *Kommersant'*, no. 26 (June 22–29, 1992): 18.

17. "Grazhdanskii Soyuz," *Rossiiskoye Vremya*, no. 2 (August 1992): 3. The economic program of Civil Union includes four main policies: (1) stimulate demand for consumer goods by loosening the money supply, (2) support state enterprises through subsidies when necessary, (3) support and protect high-technology industries, and (4) preserve low prices for oil and gas.

18. Authors' interview with Alexander Sungurov, Saint Petersburg, August 26, 1992. *Conservative* in this context means those resisting radical economic reform.

19. "DPR: The Democratic Party of Russia: Goals, Structures, and Perspective" (mimeo in English, 1991). This description of the party also includes a composition of party

membership: businessmen 9.8 percent, servicemen 0.7 percent, workers 17.2 percent, students 3.7 percent, engineers 24.1 percent, middle- and higher-level management 9 percent, artists, teachers, lawyers, and doctors 22.1 percent, government workers 7.4 percent, retired 3 percent, and part-time workers 3 percent. Eighty-eight percent of the party is male, 12 percent is female, and 70.3 percent has a higher education.

20. See "Travkin Cited on United Democratic Party," *FBIS-USSR 91–018* (July 30, 1991). The party has opened a school to train prospective candidates and campaign organizers.

21. *Moskovskii Novosti*, no. 2 (January 12, 1992): 2.

22. Travkin has consistently advocated the construction of organized and formal parties, whereas most of Democratic Russia's leaders prefer to maintain looser coalitions or united fronts, similar to those in Eastern Europe.

23. This campaign was in May 1990.

24. Gavriil Popov was chairman of the Moscow City Council. Sergei Stankevich was deputy chairman of the Moscow City Council, and Anatoly Sobchak was chairman of the Leningrad City Council.

25. Nikolai Ryzhkov was Gorbachev's prime minister for several years until he was removed in December 1991. During the election for the Russian presidency, he appealed to conservative Communists, particularly in the rural areas, for his base of support.

26. General Boris Gromov was the commander of Soviet forces in Afghanistan. In December 1991, Gorbachev appointed him as the deputy minister of internal affairs under Boris Pugo. Pugo, of course, was one of the eight leaders of the coup attempt in August 1991.

27. Tatarstan is an autonomous republic within the Russian Federation that is seeking independence.

28. At the founding congress of the Democratic Party of Russia, Travkin argued that the party needed only one chairman. Salye, Ponomarev, and Kriger argued that the party would be better served with cochairs. Travkin won the argument, and the others quit the party.

29. Vladimir Bukovsky is a famous dissident who spent several years in psychiatric hospitals in the Soviet Union during the 1960s and 1970s before being involuntarily exiled from the Soviet Union by Leonid Brezhnev. For his autobiography, see Bukovsky, *To Build a Castle: My Life as a Dissenter* (New York: Viking Press, 1978). Recently he has periodically returned to Russia to participate in the new political situation.

30. Stanislav Shatalin, an economist who was the principal author of the five-hundred–day plan, joined the Democratic Party of Russia in the spring of 1991 and was elected chairman of the party's political council at the DPR's third congress in December 1991. He resigned from the party, however, several days later, after the Democratic Party held a pro-Union demonstration at which Vladimir Zhirinovsky appeared. Although Zhirinovsky was not formally invited to the demonstration, Shatalin cited this event as a reason for resigning. Only a few days later, he was elected as one of the cochairmen of the Movement for Democratic Reform.

31. General Makashov ran as a presidential candidate in the June elections. He is a very

conservative Communist and nationalist. Nikolai Ryzhkov, as explained before, is a former prime minister who also ran in the June 1991 elections. Vladimir Zhirinovsky, the head of the Liberal-Democratic Party but a militant nationalist, also ran for Russian president. An interview with Zhirinovsky appears in chapter 12.

Chapter Five

1. Future SDPR leaders in this organization in Moscow included Oleg Rumyantsev, Leonid Volkov, and Pavel Kudiukin. Other prominent participants included Ernest Ametistov, Boris Kurashvilli, Andrei Fadin, Dmitrii Leonov, Victor Zolotarev, Vyacheslav Igrunov, Mikhail Maliutin, Boris Kagarlitsky, Victor Kuzin, and Yurii Skubko. In Leningrad, Anatoly Golov, the future SDPR chairman there, also cofounded the Leningrad Perestroika Club along with Marina Salye, Gennadii Bogomolov, Pyotr Phillipov, and Alexander Sungurov. The impetus for the Moscow club actually came from this Leningrad group.

2. See Vyacheslav Igrunov, "Public Movements: From Protest to Political Self-Consciousness," in Brad Roberts and Nina Belyaeva, eds., *After Perestroika: Democracy in the Soviet Union*, CSIS Significant Issue series, vol. 13, no. 5 (Washington, D.C.: Center for Strategic and International Studies, 1991), pp. 17–20. As Igrunov notes, part of the reason the "radicals" were purged from the club was owing to pressure from Communist Party officials who had allocated the club space to hold its meetings. When Democratic Perestroika was formed, the Central Econometrics Institute, the sponsor of the original club, supported its formation and allowed the group to continue to meet on its premises. Perestroika 88, however, could not gain access to a public facility and had to resort to holding its meetings in parks and metro stations. Needless to say, Perestroika 88 was soon disbanded.

3. Victor Kuzin and Yurii Skubko were the leaders of this organization. They later joined the Democratic Union (see chapter 2).

4. Leaders of the Social-Democratic Union either joined the Democratic Union or moved closer to the more amorphous popular fronts in Leningrad and Moscow.

5. Evidently Yurii Afanasiev was supposed to become one of the three cochairmen, but he did not appear at the congress. Instead, Pavel Kudiukin, a famous dissident who had been imprisoned by the KGB in the early 1980s, was elected.

6. Oleg Rumyantsev, member of SDPR Presidium, "Politicheskii Moment i Nashi Zadachi," mimeo (Sverdlovsk, October 25, 1990). In adopting this program, SDPR leaders claimed to be taking the first step toward creating a genuine political party (Pavel Kudiukin, Sergei Markov, Alexander Obolensky, and Oleg Rumyantsev, SDPR press conference, October 29, 1990, Moscow). A draft proposal of the program was approved in Sverdlovsk; the final program was adopted in May 1991 at the Third SDPR Congress in Leningrad.

7. "Put' Progressa i Sotsial'noi Demokratii: (Programnie Tezisi SDPR)," Proekt (Moskva: October 22, 1990), p. 18.

8. Ibid., p. 19.

9. Ibid., p. 33.

10. Ibid., part 1.

11. Because of these rather unorthodox positions, most of the social-democratic parties in Western Europe did not recognize the SDPR but continued to support the CPSU until after the coup. See Tomas Kolesnichenko, "Popitka Poslesloviya," *Pravda*, November 5, 1990, p. 5. During the three days of the coup, several West European social-democratic parties actually called Oleg Rumyantsev's office to apologize for their lack of earlier support.

12. Oleg Rumyantsev, "Our Road to Social Democracy," *Narodnii Deputat*, no. 2 (1991). This article is reprinted and quoted here from M.A. Babkina, *New Parties and Movements in the Soviet Union* (Commack, N.Y.: Nova Science Publishers, 1991), p. 59.

13. Oleg Rumyantsev, SDPR press conference, October 29, 1990, Moscow.

14. "Put' Progressa i Sotsial'noi Demokratii," part 2.

15. See Oleg Rumyantsev, "What Is Meant by a Round-Table? *Moscow News*, no. 14 (April 7–14, 1991): 9.

16. The first draft published in *Rossiiskaya Gazeta*, November 22, 1990, and in *Konstitutsionni Vestnik*, no. 4 (1990): 55–120.

17. For accusations and responses, see *Rabochaya Tribuna*, November 25, 1990, p.2; *Moscow News*, no. 50 (1990): 6; and the alternative communist draft submitted by Slobodkin and published in *Sovetskaya Rossiya*, November 24, 1990.

18. On SDPR initiatives in the Russian parliament more generally, see *Novosti Sotsial-Demokratii* (Moscow), no. 16 (April 1991): 1.

19. Rumyantsev, "Politicheskii Moment i Nashi Zadachi."

20. "Vitse-Prem'er ot Sotsial-Demokratov," *Alternativa-Novaya Zhizn'* (sovmestnii vipusk), no. 14 (December 1991): 1. Both papers of this joint publication are official organs of the SDPR.

21. "Postanovlenie II S'ezda SDPR o Politicheskoi Koalitsii SDPR, RPRF, i DPR," *Novosti Sotsial-Demokratii*, Informatsionnii Byulleten' Sekratariata Pravleniya SDPR i Ispolkoma Moskovskoi Organizatsii SDPR, no. 4 (November 1990):3.

22. See Michael McFaul, "The Social Democrats and Republicans Attempt to Merge," *Report on the USSR* 3, no. 3 (January 18, 1991): 10–13, and "Politicheskaya Resolyutsiya Prakticheskoi Konferentsii Regional'nikh Organizatsii RPRF i SDPR," *Novosti Sotsial-Demokratii* (Moscow), no. 16 (April 1991): 2.

23. *Zayavlenie o Sozdanii Bloka Politicheskikh Partii "Novaya Rossiya,"* (Moscow, undated but circulated in January 1992).

24. For a sociological portrait of the SDPR, see Leontii Byzov (codirector, "Rossika" Research Center), "The Social Democrats of the Russian Federation: Who Are They?" in Babkina, *New Parties and Movements in the Soviet Union*, pp. 65–70.

25. Under the direction of Galina Rakitskaya and Pavel Kudiukin, the SDPR has initiated contacts with strike committees, the Independent Union of Miners, and Sotsprof, but working-class membership in the party is minimal (authors' interview with Galina Rakitskaya, Moscow, June 1991).

26. Lyzlov quit the SDPR in the spring of 1991, claiming that the group was too socialist

and poorly organized. Soon thereafter, he became deputy chairman of the Executive Committee of the Democratic Party of Russia. Unlike most other splits in Russian parties, however, Lyzlov left with no ill will toward his social-democratic colleagues. (Authors' interviews with Lyzlov, Moscow, June and October 1991.)

27. Boris Yeltsin is nominal chairman of the Constitutional Commission, while Rumyantsev is the working secretary.

28. Before being coined by Gorbachev, *perestroika*, literally "rebuilding," was a concept sometimes used in socialist states to signify major reform.

29. The Interregional Group of People's Deputies was a faction of progressive deputies within the USSR Congress of People's Deputies. Among its leaders were Andrei Sakharov, Boris Yeltsin, Anatoly Sobchak, Gavriil Popov, Yurii Afanasiev, Telman Gdlyan, Nikolai Travkin, and Arkadii Murashev.

30. Arkadii Murashev, a former USSR people's deputy, was a founding member of the Interregional Group, a cochairman of Democratic Russia, and a founding member of the Liberal Union, a coalition of parties, movements, and individuals espousing radical economic reform and the establishment of a unrestricted capitalist system. He was Moscow's chief of police.

31. Rumyantsev is referring to a group of people who emerged from the Moscow People's Front (MPF) and later the Moscow Association of Voters (MOI) to dominate the Coordinating Council of Democratic Russia. For details, see the interview with Mikhail Schneider, a member of this group, in chapter 8.

32. Rumyantsev is referring to a roundtable, modeled after the process in Poland, that would lead to the constitution of a new government in the former USSR. During the spring of 1991, Rumyantsev was one of the leading advocates of this form of transition.

Chapter Six

1. These organizational divisions were not so rigid, for many of the same people belonged to several of the groups mentioned in this list.

2. "Sozdadim Demokraticheskuyu Platformu v KPSS," Obrashchenie Moskovskogo Partkluba "Kommunisti za Perestroiku" (Moscow, undated).

3. The program of the Democratic Platform was published in *Pravda*, March 3, 1990.

4. Ironically, Nikolai Travkin was one of the leading proponents of this strategy. See his speech at the January All-Union Congress of the Democratic Platform in *Demokraticheskaya Platforma*, no. 2 (April 1990): 6. Not surprisingly, delegates from the provinces also supported this approach. See, for instance, the remarks of S. Podborodhikov for the Union of Workers of Kuzbass at the Democratic Platform founding congress in ibid., p. 7.

5. Arkadii Murashev, people's deputy of the USSR, at the founding congress of Democratic Platform in *Demokraticheskaya Platforma*, no. 2 (April 1990): 6.

6. The leading proponent of this strategy was Vladimir Lysenko. See Vladimir Lysenko, "Yest' Takaya Partiya?" *Demokraticheskaya Platforma*, no. 2 (April 1990): 2.

7. See the remarks of Alexei Brechikhin (first secretary of the CPSU in Sevastopol

Rayon, Moscow) and Alexander Sungurov (Leningrad Partklub) at the founding congress, published in *Demokraticheskaya Platforma*, no. 2 (April 1990): 7. Some, including Nikolai Travkin, did want to wait, quit the Party (and therefore the Democratic Platform), and form the Democratic Party of Russia.

8. See Vladimir Lysenko's assessment of the CPSU February plenum in "Razmishleniya o Rossiiskoi Kompartii," *Demokraticheskaya Platforma*, no. 3 (June 1990): 3, and Alexander Mekhanik, "Raskol KPSS: Katastrofa ili Blago?" Ibid., p. 1.

9. Authors' interview with Igor Chubais, Moscow, June 6, 1991.

10. Authors' interviews with Valerii Lunin (a leader of the Democratic Platform at the time), Moscow, April 15, 1991, and Igor Chubais, Moscow, June 6, 1991.

11. When he was not invited to participate in this March plenum, Nikolai Travkin decided to quit the Party and form his own Democratic Party of Russia.

12. For the rationale for the new name, see V. N. Lysenko, "Kak Nazivat'sya Nashei Partii," mimeo (Moscow), October 22, 1990, distributed at the November congress, and *Nevskii Kur'er*, no. 18 (Leningrad) (1990): 4.

13. Even the leadership of the party could offer no logical explanation for the new title other than the lack of alternatives (press conference with Vyacheslav Shostakovsky, Moscow, November 18, 1990).

14. See "Programma Deistvii Partii Demokraticheskoi Platforma" (Proekt) (undated, but prepared for the November 1990 congress).

15. "Programma Deistvii Respublikanskoi Partii Rossiiskoi Federatsii," *Byulleten' Partiino-Politicheskoi Informatsii*, no. 1 (Moskva) (December 1990): 13–14.

16. Ibid., p.14.

17. Quoted in Sergei Mulin, "Mensheviks Turn Republican: Only for Three Months?" *Moscow News*, no. 47 (December 2–9, 1990): 6.

18. See "Zayavlenie o Sozdanii Demokraticheskogo Kongressa," *Dvizhenie "Demokraticheskaya Rossiya,"* Informatsionnii Byulleten', no. 5 (February 1991): 1. For the congress's latest activities, see "Informatsionnoe Soobshchenie" (Kiev, Ukraine, February 12, 1992).

19. Vladimir Lysenko, "O RPRF," *Respublika*, no. 1 (June 1991): 2.

20. See "Vystuplenie V. N. Shostakovskogo," *Tumenskii Komsomolets* (Tumen), December 11, 1990, p. 3.

21. See the interview with Stepan Sulakshin in "Respublikantsy Posle Uchreditel'nogo S'ezda," *Gospodin Narod*, no. 2 (1990): 2. After the departure of the Democratic Party of Russia from Democratic Russia in November, the Republican Party became one of the two most influential parties in the coalition. At the Second Congress of Democratic Russia, four members of the Republican Party—Lysenko, Shostakovsky, Smirnov, and Galendobaev—were elected to the movement's Council of Representatives. See Igor Yakovenko, "Daite Pravyashchuyu Partiyu," *Gospodin Narod*, no. 14 (1991): 3.

22. Interview with Vladimir Lysenko in *Demokraticheskaya Rossiya* 7, no. 1 (March 1991): 9, and Lysenko, "O RPRF," p. 2.

23. An August poll conducted by *Demokraticheskaya Rossiya* asserted that among

Muscovites, 19 percent supported the Democratic Platform over other parties, while 14 percent supported the SDPR. The Democratic Party of Russia (Travkin) received the greatest single percentage, with 21 percent. The method of polling, however, was not published. (*Demokraticheskaya Rossiya*, no. 3 [September 1990]: 13.)

24. On the Republican Party's structure, see Vyacheslav Shostakovsky, "Drugie Partii Ishchut Strukturi, a Respublikantsy ikh Imeyut," *Gospodin Narod*, no. 3 (1991): 8.

25. Surveys conducted before the opening of the RPR congress showed that 52 percent of the party supported the merger. After the congress, at which several leaders of the SDPR spoke, proponents of unification claimed that more than 80 percent of the delegates supported the merger. (Authors' interviews with Igor Chubais, Vladimir Filin, and Vladimir Lysenko, Moscow, fall 1990 and spring 1991.)

26. Disgruntled with the Republican Party's intransigence on unification, Chubais quit the party in March 1991 to cofound the People's Party of Russia with Telman Gdlyan and Oleg Borodin.

27. In a poll taken by *Postfactum* at the Republican congress regarding the delegates' choice for leader of the new party, Lysenko received a 64 percent approval rating, compared with 57 percent for Shostakovsky, 19 percent for Sulakshin, and 8 percent for Chubais. See "Rozhdenie Partii," *Gospodin Narod*, no. 1 (1990): 2. This newspaper is an official organ of the Republican Party of Russia.

28. "Ob'edinitel'naya Konferentsiya," *Gospodin Narod*, no. 2 (1991): 6.

29. See "Iz Politicheskoi Resoliutsii Sovmestnogo Soveshchaniya Koordinatsionnogo Soveta Respublikanskoi Partii RSFSR i Pravleniya Sotsial-Demokraticheskoi Partii Rossii," *Gospodin Narod*, no. 3 (1991): 11.

30. Stepan Sulakshin also shares this position. In October 1991, he joined the Liberal Union, a coalition of neo-Thatcherite conservatives who support radical economic reform without any state intervention or regulation.

31. *Zayavlenie o Sozdanii Bloka Politicheskikh Partii "Novaya Rossiya,"* (Moscow, undated but circulated in January 1992).

32. Most members of these other two organizations are former members of the Democratic Platform who did not leave the CPSU in July 1991. Although the two parties have worked together, the Republican Party has been critical of Rutskoi himself. See, for instance, "Problema No. 1—Rutskoi," *Gospodin Narod*, no. 16 (1991): 8.

33. See Vyacheslav Shostakovsky, "Smutnoe Vremya s Primeneniem Oruzhiya," *Gospodin Narod*, no. 16 (1991): 6. In February 1992, the Republican Party quit the Russian Movement for Democratic Reform, though it maintained an affiliation with the International Movement for Democratic Reform.

34. See the report on the Republican Party plenum, held December 20–21, 1991, in Moscow in *Gospodin Narod*, no. 16 (1991): 3.

35. The interview took place on June 13, 1991, the day after the election for the Russian presidency.

36. Alexander Rutskoi at the time was the head of the Communists for Democracy, a faction within the CPSU. After the August 1991 coup attempt, the group founded a new

party, the Party for a Free Russia. As Yeltsin's running mate, Rutskoi was elected Russian vice-president on June 12, 1991.

37. At the time, Alexander Yakovlev was still a member of the CPSU Politburo and one of Gorbachev's closest aides.

38. Lysenko is referring to the Movement for Democratic Reform. See chapter 13.

39. *Soviets*, the Russian word for councils, are the main governmental structure in the Russian republic.

40. The Democratic Congress is a coalition of democratic movements from all the republics.

41. Lysenko is referring to the Russian Christian-Democratic Movement headed by Victor Aksiuchits. Other Christian-democratic parties do no support necessarily this position.

42. The 9 + 1 Accord was an agreement between Gorbachev and Yeltsin in which both leaders pledged to work toward the construction of a new union consisting of nine republics plus the center.

43. Marina Salye, a Russian people's deputy and people's deputy of the Saint Petersburg City Council, now heads the Party of Free Democrats and the Russian Constitutional Assembly.

Chapter Seven

1. The Russian letter *X* is used here for this abbreviation rather than the transliterated *Kh* to more accurately reflect the Russian acronym.

2. The journal's subtitle was a *Literary-Philosophical Journal of Russian Christian Culture*; the journal included articles about Alexander Solzhenitsyn, the life of Christ, the second millennium, Russian culture, and poetry.

3. Father Gleb Yakunin, a longtime and well-known religious dissident, is also an RSFSR people's deputy and cochairman of Democratic Russia. At the time, Valerii Borshchov was a member of the Presidium of the Moscow City Council.

4. See, for instance, Vladimir Karpets, "Ideya Rossiya ili 'Russkaya Ideya'?" *Put'* (official newspaper of RXDD) 4, no. 1 (Janaury 1991): 7.

5. *Rossiiskoe Khristianskoe Demokraticheskoe Dvizhenie: Sbornik Materialov* (Moskva: Duma RXDD, 1990), pp. 4, 27, 33.

6. *Rossiiskoe Khristianskoe Demokraticheskoe Dvizhenie*, pp. 30–31.

7. "Osnovie Polozhenii Politicheskoi Programmi RXDD," *Rossiiskoe Khristianskoe Demokraticheskoe Dvizhenie*, p. 33.

8. See Victor Aksiuchits, "Natsional'noe i Ideologicheskoe," *Put'* 4, no. 1 (January 1991): 2. Most other Christian political organizations, however, are much more nationalistic than the RXDD. For a survey of their political platforms, see *Khristianskie Partii i Samodeyatel'nie Ob'edineniya* (Moskva: Akademiya Obshchestvennikh Nauk pri TsK KPSS, 1990).

9. See the section on patriotism in the RXDD declaration of principles, printed in *Rossiiskoe Khristianskoe Demokraticheskoe Dvizhenie*, pp. 31–32, and the interview with Il'ya Konstantinov in *Put'* 12, no. 9 (1991): 5.

10. See Victor Aksiuchits, "Tupiki Liberal'nogo Kommunizma," *Put'* 12, no. 9 (1991): 2.

11. The RXDD recommended that people not vote at all regarding the March 17, 1991, referendum on the preservation of the USSR. Although the RXDD supported the preservation of the Union in general, the movement was against the preservation of a *socialist* Union, as was proposed on the ballot. See "Obrashchenie Dumi RXDD," *Put'* 5 no. 2 (March 1991): 2.

12. "Rezolutsiya Konferentsii RXDD, Moskva, October 28, 1990," *Put'* no. 1 (1990): 1.

13. *Put'* 12, no. 9 (1991): 4.

14. There are dozens of Christian movements as well as monarchist and patriotic groups that pledge their allegiance to the Russian Orthodox church. See *Khristianskie Partii i Samodeyatel'nie Ob'edineniya*.

15. On the history of this movement, see *Khristiansko-Demokraticheskii Soyuz Rossii* (London: Overseas Publications Interchange, 1990).

16. For an account of the founding congress and subsequent activities of the party, see *Khristiansko-Dmokraticheskii Soyuz Rossii*. The party also publishes the newspaper *Vestnik Khristianskoi Demokratii*.

17. According to Ogorodnikov, the Christian-Demoratic Union maintains a pure Christian orientation with special emphasis on human rights and morality, which, over the long run, will be more sustainable than the RXDD's more political orientation. (Authors' interview with Alexander Ogorodnikov, Moscow, May 1991.)

18. "Vystupleniye," *Obozrevatel'*, nos. 2–3, insert (1992): 5–10; Nataliya Ganina, "Pervii shag k obyedineniyu," *Put'*, no. 2 (1992): 2.

19. "V rossiiskom sobranii," *Obozrevatel'*, nos. 2–3 (February 1992): 2. The National Republican Party of Russia should not be confused with the Republican Party of Russia, though both have leaders named Lysenko. The National Republican Party of Russia is a quasi-military organization bent on using force, not democratic processes, to strengthen the Russian state and protect Russians living outside Russia. To realize these ends, the National Republican Party has organized volunteer militia tasked with defending Russian minority populations living in former republics of the Soviet Union. See *Natsional'no-respublikanskaya Partiya Rossii*, program documents (Saint Petersburg, 1992).

20. "Zayavleniye Kongressa grazhdanskikh i patrioticheskikh sil," *Obozrevatel'*, nos. 2–3 (1992).

21. Not surprisingly, Russian delegations from ten of the newly independent states of the former Soviet Union attended the founding congress. See Victor Aksiuchits, "Chuvstvo Istoricheskoi Otvetstvennosti," *Put'*, no. 2 (1992): 3.

22. "Deklaratsiya," *Den'*, no. 11 (March 1992): 1. This courtship of Communists has fueled internal splits within the party. See "Krizis v partiyakh," *Nezavisimaya Gazeta*, April 29, 1992, p. 2.

23. Parliamentary factions that joined this bloc include Rossiiskii Soyuz, Otchizna, Rossiya, the Agrarian Union, and Communists of Russia.

24. "Vserossiiskoye Trudovoe Soveshchanie," *Izvestiya*, July 16, 1992, p. 2. On threats

of a nationwide strike, see Anna Krayevskaya, "Budut Podnimat' Narod," *Nezavisimaya Gazeta*, August 18, 1992, p. 2.

25. Such former radical democrats and anti-Communists as Yurii Vlasov and Tatyana Koryagina now vehemently criticize the government in the pages of the communist and nationalist press. See "Pervyi Laureaty," *Den'* 29, no. 1 (January 1992): 1.

26. In addition to Sterligov, the governor of Sakhalin, Valentin Fyodorov, and Valentin Rasputin, a writer and former member of Gorbachev's Presidential Council, were also elected cochairmen. *Obozrevatel'*, nos. 2–3, insert (1992): 21. More generally, see Evgenii Krasnikov, "Rossiiskoye Edinstvo Toskovalo po Putchu," *Nezavisimaya Gazeta*, August 21, 1992, p. 2.

27. "Chto Bylo na Nedele," *Kommersant'*, no. 8 (February 1992): 2.

28. "Vystupleniye General-Mayora A.I. Sterligova," *Obozrevatel'*, nos. 2–3, insert (1992): 21–25, and Elena Dikun, "Moskva," *Megapolis-Express*, August 5, 1992, p. 13.

29. Sergei Kazannov, "Kto vmesto 'Demokratov'," *Den'*, no. 31 (August 1992): 2.

30. A recent poll asked, "If there will be a change in government, who will come to power: a new team of democrats or nationalists? In March 1992, 40 percent predicted democrats and 16 percent predicted nationalists. By July, however, only 15 percent of those polled believed that democrats would come to power; 19 percent assumed that nationalists would constitute the next government. See Boris Grushin, "Ne Tak Ne Stabil'na Nineshnaya Vlast," *Nezavisimaya Gazeta*, August 20, 1992, p.2.

31. At the time of this interview, Anatoly Lukyanov was chairman of the USSR Supreme Soviet.

32. At the time, Sergei Shakhrai was chairman of the Committee on Legislation for the RSFSR Supreme Soviet. Oleg Poptsov was the head of Russian television.

33. These are all communist youth organizations.

34. As noted above, the Christian-Democratic Union is the RXDD's main rival and is led by Alexander Ogorodnikov.

35. Aksiuchits is referring to the meeting they had with the International of Christian Democracy. He also may have been referring to his own remarks at that meeting.

36. The founding principles of the bloc are in chapter 4.

37. Sergei Baburin, a people's deputy in the Russian parliament, leads the conservative, communist parliamentary bloc Rossiya.

38. Soyuz was a coalition in the USSR Supreme Soviet and did not have an affiliate in the RSFSR Supreme Soviet. See chapter 11.

Chapter Eight

1. Most of the popular names appearing on DemRossiya posters became famous through their activities in the Interregional Group of People's Deputies, a coalition of radical reformers within the Supreme Soviet of the USSR.

2. According to the Ministry of Internal Affairs, 982,700 people participated in these

meetings around the Soviet Union. See Yurii Gladish, "Den' Rozhdeniya Vesni," *Demokraticheskaya Platforma*, no. 3 (June 1990): 1.

3. For details, see Orgkomiteta po Sozdaniyu Dvizheniya "Demokraticheskaya Rossiya," *Soobshchenie*, no. 3 (1990).

4. "Democratic Russia Charter," adopted by the founding congress, Democratic Russia movement, October 20–21, 1990.

5. See Koordinatsionnogo Soveta Dvizheniya, "Demokraticheskaya Rossiya," *Soobshchenie*, no. 1 (December 1990): 6.

6. See "Protsess Polyarizatsii Zavershen," *Dvizhenie Demokraticheskaya Rossiya*, Informatsionnii Byulleten', no. 3 (February 1991): 1.

7. On the Union referendum, see "Kakaya-to Tainaya Tsel'," *Argumenti i Fakti*, no. 10 (March 1991): 3; and "Zayavlenie Koordinatsionnogo Soveta Dvizheniya Demokraticheskaya Rossiya," *Dvizhenie Demokraticheskaya Rossiya*, Informatsionnii Byulleten', no. 6 (March 1991): 1. Democratic Russia opposed the referendum because it called for the preservation of a *socialist* Union. On Democratic Russia's support for the miners, see *Moskovskii Komsomolets*, March 12, 1991, p. 1; and "Pomosh' Moskvi," *Kuranti*, March 13, 1991, p. 2.

8. Regarding DemRossiya plans for cells in the workplace, see *Dvizhenie Demokraticheskaya Rossiya*, Informatsionnii Byulleten', no. 4 (February 1991): 2. For a list of all local branches, see *Dvizhenie Demokraticheskaya Rossiya*, Informatsionnii Byulleten', no. 6 (March 1991): 3.

9. Authors' interview with Lev Ponomarev (Moscow, April 15, 1991).

10. At the opening session of the RSFSR Congress of People's Deputies that same day, the deputies passed a resolution that suspended their activities until the troops were removed. Many communist deputies broke ranks on this vote and sided with Yeltsin's supporters.

11. Many Western observers scoffed at the numbers that turned out at DemRossiya demonstrations, claiming that they did not compare with the larger crowds in Czechoslovakia in 1989 or even Lithuania in 1990. Calculations about crowd size, however, must be understood in the context of Russian history and culture. First, as Russia's history demonstrates, a handful of organized revolutionaries can orchestrate revolutionary events without millions of supporters. Second, and more important in the contemporary Soviet context, the Russians are *supposed to be* complacent, apathetic, and timid. That anyone showed up to these demonstrations was significant; that tens of thousands assembled regularly was revolutionary.

Retrospectively, Democratic Russia cochair Lev Ponomarev called the successful demonstration a dress rehearsal for the resistance effort in August 1991. See his speech in *Materiali: II S'ezda Dvizheniya Demokraticheskaya Rossiya,* (Moskva: DR-Press, November 1991), p. 5.

12. See "Zayavlenie, Plenuma Soveta Predstavitelei Dvizheniya Demokraticheskaya Rossiya o Kruglom Stole Politicheskikh Sil, April 13, 1991," *Dvizhenie Demokraticheskaya Rossiya*, Informatsionnii Byulleten', no 10 (May 1991): 4.

13. See Lev Ponomarev's account of DemRossiya activities in *Materiali*, p. 6.

14. The core of Democratic Russia's apparat—people such as Vera Kriger, Mikhail Schneider, and Vladimir Boxer—had emerged from the Moscow Popular Front (MNF) and the Moscow Association of Voters (MOI), neither of which were active political movements at the time of the founding of Democratic Russia. In fact, these organizations essentially merged into Democratic Russia, giving former MNF and MOI activists a new single, political identity—the Democratic Russia movement. In contrast, people who joined Democratic Russia as representatives of active political parties owed their first allegiance to their parties. Authors' interview with Oleg Rumyantsev (Leningrad, May 3, 1991).

Divisions between the Democratic Party of Russia and Democratic Russia are outlined in statements by Nikolai Travkin and Arkadii Murashev in "Krov'—Kto za Nee Otvetit?" *Demokraticheskaya Rossiya* 18, no. 12 (June 14, 1991): 5.

15. The idea of transforming Democratic Russia into a mass political party first appeared after the Soviet invasion of Lithuania in January 1991. See "Vozglavit li Yeltsin Novuyu Partiyu?" *Gospodin Narod*, no. 3 (1991): 3.

16. On the necessity of unity, see the speech by DemRossiya cochair Father Gleb Yakunin in *Materiali*, p. 8.

17. See the speech by Victor Aksiuchits in *Materiali*, p. 25.

18. See Popov's speech in *Materiali*, p. 9. Several local branches of the Democratic Party of Russia, however, refused to leave the Democratic Russia coalition. See Igor Yakovenko, "Daite Pravyashchuiu Partiyu," *Gospodin Narod*, no. 14 (1991): 1.

19. Popov resigned as a cochairman of Democratic Russia soon after becoming chairman of the Moscow City Council. He resigned to adhere to a Yeltsin decree on the departycization [*sic*] of top government positions, and not because of poor relations with the Democratic Russia movement. The poor relations developed later and exploded in October 1991.

20. See "Politicheskaya Deklaratsiya Koalitsii Demokraticheskikh Sil Moskvi" (mimeo, undated) and "Obrashchenie k Uchastnikam i Storonikam Dvizheniya 'Demokraticheskaya Rossiya'" (mimeo, October 10, 1991).

21. As explained to the author by two leading proponents of these new committees, Mikhail Schneider and Vladimir Boxer, these structures will make do until a true civil society develops. (Authors' interviews, Moscow, December 1991.)

22. "Vystuplenie Popova na Vtoroi Konferentsii Moskovskogo Obiedineniia Izbiratelei," *Nash Vybor*, no. 2 (November 1989): 1.

23. In 1990, Schneider and Sergei Stankevich published a guide for campaign strategy. See S. Stankevich and M. Schneider, *Rekomendatsii po Taktike Kandidatov Demokraticheskogo Bloka i Ikh Kompanii, 1989–90 g.g.* (Moskva: Informtsentr Moskovskogo Narodnogo Fronta, 1990).

24. In March 1990, Gavriil Popov appointed Mikhail Schneider as first assistant to the mayor, but this position simply gave Democratic Russia office space and equipment in the city hall building.

25. The Cheremushkinskii borough was an electoral district in Moscow.

26. After the failed August putsch, Sevastyanov was appointed by Moscow mayor Gavriil Popov as head of the Moscow KGB.

27. Shchit', an independent union for military officers, was involved in radical, anti-communist activities.

28. Several months earlier, in March 1990, Travkin had created the Democratic Party of Russia. Ponomarev and Kriger were members of the party until its first congress, when Travkin rejected the idea of cochairs. Travkin became chairman, and Ponomarev, Kriger, and Maria Salye of Saint Petersburg quit to form the Free Democratic Party of Russia.

29. At the congress, Beloserdtsev accused Lev Ponomarev of working for the KGB.

30. At the time, both Kalugin, the former KGB officer, and Gdlyan, the former head of the procurator's office, were popular figures. Both were much more radical than the majority of Democratic Russia's original organizing committee.

31. Ironically, this commission is located in the former offices of the Ideological Department of the CPSU on Staraya Ploshchad.

32. Lev Ubozhko heads the Conservative Party. Vladimir Zhirinovsky heads the Liberal-Democratic Party.

33. In October 1991, Victor Dmitriev was one of the founding members of the Liberal Union, a coalition of conservative parties and individuals. Other founding members included Garry Kasparov, Arkadii Murashev, Larisa Piyasheva, Boris Pinsker, Galina Starovoitova, Victor Zolotarev, Igor Korovikov, and Alexander Tikhonov.

34. At the time, Anatoly Lukyanov was chairman of the USSR Supreme Soviet. He was later charged with conspiring with the Emergency Committee.

35. Manezh Square was the traditional meeting place of the democratic forces for mass demonstrations.

36. At this time, the White House had received reports that a special unit was ordered to storm the building.

37. These are the three people who died during the coup.

Chapter Nine

1. See Vitaly Ponomarev, *Obshchestvennie Volneniya v SSSR* (Moskva: Levii Povorot, 1990), p. 5; and Vadim Belotserkovsky, "Vostaniya, o Kotorikh Ne Znala Strana," *Novie Vremya*, April 1991, p. 8.

2. For an analysis of the 1989 strikes, see Peter Rutland, "Labor Unrest and Movements in 1989 and 1990, *Soviet Economy* 6, no. 3 (1990): 345–84.

3. Salary increases were not part of the list of demands from striking miners in Vorkuta. See *Vestnik Rabochego Dvizheniya*, no. 3 (November 1989): 1. For a survey of miners' grievances, see L.L. Mal'teva and O.N. Pulyaeva, "What Led to the Strike?" *Soviet Sociology* 30, no. 3 (May–June 1991): 41–48. This article first appeared in *Sotsiologicheskie Issledovaniia*, no. 6 (1990).

4. Because individual strike committees drafted their lists of demands independently, the kinds of demands were wide-ranging. Some strike committees were overtly political,

whereas others limited their demands to economic issues. Some committee demands focused solely on local issues; others had national consequences. The Vorkuta strikers had some of the most overtly political demands, including repealing Article Six of the Soviet constitution and ending aid to Cuba. See Ludmilla Thorne, "What the Soviet Miners Want," *Freedom at Issue*, March-April 1990, p. 27. See also Rutland, "Labor Unrest and Movements in 1989 and 1990," pp. 356–57.

5. Authors' interview with Ilya Shablinsky, executive secretary of the Confederation of Labor (Moscow, May 1991).

6. *Konfederatsiya Truda* (Moskva: May 1990), p. 5. This charter was approved on May 1, 1990, in Novokuznetsk, Kemerovo region, at the founding congress of the confederation.

7. Authors' interview with Galina Rakitskaya (Moscow, June 1991). Galina Rakitskaya, along with her husband, Boris Rakitsky, is one of the Moscow intellectuals who helped found the Confederation of Labor and who has since been involved in assisting the development of the Independent Union of Miners.

8. "Rabotaet Shakhterskii S'ezd," *Pravda*, October 23, 1990, p. 2.

9. The NPG, of course, could not speak for all miners, though the union did claim to be the leading representative of the miners during the 1991 strikes. See the interview with Alexander Sergeev, assistant chairman of the Executive Bureau of the Independent Union of Miners, in *Izvestiya*, April 2, 1991, p. 2.

10. The spontaneous strikes that erupted in Minsk after the price hikes are an example. By April, however, the strikes at the mines were already losing their momentum. Many believe that the Union government deliberately provoked the strike in March to diffuse public reaction and the miners' reaction in particular to the price hikes in April.

11. Pavel Shushpanov, chairman of the Executive Committee of the Independent Union of Miners, and Anatoly Malykhin, chairman of the Interregional Coordinating Council of Workers' Strike Committees, "Obrashenie Nezavisimogo Profsoyuza Gornyakov and Mezhregional'nogo Koordinatsionnogo Soveta Rabochikh Komitetov k Verkhovnim Sovetam, Pravitel'stvam i Narodnim Dvizhenim Suverennikh Respublik" (undated but delivered at the end of March 1991).

12. These were some of the striking miners' cardinal demands. See *Ekspress-Khronika* 187, no. 10 (March 5, 1991): 1.

13. In disgust, the miners began to return to work before a settlement had been negotiated, forcing the strike leaders to move quickly to find a face-saving settlement. Drunkenness and crime, two problems absent during the first strike, also began to increase dramatically during the second month of the strike.

14. In general, the coal miners have been critical of both the dissolution of the Soviet Union and the subsequent disputes arising from the creation of independent states, claiming that these debates about sovereignty have distracted government officials from focusing on the more important issues of economic reform. See, for instance, Henry Kamm, "Struggling Ukrainian Miners Are Put Off by Diet of Nationalism," *New York Times*, February 16, 1992, p. 6.

15. On the strike threat, see V. Sharipov, "Obrashchenie, Sovet Predstavitelei NPG Kuzbassa" (Kemerevo), December 12, 1991.

16. See Ilya Shablinsky, "Where Is Our Labor Movement Going? Reflections on Its Sources and Prospects," *Soviet Sociology* 30, no. 4 (July-August 1991): 41–48.

17. In 1987, the Council of Workers' Collectives was established to coordinate activities between individual collectives. In December 1990, the Union of Workers' Collectives, a more politically oriented organization, was established that claimed to represent seven million workers from six hundred enterprises. The main objective of this union is to promote worker ownership and worker self-management at the enterprise level. (Authors' interview with Galina Rakitskaya, one of the cofounders of the Union of Workers' Collectives, Moscow, June 1991.)

18. For a brief description, see "Alternative Trade Unions: Possibilities and Realities, *Soviet Sociology* 30, no. 1 (January-February 1991): 55–56. This article originally appeared in *Sotsiologicheskie Issledovaniia*, no. 2 (1990).

19. Sergei Khramov, cofounder of Sotprof, as quoted in ibid., p. 61.

20. Sotsprof, for instance, joined Democratic Russia, an action that the Independent Union of Miners refused to take. See "Postanovlenie 2 S'ezda Ob'edineniya Profsoyuzov SSSR SOTSPROF" (Donetsk), February 11–13, 1991, reprinted in "Dvizhenie 'Demokraticheskaya Rossiya' " *Informatsionnaya Bulletin'*, no. 6 (March 1991): 4.

21. "Initsiativnaya Gruppa za Sozdanie Partii Truda," *Obozrevatel': Spetsial'nii Vipusk* (1991): 11. The activities of the Moscow Federation of Trade Unions as well as the Party of Labor and other new manifestations of workers' organizations are closely chronicled in *Byulletin KAS-KOR* and *Solidarnost': Gazeta Moskovskikh Profsoyuzov*.

22. At the time of this interview (May 1991), the miners were out on strike for the second time in two years.

23. At the time, Ivan Silaev was the Russian prime minister and Ruslan Khasbulatov was the acting chairman of the Russian Supreme Soviet. Yeltsin, of course, was president of Russia.

24. This interview took place at the second congress of the Independent Union of Miners to which an American delegation, called the Joint Labor-Management Mission to the Soviet Union, sponsored by the Coal Industry Project, was invited. The delegation included W. J. Usury, a former secretary of labor and director of the Federal Mediation and Conciliation Service, John Banovic, secretary treasurer of the United Mine Workers of America, and Richard Wilson, director of Central and East European Affairs of the Free Trade Union Institute of the AFL-CIO.

25. Shushpanov is referring to the congress of official trade unions controlled by the Communist Party.

26. The tariff agreement outlined the conditions of work that the miners demanded from the government. The government's failure to meet the conditions of the agreement was the basis for the second wave of strikes in the mining areas during the spring of 1991.

27. Mikhail Sobol' was the leader of the coalition of trade unions in Minsk that led the massive strikes against price hikes in April 1991. He is also the chairman of the Executive Committee of the Confederation of Labor in Minsk.

28. Vorkuta, in northern Siberia, is one of three bases of the Independent Union of

Miners. The other two areas of concentrated support for the union are the Kuzbass in Russia and the Donbass in Ukraine.

Chapter Ten

1. See Roy Medvedev, *K Sudu Istorii* (Let History Judge: The Origin and Consequences of Stalinism) (New York: Knopf, 1971); Roy Medvedev, *Lichnost' i Epokha* (Brezhnev's Political Portrait) (Moscow: Novosti Press, 1991); and Alexander Chakovsky, *Pobeda* (Moscow,1980).

2. Terms such as *liberal, conservative, left wing,* or *right wing* are confusing when discussing this period of political formation in Russia. In the beginning, those who supported reform were called *liberals* while those who resisted change were labeled *conservatives.* Later, as the political debate expanded to included people and organizations outside the Communist Party, those who supported more radical reform were called *democrats* while those who resisted were referred to as *Communists.* Since the collapse of the CPSU in August 1991, however, the discourse about the Russian political spectrum is beginning to parallel the Western lexicon. Those who support the old Soviet system are called *leftists, ultraleftists, Communists,* or *neo-Communists* while those still advocating radical economic reform now call themselves *liberals, conservatives,* and even *Thatcherites.* A third force, which often overlaps with the communist groups, is called *nationalists, patriots,* or *Fascists.*

3. The development of self-organized communist groups developed much more slowly than democratic organizations, as many hard-line Communists hoped that the CPSU could be reinvigorated and cleansed of its reformist "traitors" in the leadership.

4. At the time of its formation, OFT was considered a major threat to the democratic forces; Andrei Sakharov even flew to Sverdlovsk, where the OFT founding congress was held, to urge people not to join the organization. "Narodnii Deputat SSSR A.D. Sakharov na Urale," *Pozitsiya,* no. 1 (1989?): 4.

5. Yarin was later expelled from the United Workers' Front for supporting Gorbachev's reforms.

6. On the Marxist Platform, see V. Berezovsky, N. Krotov, and V. Chervyakov, *Rossiya: Partii, Assotsiatsii, Soyuzy, Kluby* tom 1, chast 2 (Moskva: Rau Press, 1991), pp. 281–85.

7. "Informatsionoe Soobshchenie o Pervom S'ezde OFT," *Shto Delat'?* no. 3 (August 1989): 1.

8. "Nasha Pozistiya," *Shto Delat'?* no. 1 (June 1989): 1.

9. See Vera Tolz, "The United Front of Workers of Russia: Further Consolidation of Antireform Forces," *Report on the USSR,* September 29, 1989, pp. 11–13.

10. Among other standard communist notions, their platform called for property to be given to workers' collectives and not private hands, the reinstatement of the planned economy, and the end of the theft of Russia's treasures by Western capitalists. ("Patriotism i Znanie Spasut Rossiyu," 1990 mimeo.)

11. Authors' interview with Igor Malyarov (Moscow, April 21, 1991). After helping to

found OFT, Malyarov founded the Communist Initiative youth movement, which served as the basis for reconstituting the Komsomol in February 1992 after it had been disbanded in the wake of the August putsch.

12. "DKI Nabiraet Silu," *Russkii Golos*, no. 6 (July 1991): 6.

13. For details and copies of the founding documents, see Kobal', *Rossiya Segodnya*, pp. 51–71.

14. See Dawn Mann, "The Democratic Party of Communists of Russia," *Report on the USSR*, August 30, 1991, pp. 26–30.

15. See the interview of Dmitrii Igoshin, *Narodnaya Pravda*, no. 18 (May 1992): 3; *Rabochii*, no. 1 (December 1991); "Informatsionnoe Soobshchenie," *Nasha Rossiya*, no. 20 (1991): 2; "Oktyabr'skii Manifest Kommunisticheskikh Dvizhenii," *Nasha Rossiya*, no. 21 (1991): 4; "Uchrezhdena RKPR," *Molniya*, no. 28 (December 1991): 2; "OFT," *Kontrargumenti i Fakti*, 10, no. 1 (1992): 3; V. N. Berezovsky, N.I. Krotov, V.V. Chervyakov, and V.D. Solovei, eds., *Rossiya: Partii Assotsiatsii, Soyuzy, Kluby*, Kniga 6 (Moskva: Rau Press, 1992).

16. On the demonstration on November 7, 1991, see "100,000 Demonstrantov Krasnoi Ploshchadi," *Nasha Rossiya*, no. 21 (1991): 1.

17. See Victor Anpilov and Vladimir Yakushev, "Nizlozhit' Uzurpatorov!" *Molniya*, no. 28 (December 1991): 1; and the interview with General Albert Makashov, "Makashov: Narod Obmanuli," *Molniya*, no. 29 (1991): 3. On March 17, 1992, the neocommunist organizations convened the defunct USSR Congress of People's Deputies, where they declared that the Soviet Union still existed. Of the 2,250 original USSR people's deputies, 450 supported the idea. See V.P.Nosov, "Informatsiya," *Nasha Rossiya*, no. 5 (1992): 4; "Zayavleniye VI Chrezvychainogo S'ezda Narodnykh Deputatov SSSR," *Sovetskaya Rossiya*, March 19, 1992, p. 1; and "Den' Sovetskogo Soyuza," *Narodnaya Pravda*, no. 12 (March 1992): 1.

18. Even before the coup, the nationalists and the neo-Communists had begun to work together. Most important, on February 27, 1991, two dozen nationalist and communist organizations joined in For the Great and Unified Russia movement. See "Kommunisti i Patrioti Reshil Spasti Rossiyu. Ot Demokratov," *Kommersant'*, no. 9 (February 25–March 4, 1991): 13.

19. "Krovavoe Voskresenie," *Den'*, no. 9 (March 1992): 1–2.

20. Evgenii Krasnikov, "Trudorossii Naznachili Voinu na 22 Iyunya," *Nezavisimaya Gazeta*, June 20, 1992, p.2.

21. V. Anpilov, "Ostankino: Shag k Pobede," *Molniya*, no. 38 (July 1992): 1.

22. Authors' interviews with leaders from each of these parties (June 1992). See also "U Levykh Sil Mnogo Obschikh Zadach," *Nash Kompas*, no. 7 (June 30, 1992): 1. The Russian Communist Workers' Party also claimed to have established large cells within the former Soviet army. See "Materialy Iyunskogo Plenuma TsK RKRP," *Za rabochee delo*, no. 7 (July 31, 1992): 3.

23. See *PIA* (Povolzhye Information Agency), no. 108 (August 1992).

24. See, among many other examples, "Trudorossii Protestuyut," *Nezavisimaya Gazeta*, August 19, 1992, p.2; "Rasprava nad Patriotami," *Nasha Rossiya*, no. 24 (1992): 1–4;

"Pravitel'stvo v Ot'stavku!" *Glasnost'*, no. 15 (April 1992): 1–2; "Mitingi. Rezolutsii. Bor'ba." *Molniya*, no. 24 (April 1992): 1; "Doloi Mafiyu!" *Nasha Rossiya*, no. 8 (1992): 1; "Primireniya ne budet," *Molniya*, no. 34 (April 1992): 1.; Evgenii Yanayev, "Viktor Anpilov: Krasnykh i Belykh," *Kommersant'*, no. 34 (August 1992): 24; and M. Razdobreev, "Ono budet—Pravitel'stvo Trudovogo Naroda!" *Narodnaya Pravda*, no. 32 (August 1992): 2.

25. Most were lecturers from Departments of Scientific Socialism.

26. Although confusing, Kosolapov is trying to explain how the Central Committee of the CPSU attempted to co-opt the initiative to create an independent Russian Communist Party. The co-option failed.

27. Gennadii Zyuganov was elected to the Politburo of the Russian Communist Party on September 7, 1990, and is considered one of the leading ideologists of the Party. See "Plenum TsK Kompartii RSFSR," in Kobal', *Rossiya Segodnya*, p. 60. After the August coup, Zyuganov became chairman of the Russian patriotic forces. See *RFE/RL Daily Report*, no. 44 (March 4, 1992): 1.

Chapter Eleven

1. See Eduard Shevardnadze, *The Future Belongs to Freedom* (New York: Free Press, 1991). Much of this book is devoted to refuting these Soyuz accusations.

2. "New Arms for the Army! Ban the CPSU!" (interview with Colonel Victor Alksnis), *Moscow News*, no. 6 (February 10–17, 1991): 7.

3. Had the coup leaders sought parliamentary approval of their actions, Soyuz would have been able to provide the necessary votes to win a majority on a resolution supporting the actions of the Emergency Committee.

4. Besides Soyuz, the Rossiya faction of the Russian parliament was one of the main forces behind this new movement. Sergei Baburin, the Rossiya leader, also was elected to the coordinating council.

5. On March 17, 1991, the Soviet Union held a Unionwide referendum asking voters whether the Union should be preserved. The referendum passed. Several republics, however, refused to participate.

6. The poll was published in *Nezavisimaya Gazeta*, February 5, 1992.

7. The interview took place in the Rossiya Hotel, where most of the USSR people's deputies lived.

8. Colonel Alksnis is referring to refugees from different republics who have been displaced because of ethnic clashes.

9. Grigorii Yavlinsky, an economist, was one of the authors of the famous "five-hundred-day plan."

10. Kazan is the capital of Tatarstan.

11. The Interregional Group was a coalition of democratic deputies in the USSR Congress of People's Deputies that included Yurii Afanasiev, Gavriil Popov, Andrei Sakharov, Anatoly Sobchak, Sergei Stankevich, and Boris Yeltsin.

12. See the following chapter on the Liberal-Democratic Party that explains Vladimir Zhirinovsky's relation to the Centrist Bloc.

Chapter Twelve

1. The year before, Vladimir Bogachev and Lev Ubozhko founded a small party called the Liberal-Democratic Party of Russia. Bogachev later joined forces with Zhirinovsky to form the Liberal-Democratic Party of the USSR, whereas Ubozhko went on to found the tiny Conservative Party. See Vladimir Pribylovsky, "Slovar' Oppositsii: Novie Politicheskie Partii i Organizatsii Rossii," nos. 4–5 (Moscow), *PostFactum Analytical Review* (April 1991): 16.

2. See the interview with Vladimir Zhirinovsky in *Argumenti i Fakti*, no. 12 (1990), reprinted in B. Kobal', ed., *Rossiya Segodnya: Politicheskii Portret, 1985–1990* (Moskva: Mezhdunarodnye Otnosheniya, 1991), pp. 188–89.

3. After the August 1991 putsch, Yeltsin appointed a committee to investigate the activities of the security agencies during the coup; that committee charged Zhirinovsky with conspiring with the KGB and the state Emergency Committee.

4. "Program of the Liberal-Democratic Party of the Soviet Union," adopted unanimously by the first LDP national congress on March 31, 1990, in Moscow; reprinted in *Liberal'no-Demokraticheskaya Partiya Sovetskogo Soyuza: Dokumenti i Materiali* (Moskva: 1991), p. 17.

5. Allegedly, the Institute of Social Sciences for the CPSU wrote the document for Zhirinovsky. The typesetting, paper, and booklet size exactly replicated CPSU program publications.

6. "Coup or Operetta?" *Moscow News*, no. 45 (November 18–25, 1990): 6.

7. See the interview with Vladimir Zhirinovsky, "Narodu Nechego Teryat," in *Den'* 29, no. 1 (December 29, 1991—January 9, 1992): 2.

8. Zhirinovsky and Vladimir Voronin, the head of the A.D. Sakharov Union of Democratic Forces, were the two cochairmen of the bloc. Despite its name, the A.D. Sakharov Union had nothing to do with Sakharov himself. His wife, Ylena Bonner, was furious that this organization had used his name.

9. See Olga Bychkova, "The Invisible People," *Moscow News*, no. 7 (February 17–24, 1991): 8.

10. Zhirinovsky received 7.81 percent of the vote compared with 57.3 percent for Yeltsin and 16.85 percent for Ryzhkov.

11. See, for instance, the cover of *Stolitsa* 42, no. 36 (1991).

12. Zhirinovsky's education and employment record fuel suspicion of his ties to the KGB. He received his first degree from the Institute of Asian and African Countries at Moscow State University, which was notorious as a training center for KGB agents. Likewise, before perestroika, the Soviet Peace Committee was widely regarded by both the West and the Soviet Union as a KGB front. According to his official biography, however, Zhirinovsky has been struggling for the creation of a multiparty system since

---

1967. See "Zhirinovsky Vladimir Bol'fovich," *Liberal* (organ of the Liberal-Democratic Party of the Soviet Union), nos. 2–3 (November 1990).

13. There were many polls taken at this congress, but we have not been able to verify this particular vote count.

14. Zhirinovsky is referring to General Gromov, Nikolai Ryzhkov's running mate, and Colonel Rutskoi, Yeltsin's partner. Note that he makes no distinction between the CPSU ticket and the Yeltsin ticket.

15. Arkadii Murashev and Yurii Afansiev are two of the original six cochairmen of Democratic Russia.

16. The Centrist Bloc was created on June 8, 1990, by Zhirinovsky from the Liberal-Democratic Party and Vladimir Voronin of the Sakharov Union of Democratic Forces. Although the bloc included more than two dozen political parties and movements, most were ghost organizations or clubs with three or four members. At the time, however, the official press gave the bloc much publicity and senior ministers in Gorbachev's government met with the bloc's leadership.

17. When Soviet special forces (OMON) seized government buildings in Lithuania and Latvia in January 1991, "national salvation committees" in these republics claimed responsibility. Thereafter, several right-wing organizations began calling for the formation of a national salvation committee for the entire Soviet Union. The coup attempt in August 1991 was one such attempt.

18. These were senior officials in the Soviet Union government with the exception of Ivan Silayev, who was Russia's prime minister.

19. These people are heads of former republics.

20. Note that the Republican People's Party is not the same organization as the Republican Party of Russia. The former is a nationalistic organization headed by *Nikolai* Lysenko, whereas the latter is a left-of-center party headed by *Vladimir* Lysenko, one of the leaders interviewed in this book.

Chapter Thirteen

1. As noted earlier, the CPSU had several factions, not just two. The Party was polarized into two camps, however, over certain issues, most important, the collapse of the Soviet Union.

2. Retrospectively, Gorbachev has admitted that this particular turn to the right was one of his most critical mistakes. See an interview with Gorbachev as reported in the *RFE/RL Daily Report*, no. 23 (February 4, 1992): 2.

3. For the full explanation of his resignation, see Eduard Shevardnadze, *The Future Belongs to Freedom* (New York: Free Press, 1991).

4. These pleas were very similar to those made by the organizers of the Democratic Platform a year earlier. See "A Calamity of Bolsheviks Can't Survive: An Interview with Eduard Shevardnadze, *Moscow News*, no. 25 (June 23–30, 1991): 6.

5. People like Shevardnadze and Yakovlev were from a different generation of poli-

ticians than those leading movements and parties like the SDPR or Democratic Russia. As such, their tactics and style are very different, if not incompatible.

6. The original nine founders of the organization were Eduard Shevardnadze, Alexander Yakovlev, Stanislav Shatalin, Nikolai Petrakov, Alexander Rutskoi, Ivan Silayev, Arkadii Volsky, Gavriil Popov, and Anatoly Sobchak.

7. See Elizabeth Teague and Vera Tolz, "Prominent Reformers Create Opposition Movement," *Report on the USSR* 3, no. 28, (July 12, 1991): 1–4.

8. In addition to these official government positions, Popov used his authority as mayor to grant the Movement for Democratic Reform several former communist buildings and equipment. Needless to say, this action was very unpopular among both Communists and other democrats.

9. Yakovlev still holds a position in the Moscow city government. Shevardnadze has become active in Georgian politics. Both Yakovlev and Shevardnadze also took positions with the Gorbachev Foundation.

10. Neither Shevardnadze nor Yakovlev participated in the founding congress of the Russian Movement for Democratic Reform. The Republican Party of Russia also left the founding congress of the Russian Movement for Democratic Reform, fearing that the organization had become "a party of one man": Gavriil Popov. (See the remarks of Vladimir Lysenko in *RFE/RL Daily Report*, no. 38 [February 25, 1992]: 2.) Eventually, the International Movement for Democratic Reform was created, but none of the prominent figures who founded the DDR have assumed active roles in this organization.

11. See the interview with Gavriil Popov, "Za Nami Poidut Predprinimateli," *Dvizhenie Demokraticheskikh Reform* (Moscow) (December 1991): 1. In a survey conducted at the congress, more than 90 percent of the delegates identified themselves as members of the intelligentsia. Only 1 percent of the delegates were "workers." See *DDR—Vozniknovenie i Razvitie* (Moskva: Moskovskii Regional'nii Tsentr DDR, 1991) Vipusk 1, p. 16.

12. Arkadii Volsky later formed his own party, Obnovlenie (Renewal), in May 1992. This party then joined forces with Alexander Rutskoi, another DDR cofounder, and his People's Party for Free Russia and Nikolai Travkin's Democratic Party of Russia to form the coalition Grazhdanskii Soyuz in June 1992. See Grazhdanskii Soyuz, *Dokumenti Foruma Obshchestvennikh Sil* (Moskva: n.p., June 21, 1992).

13. He eventually did resign in June 1992.

14. See *RFE/RL Daily Report*, no. 39 (February 27, 1992): 2.

15. Gavriil Popov resigned as mayor of Moscow in the summer of 1992 to devote his full attention to building the Russian Movement for Democratic Reform.

16. For full details, see Shevardnadze, *The Future Belongs to Freedom*.

17. Hundreds of books and articles have been written on this subject. See, for instance Allen Lynch, *Gorbachev's International Outlook: Intellectual Origins and Political Consequences* (New York: Institute for East-West Security Studies, 1989).

18. *RFE/RL Daily Report*, no. 38 (February 25, 1992): 3.

19. In the spring of 1991, Alexander Yakovlev, Yegor Yakovlev, and Anatoly Sobchak published articles in *Moscow News* promoting the creation of such a party or movement.

20. Among the leadership of the Movement for Democratic Reform, Shevardnadze is

the most nonideological. Alexander Yakovlev has proposed a social-democratic platform for the movement, whereas Gavriil Popov favors a classical liberal program.

21. These three—some of the most famous economists in Russia—contributed to the five-hundred-day plan.

22. This interview was conducted in November 1991, before the dissolution of the Soviet Union and the creation of the Commonwealth of Independent States.

Index

Kirkland, Lane, 186
Kislyuk. Mikhail, 179
Klyamkin, Igor, 87
Klyuchevsky, Vasilii, 57
Kobets, General, 39
Kogan, Yevgenii, 229
Komar, Dmitrii, 168
Komarov, Georgii, 229, 233
Komissarov, General, 25, 40, 280n.15
Kommersant', 87
Kommunist, 204, 206
Komsomol (Young Communist League),
    5, 7, 17, 27, 86, 120–54 passim, 197–
    216 passim, 260, 264
Konstantinov, Ilya, 61
Korea, South, 236
Korotich, Vitalii, 142, 147
Korovikov, xiii, 267n.3, 295n.33
Kosolapov, Richard, 201, 203–12
Kostomarov, Nikolai, 57
Kovalenko, Mikhail, 28, 29, 30
Kovalev, Sergei, 102
Kovcheg (Ark), 124
Krasnodar, 112
Krasnoyarsk, 13, 125
Kratovo, 22
Kravchuk, Leonid, 235, 253
Krichevsky, Ilya, 168
Kriger, Vera, 61, 62, 72, 73, 108, 140,
    149, 150, 294n.14
Kronstadt, 30
Krotov, Nikolai, 146
Kryuchkov, Vladimir, 38, 163, 244, 252
KSI. See Club of Social Initiatives
Kudiukin, Pavel, 82–91 passim, 142,
    274n.67, 285n.5,n.6, 286n.25
Kuibyshev, 210
Kursk, 216, 250
Kuzbass, 15, 169, 171–84, 189, 193–96
Kuzin, Victor, 22–41, 87, 88, 100, 101,
    147

Landesbergis, Vitautas, 240, 247, 250,
    253
Laptev, Ivan, 252
Latvia, 63, 137, 230, 232, 256

Leaflets, 8, 9, 29, 36, 131–52 passim
Left-wing parties, 78, 127, 130, 216, 228,
    298n.2
Lemeshev, Alexei, 145, 146
Lenin, Vladimir, 46–48, 58, 128, 158,
    208–51 passim
Leninism, 3, 31, 161, 226
Lennon, John, 86
Leonov, Dmitrii, 101
Leonov, Yurii, 214
Levashov, Alexei, 155
Liberalism, 13, 111, 218
Liberalization, 2
Liberals, 3–42 passim, 65, 91, 139, 160,
    298n.2
Liberal Democratic Party of the USSR,
    14, 19, 243–57, 267n.1
Liberal Union, 153, 273n.57
Ligachev, Yegor, 4, 5, 101, 105, 201,
    229, 239, 271n.29
Lingua, 140–42, 269n.14
Lithuania, 15, 27, 63, 137, 234, 240,
    241, 247, 250, 256
Lopatin, Vladimir, 240
Lugansk (Voroshilovgrad), 183
Lukashov, Alexander, 32
Lukyanov, Anatoly, 30, 121–22, 164,
    233, 292n.31
Lunin, Valerii, xi, 298n.10
Luzhkov, Yurii, 38–40
Luzhniki, 7, 8, 140, 147
Lysenko, Anatoly, 112
Lysenko, Nikolai, 119, 255, 291n.19,
    302n.20
Lysenko, Vladimir, 9, 10, 30, 68, 69, 94–
    113, 160–61, 291n.19, 302n.20
Lyzlov, Vyacheslav, 84

MacArthur, General Douglas, 236
Magaril, Sergei, 87
Makashov, Albert, General, 75, 202, 242,
    250, 284n.31
Malyarov, Igor, 201
Maliutin, Mikhail, 94, 101, 142, 270n.14,
    272n.43

About the Authors

MICHAEL MCFAUL is a research associate at Stanford University's Center for International Security and Arms Control and a research fellow at the Hoover Institution. A Rhodes scholar, he has been a field program officer for the National Democratic Institute in Moscow, a consultant for the "McNeil/Lehrer NewsHour," and an International Research and Exchanges Board scholar at Moscow State University.

SERGEI MARKOV is an assistant professor at Moscow State University in the newly created faculty of Russian Politics and has been a visiting scholar in the Political Science Department at the University of Wisconsin at Madison. He has served as a political consultant on the Russian government and parliament.